P9-EAJ-744

CRC
LIBRARY

Fourth Edition

Principles of AGRIBUSINESS MANAGEMENT

James G. Beierlein
The Pennsylvania State University

Kenneth C. Schneeberger
University of Missouri

Donald D. Osburn
University of Missouri

Long Grove, Illinois

To all our students who have given us immense pleasure

For information about this book, contact:
Waveland Press, Inc.
4180 IL Route 83, Suite 101
Long Grove, IL 60047-9580
(847) 634-0081
info@waveland.com
www.waveland.com

10-digit ISBN 1-57766-540-6
13-digit ISBN 978-1-57766-540-3

Printed in the United States of America

7 6 5 4 3 2

Contents

6T

PART II
The Planning Function 35

PART IV
The Controlling Function 155

Preface

The fourth edition of *Principles of Agribusiness Management* is a significant revision and refinement of this book that represents our continual desire to give our students the best agribusiness management education possible, and to maximize their learning by incorporating the most effective teaching/learning techniques.

The new edition:

1. Presents material that has been extensively classroom tested.
2. Incorporates the latest thinking on what makes good business management.
3. Addresses the need for ***strategic planning and management*** for an agribusiness to remain competitive in the market.
4. Gives greater attention to the role of ***leadership*** in business management, marketing management, human resource management, and economics in developing a successful approach to business management.
5. Strengthens the connection of everything a manager does to our ***unifying theme*** so students can more easily construct their own personal, workable approach to agribusiness management.
6. Presents all the material using the best instructional design methods so that the teaching/learning process has the greatest chance for success.

Comprehensive Scope

Students who use this book will be presented with a complete exposure to the principles of agribusiness management that will help them take a giant stride toward being an effective agribusiness manager in the twenty-first century. The U.S. Department of Agriculture tells us that over the next 10 years nearly 50 percent of the job openings in the agri-food system will be for people with business management backgrounds. This text prepares students to fulfill this need.

Specifically, the following changes have been made:

- A new chapter (***Staying Competitive***) on strategic management has been added. The need to stay competitive by constantly adapting to a changing market has never been greater than today. The speed and magnitude of change will only grow. Our students need to be prepared to deal with the future.
- From the third edition, chapter 16 has been rewritten and retitled ***Human Resource Leadership*** to reflect the importance of the message that you must be a good leader before you can be a great manager.

- The discussion of the ***futures market*** has been returned to the forecasting chapter. For those who wish to devote more time to the mechanics of futures and options trading a reference to a great tutorial at the Chicago Board of Trade Web site is given.
- The learning objectives at the start of each chapter have been refined so they better conform to good instructional design by giving measurable objectives.
- The chapter quiz at the end of each chapter encourages student critical thinking about what they have read; it has been expanded and can be used for classroom discussions or homework assignments.

KEY FEATURES

Since the first edition of this book appeared in 1986, many of the changes in agribusiness that we prepared students for have come about. Now it is time to anticipate the next round of changes so we can properly prepare the next generation of agribusiness managers who will lead us. Because we focus on principles that endure, many of the key parts of the book that readers have told us they enjoy, such as the detailed financial management section, have been retained, while many major advancements in business management (supply chains, strategic management and leadership) have been incorporated.

Intended Audience

Principles of Agribusiness Management is designed for students taking either their first or only course in agribusiness management. For agribusiness students, it is a solid foundation for higher-level agribusiness courses. For nonmajors, it provides a broad and necessary understanding of basic agribusiness management skills that will complement a technical major. For working professionals who need to enhance their management skills, it provides a comprehensive, straightforward presentation of all the key management concepts and skills needed for success.

Maximizing Learning

Much of the material and many of the examples in this text come from our real-world experiences with practicing agribusiness managers. We have combined this practical experience with our many years of classroom teaching to maximize learning from this book. This is done by consulting with educational designers so we can employ the best teaching/learning practices.

To help students improve their reading comprehension:

- Learning objectives are clearly listed on the first page in measurable terms so students will know what the important points of the chapter are and can look for them as they read.
- Chapter highlights are listed at the end of the chapter so students can check their understanding of the key ideas and concepts presented.

To help students improve their critical thinking skills, each chapter comes with a decision case that gives them a chance to apply the learning points in the chapter.

- Cases promote active and collaborative learning that engages students' minds.
- Agribusiness management is about the application of knowledge to business decision making.
- Students learn more when they can see the practical value of what they are learning.
- Students learn more when they can put their new knowledge to work immediately.
- Cases are an engaging, fast, inexpensive way to bring the real world into the classroom.

Readability

Principles of Agribusiness Management is written in a straightforward, jargon-free style that facilitates student learning. It uses a step-by-step approach with many worked examples and emphasizes the application of basic, practical business management skills in marketing, demand analysis, forecasting, production, finance, leadership, and human resource management.

This book is arranged to tell the story of agribusiness management. New ideas and concepts are presented as they are needed. First, a need is established. Second, a procedure is developed to meet it. Finally, the new material is integrated with what has already been presented. This approach helps students to process all the material into a workable approach to agribusiness management.

A Unifying Theme Integrates All the Material Presented

Topics are presented in a logical sequence built around the application of the four functions of management—planning, organizing, controlling, and directing. What connects each of these topics in a meaningful way is the unifying theme that *every manager's primary objective is to maximize the long-term profits of the firm by profitably satisfying customers' needs.*

- The first part of this theme—every manager's primary objective is to maximize the long-term profits of the firm—means the manager must be economically *efficient*. Managers who maximize their long-term profits are using all their resources in the most efficient ways possible. Accomplishing this means the firm is practicing a *sustainable approach* to management that is compatible to good environmental stewardship.
- The second part of this theme—profitably satisfying customers' needs—means the manager must be *effective*. The manager must do the right things in order to satisfy customers' desires and do so at a profit.
- Thus, a successful manager is both *efficient* and *effective*. Managers must not only do things well, but must also do the right things (what the customers want) profitably.

Each topic covered is integrated into this unifying theme. Marketing helps managers uncover their customers' needs; production and inventory management help managers operate efficiently; good leadership and human resource management help to make workers more efficient and effective; and so on. Everything a manager does is related to the accomplishment of this central theme. This approach makes it easier for students to build, relate, and integrate all the material that is presented, and leave the course with a workable approach to agribusiness management. The result is better learning and better agribusiness managers.

Glossary

The glossary at the end of the text defines more than 250 important agribusiness terms in straightforward language.

BROAD COVERAGE

With the revisions and additions made to this edition of *Principles of Agribusiness Management*, instructors have more than a complete one-semester introductory course to agribusiness management. Not only is the topic coverage comprehensive, but in-depth coverage is given to each of the following topics:

- *The size and scope of the global agribusiness system.* Few students, including those who grew up on farms, understand the dynamics of the world agri-food system and the role that technology application has played in its progress. Chapter 1 sets the stage and establishes the need for good business management to keep the progress alive.
- *The role of marketing in the economy and the firm.* Students have an easier time grasping the concepts of marketing when they understand why marketing exists and the role it plays in our economic system.
- *How marketing relates to the other functions of business management.* Students find it easier to understand marketing when they understand how it relates to the other functions of the firm.
- *The need to stay competitive in rapidly changing global markets.* Staying competitive has opened a whole new area of business management called strategic management. The urgency of this issue is best summed up in the well-known management maxim that it is not the strongest but the most adaptive firms that survive.
- *How economics can help agribusiness managers make marketing decisions.* The direct application of microeconomics helps students understand the factors that influence consumer demand and how understanding consumer demand elasticity can help managers make pricing decisions.
- *The value of forecasting in making business decisions.* A variety of forecasting procedures—including futures prices and seasonal price indices—are developed and applied to agribusiness decision making.

- *The importance of a good organizational design for a firm to achieve its goals.* Students see how the organizational scheme and the levels at which decisions are made affects a business's performance.
- *The impact of a firm's legal structure on its taxes and longevity.* Managers must choose carefully when deciding whether to be a sole proprietor, join a partnership, or form a corporation. Limited liability partnerships and corporations can offer firms the best of both worlds.
- *The importance of a good management information system to accurately measure costs.* Students see the direct application of cost information on making business decisions using break-even analysis, determining the shutdown point, and good inventory management.
- *The use of basic accounting information to develop a sources and uses of net working capital document.* This increasingly popular financial document gives managers the ability to determine where a firm gets its money and where it spends it.
- *The use of the pro forma cash flow budget to forecast future cash needs and to plan loan repayments.*
- *A comprehensive discussion of the major capital budgeting procedures with applications.* This discussion includes a worked example of a buy-borrow-lease decision.
- *How the directing business management function is about leadership while the other three functions are about managing things.* Once understood, this important difference is what separates good managers from great managers.
- *The importance of personal selling to an agribusiness's success.* Regardless of your position in the firm, everyone is in sales—of themselves and their ideas. The eleven elements of successful personal selling are presented.
- *A decision case is included at the end of every chapter to give students the chance to immediately apply their new knowledge in an agribusiness setting they are likely to encounter.* Case learning leads to better student learning.
- *The final chapter assists students in putting all the pieces back together so they leave the course with a workable approach to agribusiness management that they can apply right away.*

This fourth edition of our text is based on our long experience of teaching a large introductory course on agribusiness management every fall and spring semester for many years. We offer classroom-tested presentations of the latest agribusiness management material using the best teaching and learning techniques available.

We are fortunate to live in exciting times!

Acknowledgments

No project like this is ever possible without the support and guidance of a number of people. We extend our thanks to our colleagues and students at The

Pennsylvania State University and the University of Missouri for their assistance and comments. Students' patience with the seemingly endless tinkering with presentation approaches and last-minute changes is greatly appreciated. We feel we all have benefited from these changes.

A special thank you goes to Al Beliasov for sharing his many years of successful selling with our students each semester. He is a master teacher. This is why we invited him to help us write the personal selling chapter. As Al is quick to remind us, we are all in sales because we must always sell ourselves and ideas to others.

We extend thanks to our families for allowing us to pursue projects such as book writing.

Finally, a special thank you to Neil Rowe at Waveland Press. His professionalism and support is greatly appreciated. Neil's good practice of business management is reflected in our editors Don Rosso and Diane Evans. Their care and feeding of dazzled authors helped make our book better. We appreciate your help!

James Beierlein
Kenneth Schneeberger
Donald Osburn

PART I

Introduction to the Business of Agriculture

When most people hear the term "agriculture," they often conjure up an image of a poorly educated, exhausted soul nobly tilling the good earth for a meager but honest income. Nothing could be further from the truth. Today's agri-food system is a global, fast-paced, high-technology industry that is one of the most effective adopters of scientific innovation. Managers in this industry must be well grounded in the technical aspects of food and fiber production as well as the principles of business management. This is a tall order but one that is routinely met every day when agribusiness managers integrate technology with business management to feed a hungry world.

The two chapters in this first section set the stage for all that follows by describing the evolution of agriculture from simple self-sufficient farming to a global agri-food system and the critical integrative role that business management plays in its success.

- ***Chapter 1—The Global Agri-Food System*** A prerequisite for being a successful manager is to understand the environment in which agribusinesses operate. The first chapter describes the evolution of the global agri-food system. It documents how more progress in food production was made during the past 100 years than in the previous 10,000. The chapter also points the way to the future and sets out the management skills that will be needed to continue this growth during the twenty-first century.
- ***Chapter 2—The Agribusiness Manager*** Because the agri-food system works so smoothly most people have never given a thought to the pivotal role that business management plays in its success. The second chapter is devoted to explaining how business management integrates new technologies with consumer needs to bring Americans the safest, greatest assortment of the lowest-priced food in the world. The battle to end world hunger is not yet won but agribusiness management will continue to play an important part in its success. The chapter sets out the unifying theme of this book—*that the goal of all managers is to maximize the long-term profits of their firms by profitably satisfying customers' needs*. The book's overall framework, the four functions of management—planning, organizing, controlling, and directing—is introduced.

Chapter 1

The Global Agri-Food System

Chapter Learning Objectives

- Describe how agribusiness firms operate in a global agri-food system that includes everyone from the suppliers who provide farmers and ranchers with the materials needed to produce a crop to the retailers who put food on our tables.
- Explain why agribusiness managers must integrate rapidly changing technology with business management skills in order to succeed in a volatile global market.
- Explain why agribusiness is a high-tech industry with a crucial mission that offers a challenging future for those who have the right technical and business management skills.

Introduction

Agribusiness is one of America's best kept secrets. It functions so flawlessly that few people realize the extent of its reach. For over 150 years, U.S. agribusiness firms have led the industry by consistently applying new technology and effective management to the **production**, **processing**, manufacturing, **distribution**, and **retailing** of food and fiber. As a result, Americans have the safest food supply and the highest variety of food available at the lowest cost in the world. This surplus has made the United States a major food supplier for the world. By the close of the twentieth century, food had "gone global" more than any other commodity. On nearly any day of the year, in nearly any food store or restaurant in the United States, consumers can find an overwhelming assortment of safe, fresh, exotic foods from around the world. This food abundance is increasingly being replicated around the world and is unprecedented in world history.

Despite our success, much work needs to be done. Currently, the global agri-food system is expanding the world's food supply at a rate that exceeds population growth. It is vital that this rate of growth be maintained until the middle of the twenty-first century, when world population is expected to stabilize. This means that what you do during your career to expand and improve the global food system will help determine whether the world will achieve this critical goal.

The Scope and Size of the Agri-Food System

Unfortunately, few people in this country recognize the grand system that surrounds them. The U.S. agri-food system is the largest part of our economy. It generates about one-sixth of the total **gross domestic product (GDP)** and one-eighth of all employment. If these numbers surprise you, you are not alone. Few people, even those who work in the system, have ever stopped to grasp its size and importance.

The **agri-food system** is made up of a variety of different agribusiness firms and includes more than just farmers and ranchers (see figure 1-1). Component industries of the agri-food system include:

- *Input Suppliers*—Agribusiness firms that prepare and sell things like feed, seed, fertilizer, and credit to farms and ranches.
- *Producers*—Agribusiness firms (farms and ranches) that purchase items from input suppliers and produce agricultural commodities such as wheat, corn, raw milk, cattle, fruits, and vegetables.
- *Commodity Processors*—Agribusiness firms that buy agricultural commodities such as raw milk, wheat, and live cattle from farms and ranches for processing into pasteurized milk, flour, boxed beef, and so on.
- *Food Manufacturers*—Agribusiness firms that purchase the processors' products to manufacture prepared food products. An example is a bakery that buys flour, processed eggs, and pasteurized milk to make bread and other baked goods.
- *Food Distributors*—Agribusiness firms that transport agricultural commodities as well as processed and manufactured food products between different parts of the agri-food system.

Figure 1-1 Product Flow in the Global Agri-Food System

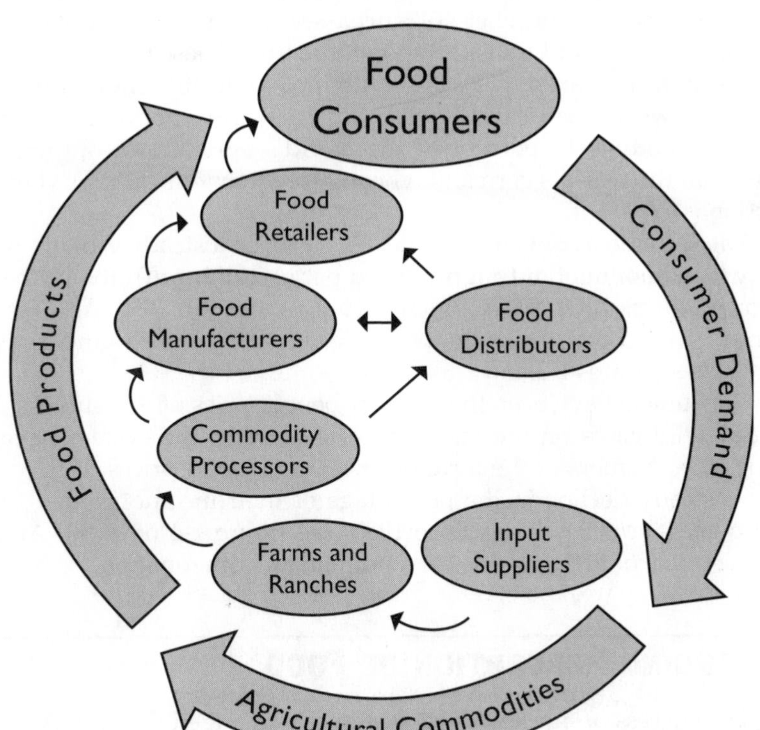

- *Food Retailers*—Agribusiness firms that sell agricultural commodities such as fresh fruits and vegetables, processed food products such as flour and pasteurized milk, manufactured food products, and prepared foods to consumers. Food stores and restaurants fall into this category.

This is a much broader definition than most people use when they consider agriculture. But everyone included in this definition plays an important part in bringing us food. They all must work together efficiently and effectively or nothing happens. The term *agri-food system* is increasingly used to capture the full dimension of interaction between all these parts. The term *agri-* captures all the activities associated with the production of agricultural commodities. *Food* captures all the activities between production and final consumption of food products.

U.S. agribusiness firms are a leading force in this global system. Every day they provide each American with approximately six pounds of food. They bring us around 1,000 new food items each month. Each farm worker produces enough food to feed more than 100 people, with more than a quarter of them living abroad. In return, farmers and ranchers receive approximately 19 percent of each dollar spent on food. The average U.S. consumer spends just 9.9 percent of their disposable (after-tax) income on food, with 5.8 percent spent on food prepared at home and 4.1 percent on food offered outside the home.

The **production sector** is a major part of this system. It comprises 13 percent of the combined dollar value of the system's output and 16 percent of its employment. While farm workers make up a small part of the general economy (less than 2 percent), the total number still surpasses the combined sum of workers in the steel, automobile, and transportation industries. These few people feed the nation and a significant part of the world with incredible efficiency. With less than 7 percent of the world's land and 5 percent of the world's population, U.S. farmers and ranchers produce 12 percent of the world's agricultural output. This includes about half the world's corn and wheat. More than one quarter of each year's production is exported.

The secret to agribusiness's success has been a steady growth in farm **productivity** (the amount of **output** produced per unit of **input**). Today, the same level of input produces 2.8 times as much output as it did in 1950. As a result, each farm worker now produces enough food to feed five times the number of people he did in 1950 (see figures 1-2 and 1-3).

Consumers have been the primary beneficiaries of this success. Nearly all the productivity gains on the farm and elsewhere in the system have been passed along to consumers in the form of lower retail food prices. U.S. consumers have seen a steady decline in the percentage of their income needed for food—from 24.2 percent to 9.5 percent since 1930 (see figure 1-4 on p. 8). Americans pay a smaller share of their income for food than any other nation.

THE CHANGING PERCEPTION OF FOOD

The success of our agri-food system has changed the way Americans look at food. Abundance, variety, safety, and low cost give U.S. citizens the luxury of

Figure 1-2 Farm Productivity Index

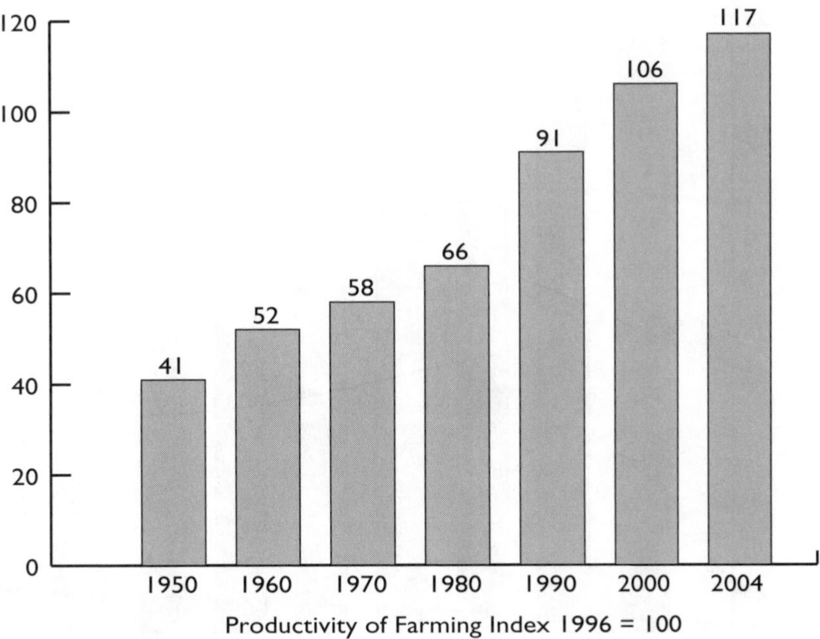

Figure 1-3 People Fed per Farmer

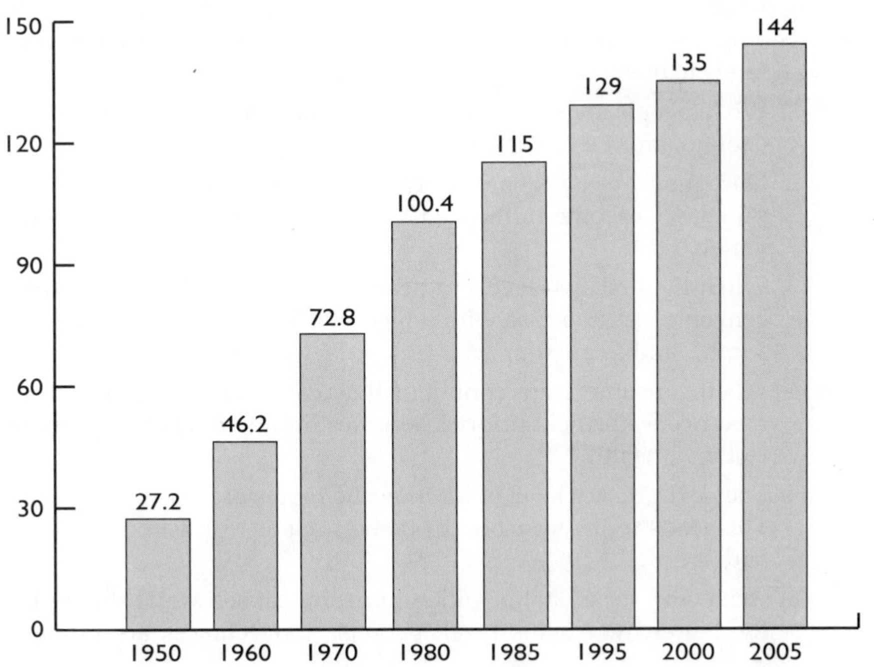

Figure 1-4 Percent of Income Spent on Food

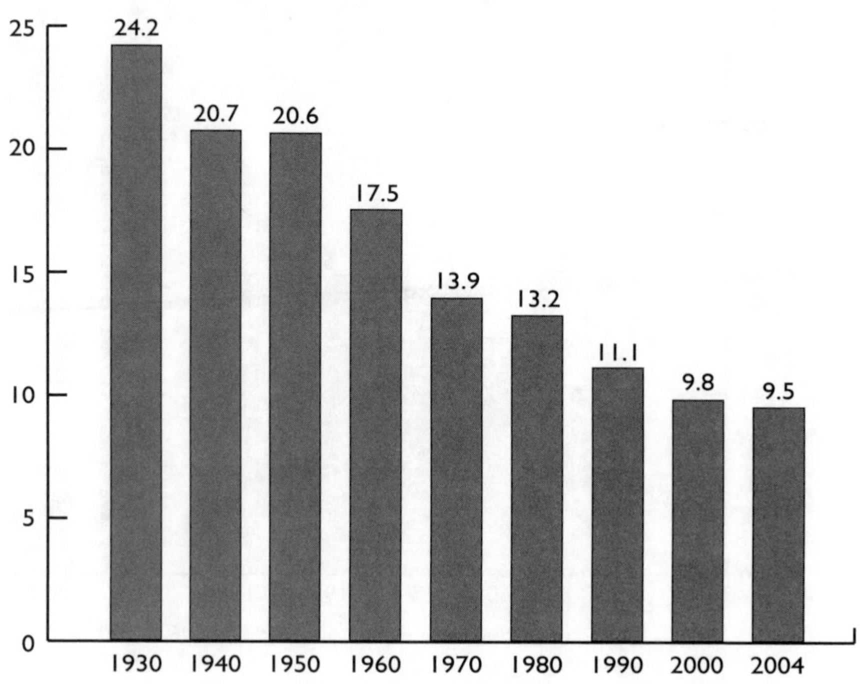

being highly selective in their food purchases. Jean Kinsey, a well-known agricultural economist, found a hierarchy of reasons that people consider when deciding which foods to buy (see figure 1-5).

1. When people are struggling to find enough to eat, they simply want to find enough affordable, safe, and nutritious food.
2. Once they are confident they can achieve this on a regular basis, their food purchases become influenced by whether the food tastes good and offers variety.
3. When the first two levels of needs are assured, the next priority becomes convenience—the ease with which this food or meal can be prepared, consumed, and cleaned up.
4. When consumers are confident they can achieve the first three levels of food needs, the next priority becomes finding foods that promote and protect their health.
5. The next priority level is whether the food purchase helps one to live well. This leads to the selection of items such as exquisite wines, exotic foods, and so on.
6. Achieving social status and supporting causes are at the highest level of the hierarchy. At this level, people's food choices are guided by issues

Figure 1-5 People Buy Food for a Hierarchy of Reasons

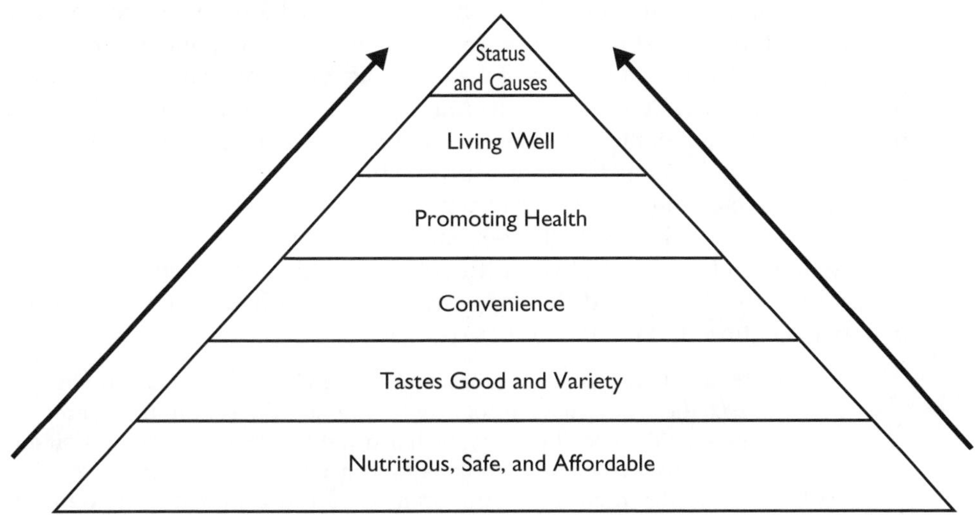

other than nutrition. Causes vary from buying canned tuna fish only from firms that certify they have not harmed dolphins to eating chickens that were raised humanely. In some people's eyes, one gains status by opposing food products that utilize biotechnology in their production or irradiation in their processing.

Because of the affluence and success of the U.S. agri-food system, increasing numbers of consumers are basing their food-buying decisions on the items at the top of Kinsey's hierarchy. Intense market competition for the consumers' food dollar combined with the growing size of this market segment means that agribusiness firms throughout the agri-food system must pay greater attention to these issues if they wish to be successful in the future.

Combining Science, Technology, and Business Management

Nearly all the benefits we derive from our world-class agri-food system come from the transformation of science into **technology** and the application of effective business management. Don and Philip Paarlberg explained it this way in their book *The Agricultural Revolution of the 20th Century* (p. 59): "Science remains in the laboratory unless there is incentive to adopt the knowledge. This is the difference between science and technology."

The conditions that made this happen in U.S. agriculture came from three sources: a free-enterprise, democratic system of government that rewards those who successfully take risks, the human race's perpetual desire to generate an adequate food supply, and vast tracts of high quality, inexpensive, available land.

The Role of Science and Technology

Since the beginning of time man has worked hard to secure an adequate amount of food. Those farmers who could profitably expand their production knew that they could achieve great wealth. This typically meant hiring more farm workers. From colonial times, the seemingly endless supply of low-priced land in the United States meant that farmers were always hard-pressed to find enough laborers to permit them to expand production. Most workers stayed just long enough to save enough money to buy their own farms. Thus, U.S. farmers were a ready audience for the production-enhancing and labor-saving devices that technology had to offer. The Industrial Revolution, which engulfed the latter half of the nineteenth century, laid the foundation for the agricultural revolution of the twentieth century that the Paarlbergs describe:

> If a farmer from Old Testament times could have visited an American farm in the year 1900, he would have recognized—and had the skill to use—most of the tools he saw: the hoe, the plow, the harrow, the rake. If he were to visit an American farm today, he might think he was on a different planet.
>
> The changes that occurred in American agriculture during the 20th century exceeded in magnitude all the changes that had occurred during the 10,000 years since human beings first converted themselves from hunters and gathers to herdsman and cultivators. (p. xiii)

The Role of Business Management

The presence of new technologies is important to the growth of agriculture, but without a way to organize these scientific advances, their full potential would be lost. Farm management began to emerge in the last two decades of the nineteenth century. The goal of farm management (which later evolved into agribusiness management) was to find a way to integrate the workings of technology to maximize benefits to farmers and consumers. As the Paarlbergs described, "Throughout history, farmers exercised the role of management, putting together the products of these overlapping and reinforcing [scientific] disciplines, together with finance, economics, and business, in an effort to make a profit."

Modern agribusiness **managers** have successfully met this challenge. They integrate knowledge of rapidly evolving production technology in agronomy, animal science, food science, and plant science with the business management skills of marketing, human resources, finance, and **economics** to profitably produce food and fiber. In recent years advances in logistics, telecommunications, and operations management have made agri-food one of the first truly global industries.

The Evolution of the Agri-Food System

Until the middle of the nineteenth century, most Americans lived on farms. The typical farm produced little more than what the farmer and his family needed to survive. Because there was little to sell to others to generate cash, many farms became self-sufficient operations that did most of their own input preparation and food processing. Large-scale agricultural operations developed only in the southern cotton industry following Eli Whitney's 1793 invention of the cotton gin. Cotton was the leading U.S. export from colonial times until after the Civil War.

Beginning around 1840, the first applications of the expanding Industrial Revolution found their way to the farm. Cyrus McCormick introduced the first mechanical wheat-harvesting equipment in 1840. The 1847 invention of John Deere's moldboard plow made it possible to cut through the tough prairie sod; as a result, the number of acres under cultivation nearly doubled during the 1870s. The Industrial Revolution also brought improvement in large-scale food processing operations such as flour milling.

As a result of this revolution in agriculture, two new sectors of agriculture emerged (see figure 1-6). Large-scale commodity processing and food manufacturing moved off the farm; it became cheaper, easier, and less time-consuming to buy things such as flour and canned foods at a store than to prepare them at home. Similar forces were at work on the input side of the farm as well; it became cheaper, easier, and less time-consuming to buy production inputs such as seed, fertilizer, and feed from others than to produce it on the farm. The end result of these changes was the development of two independent industries: one devoted to producing inputs and another to commodity processing/food manufacturing.

Both of these changes benefited producers. Farmers were able to buy inputs that were more productive and cheaper than those they could produce themselves, thus reducing their production costs. Farmers were also freed from time-consuming chores such as butchering their own meats and canning their own fruits and vegetables. This gave them more time to devote to the thing they did best—producing more commodities. As a result, the whole system became more efficient overall. Output soared. Farmers and ranchers achieved their long-term goals. Fewer farm workers were needed; the released workers were quickly re-employed in the growing factories of the Industrial Revolution. Farmers evolved into specialists in the efficient production of agricultural commodities.

Figure 1-6 The Agri-Food System

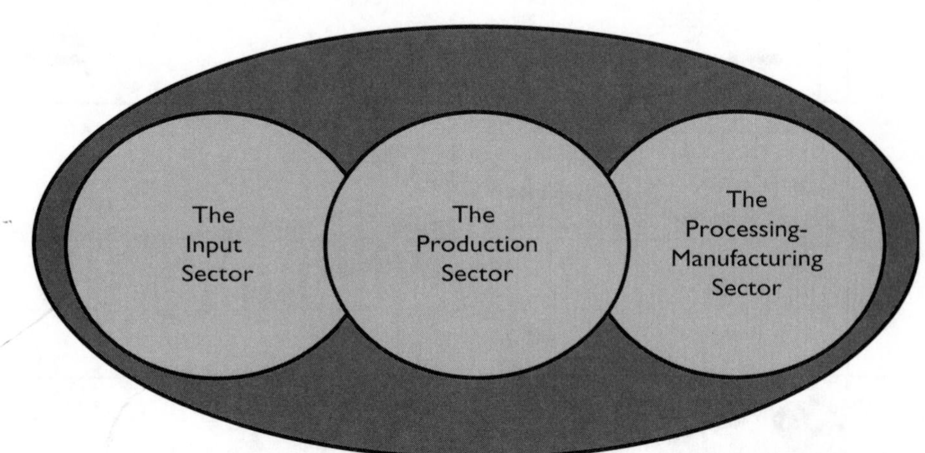

The Future of the Agri-Food System

The agricultural revolution of the twentieth century created today's three-part global agri-food system. The forces that shaped this system are still at work. The system has become more interdependent with the rest of the economy than it was in the past, and this will continue in the future. The abundance of food supplies has given consumers greater choices than ever before. As a result, more consumers around the world are moving up Kinsey's hierarchy and demanding more than just safe, affordable, nutritious food. Agribusiness firms throughout the system must be responsive to these desires, since consumers have many potential food suppliers from whom they can buy their food. Only those who remain responsive will prosper.

Consumers' desires for greater accountability and specific product attributes must be translated back through the system if these needs are to be met. A recent example is the rapid shift in consumer preference to organically grown food. Demand for beef has stabilized in the past several years after many years of decline. Success today requires full coordination and a quick response of the agri-food system to these changing consumer preferences. Merely supplying affordable, safe, nutritious food is not enough anymore.

The Input Sector

The impact of technology clearly can be seen in the evolution of the **input sector**. Scientific advances, many coming from land-grant universities, led the way to many of the sector's technological improvements. These improvements made it possible to more than double agricultural production since 1950 while inputs remained fairly constant (see figure 1-7).

Figure 1-7 Farm Productivity

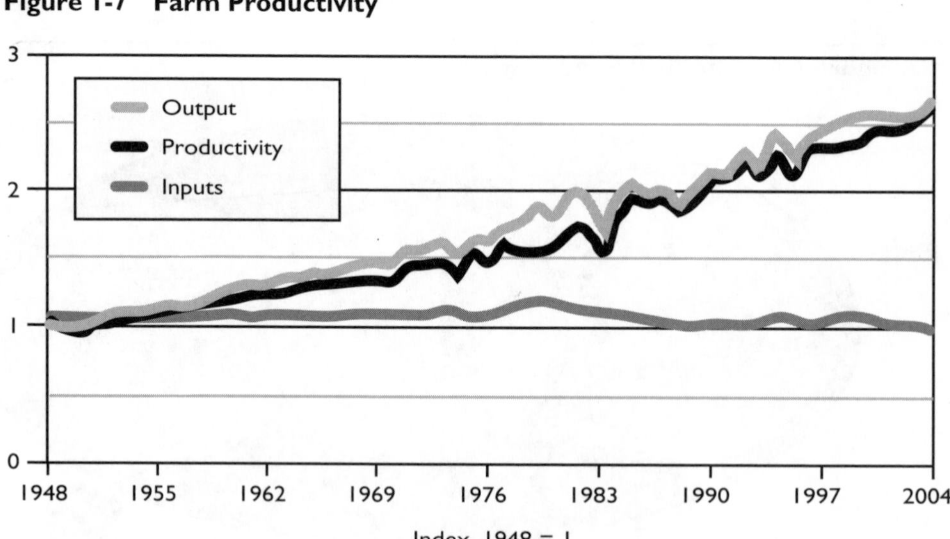

The most profound change is the continuing decline in labor use. This trend reflects producers' long-standing desire to lower production costs by substituting different inputs for relatively higher-priced farm labor. The major substitutes for labor have been chemical (herbicides and pesticides) and mechanical (tractors and combines). It is no longer necessary to hire workers to remove weeds using hoes or to plant and harvest a crop by hand. Since 1980, the use of all inputs has fallen slightly while output has continued to grow as producers have improved their business management skills and acquired more productive inputs. The return from the use of better inputs and better management practices is seen in the continued decline in the number of hours of farm work required to plant an acre (down 70 percent) and in the steady rise in crop and animal yields since 1950 (figure 1-8).

Figure 1-8 Labor Use

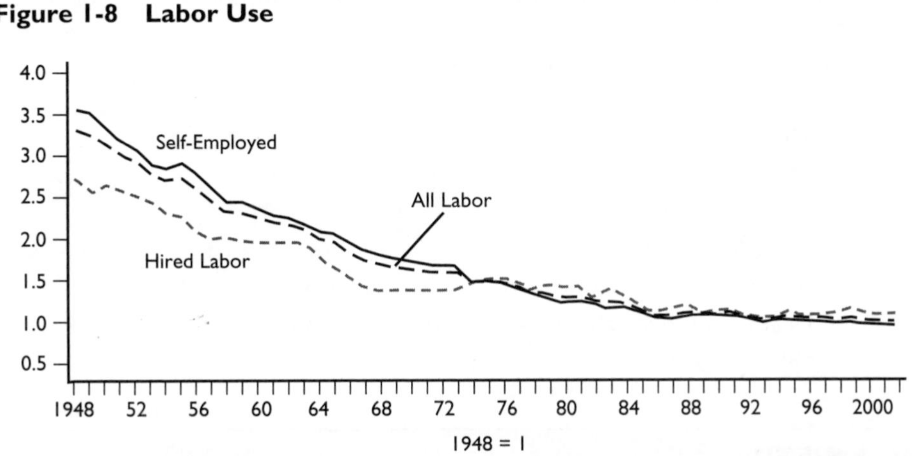

The input sector evolved slowly during the twentieth century. Much of the work on developing and certifying high-yield seed varieties began in the late 1920s at colleges of agriculture. The growth of commercial fertilizer-production capacity came partly as a by-product of World War II. The same products used as fertilizer—nitrogen, phosphorus, and potassium—are key ingredients in bombs and bullets. At the end of the war, the government sold its munitions plants to private-sector owners, who often converted these plants to fertilizer production. In the 1930s, Franklin Roosevelt's New Deal Rural Electric Administration brought electricity to many farms and the Farm Credit Administration set up a banking system better suited to the special needs of farmers and ranchers.

Thus, government activity, research, and private enterprise have combined to build a separate stand-alone input sector whose firms' sole purpose is to meet producers' input needs.

The Production Sector

The development of a separate input sector was one of several forces that changed the way the production sector operates. First, the development of these two new sectors of the agri-food system enabled farmers and ranchers to concentrate their efforts on producing greater quantities of agricultural commodities. Because of the inelastic nature of **supply** and **demand** for most commodities, the increases in output led to declines in market prices. Second, because of declining prices brought on by the adoption of new technology, farmers and ranchers had to seek out lower cost-per-unit production methods. Third, many of these lower-cost production methods and productivity-enhancing inputs are expensive and need to be utilized to produce large volumes in order to gain the maximum benefit for the producer.

Since 1950, these forces have brought about a number of significant changes in the production sector:

- The number of farms in the United States has shrunk by nearly two thirds (5.6 million to 1.9 million).
- The average farm size has more than doubled (213 to 471 acres).
- Net farm income as a percent of farm receipts has been halved (from 41 percent to 19 percent).
- The distribution of farm numbers and annual sales has become skewed to where 2 percent of the farms produce approximately 50 percent of the output.
- Despite all these changes, more than 99 percent of all farms and acreage are still family owned.

The Shifting Roles of Exports and Imports

American agriculture has always looked to export markets as a way to boost demand for its agricultural commodities. During our country's first hundred years the vast majority of our exports were agricultural products. Like the rest of the agri-food system, exports are now undergoing profound change. Major portions of our wheat (almost half), corn (almost one-fifth), and soybeans (more than one-third) are exported each year. The changing world scene, as well as the economic landscape of the 1990s, has also brought about alterations in what is traded and who our trading partners are.

U.S. Role as Exporter

The United States has been a net exporter of agricultural products since 1959. However, since 1996, the agricultural trade surplus shrunk from $27.3 billion (an all-time high) to $10.5 billion. Although the United States is still the world's leading exporter of farm products, imports are increasing nearly twice as fast. In 2003, U.S. agricultural exports grew by almost $3 billion. However, imports increased by more than $13 billion, from $32 billion in 1996 to $46 billion in 2003.

Only 20 years ago, almost half of U.S. exports consisted of major bulk commodities (grains, oilseeds, cotton, and tobacco). Today, this share has fallen to 36 percent. There are several reasons why this shift occurred, many of which originated outside the United States. In 1997, a financial crisis began in Asia, stifling demand for U.S. products in markets such as Korea, Taiwan, Hong Kong, Thailand, and Indonesia. As this crisis spread to Russia and South America, exports fell even further. Concurrently, the U.S. economy experienced a boom, which effectively drove up export prices at a time when those we exported to were experiencing a major decline. As a result, demand for U.S. products fell, and the value of agricultural exports dropped by more than $10 billion during a three-year period (1996–1999).

Processed foods have buoyed U.S. agricultural exports in the past, but today high labor costs limit U.S. competitiveness. The booming economy of the 1990s in the United States also allowed U.S. consumers to spend more on processed foods, foods that could be produced cheaper in foreign markets. In 2003, processed foods, feed products, and beverages accounted for $28 billion (62 percent) of U.S. imports. These imports exceeded U.S. agricultural exports by more than $2 billion, the first time since 1989. Processed food imports increased by an average of 7 percent per year from 1994 to 2003, for a total of 96 percent over a decade (see figure 1-9).

Figure 1-9 U.S. Processed Food Imports and U.S. Exports

The Future of Imports and Exports

Agricultural economists Philip Paarlberg and Phil Abbott from Purdue University predict that, if these trends continue, the current agricultural trade surplus will turn into a deficit toward the end of the decade. This type of prediction raises questions about the competitiveness of the United States in the world agricultural market as well as consumer preferences at home.

A number of key economic and demographic forces (continued U.S. population growth, higher real disposable income, a relatively strong dollar, and comparatively weaker economies in Japan and the European Union) suggest that recent trends in import and export growth are likely to continue over the next few years. As noted previously, changing consumer preferences in food and beverages, driven in part by healthier lifestyles and increasing ethnic diversity, are evident in the products that are increasingly imported today.

Agriculture and the Environment

The production sector has made tremendous progress in improving its environmental record. Better production practices such as minimum tillage, integrated pest management (IPM), the Conservation Reserve Program (CRP), and biotechnology all have lessened this sector's impact on the environment. In 2004, 41 percent of planted acreage used some form of conservation tillage (no-till, ridge till, or mulch till). These tillage practices are believed to reduce input costs with either a neutral or slightly positive impact on yield.

Soil Erosion

Since 1982, new production processes have helped to reduce soil erosion by 38 percent to 1.9 tons per year during the late 1990s. Reduced soil erosion also improves water quality by keeping nutrients and pesticides in the field where they can be used by crops, reducing their movement into nearby lakes, streams, and groundwater. Crop residues left on the soil surface improve air quality by reducing wind erosion, therefore lowering dust. Despite this progress, excessive erosion continues to be a serious problem in many parts of the country.

Land Use

The United States has a total land area of nearly 2.3 billion acres. In 2002, 587 million acres (25.9 percent) was used for rangeland, 651 million acres (28.8 percent) for forestland, and 442 million acres (19.5 percent) was used for cropland. Special uses (parks and wildlife areas) accounted for 297 million acres (13.1 percent) while urban land accounted for 60 million acres (2.6 percent). From 1997 to 2002, cropland declined by almost 3 percent (14 million acres). However, during this same period grassland pasture and range, as well as forest and special-use areas, increased. The most consistent trends in major uses of land in the United States have seen an upward trend in special-use and urban areas and a downward trend in total grazing lands.

Some people have been concerned about whether we are losing our valuable cropland to urban development. The figures presented above indicate that it is a concern but not a threat. Prime farmland is declining, but in 2002 it declined only 1 percent below the previous low recorded in 1964. A comparison of land use over the 53-year period from 1949 to 2002 shows the total cropland usage decreasing slightly from 478 million acres to 442 million acres. Thus, while we are losing some prime farmland it is at a rate that could be stopped easily (see figure 1-10).

Figure 1-10 Changes in U.S. Land Use, 1945 vs. 2002*

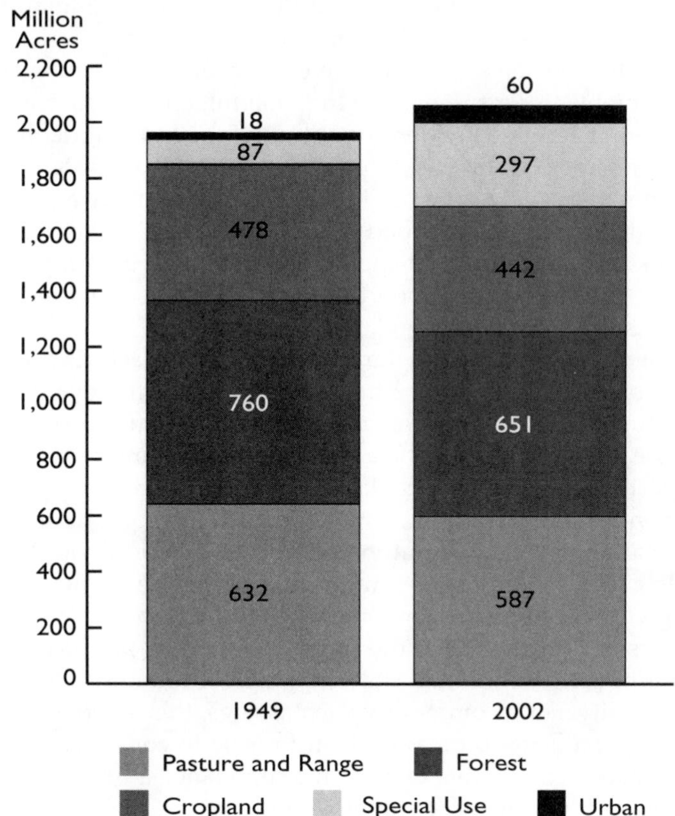

*Until 1959, the area for special uses only included the 48 contiguous states.

THE COMMODITY PROCESSING AND FOOD MANUFACTURING SECTOR

Like the input sector, the commodity processing and food manufacturing sector's growth has come from improving technology and good business management. Large-scale industrial production in the mid-1800s brought increased use of canned food and milled flour. Railroads gave farmers access to urban markets.

During this period, Minnesota and the Dakotas were major growing areas for soft red winter and spring wheat. Minneapolis grew as a flour-milling center because of its proximity to the crop and its access to inexpensive waterpower. Railroads could then take the flour to major consumer centers. Consumers could have store-bought flour that was better and less expensive than what they could mill at home. Improved, safer canning techniques enabled people to eat a wider variety of food year round, and they no longer had to live near a farm to do it. The widespread use of canned food during the Civil War expanded its acceptance. Improvement in the processing and manufacturing procedures made it safer, cheaper, and easier to buy food in stores than to do the work yourself.

Two types of firms emerged from this transition: commodity processors and food manufacturers. *Commodity processors* take a raw agricultural commodity from a producer (such as raw milk, live cattle, or wheat) and process it into a form more acceptable to consumers and food manufacturers (such as pasteurized milk, boxed beef, or flour). The identity of the original raw agricultural commodity is normally retained at the end of processing. *Food manufacturers* mix raw agricultural commodities and processed food together to make a product that does not resemble the ingredients. A good example is a pizza maker who starts with flour, eggs, milk, tomato sauce, and cheese and ends up with a ready-to-eat pizza. This sector also includes all the food transporters and food retailers (food stores and restaurants) who distribute food to consumers.

Much of what happens in the **processing/manufacturing sector** is designed to provide consumers food in the time, place, and form they desire. Processors and manufacturers do this because consumers are willing to pay more for products with these characteristics. When you go to a restaurant and order a hamburger, you expect to receive a fully cooked patty on a bun ready to eat. You do not want to be given a lead rope to a live cow and a gun! To avoid this you are willing to pay extra to have someone else put the product in the form you desire. Likewise, you are willing to pay extra to get your product at the right time and in the right place.

To give consumers the convenience they want in their food typically requires that others perform much of the labor. This is why producers' earnings average 19.5 cents of each food dollar. Is this too high or too low? The answer depends on the commodity. For a commodity such as eggs, this is too low because eggs need very little processing to prepare them for sale to consumers. For a food product such as bakery goods, this may be too high since a great deal of work must be done to produce an item acceptable to consumers.

Labor accounts for nearly 40 percent of all money spent on food. This money pays others to do the food preparation work we want. Many people are surprised to see how little goes to **profit** (4.5 percent). This level is typical of most businesses (see figure 1-11).

Food sales generally grow at the same rate as the population (1 percent). Like other firms, food processors and manufacturers are constantly looking around the world for new products that will increase their sales and profits. To accomplish this, the industry brings out approximately 1,000 new food items per month. Some of these are small changes such as new flavors and different container sizes. Others are totally new concepts such as frozen pudding on a stick. Few of these products survive.

Figure 1-11 What a Dollar of Food Pays For

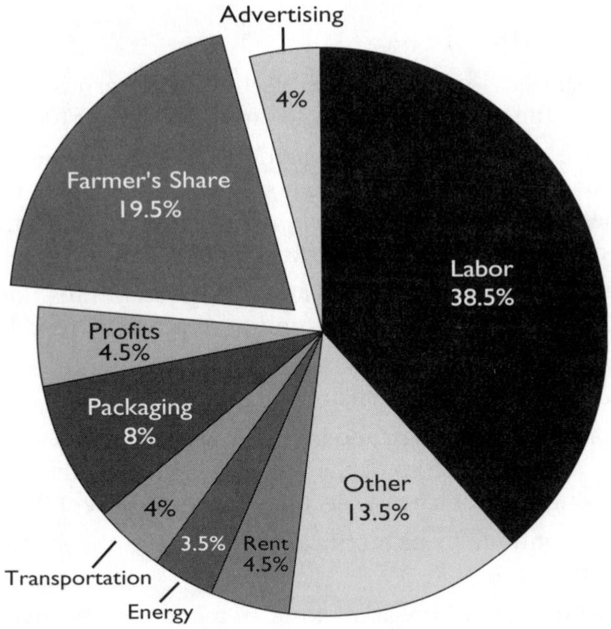

Food Retailing

Consumers' food dollars are now nearly evenly split between food eaten at home and food eaten away from home. The restaurant and supermarket industries are always striving to keep up with changing consumer preferences. As market competition intensifies and more of their consumers move up to higher levels of Kinsey's food buying hierarchy, food retailers are under relentless pressure to search for new and better food products and services.

The typical supermarket stocks nearly 45,000 food items from around the world in a store that covers slightly more than a full acre of space (48,750 square feet). The nation's grocery stores employ 21 percent (3.5 million) of the people in the agri-food system in over 127,000 stores. Shoppers visit these stores an average of 1.9 times per week and spend an average of about $29 per visit, ringing up average weekly total sales for the store of $327,000. Supermarkets earn a profit of 1 percent of sales. They survive by generating high sales volumes and turning their inventories over several times each year.

Restaurants, like supermarkets, also need to keep abreast of consumers' changing tastes. The competition is intense. Restaurants are the most popular type of business to open. They are also the most likely type of business to fail. Restaurants are the largest private employer in the agri-food system and in the United States. They employ over 12.8 million workers (9 percent of all workers) in over 900,000 establishments and serve 70 billion meals a year. Despite their size, most restaurants are single-unit operations that employ less than 20 people and whose customers' average bill is less than $7 per person.

Chapter Highlights

1. Agribusiness is one of America's best-kept secrets because it flawlessly brings us the safest, freshest, and largest variety of food in the world.
2. The term agri-food system was developed to capture the full impact of how food is brought to consumers. The agri-food system includes the agribusiness firms that are input suppliers, producers, commodity processors, food manufacturers, food distributors, and food retailers.
3. The agribusiness firms in the agri-food system must keep abreast of rapidly changing consumer needs and perceptions of food in order to survive.
4. The development of the agri-food system depends on the application of science, technology, and business management.
5. The forces of technology and business management led to the development of two separate sectors of the agri-food system—the input sector and the processing/manufacturing sector—that supplement the production sector.
6. Exports continue to be a critical ingredient in the success of U.S. production agriculture.
7. Production agriculture is making tremendous improvements in its environmental record.

Chapter Quiz

1. List and briefly describe the six parts of the global agri-food system.
2. Define and describe each word in the term agri-food system.
3. Why was agriculture a prime market for the adoption of production-enhancing and laborsaving devices during the Industrial Revolution?
4. How has Americans' perception of food changed in recent years? What does this mean for the agribusiness firms in the agri-food system?
5. What is the difference between science and technology?
6. What is the role of business management in the success of the agri-food system?
7. Identify the three major sectors of the agri-food system. Describe the evolution of agriculture into the agri-food system.
8. How do you think the agri-food system will meet the food needs of the world's population in the future? How will it change as a workplace?
9. Explain why you are optimistic or pessimistic about the agri-food system's ability to produce enough food to feed a hungry world. What are the biggest challenges it will face in achieving this crucial goal?
10. Describe the role of export markets and how they have changed.
11. Describe the production sector's environmental record.

12. What is the difference between an agricultural commodity and a food product?
13. Describe the steps in the agri-food system and what happens at each step in the journey from "dirt to dinner."
14. Explain Kinsey's hierarchy of why people buy food (figure 1-5), and then use it to explain the success of grocery store chains such as Whole Foods.
15. Describe the role of agribusiness management in the evolution of the agri-food system.
16. Describe the role of exports and the composition of exports in the financial success of the U.S. agri-food sector.
17. Develop your response to people who tell you U.S. agriculture is destroying the environment and we are losing prime farmland at an alarming rate.
18. If the farmers, processors, manufacturers, and retailers are all making small profits, who is profiting from our global agri-food system?
19. Why was the agri-food system the first application of the benefits of the Industrial Revolution in the United States? How did this influence the industrial growth of our country?
20. What is **agri-phobia** and what is the best way to overcome it?
21. Compare and contrast the terms agribusiness management, technology, and science. Explain how they interact to make our agri-food system work efficiently and effectively.

CASE 1
Angela's Agri-Phobia

The warm October sun felt good on Julie's face as she headed back to her dorm. It was Friday afternoon, and the week was finally over. Because of tomorrow's football game she had decided to stay at school this weekend. While the game would be great, she would miss being home since October was one of the prettiest times of the year at her family's 650-cow dairy farm located in the picturesque mountains in the central part of the state.

Julie did not have much choice about where she went to college. It seemed as though everyone in her family had graduated from this school. She came to college with the firm goal of continuing her family's long involvement with production agriculture. She and her younger brother had talked about expanding the family's dairy farm once they both graduated from college. Where she came from it seemed that nearly everyone either worked on a farm or for a business that was linked to one.

It came as a pleasant surprise when she learned that her roommate this year also was majoring in agriculture. Unlike Julie, Angela came from a suburban area outside of the largest city in the state. Nobody in her family had ever really had any strong involvement with agriculture. She had enrolled so she could combine her interests in horticulture and the environment.

When Julie got to their room, she saw that Angela was upset and packing her suitcase. She seemed to be packing more than just what she needed for the weekend. When Julie asked her what was wrong, Angela nearly exploded. "I'm tired of everyone asking me why I want to be a farmer and telling me how sad it is that someone with my good grades and high test scores is wasting her time preparing for a career in a dead-end field like agriculture. Besides, if I were going to be a farmer, why would I waste my time going to college? If I can't get my major changed quickly to something with a decent future, I'm out of here!"

In the six weeks they had lived together, Julie had sensed that Angela was uncomfortable being labeled an "aggie." It did not seem that her parents were very happy about it either. Angela had told her a story about how she and her mother had met one of her mother's friends in the supermarket just before school started. When the friend asked her mother what Angela was planning for a major, her mother looked very embarrassed and mumbled something about flowers.

Once Angela calmed down she said, "You're a bright person. How come you aren't getting out of agriculture and doing something useful with your life? I just can't see myself working on a farm in the middle of nowhere the rest of my life."

If you were Julie what would you tell Angela about the future of agriculture that might change her mind?

Chapter 2

The Agribusiness Manager

Chapter Learning Objectives

- Summarize how business management plays a crucial role in the success of agribusiness firms.
- Explain why business management is an art supported by science.
- Describe how the unifying theme of this text ties together everything a manager does.
- Explain how firms earn their right to make a profit when they give their customers value.
- Explain why long-run business success requires that firms be the first choice of their customers, employees, and investors.
- Explain how being the first choice of customers, employees, and investors means a business must be efficient and effective in all it does.
- Explain the difference between managing things and leading people.
- Describe why it is important to be a good leader before being a great manager.
- Summarize the six-step process used in business decision making.
- Identify the four functions of management and explain their role in agribusiness success.
- Discuss the unique management challenges facing agribusiness managers.
- Explain why agribusiness management is a dynamic, continuous process.

Introduction

Chapter one showed how the success of the agri-food system depends heavily on the continual adoption and integration of new technology. New technology improves the **technical efficiency** of the system by increasing the amount of output per unit of input. Business management improves the **economic efficiency** of agribusiness by finding profitable ways to apply new technology. As Paarlberg and Paarlberg reminded us in their history of twentieth-century agricultural research, science stays science if it stays in the laboratory. Science becomes technology when it can be applied to make peoples' lives better.

Agribusiness management is all about adoption and integration of technology in ways that maximize the business's long-term profits. This process is worthwhile because businesses earn their right to make a profit *only* when their products provide their customers with **value**—satisfaction that exceeds cost—and enhance their well-being. The better they do this, the greater the business's profits. Thus, agribusiness managers play an important role in the overall success of the agri-food system by putting technology to work in a way that ensures that producers and consumers gain the maximum benefit from the available technology.

THE DEVELOPMENT OF THE BUSINESS MANAGEMENT PROFESSION

Like science and technology, business management traces its origins to the Industrial Revolution. Until the late 1800s, little need existed for business management. Most businesses were small, owner-operated enterprises with few employees. The advent of the Industrial Revolution brought large-scale production facilities with more complex production processes and greater numbers of employees. The growth in the size of business created a separation between the functions of owners and managers, and forced owners to deal with the question of what makes a good manager.

Until then, the only large organizations that had existed for any length of time had been the military and the church. As the number of large firms grew, the level of interest in business management expanded. In the beginning, the subject of business management was examined from the perspectives of engineering, economics, psychology, and other subjects. It was not until the 1930s that business management became a separate **profession**, such as engineering, medicine, and law, to be studied at the college level. If you look closely at what business managers do, you see a profession that applies knowledge from a diverse set of academic **disciplines** such as economics, statistics, psychology, and mathematics to accomplish its objectives. Because it applies knowledge and draws from so many separate disciplines, it stands as a separate profession.

THE ROLE OF MANAGEMENT IN SUCCESSFUL BUSINESSES

Managers must perform a variety of tasks to succeed. Each task requires a degree of technical ability, but also embodies general **management** functions and problem-solving procedures. *The unifying theme that ties together everything a manager does is the desire to maximize the long-term profits of the firm by profitably satisfying customers' needs.* This unifying theme places two major responsibilities on business managers. First, they must successfully integrate all their assets (technical, financial, physical, and human) in order to produce a saleable product. Second, they must do this better, faster, cheaper, and quicker than their competitors before they earn the right to make a profit.

This requires that businesses be **efficient** (do things well) by using all their resources in the best possible ways over the long run. Firms do this when they maximize their long-run profits. They evaluate their efficiency by calculating the firm's return on invested **capital** (profit/assets). Efficient firms are *sustainable* because they operate from this long-run perspective. It also requires that businesses be **effective** (do the right things). Firms accomplish this when they profitably satisfy their customers' needs. Thus, businesses that accomplish the unifying theme meet management expert Peter Drucker's definition of what it takes for long-run business success—be efficient and effective.

Long-run business success requires one more ingredient. Well-known business management expert Stephen Covey says that an organization must also enhance the economic well-being of all its stakeholders—customers, employees, and investors—in order to achieve long-run success. Thus, the recipe for long-run business success can be represented by the three Es:

Efficiency + Effectiveness + Economic Well-Being

Business managers can achieve the three Es when their firms are the first choice of:

- ***their customers***—their products must provide their customers with the greatest value;
- ***their employees***—their jobs must provide their employees with the greatest overall satisfaction; and
- ***their investors***—their investments must provide their investors with the greatest financial return.

In order to become the first choice of your stakeholders business managers must be technically knowledgeable about their firm's products and services; a good communicator and motivator; proficient in the technical skills of business management such as **inventory** management, accounting, and forecasting; and most important, managers must have the ability to mix each of these skills in just the right proportion in each business situation to accomplish our unifying theme. This is why Peter Drucker saw business managers as practicing management just as a physician practices medicine or a lawyer practices law.

Successful business managers must be good leaders before they can be great managers. They must efficiently and effectively *manage* their technical processes, and they must also effectively *lead* their employees by being good communicators and motivators. This is what makes agribusiness management an art supported by science. It requires the use of just the right combination of technical know-how, leadership, logic, and judgment in order to be successful in each situation.

Business Management versus Leadership

A distinction must be made between business management and **leadership**. Those that only apply the technical skills of business to the management of things (inventory, production, and so on) are just managers. Leaders lead people, and get results that exceed the sum of the parts. The size of the difference reflects the leader's role and separates great leaders from people who are just managers. Leaders achieve their goals by remembering that managing things and processes gains maximum technical efficiency, but leading people gives the greatest overall result.

Thus, the best definition of business management is the accomplishment of tasks through people. Successful business managers are efficient (do things well) and effective (do the right things) managers of their technical processes, *and* they also are effective leaders who can communicate and motivate people. No one can be a truly great business manager without being a good leader first.

Business Decision Making

A major part of the manager's time is spent making decisions that affect the future success of the organization. Good decision making is at the heart of successful business management. Just as there are fundamental principles associated with management, there are fundamental principles associated with decision making. The goal is to identify these principles and develop a sound decision-making procedure that will (1) make decision making easier, (2) improve the quality of those decisions, (3) reduce the time necessary to make good decisions, and (4) improve the frequency of good decisions.

Good decision making requires clear and logical thinking. Good decision making means clearly understanding the problem; objectively weighing the alternatives; and efficiently/effectively implementing the best solution. However, to translate these general principles into practice requires more detail.

The Six Steps in Decision Making

1. Identifying the problem.

Clear identification of the problem is the most important and difficult step in decision making. How the problem is defined has a great deal to do with the type of decision that is made.

The first task is to find out exactly what the problem is. This usually requires a great deal of investigation. It is important that any problem solver keep digging until he or she really understands what is going on. Valuable sources of information are those people directly affected by the problem. They usually have insights into what the real problems are and often have one or two good solutions already worked out. The important point is to listen carefully. Listen to what is said, to what is not said, and to how it is said.

During the investigation, it is important to separate the symptoms from the problem to ensure that you are dealing with the real problem. If the real problem is not identified, the solution will not work and you will be forced to repeat the process until you get the problem right. It is better to take the time to correctly diagnose the problem. Once it is properly identified, it needs to be expressed in the most exact and concise terms possible. Then it is possible to make a good decision that solves the real problem the first time.

2. Determining alternative courses of action.

Once the problem has been correctly identified and concisely expressed, it is necessary to develop a list of all the pertinent courses of action that may solve the problem. The list should run from making major changes (such as closing the plant and filing for bankruptcy) to minor adjustments (such as tightening a screw). Sometimes doing nothing is the best solution. What is important is to identify *all* the relevant alternatives, which is impossible unless the problem is correctly identified. After some reflection, you should be able to select several alternatives that look promising for further consideration.

3. Analyzing the alternatives.

Analysis of the alternatives is a three-step process. First is the selection of an appropriate, measurable criterion (for example, sales, cost/unit, profit, return on investment, or units produced) that will be used for the evaluation of each alternative. The second step is to select a method of analysis that will give you an objective reading of the criterion chosen. The final step is to carry out the chosen analysis.

4. Selecting the best alternative.

If the preceding three steps are carried out satisfactorily, the best alternative will present itself. The best alternative gives the best result on the criterion that was objectively measured. The selection of the best alternative should be done in light of what maximizes long-run profits and helps profitably satisfy customers' needs.

5. Implementing the decision.

Now that the decision has been made, it is important to establish a mechanism to ensure that the decision is transformed into reality as efficiently and effectively as possible. Although this step seems relatively simple, it is often the most poorly done. Poor implementation can take a great decision and quickly turn it into a disaster.

6. Following up.

Once the first five steps have been completed, it is beneficial to review the results of the decision and the decision-making process. This review can be worthwhile for several reasons. First, it provides a way to assess general decision-making skills. Second, if the decision involves a recurring problem, the follow-up can help to better understand the problem so it can be handled more efficiently in the future. Third, it can help a high-level manager to identify the good managers who work for him or her: those who can accurately assess a situation, select and analyze alternatives, and efficiently/effectively implement a solution.

To make good decisions in business, a manager must complete all six steps in the above procedure. At the conclusion of each step, it is advisable to reevaluate the problem in light of any new information or insight that might have emerged during analysis. If the new data dramatically changes the assessment of the problem, the procedure must be started over. It is through constant reevaluation and updating that the manager ensures that the proposed solution best solves the problem.

THE FOUR FUNCTIONS OF MANAGEMENT

Managers do many things in order to be successful. They plan sales campaigns. They prepare budgets. They review the performance of businesses and people. The list goes on and on. In order to make the study of business management easier, it is necessary to shorten the list. One method is to separate these tasks into larger categories called functions. Each management function deals with a specific aspect of what managers do. The **four functions of management** are planning, organizing, controlling, and directing.

The Planning Function

The **planning function** includes all activities that determine the future of a business. The objective of planning is to put the firm in the best possible position relative to future business conditions and customer demands. This allows the firm to reap the highest profit from its activities. The scope of the plan may be grander for the head of the business, but planning must be done at every level. Business planning covers anything from what is going to be done this afternoon to meet the needs of a single customer to deciding whether to start a new line of business and open a new multimillion dollar plant to support it.

Planning concerns what will happen in the future, so being able to forecast future business conditions is important. Business forecasting involves evaluating both past and current conditions and making predictions of future customer demands and business conditions. Forecasting can be done in many ways, from making a simple intuitive guess to developing elaborate computer models. Planning can be applied to nearly every area of business, including sales, marketing, production, inventory, cash flow planning, and finance.

Planning begins with the development of the organization's **marketing plan**. The marketing plan is the business's road map to success. It shows the owners, the managers, the employees, and everyone else how the firm is going to be successful. The first item in the marketing plan is a definition of the firm's **purpose**. The purpose tells the owners, employees, investors, and the public in clear, concise terms what the firm intends to do. The purpose may be to provide a full line of liquid fertilizer applications to all the farmers in a county. It could be to sell cattle-feeding equipment to ranchers in eastern Oklahoma. Whatever it is, the purpose is what gives the firm its identity.

The second item in the marketing plan is a statement of the firm's objective. The **objective** is a statement of how the business is going to accomplish its purpose. It explains what the firm is going to do better, faster, cheaper, and so on that will give it a competitive advantage in the market (i.e., why someone would buy from them rather than someone else). For example, a business's objective could be to have the largest selection, the lowest price, the best credit terms, or the best service in the area.

The Organizing Function

Once the firm has made its plans, it is necessary to develop a way to convert them into reality. The **organizing function** covers all the issues surrounding how to set up a business. This requires the development of an organizational scheme that accomplishes the firm's purpose and objective efficiently (so things are done well) and effectively (so the right things are being done). The business must be concerned not only with the flow of work through the system but also with the people involved and their interrelationships. The well-being of employees is important because happy workers are productive workers, happy workers make happy customers, and happy customers mean a successful business.

How the firm is structured has a great deal to do with how employees perceive their work, sense of accomplishment, productivity, and how they make decisions. The biggest goal is to give employees a sense of belonging and a feeling of influence in what happens. To do this, businesses use a mixture of organizational approaches. Some use teams. Some organize by product. Some organize by market. The goal is to develop an organizational structure that best permits the accomplishment of the firm's purpose and objective.

Another aspect of organization is the selection of a legal structure (e.g., sole proprietorship, partnership, cooperative, or corporation). Each of these forms and their variations brings some advantages and disadvantages. Agribusiness managers need to understand what each has to offer in order to select the best one for their business.

The Controlling Function

The **controlling function** concerns giving management feedback on the firm's progress in achieving the goals set in planning. The amount and type of controls are usually decided by the size and complexity of the organization.

Controls are found at all levels and include measures of an individual's progress as well as the progress of entire departments and businesses. The level of progress should be measured against standards set in the planning and organizing functions. The achievement of some key standards, such as production rates per hour, cost per unit, or annual dollar sales, will determine the success or failure of the business. Severe deviations from these standards need to be detected early and warrant careful investigation. The fault may rest in the standard as well as in the performance of an individual or the organization.

Deciding the proper corrective action is often a judgment call by the manager. When only minor adjustments are needed, that is all that should be done. When a major overhaul is required, that is what should be done. The art is knowing the difference. Managers' control systems should give them enough information about how serious a problem is to correctly determine the appropriate response.

Controls (feedback mechanisms) should not impede the progress of the organization toward its purpose and objectives, but should provide an early warning of deviations. In this way, business controls assist managers in achieving their purpose and objective. This subject is covered in detail in the chapters on the organizing function.

The Directing Function

The fourth management function—**directing**—is where the planning, organizing, and controlling functions are brought together to convert the plan into reality. Directing is the actual implementation of the other three management functions and normally consumes about 90 percent of a manager's time. This is where agribusiness managers mesh plans, organizational schemes, and controls with human resources to accomplish the purpose and objective of the firm efficiently, effectively, and profitably. While the first three management functions are mainly about managing things, directing is about leadership. The focus of the directing management function is devoted to the leadership of people and how to set up a work environment where everyone seeks to excel.

Successful directing relies strongly on good leadership to accomplish its mission. If employees can see and understand the firm's purpose and objective, accept their importance, and recognize how what they do each day helps the firm accomplish them, then they are more likely to be productive employees. Their acceptance can usually best be accomplished if the workers are advised and consulted during the whole business planning process. Often they will have special insights that will improve the chances for success. Wise managers carefully *manage* their technological, financial, and physical resources, but are careful to *lead* their most valuable business asset—the people who do the work. A business can never be better than the people who work there. With good leadership, even a poor business plan can be successful.

THE AGRIBUSINESS MANAGEMENT CHALLENGE

In addition to all the normal challenges found in other types of businesses, the agribusiness manager must confront the extra burdens of uncertain weather, disease, changing technology, changes in government policies, fluctuations in foreign currency exchange rates, and the perishable nature of their products. The agribusiness manager needs all the management skills mentioned above plus a strong understanding of the biological and institutional factors surrounding the production of food and fiber as well as the ability to adapt quickly to volatile market conditions arising from changing government policies, weather, and technology. Successful agribusiness managers are effective leaders who can apply the right combination of technical and management skills at the proper levels to fit each new situation.

Agribusiness Management Is a Dynamic, Continuous Process

By using the functional approach to business management, it is possible to examine systematically the many tasks performed by managers. These functions are separate but interrelated. It is best to look at them as parts of a dynamic system where the general flow moves from planning, to organizing, to controlling, to directing, with constant feedback being given from each function to all the others. Each day managers must adjust to changing market conditions and shifting consumer needs in order to retain their competitive edge in the market. The best way to describe this relationship is to invoke the old cliché that remaining successful in the global agri-food system is "a journey, not a destination."

CHAPTER HIGHLIGHTS

1. The success of the agri-food system rests heavily on the adoption of technology *and* the application of good business management. Business management contributes to this success by integrating technology, physical assets, financial assets, and human assets in a way that maximizes the business's long-term profits. Business managers secure their right to these profits by satisfying the needs of their customers more efficiently than their competitors. Thus, agribusiness managers play a pivotal role in the overall success of the agri-food system.
2. The long-run success of agribusinesses requires that they be the first choice of their customers, employees, and investors.
3. To be the first choice of customers, employers, and investors means firms must be efficient (do things well) and effective (do the right things) in everything they do.

4. Business management is a profession that applies knowledge from a diverse set of academic disciplines such as economics, statistics, psychology, and mathematics.
5. Business management is an art supported by science.
6. The common business management principle that unifies everything a manager does is the desire to maximize the long-term profits of the firm by profitably satisfying customers' needs.
7. Successful business managers can efficiently and effectively manage their technical processes *and* they are also effective leaders who can communicate and motivate people.
8. Agribusiness managers face a unique challenge. In addition to all the normal problems that confront managers, agribusiness managers must have a strong understanding of the biological and institutional factors surrounding the production of food and fiber along with the ability to adjust quickly to changes in the market.
9. The six steps in the decision-making process are identifying the problem, determining alternative courses of action, analyzing the alternatives, selecting the best alternative, implementing the decision, and following up.
10. The four functions of management are planning, organizing, controlling, and directing.
11. A key part of the planning function is the marketing plan, in which the firm clearly and concisely explains its purpose (what the firm will do) and objective (how the firm will gain its competitive edge in the market).

Chapter Quiz

1. Why is business management referred to as a profession rather than a discipline? What is the difference between a discipline and a profession?
2. Business managers practice management just as a physician practices medicine or a lawyer practices law. Do you agree or disagree with this statement? Explain your answer.
3. What do you mean when you say a business has to earn their profit?
4. Identify and explain the three Es of long-run business success.
5. Explain how being the first choice of your customers, employees, and investors leads to long-run business success.
6. What is the difference between business management and leadership?
7. Describe the business decision-making process.
8. List the four functions of management and describe how they interact to allow a firm to succeed.
9. Agribusiness management is described as a dynamic, continuous process. Do you agree or disagree? Explain your answer.
10. What is the difference between efficiency and effectiveness?

11. Explain how the unifying theme of this book leads to greater success by agri-food managers.
12. If I have a technical or production major why should I have to take a course in business management?
13. Which is more important: to be a great manager or a great leader? Explain your choice.
14. Why do employers look for managers who have industry-based educations?
15. Rank the six steps to business decision making from the most important to the least important. Explain your ranking.
16. Identify, define, and explain how the four functions of management work together to make an agri-food firm successful.
17. Rank the four functions of management from the most important to the least important. Explain your ranking.
18. Where do people fit into this discussion of agribusiness managers?
19. What is meant when we say we have taken a functional approach to the subject of agribusiness management? What are some of the advantages of using this approach?
20. Explain the role of business management in the overall success of an agribusiness.

Case 2
Mike's Epiphany

Mike remembered how excited he had been when he landed his dream job as production facility manager for the region's largest hog producer. The salary and benefits package had been competitive, but what really caught his eye were the performance incentives. It seemed entirely possible that he could double his base salary after a year on the job and then move up to district manager. Those dreams were fading away as he stared at this month's production report that showed his operation dead last for the third consecutive month. The unit was performing close to the company average when he took over six months ago. How could this have happened?

In Mike's mind, a 1,000-acre hog-corn-bean farm in Indiana was the perfect place to grow up. From his earliest days he knew he wanted to stay in agriculture. However, he also knew from the time he was ten years old that he and his younger brother, Ken, would have to find something else to do since their oldest brother, Larry, was going to inherit the farm.

It took a while for him to sort out his life. After high school, he knew more school was not for him so he joined the army, which sent him to medical technician school. For a kid who didn't like school, Mike found himself fascinated by what he could do in a biology lab. He went straight from the army to college where he earned a degree in animal science and was on the dean's list nearly every semester. He had found the perfect way to combine his love of science with his desire to remain in agriculture. This job was the perfect capstone in his career plan.

His lack of job success was not because he was lazy. He was always the first one in every morning and the last one out at night. He worked side by side with the company's nutritionists and closely supervised the employees in his unit. Mike always volunteered his unit to be the first one to employ new technical innovations. He always felt his unit turned out the best hogs of any unit in the company even if they did not always match the company's specifications. How could his unit produce such a top-grade product using all the best technology and fail to be a highly productive, successful operation?

If Mike asked you for advice on how to turn things around, what would you tell him?

PART II

The Planning Function

The planning business function deals with what an agribusiness must do to put it in the best possible position relative to the future so it can fully meet the needs of its consumers and maximize its long-term profits. The four planning activities dealt with in this section are marketing, strategic management, forecasting, and budgeting.

- *Chapter 3—The Role of Marketing* To be successful a manager must understand the important role that marketing plays in the success of a free-market economy and how this has changed in recent years. Having the right outlook on the market is a critical first step in business planning.
- *Chapter 4—Marketing Management* Managing the marketing function is an important part of what managers do. Understanding how marketing helps the firm realize its objectives enables managers to do a better job of carrying out their planning function. This knowledge enables them to develop more effective marketing mixes (product, price, place, and promotion) and business plans.
- *Chapter 5—Understanding Consumer Demand* Successful business planning requires that managers understand what motivates their consumers to buy their products. Economics tells us a great deal about consumer behavior, such as the factors that affect consumers' demand for specific products and what impact changes in product prices or competitive products' prices will have on sales and profits. This knowledge enables agribusiness managers to make better pricing decisions when developing the marketing mix in their business plans.

Chapter 6—Staying Competitive Globalization has made just about every agribusiness a player in the world market. Now firms must compete not just against firms around the corner but also against firms around the world for their customers' business. This new market environment means agribusinesses need to constantly assess the competitiveness of their products and services if they hope to survive. This process is called strategic management. It is now an essential part of the skills every agribusiness manager needs to have in order to achieve long-run business success.

- *Chapter 7—Forecasting* In addition to knowing the factors that affect current consumer demand for products, it is also valuable to be able to anticipate changes in customer desires and the impact of changes in the prices of the goods and services you buy and sell. This knowledge improves agribusiness managers' ability to place their firms in the best possible position relative to the future.

- ***Chapter 8—Budgeting*** While it is important to be able to completely meet the needs of customers, managers must not forget that businesses also have financial objectives. Budgeting is the financial part of business planning. It puts all of the other parts of the planning function into a common denominator (money) so managers can easily decide the best uses for their money.

Chapter 3

The Role of Marketing

Chapter Learning Objectives

- Explain the mission of marketing.
- Describe the role of marketing in the economy.
- Summarize how the five barriers to consumer satisfaction, the nine marketing functions, and the four utilities of marketing combine to accomplish the mission of marketing.
- Summarize how the marketing system is evaluated using the structure-conduct-performance model.
- Summarize how agribusiness firms use the information from the structure-conduct-performance model to develop effective marketing plans.

The Misunderstood Mission of Marketing

Marketing is one of the most misunderstood areas of business management. This is unfortunate since marketing has had so much to do with the prosperity that most of us enjoy. This is especially true in the agri-food system, where marketing plays a significant role in providing an overwhelming assortment of food and fiber products that meet consumer needs at the lowest prices found anywhere in the world.

Whether or not your future includes a job in marketing, you will find yourself affected by it. Marketing activities are the largest part of the agri-food system and account for over 80 percent of the employment and value-added utility in the system. Whether you are a producer, a processor, or a consumer, an understanding of the role of marketing is important in understanding the economic world in which we live.

The Mission of Marketing

The mission of **marketing** is to bridge the gap between the conflicting needs of producers and consumers by completing the production process. Most of its activities involve helping producers better understand the needs of consumers so that they will be more likely to produce the goods that consumers want. Thus, marketing helps find answers to the five key questions that drive every economic system:

1. What products to produce.
2. How much to produce.
3. When production should be initiated.
4. Who should do the producing.
5. For whom goods should be produced.

When done efficiently and fairly, marketing improves the overall efficiency of the economy, increases producers' profits, and increases consumer satisfaction.

Regardless of the location, there is an economic system that seeks to meet human needs and desires for food, shelter, clothing, and other things. Human needs are normally unlimited. People always want more and better goods and services. Unfortunately, the resources required to meet these needs—time, money, and energy, for example—are limited. As a result, people must make choices about where to spend their time, money, and energy. Economics gives people the ability to make good decisions when faced with these choices. Much of the evolution of the marketing system reflects the result of good economic decision making.

Evolution of the Marketing System

In a subsistence economy finding the answers to the five economic-system questions is easy. Everyone produces all the things they can and consumes everything they produce. Although each person may not produce all that he or she needs, everyone must make do with what he or she produces. The following describes the evolution of trade and economy.

Specialization and Trade. Even in a subsistence economy, an uneven distribution of human talents exists. Some people are better than others at producing some things. Those who are better at producing certain products will find that they are better off specializing in the production of those goods and then trade what they produce beyond their personal needs for the other goods they require. Specialization and trade provide more goods for everyone because each product is produced by its most efficient producers. Everyone is still a producer and a consumer, but each person produces only a few products. This very simple economic system is called a barter economy.

Central Markets. Trading sounds easy: everyone exchanges his or her surplus production for the surplus products of others. However, because of difficulties in time, distance, and information, buyers and sellers have a hard time finding each other. A better solution is to have everyone meet at one place and time to exchange his or her surplus production. The result is the formation of a central market. Central markets are valuable because they increase the efficiency of the economic system. All the buyers and sellers come to a single location so they can see and trade for all the surplus production at once rather than spend their time visiting all the other producers of the goods they need. As a result of using central markets, each person has more of everything. Producers have more time to produce more surplus, and consumers have more time to consume and enjoy the products they buy.

Money. Specialization of production, trade, and central markets improves the efficiency of an economic system. Yet even with a central market, producers still must barter for each item they need, such as ten bushels of corn for three chickens or four goats for a wagon wheel. This can leave the trader with more of some items than he or she wants and too little of other items. Bartering can result in long and complicated trails of exchanges to get to what the trader wants. Thus, if a producer has corn to barter but needs a wagon wheel, he must find someone who has wagon wheels and who wants corn. It may require several extra trades to finally get what he really wants. A better solution would be to use a common denominator of value—money. Placing the value of all goods in terms of this single unit—dollars, euros, yen, etc.—increases the efficiency of the economic system and allows the economy to expand. Now the corn producer only needs to sell his ten bushels of corn for $30 and buy the wagon wheel directly.

Middlemen. As central markets grow larger it becomes necessary for someone to oversee their operation. Someone has to provide a place to hold the market and keep it going. Someone has to build the stalls used by sellers. Someone has to store the goods between sales. Some producers may hire someone to transport their goods to the central market. Others may even hire someone to sell his or her goods for them. The people who perform all these tasks are called *middlemen*. Middlemen complete the production process by preparing the producers' goods for sale to consumers. They are neither producers nor consumers, but in the middle.

Marketing Resolves the Conflicting Needs of Producers and Consumers

Regardless of how an economic system is organized, it must have a marketing system to bridge the gap between the conflicting needs of producers and consumers. On one side of the gap are producers, who seek to maximize their long-term profits by specializing in the production of a large quantity of a few products that they can sell at the highest possible prices. On the other side of the gap are consumers, who seek to maximize the total satisfaction they get from consuming small quantities of many products with their limited incomes by purchasing them at the lowest possible prices. The goal of the middlemen in the marketing system is to resolve these differences.

THE ROLE OF MARKETING IN THE ECONOMY

It is important to understand what marketing does to increase the level of consumer satisfaction in the economy. For this concept to be useful to agribusiness managers, it is necessary to look more closely at the process that makes this happen.

The Five Barriers to Consumer Satisfaction

In every economic system five barriers exist that prevent producers from satisfying a consumer's need or ability to participate in that system. These barriers include: (1) **ownership separation** (inability to transfer ownership), (2) **time separation** (product is not available when it is desired), (3) **space separation** (location of product is inaccessible), (4) **value separation** (product is not in the proper form), and (5) **information separation** (lack of relevant information). In order to raise the level of consumer satisfaction, a marketing system must find ways to overcome these separations.

The Nine Marketing Functions

The marketing system performs nine separate functions to overcome the barriers to consumer satisfaction. The most familiar marketing functions are the **buying function** and the **selling function**, which overcome the separation of ownership by transferring legal title of the product from the buyer to the seller. The marketing system must include both functions for product exchanges to occur. The **storage function** overcomes the separation of time by maintaining the product in good condition between production and final sale. The **transportation function** overcomes the separation of space by moving the product from where it is produced to where consumers desire it.

The **processing function** overcomes value separation by transforming a commodity to a form that has greater value to the consumer. Processing is included as one of the nine functions of marketing because consumers determine what is produced in a free-market economy.

The facilitating functions of marketing include those functions that make the system work more efficiently. The **grades and standards function** overcomes information separation by providing uniform physical descriptions of commodities and products. Reliable third parties, such as the U.S. Department of Agriculture (USDA), have the authority to set standards and establish a grading process. Buyers do not have to be present to physically inspect each item to be purchased to be assured that the products will conform to minimum or acceptable standards. The **financing function** overcomes value, time, and space separations by providing the funds necessary to pay for the production, processing, storage, and transportation of a product before the money is received from its sale.

The **risk-taking function** overcomes time separation by assuming the physical and price **risks** between purchase and sale. Wide dissemination of information on prices, inventory levels, embargoes, or anything else that could influence the buying and selling of products also enhances the efficiency of the marketing system. The **market information function** overcomes information separation by disseminating this type of information.

Middlemen in a free-market economy perform these nine marketing functions. Buyers and sellers can bypass middlemen by performing some of these functions themselves, but rarely can they be eliminated if the system is to function efficiently. A single middleman may not perform all these functions. Some may perform just one, while others may do three or four. In some cases, producers may carry out some of the marketing functions, such as when they do their own retailing. Consumers perform marketing functions when they buy from a roadside stand or pick their own strawberries at a direct marketing outlet.

The Four Utilities of Marketing

One way to describe marketing is to look at it as adding value to products by completing the production process. Middlemen or marketers exist because they add value to products that consumers want and are willing to pay extra to receive. The result of this process is greater consumer satisfaction. Economists call this satisfaction **utility**. Consumers receive four types of utility from using products after marketers have handled them: form, place, time, and possession.

Form utility comes from processing the product into a form more desirable to consumers. This may be nothing more than cooking eggs for someone who is willing to pay you to make a ready-to-eat omelet. For those who want French fries at a fast-food restaurant, the farmer may begin the process of providing form utility by converting seeds, water, fertilizer, and other inputs into a full-grown potato that is ready to harvest. Those that process the raw potato into frozen French fries are also involved in the process of providing form utility, as are the people who cook it at the fast-food outlet. Merely handing the customer a raw potato will probably do very little to give him any positive utility when what he really wants is hot, sizzling, ready-to-eat French fries. Marketing people recognize the profit potential in this desire and transform the raw ingredients into cooked French fries through processing.

Place utility involves transporting the product to a location desired by consumers. To continue the French fry example, turning the potato into ready-to-eat fries only does part of the job. If the fries are in Idaho while the customer is in New Jersey, little is added to consumer satisfaction. The product needs to be transported to the consumer, since consumption of the ready-to-eat fries in New Jersey will give him more utility than driving to Idaho to get them.

Time utility results from storing the product until the consumer needs it. Time utility is important to agribusinesses since many commodities such as potatoes are harvested once a year but are consumed year-round. Returning to the French fry example, without storage we could only enjoy French fries for a few weeks each year after the potato harvest. Again, marketing people recognize the profit potential in consumers' year-round desire for fries and develop ways to store potatoes and French fries successfully to meet this need.

Possession utility facilitates the process of gaining ownership of the product so buyers can use it fully. The marketing system strives to make this transfer process as quick and easy as possible to increase consumer satisfaction. This is why restaurants and food stores offer their customers a variety of ways to pay for their purchases, such as cash or debit and credit cards. Possession utility normally completes the utility process as ownership and control pass ultimately to the consumer of the product.

The function of marketing in our economic system makes sure that consumers get the products they desire. This means ensuring that the right product (form utility) is available at the right place (place utility), at the right price (possession utility), and at the right time (time utility) to fully satisfy the consumer.

The Relationship of Marketing Principles

The relationships between these marketing principles ultimately perform multiple functions that enhance consumer satisfaction and the proper functioning of the marketing system, which ensures the success of every economy. They bridge the gap between the conflicting needs of producers and consumers; they complete the production process by adding four utilities to products (which overcome the five barriers to consumer satisfaction); and they raise the level of economic efficiency within the system. As a result, consumers receive greater satisfaction, production operations are more profitable, and the general welfare of society is increased because society's resources are being efficiently allocated.

The Role of Marketing in the Future of Agribusiness

At the core of the contemporary agri-food system are producers both in the United States and around the world with a productive capacity for most raw commodities that greatly exceeds domestic demand. The export markets that were expected to absorb the excess supply have not developed as expected. Competition for foreign markets has intensified as more countries have expanded production in the name of food security and increased their involvement in international commodity and food markets as a way to earn foreign exchange. Many have targeted the United States as an outlet for their food products. As a result, American agribusinesses face increased domestic and global competition for the consumers' food dollar. Success comes to those agribusiness firms and managers who can most efficiently and effectively meet the changing needs of the world's consumers in this demanding marketplace.

In this global market environment, a more sophisticated approach to marketing and closer attention to consumer needs is needed to remain profitable. It is no longer sufficient to find ways to dispose of what farmers have already produced. Agribusiness firms throughout the agri-food system need to devote the same level of effort to marketing management as they have to production management. Marketing can help agribusiness firms compete successfully in this competitive global marketplace and assure the future success of the agri-food system. This is why marketing is defined as all the business activities that satisfy consumers' needs by coordinating the flow of goods and services from producers to consumers.

The Marketing Approach

A major change in contemporary marketing management is the shift away from a production-and-selling orientation to one that focuses on profitably satisfying consumer needs. This sophisticated attitude is called the **marketing approach**. The marketing approach is based on the premise that a firm's success does not come from producing a technically superior product, but how completely it satisfies consumers' needs. This is a subtle but very important change.

Consumers purchase the satisfaction that products give them rather than a physical product. For example, when consumers buy CDs with the latest music, they are not only buying the latest album from their favorite artist. They are also buying the satisfaction derived from being able to listen to high-quality music. Therefore, some consumers quickly switched to MP3s when they became available. The marketing goal of a firm is not to make the best CD or MP3, but to provide consumers with the best way to listen to music. The actual product, whether a CD or MP3, is just the best way to do this at a particular point in time. The difference is important. Many businesses have failed because they focused on making the best physical product rather than remembering they are satisfying a customer need. The goal of every firm should be to meet the needs of its customers more efficiently, effectively, and completely than its competitors. The level of their profits is directly related to how well they do this.

The marketing approach proposes that the profitable satisfaction of consumer needs should be the driving force behind everything a business does. The marketing approach will succeed in making a firm profitable when all the functional areas of the firm, such as production, accounting, shipping, and warehousing, accept the idea of **consumer sovereignty** (that is, the consumer is king and queen). The profitable satisfaction of consumer needs must be of paramount importance to everyone in the firm if it is to succeed. This is why the unifying theme of this book is *the goal of every manager is to maximize the long-term profits of a firm by profitably satisfying customers' needs.*

The biggest challenge agribusiness firms face is to accept this reorientation of the way a firm looks at itself. Each function in a business exists because it plays a role in the accomplishment of customer satisfaction. Whether an employee works in research and development, sales, information technology, shipping, or maintenance, his or her job is customer service. Marketing does not take over the business, but it does give direction to every business function. Marketing identifies consumers' wants and transmits these needs to the rest of the firm.

Evaluating the Performance of a Marketing System

Regardless of the economic system a society chooses, it must develop a marketing system that meets the needs of its citizens. How well that marketing system accomplishes this objective is important because it determines the level of consumer satisfaction, producer profits, and the overall welfare of society. This is why society (through government) devotes considerable effort to evaluating the performance of its marketing system.

Prerequisites to an Efficient Economic System

A marketing system can efficiently meet the needs of producers and consumers and provide society with an efficient allocation of its scarce resources when three prerequisites are met: a free-market economy, prices that reflect the full value of resources, and a high degree of interaction between consumers and producers.

A Free-Market Economy. A free-market economy is an economy in which consumers, with little government interference, provide the answers to the five economic-system questions listed earlier, and the level of producers' profits measure how well producers meet consumer needs. In planned economies, the government provides the answers to these questions with little direct information from consumers, which typically results in shortages of goods people really want and surpluses of things few people want.

Prices Reflect the Full Value of Resources. When prices accurately measure the true value of resources, resources are used efficiently. How close an economic system comes to achieving this is a measure of its *pricing efficiency.* A high degree of pricing efficiency is desirable because:

- Producers use the most efficient technology available and the cheapest combination of inputs to make their products. They are driven to do this by their desire to maximize their long-term profits. By paying the market price for an input, producers imply that its value in the production process is greater than or equal to that price. If its value is less than the market price, they should not use it. In this way, the market system uses scarce resources in the most efficient way possible.
- Consumers purchase only those products that increase their total happiness (satisfaction). By paying the market price for a product, they indicate that they are receiving satisfaction greater than or equal to the dissatisfaction they feel at giving up the money needed to buy the product. If the added satisfaction consumers receive is less than the price of the product, they should not buy it. In this way, consumers direct the marketing system to produce the goods they want and to stop producing the goods they do not believe are worth the price.

A High Degree of Interaction between Consumers and Producers. When consumers and producers have a high level of interaction, both parties know a lot about what is going on in the market. If consumers know a great deal about producers and the variety and prices of goods for sale, they make informed buying decisions. Producers' knowledge about consumers and their desires helps them make informed production decisions.

How well these three prerequisites are met largely determines the level of economic efficiency present in an economic system. A higher level of economic efficiency creates a higher level of overall consumer satisfaction and producer profits. Therefore, maintaining a high level of economic efficiency should be a major concern of a society.

Criteria Used to Evaluate Performance

The goal of economic efficiency is of sufficient importance in the United States that citizens have empowered the government to establish laws to protect its existence. These laws ensure that everyone plays by the same rules and that all consumers and producers are given an equal opportunity to prosper in the marketplace. The government does this by passing laws that provide for enforcement of contracts, protection of private property rights, fairness in the pricing system, and fair rules of trade. Through the legislative process, the people make known what type of economic system and the level of economic efficiency they desire.

The marketing system is evaluated on two criteria: *efficiency* (how efficiently goods and services flow from producers to consumers) and *fairness* (how well the marketing system meets the needs of consumers). Consumers show how they feel about their system directly by voting with dollars in the marketplace for the goods they want, and indirectly by expressing their opinions through political action.

The Structure-Conduct-Performance Model

Economists analyze the fairness and efficiency of the marketing system by examining the structure, conduct, and performance of individual markets in the economy. The model is based on the notion that the way firms are organized in a market (their structure) tells a great deal about how they make decisions (their conduct), which in turn influences the level of efficiency and fairness present in a market (their performance). Therefore, if society wants to affect the efficiency and fairness of its markets, it must alter their structure.

Markets with few suppliers operate less efficiently than markets with many suppliers. When fewer suppliers are present, consumers pay higher prices and suppliers have larger profits. When a sufficient number of suppliers are present in a market (structure), individual firms must respond to the market rather than try to control it (conduct). This leads to more reasonable levels of prices and profits (performance). The result is more efficient markets with higher levels of consumer satisfaction and no undue price enhancement (excess profits) on the part of producers or middlemen. The Federal Trade Commission and the U.S. Department of Justice use things such as the structure-conduct-performance model to monitor the efficiency and fairness of our economic system. They use these models to evaluate the impact of corporate mergers and acquisitions on competition in the economy.

Structure. To be fair and efficient, a market structure must have:

- A sufficient number of firms in the market and firms that are large enough to have low operating costs per unit of output.
- Few barriers to market entry or exit.
- Firms that differentiate and improve products as they compete against each other.

Market evaluators use *concentration ratios* to measure market structure. The concentration ratio is the proportion of total sales in a market accounted for by the sales of the largest firms. The number of firms included in this group depends on the situation, but normally involves the top four to ten firms. Market evaluators typically become worried when fewer than four of the largest firms account for more than 50 percent of total market sales. When this occurs the firms in these markets tend to behave as oligopolies. This means they begin to compete on things other than price, such as advertising, packaging, coupons, and so on. Efforts to improve and differentiate products may lag also. The result is loss of economic efficiency and consumer satisfaction. To increase competition and raise economic efficiency, the government may step in to limit further market concentration in the form of mergers and acquisitions.

Conduct. In a market with many firms, conduct that enhances an individual firm's ability to maximize its long-term profits can be beneficial to consumers. However, when only a few firms are present in the market, such conduct pushed to the extreme could lead to monopolistic behavior that would not be acceptable to society.

To be considered fair and efficient, market conduct must include:

- A number of firms in the market sufficient to create some managerial uncertainty whether competitors will follow another firm's price changes (both up and down).
- No unjustified price discrimination.
- No collusion in the market on pricing and other items.
- No unfair trade practices.
- Truthful product claims.
- The existence of product differentiation based on meaningful differences.

Performance. The structure and conduct of the firms in a market affect their economic performance. Markets that meet the above criteria for structure and conduct should be efficient and fair. When this is the case, the market and the firms in it should meet these performance criteria:

- Optimum output levels at the minimum cost per unit.
- Reasonable profits, given the amount of risk, management skill, and new product development involved.
- Innovations and improvements in product and process.
- Reasonable levels of investment, reinvestment of profits, and research and development.

Why Study Market Performance?

While the structure-conduct-performance model provides a way for economists to evaluate the efficiency and fairness of a market, much of this evaluation deals with topics normally considered part of marketing. It is important for managers to know what government evaluators are looking for when they review market performance. These same items can be valuable to individual firms who are seeking to formulate effective marketing plans. Michael Porter, a well-known business strategist, and others have shown how to use the structure-conduct-performance model for this purpose.

Under their approach, a firm's managers analyze their industry's structure to determine the forces that affect its organization. Based on what they learn about the structure of their industry, firm managers formulate a strategy (their conduct) to take advantage of their firm's strengths, their competitors' weaknesses, and opportunities to fill unmet consumer needs. Performance, instead of being measured in terms of market fairness and efficiency, is judged by the level of profits and market share of their firm. This is not what the formulators of the structure-conduct-performance model had in mind when they developed their model, but it has proven to be very effective for individual firms seeking to enhance their economic performance.

Government Intervention in Markets

The initial role of the U.S. government in the marketplace was limited to providing for the common defense, ensuring domestic tranquility, protecting private property rights, and enforcing contracts. The growth and concentration of corporate power arising out of the industrial age left many citizens, especially farmers, afraid of losing control of their country. Congress responded to this public pressure to make the system fairer by enacting a series of laws to correct this imbalance of power.

The first major piece of legislation affecting the operation of the economic system was the **Sherman Antitrust Act** of 1890, which states in part that "every contract, combination in the form of trust or otherwise, or conspiracy, in restraint of trade or commerce among the several States, or with foreign nations, is declared to be illegal." This was the first attempt by the government to affect the structure of the economy so it would perform as its citizens desired. In 1914, the **Clayton Antitrust Act** supplemented the Sherman Act by specifically prohibiting activities that lessened competition and tended to create monopolies. Among the prohibited activities were price discrimination, tie-in contracts, exclusive deals, and interlocking directorships and stock holdings. The Robinson-Patman Act of 1936 strengthened the Clayton Act's bars against price discrimination.

In addition to laws, Congress also established a variety of federal agencies to enforce these new rules. Congress created the Food and Drug Administration in 1906 to regulate the quality of food and drug products and the Federal Trade Commission in 1914 to regulate price competition in interstate commerce.

A number of federal laws have been enacted to ensure fair trade in agricultural products. These laws were passed because farmers and consumers felt they were not being treated fairly by some of the larger agribusiness firms. The first of these was the Meat Inspection Act of 1906, which called for the enforcement of sanitary regulations and the federal inspection of meat sold in interstate commerce. The Food Products Act of 1917 established the role of the federal government in food grading and gave the enforcement job to the Agricultural Marketing Service of the USDA.

The Packers and Stockyards Act of 1921 established the rules for fair trade in livestock markets. It required that all fees be nondiscriminatory, that all weights and measures be accurate, that all transactions be conducted in an open market, and that livestock be sold in a competitive bidding system. The Perishable Commodities Act of 1930 established the same types of regulations for perishable commodities. The **Capper-Volstead Act** of 1922 exempted farmers from antitrust laws so they could come together to organize **agricultural cooperatives**.

Each of these acts and others since then are directed at assuring that trade remains efficient and fair. Market regulation is designed to ensure that competition and innovation are encouraged and prices reflect true social value. This ensures greater economic efficiency, fairness in the marketplace, and greater consumer satisfaction.

CHAPTER HIGHLIGHTS

1. Marketing plays an important role in the success of the agri-food system and the economy as a whole.
2. The mission of marketing is to bridge the gap between conflicting needs of producers and consumers by completing the production process.

3. When done efficiently and fairly, marketing improves the overall efficiency of the economy, increases producer profits, and increases consumer satisfaction.
4. The use of specialization and trade, central markets, money, and middlemen has increased the efficiency of the marketing system.
5. Marketing resolves the conflicting needs of producers and consumers by performing nine marketing functions that add utility to products that overcome the five barriers to consumer satisfaction.
6. The five barriers to consumer satisfaction are ownership, time, space, value, and information separation.
7. The nine marketing functions are buying, selling, storage, transportation, processing, grades and standards, financing, risk-taking, and market information.
8. The four utilities of marketing are form, place, time, and possession utility.
9. Marketing encompasses all the business activities that satisfy consumers' needs by coordinating the flow of goods and services from producers to consumers.
10. The marketing approach is the concept that a firm's success comes from satisfying consumer needs rather than producing a technically superior product.
11. The unifying theme of this text is that the goal of every manager is to maximize the long-term profits of the firm by profitably satisfying customers' needs.
12. The prerequisites to an efficient economic system are a free-market economy, prices that reflect the full value of resources, and a high level of interaction between consumers and producers.
13. The marketing system is evaluated on how efficiently and fairly it meets consumer needs using a structure-conduct-performance model.
14. Firms can use the structure-conduct-performance model to develop effective marketing plans.
15. In a democracy, people use government to keep their economic and marketing systems fair.

CHAPTER QUIZ

1. Describe marketing in your own words. Explain why you think marketing is not well understood. Explain why you feel it is important for people to understand marketing.
2. Describe the forces that led to the development of the marketing system.
3. Explain how completing the production process resolves the conflicting needs of producers and consumers and leads to greater consumer satisfaction.

4. Define the five barriers to consumer satisfaction, the nine marketing functions, and the four utilities of marketing. Explain how they combine to raise the level of economic efficiency in the economy.
5. The goal of the U.S. marketing system is to dispose of what farmers have already produced as quickly and efficiently as possible. Do you agree or disagree? Explain the reasons for your answer.
6. Define the marketing approach. Discuss its relevance to the agri-food system.
7. Explain why a society should spend time evaluating the performance of its marketing system.
8. Define the prerequisites to an efficient economic system. Explain their importance.
9. What criteria should be used to evaluate the performance of a marketing system? How do these criteria relate to the structure, conduct, and performance of a market?
10. Explain why an agribusiness manager should be interested in understanding market performance.
11. Explain the role of government in keeping markets fair and efficient. Give examples of when this occurred and describe why it worked or did not work.
12. Explain why marketing is an important part of any economic system.
13. Explain how specialization and trade, central markets, money, and middlemen benefit producers and consumers.
14. What is meant when we say marketing adds utility to a product?
15. Explain the difference between an agribusiness firm supplying great physical products and supplying consumer satisfaction. Which approach is best? Explain your choice.
16. The unifying theme of this book has two parts. The first part (maximizing long-run profits) deals with efficiency. The second part deals with effectiveness (profitably satisfying customer needs). Rank the two parts. Explain your choice.
17. Explain why a free market with voluntary exchange is important to an efficient economic system.
18. Explain why it is important for prices to reflect the full value of an item in the market.
19. Adam Smith, father of modern economics, says you should always buy from the lowest price provider. Do you agree of disagree? Explain your choice.
20. What are the two criteria for measuring the performance of the marketing system? What is the best way to improve market performance?
21. In a global market world, is it still appropriate to measure market efficiency on a national level?

Case 3
Dave's Dollar Dilemma: Part I

Last night's snow had given a clean, crisp look to the landscape. Dave was glad that the road crews had done a good job of clearing the road down to the hard surface as he sped along toward town. As he drove he thought about how the area had changed in the past few years. The upgrading of U.S. 39 had changed everything. A lot of new housing was going up at this end of the county. They weren't small houses either. What had been prime farmland was now being turned into 3–5 acre mini-estates. It seemed that none of these people cut their own lawns.

Even though he was on his way to pick up the year-end financials from his accountant, he was thinking about how this year might mark the turnaround his operation needed. Business had been good at the family-run farm-equipment dealership for as long as he could remember. His father had been sure to keep things up to date and to grow with the changing needs of the farmers in their area. Up until about five years ago, they felt they knew what they were doing. They had always been the dealership that took over extra territory as equipment manufacturers closed dealerships and consolidated.

Dave had continued his father's commitment to provide the best service in the area. His large-equipment mechanics attended as many training schools as he could afford. The shop had the best diagnostic equipment and online inventory system in the area. It just seemed that sales started to stagnate despite the expansion of their market area as they absorbed other dealerships. It was true that the total farm acreage in the area was unchanged, but fewer operators who used larger machines were farming it. Because of the Internet these producers knew the price of every piece of equipment within 500 miles and used this information to get the best deals from people like Dave. While he understood the situation of these farmers, it was hard for him to accept a profit on the sale of a big piece of equipment that approximately equaled his profit on a small tractor for some guy to cut his three-acre lawn.

Dave was always amazed by how much time he would have to put in to sell a big piece of equipment when it seemed those part-time country gentlemen farmers would see a small tractor they liked as they drove past the dealership and buy it on the spot. Many just put it on a credit card, loaded it into their fancy pick-up trucks, and drove away. After the purchase, they would come back to ask about how to get all sorts of accessories such as headlights, front loaders, and wagons. Since this was a farm-equipment dealership and not a lawn-and-garden store, Dave had resisted his manager's request that they stock these items and other hobby farming items.

When Dave got his financials he was surprised to see sales had declined, costs had risen, and profits were almost zero. With his kids getting ready for college, this really caused him to worry. When Dave asked his accountant about what he should do, he said he should do a better job of marketing.

Is the accountant right? What does it mean to "do a better job of marketing?" How does marketing help an agribusiness succeed? If Dave asked you what you would do, how would you tell him to increase the dealership's profits?

Chapter 4

Marketing Management

CHAPTER LEARNING OBJECTIVES

- Summarize the changing role of marketing within the firm.
- Explain why it is important to adopt the marketing approach.
- Describe the relationship between marketing and the four functions of management.
- Summarize the four Ps of marketing and describe their role in the marketing mix.
- Explain the role of a business plan in the success of an agribusiness.
- Summarize the elements of a marketing plan and its role in strategic planning.

THE CHANGING ROLE OF MARKETING WITHIN THE FIRM

Chapter 3 was devoted to explaining the role of marketing in a free-market economy. Now it is time to bring these concepts down to the level of the individual firm so they can be incorporated into the management of an agribusiness. By constructing the general framework first, it will be easier to see how marketing helps an agribusiness succeed.

Transition from Efficiency to Selling to Marketing

Like most aspects of business management, marketing has changed over the years. In the earliest days of market development, demand greatly exceeded supply for most items and consumers were thankful to receive any product, as long as it met some minimum quality standards. Faced with a situation where demand seemed endless, producers focused on expanding output in order to maximize long-term profits. In this market environment, marketing dealt only with ways to lower costs and improve the physical efficiency of moving products from producers to consumers. Because simply acquiring a product satisfied consumers, producers often became insensitive to their needs.

As producers became more adept at manufacturing, they began to pay more attention to their products. They felt that consumers recognized improvements in product quality and better product features. Thus, a producer could gain a competitive edge by making high-quality products and improving them over time. At this stage marketing activities were still focused on producer-developed products and features that they hoped would be accepted by consumers.

By the middle of the twentieth century, the production capacity for most products exceeded demand. Many producers, including agri-food firms, found themselves faced with the situation of how to get rid of large quantities of what they had already produced. During this era the focus of marketing shifted from physical efficiency to selling. It was assumed that anything could be sold with enough sales pressure. The most prized salespeople were those who could "sell eggs to a chicken." Products that need a hard sell probably do not fit consumer needs very well since consumers must be persuaded to buy them. Hard selling is a short-term solution at best. It may get the firm the first sale, but may so alienate consumers that they will not buy from that firm again. This is true even if the consumer is satisfied with the product.

A major advance in the sophistication of marketing came with a shift away from product, production, and selling orientations to one that concentrates on meeting consumer needs. This is the marketing approach discussed in detail in chapter 3. The marketing approach is based on the idea that first it is important to find out what consumers want and then develop a product that meets those needs. Success comes from satisfying consumers' needs rather than producing a superior product. The product is just the means to achieve that satisfaction.

Under the marketing approach, a firm's chances for success increase and the efficiency of the economic system rises because the likelihood increases that consumers will want what is produced. The adoption of the marketing approach is especially important today, since the production capacity for most commodities and food products exceeds demand and there is stiff competition among producers for the consumers' food dollar. The level of a profit margin can indicate how completely a product fills the needs of its consumers. The goal of good marketing is to make selling unnecessary. You know your customers so well that your product completely satisfies their needs and gives them the greatest value, so they instantly want to buy it. The classic example is Girl Scout cookies. Often all that is needed to make a sale is to tell people where and when they will be available.

Adopting the Marketing Approach

Adoption of the marketing approach by agribusiness firms is important for success. Firms that adopt it are more likely to survive and prosper. Those that do not will perish. Adoption of the marketing approach calls for a commitment to a whole new way of doing business. Marketing becomes the eyes and ears of the business and gives direction to everything it does. It is the job of management to make this happen. Management must implement the marketing approach and see to it that it reaches every corner of the firm, every day. The act of satisfying a consumer need is what gives a business its right to earn a profit. To do this successfully and profitably requires a coordinated effort on the part of all the people in the business, regardless of what they do.

Marketing and the Four Functions of Management

The management of marketing activities within the firm can be studied within the confines of the four management functions—planning, organizing, controlling, and directing. The planning function is most directly associated with marketing. The goal of planning is to put the firm in the best possible position relative to the future. When a firm employs the marketing approach, this job is easier. The major planning objectives should consider: (1) *what* consumer needs the business is going to fill, (2) *how* it is going to gain its competitive edge in the market (i.e., what is it going to do that is better or different than other firms so people will buy from it), and (3) how can it do all this *profitably*? These questions should be continuously raised and answered to everyone's satisfaction. The quality of the answers indicates whether management has a clear idea of what the firm does and what it must do to be successful. These issues are at the heart of a firm's success and are the cornerstone of its marketing efforts.

Within the organizing function, the marketing approach can serve as a guiding principle that increases the chances for business success in three ways. First, the definition of what the firm is going to do and how it is going to do it must be in terms of consumer needs rather than a physical description of a product. Consumers purchase the satisfaction that products give them, not goods and services. Second, the company should be organized so that its primary emphasis is on meeting the needs of consumers. Third, the organization of the firm needs to include mechanisms for the constant and continued reassessment of consumer needs and the search for new, better, more efficient ways to meet them. How a firm is organized reveals a great deal about how it views its market and customers. When a company adopts the marketing approach, marketing activities are given prominence in the organizational structure and the flow of work.

The controlling function measures progress toward the marketing goals that were established in planning as well as the effectiveness of the organizational scheme. Marketing managers need information on sales, prices, market shares, profit levels, and so on to evaluate their decisions in these areas and to determine whether they need to be changed. Controls give early warning of deviations from what was planned.

The directing function combines all the planning, organizing, and development of controls under the goal of producing goods and services that profitably meet consumer needs. If the marketing approach has been adopted successfully across a firm, the directing function becomes easier since the answers to the questions of what to produce, why to produce it, and how to produce it are clear. Managers can go about their daily activities confidently because they have good, solid answers to these basic questions.

The Four Ps of Marketing and the Marketing Mix

Managers confront many things that are beyond their control. However, they always can exert control over four variables. These variables make up the **marketing mix**. The goal of the manager is to combine the four elements of the marketing mix to fully satisfy consumer needs. When used together as part of a manager's tactical plan, the four controllable variables (or the four Ps) of the marketing mix allow a business to completely satisfy consumers' needs in a target market.

The Four Ps of Marketing

1. *Product*—The firm must provide consumers in the target market with a product that gives them maximum satisfaction.

2. *Price*—The right product must carry the right price in light of market conditions.

3. *Place*—The right product carrying the right price must be in the right places to be purchased by the members of the target market.

4. *Promotion*—The firm must tell the members of the target market in the right way that the right product, carrying the right price, is available at the right locations.

Developing the proper marketing mix of product, price, place, and promotion in order to satisfy consumer needs is what marketing is all about and what marketing managers do to earn their living. By manipulating the marketing mix they are able to implement the company's plans using its organizational structure. The firm's progress toward the accomplishment of these goals is measured by the control mechanisms. The objective is to position the firm so that it can maximize its advantage over its competitors with respect to changing customer, economic, and business conditions. Besides marketing to current customers, marketing managers are always looking for new products, new market opportunities, new customers, and better ways to meet customer needs.

THE BUSINESS PLAN

The success of a business is directly attributed to good planning, communication, and execution. The first step on the road to success is to get the values right. Once the values are set the firm is ready to develop a good business plan. The business plan explains how an agribusiness intends to be successful; more specifically, what a firm is going to do and how it is going to do it.

Get the Values Right—How the Firm Is Going to Conduct Itself

The business planning process begins by deciding how the firm is going to conduct itself in dealing with its suppliers, employees, customers, investors, the communities in which it operates, and with all other stakeholders. This is where a firms sets out a clear and concise code of conduct for all to see that will tell the world what this organization stands for. What the firm decides will influence the type of people and organizations that are willing to do business with it. In today's very competitive markets customers, employees, suppliers, and investors have many choices and they will typically avoid firms that do not operate honorably.

The Firm's Purpose—What the Firm Is Going to Do

A business plan begins with a clear, concise statement of a business's purpose—what specific consumer needs the firm intends to meet. The purpose must be written down and widely publicized so that its investors, employees, lenders, and even customers know and understand it. Everyone that works for the firm should accept it as a good and worthwhile thing to do. When an employee feels that what he and his business does is worthwhile, it gives greater meaning to the work being done. When all employees share this idea, it gives them a meaningful, common goal that everyone strives to achieve.

An agrochemical company once had an advertisement that stated the firm's purpose was to solve the scientific mysteries that stood in the way of an adequate world food supply. It is easy for everyone—scientists, managers, warehouse people, information technologists, and so on—to get excited about joining a firm on such a worthy mission.

The Firm's Objective—How the Firm Will Accomplish Its Purpose

The firm's objective is a clear, concise statement that describes how it is going to accomplish its purpose. Just like the firm's purpose, it is important that the objective be written down and widely publicized so everyone knows what it is, understands it, and feels it has value. The objective describes how the firm is going to gain its competitive edge in the market. It describes how the firm is going to do things better, faster, and cheaper than its competitors in meeting customers' needs so that they will buy their company's products rather than someone else's. The objective could be to have the lowest prices, highest quality, largest selection, or fastest service. Regardless of what it is, the objective is what separates a firm from all of its competitors. The objective should always be built around the efficient, effective, and profitable satisfaction of consumer needs. Remember that this is exactly the type of analysis that potential customers conduct when they decide where to buy.

To gauge how well a firm understands its purpose and objectives, managers need to see how well they can answer the following five tough questions first posed by famous management expert Peter Drucker in his classic book *Management: Tasks, Responsibilities, Practices*:

1. What is our business?
2. Who are our customers?
3. What is value to our customers?
4. What will our business be?
5. What should our business be?

The task of developing a firm's purpose and objective is of such importance that it must be decided at the highest level of management. This is normally the board of directors. The board has the responsibility to set the major direction of the firm and then to hire managers to carry it out. The plan will succeed only if top management understands and enthusiastically accepts the purpose and objective established by the board of directors in the firm's business plan. It is the job of top managers to develop the plans, organization, and controls to implement the company's business plan.

Strategic Planning and Management

When establishing a new business, the process of selecting a purpose and objective is called developing a business plan. This process (following the same procedures used to create a business plan) is called strategic planning when done by a firm that is already in business. It also includes an analysis of existing lines of business in order to determine which should be terminated or expanded, as well as whether new ones should be added so the firm will be in the best possible position relative to the future. The next step is to match profitable business opportunities with the firm's current resource base (e.g., people, talents, technology, and equipment) or to develop a plan to acquire the necessary additional resources (see figure 4-1). This process is so critically important to a business's long-run success that a whole chapter (chapter 6) is devoted to it.

Figure 4-1 The Business Planning Process

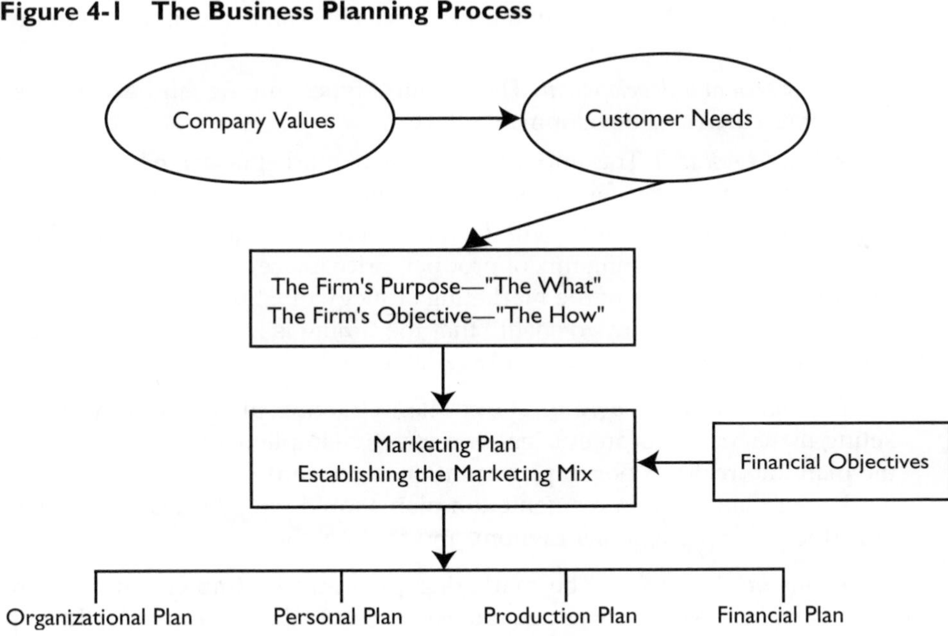

Marketing Strategy. The firm sets its basic marketing objectives, which include broad decisions such as the selection of target markets, market positioning, marketing mix, and marketing expenditure levels. The goal is to create the firm's basic marketing plan and determine the best combination of the four Ps that will enable it to achieve its financial and marketing objectives.

Specific items that should be considered in the marketing strategy include:

- *Identification of target markets.* Exactly which consumer needs the firm is going to fill and for which groups of consumers.
- *Product positioning.* Consumers' mental image of the product (e.g., best quality, lowest price, or best service).
- *Size of the product line.* The number and types of products the firm will offer.
- *Price.* The product's price relative to that of competitors' prices for similar products.

- *The number and type of distribution outlets.* How, where, and by whom products will be distributed to consumers.
- *The size and type of sales force.* What type, size, and quality of sales force is needed to accomplish marketing objectives.
- *The level and quality of service.* The type and number of service facilities and level of service offered by each type.
- *Advertising.* The amount of advertising and media to be used in reaching the firm's target markets, as well as an evaluation of the success of previous advertising efforts.
- *Sales promotion.* The amount and types of sales promotions to be used in reaching the firm's target markets, as well as an evaluation of the success of previous sales promotion efforts.
- *Research and development.* The amount, types, timing, and expected success of research and development efforts.
- *Market research.* The amount and types of market research being undertaken to help the firm achieve its financial and marketing objectives.

Each of these items deals with factors that the firm can control and that can be made part of its marketing mix of product, price, place, and promotion. To be successful, these elements of the marketing strategy must be coordinated with other activities of the company to ensure that the timing is right and that the resources needed to support these efforts are available.

Implementation Program. Once the marketing plan is approved, the marketing manager needs an efficient and effective implementation program to turn the plan into reality. Poor implementation is the cause of more failure than poor marketing plans. The implementation plan should include clear statements as to who does what, by when, for whom, and for how much.

Financial Analysis. The marketing plan and its implementation program must be translated into revenues and expenses. On the revenue side, the impact of decisions on price, product positioning, changes in sales force, changes in distribution channels, levels of service, and so on are transformed into forecasts of future sales and revenue levels. On the expense side, the cost of additional service facilities, sales, personnel, information technology, advertising, and so on are tallied. Revenues and expenses are combined to show how the marketing strategy contributes to the attainment of financial and marketing objectives. Putting the marketing strategy and the implementation program into financial terms enables marketing managers to see the consequences of their decisions and how all the pieces fit together.

Controls. The last step is to decide what types of controls (feedback mechanisms) are needed to measure the firm's progress toward its financial and marketing objectives. The controls often take the form of quarterly or monthly reports that help managers spot any serious deviations from expectations so corrective action can be taken early.

The marketing plan gives the firm a systematic way of assessing all the factors surrounding the consumer needs the firm hopes to fill. Conducting this comprehensive review increases the chance for success.

The Relationship between Purpose, Objective, and Long-Term Profits

Firms achieve higher *rates of return on invested capital* when they have a clear set of values, as well as a well-defined purpose and objective that is reflected in a carefully drawn strategic plan. The objective might be to offer the lowest prices, the highest quality, or the best service as defined by customers. Those firms that do not have a well-defined business purpose and objective, or just copy the actions of competitors, often have returns on invested capital that are average or below average. Without a well-defined purpose and objective, the firm has no competitive edge in the market. Consumers see little reason to buy an average product from an average firm when they can get exactly what they want from a firm that gives it to them exactly the way they want it. By being aggressive and following a well-thought-out strategic plan, a firm can be a market leader and enjoy greater profitability.

Analyzing Market Potential

One of the most important tasks in developing a marketing plan is an analysis of the current market situation. It is a critical part of the firm's strategic plan, whose goal is to match the company's resources with profitable business opportunities. This planning process is easier when a number of solid business opportunities have been identified and analyzed.

Transition from Mass to Target Marketing

Firms in the agri-food system have changed their market approach from a mass marketing to a target marketing approach. Mass marketing operates on the idea that all consumers have the same needs, so a firm can produce a single product and use a single marketing approach to meet the needs of all its customers. This can be summarized as the "one-size-fits-all" approach to marketing. If a firm sells hamburgers, for example, and most people like a well-done burger with ketchup, it will offer only that one product since that will satisfy most people. The **product mix** is standardized, the same product is offered to all customers at the same price and at the same types of locations using the same promotion nationwide. Mass marketing is low-cost, efficient, and easy to do. In today's market it leaves too many consumers at least a little bit unsatisfied.

In recent years, agribusiness firms have come to appreciate the added profits possible from target marketing. Target marketing operates on the idea that consumers do not all have the same needs and that products should be developed that meet the needs of specific groups of consumers. Because these products do a better job of meeting a group's needs, consumers will buy more of these products and are usually willing to pay a higher price for them because they more completely satisfy their needs. To gain the benefits of target marketing, producers must be able to correctly identify and assess the profit potential of these market segments.

Identifying Target Markets

The market identification process begins by defining consumer needs, desired benefits, and preferences. These have to be narrowed down to something specific so a single product can meet these needs. While the identification process should not be tied to any existing product, it should be conducted in product-satisfaction terms. The needs can then be matched on several sought-after characteristics to see if any patterns emerge. The next step is to match these sets of preferences with the demographic information of the potential consumers who gave the product preferences. By combining product preferences and demographics, a picture of the types of consumers who prefer a potential product should emerge.

The result of the market research may end up like this: consumers are looking for a healthy, nutritious, low-calorie, handheld snack food that can be prepared in a microwave and costs no more than $2.50 per serving. The demographics of those consumers requesting this preference could be: equal numbers of males and females who work more than 60 hours per week in professional and technical jobs, are health-conscious but often skip regular meals, have at least four years of college, and live in urban areas. Once this information has been discovered, the next step is to see if this target market (or market segment) can be serviced profitably.

Estimating Market Potential

A number of methods can be used to estimate the economic potential of a market, but before proceeding it is important to define several terms. *Market potential* is the total level of sales possible in a target market for all firms. *Sales forecast* is the level of sales a single firm can expect to receive from a target market. *Market share* is the percentage of total sales from the target market achieved by a single firm.

$$\frac{\text{Sales forecast}}{\text{Market potential}} = \text{Market share}$$

The Macroeconomic Approach. One way to estimate market potential is to derive the consumption of a product from an easily obtained macroeconomic statistic such as the gross domestic product (GDP), retail sales, industry production, or sales.

For example, if total retail food sales are typically 15 percent of the GDP, and the GDP is forecast to be $15 trillion next year, retail food sales can be projected to be:

$$\$15 \text{ trillion} \times 0.15 = \$2.25 \text{ trillion}$$

If a major supermarket chain's sales normally represent 2 percent of national retail food sales, the next year's sales can be estimated to be:

$$\$2.25 \text{ trillion} \times 0.02 = \$45 \text{ billion}$$

If the real concern is fresh produce sales, which normally account for 10 percent of the chain's total sales, next year's expected fresh produce sales will be:

$45 billion × 0.10 = $4.5 billion

The Population Approach. A second approach for determining market potential is to develop estimates from the consumer side using population statistics. For example, if market research shows that the consumers of a proposed new product are highly educated (top 25 percent of the population), male (50 percent of the population), high-income (top 25 percent of the population) people who live in cities (40 percent of the population) in the southwestern United States (20 percent), and are between 45 and 60 years of age (10 percent of the population), the figures can be combined to estimate the size of the market for this new product.

U.S. population	300,000,000	people
times highly educated	× (0.25)	
	75,000,000	people with higher education
times % males	× (0.50)	
	37,500,000	males with higher education
times % with high income	× (0.25)	
	9,375,000	males with higher education and income
times % urban	× (0.40)	
	3,750,000	urban males with higher education and income
times % living in the SW	× (0.20)	
	750,000	urban males in SW with higher education and income
times % 45–60	× (0.10)	
	75,000	urban males in SW with higher education and income who are 45–60 years old

If each of these consumers in the target market are buying on average two boxes of this product a week at an average selling price of $2.00 per unit, the per capita (per person) sales are $4.00 per week and $208 per year ($4/week × 52 weeks).

The total annual market potential is calculated by multiplying the per capita sales by the number of people in the target market:

$208 × 75,000 = $15,600,000

Based on the intensity of the responses received during market research, the firm feels it could expect to get a 20 percent market share (20 percent of the people in the target market would become regular buyers of the product) in the first year the product is offered. This gives a sales forecast for the first year of $3,120,000 ($15,600,000 × 0.20).

The Consumption Approach. A third approach for projecting market potential is to determine local consumption from national consumption figures. For example, if data from the USDA shows per capita consumption of French fries to be two pounds per year, it is possible to forecast market potential for French fries in Indianapolis by multiplying the per capita consumption by the population size:

$$2 \times 800{,}000 = 1{,}600{,}000 \text{ pounds per year}$$

This can be converted to dollar sales using the average price per serving. If the average serving size is ¼ pound and it sells for $1.00, the price per pound is $4.00. Thus, the annual market potential for French fries in Indianapolis can be calculated by multiplying the price per pound by the per capita consumption:

$$\$4.00 \times 1{,}600{,}000 = \$6{,}400{,}000$$

If the firm expects to obtain a 10 percent market share, they can estimate first-year sales of French fries by multiplying the estimated market share by the annual market potential:

$$0.10 \times \$6{,}400{,}000 = \$640{,}000$$

These analysis techniques can be applied to nearly any item to give a reasonable estimate of market potential. Such estimates are an important ingredient in formulating a successful marketing plan.

Chapter Highlights

1. The focus of marketing has changed from physical efficiency to selling to meeting consumer needs.
2. The marketing approach is based on the idea that a successful firm first finds out what consumers want and then develops a product that meets those needs.
3. Consumers do not buy a product; they buy the satisfaction the product gives them.
4. The satisfaction of a consumer need is what gives a firm its right to make a profit.
5. The marketing approach gives direction to the performance of the four functions of management.
6. The marketing mix is the combination of four variables controlled by managers that allow a firm to completely satisfy consumers' needs.
7. The marketing mix is made up of the four Ps of marketing—product, price, place, and promotion.
8. A business plan starts with a good set of values, and a clear definition of the firm's purpose (what the firm is going to do) and objective (how the firm will accomplish its purpose).
9. A marketing plan is a key part of the business plan.
10. Firms achieve higher rates of return on invested capital when they have a clear purpose and objective that is reflected in a well-thought-out marketing plan with an effective marketing mix.

Chapter Quiz

1. Explain why an agribusiness manager should be interested in having clear values and a well-defined purpose and objective.
2. Explain the relationship between marketing and the four functions of management.
3. Describe and explain how the role of marketing has changed the way agribusinesses operate.
4. Explain why it is important to adopt the marketing approach to be successful in agribusiness.
5. Describe the business planning process and explain the role of consumer needs in this process.
6. The unifying theme of this book is maximizing the long-term profits of a firm by profitably satisfying consumer needs. Explain this in your own words. Do you agree with it or not? Explain why you feel this way.
7. In this chapter you will find the phrase "by meeting a consumer need the firm earns its right to make a profit." Explain this in your own words. Do you agree with this statement? Explain why you feel this way.
8. Use of the marketing approach in an agribusiness leads to greater economic efficiency and greater consumer satisfaction. Do you agree or disagree with this statement? Explain why you feel this way.
9. Identify the four Ps of the marketing mix and explain why they are called controllable. Explain why firms want to control them.
10. What is the difference between business planning and strategic planning?
11. Has information technology changed the marketing management process? Explain your answer.
12. Explain the market forces that brought the transition from management focusing on production to efficiency, to selling, and to marketing.
13. How does great marketing make selling unnecessary?
14. Under the marketing approach, why does marketing become the primary job of everyone in the firm?
15. Which of the four functions of management is most closely associated with marketing? Explain your choice.
16. How does the success of an agribusiness come from good planning, communication, and execution?
17. Before a firm develops its purpose and objective, it must get its values—honesty and fairness—right first. Why?
18. Why is it important for an agribusiness to have clear, concise answers to the five questions posed by management expert Peter Drucker?
19. Why is it critical for agribusiness firms to do strategic planning?
20. Implementation is the most important part of strategic planning. Do you agree or disagree? Explain your answer.

Case 4
Dave's Dollar Dilemma: Part II

Develop a marketing plan for Dave's farm-equipment dealership based on what you learned in part I of this case.

What is the proper marketing mix for this firm?

Will a well-conceived marketing plan and an effective marketing mix help Dave solve his dilemma? Explain the reasons for your answer.

Chapter 5

Understanding Consumer Demand

Chapter Learning Objectives

- Summarize the value of economics in explaining how consumers make decisions and respond to price changes and other factors.
- Explain how price, in a free market, is the best allocator of scarce resources and helps society achieve the highest level of happiness.
- Describe the factors that influence consumer demand and recognize which factors lead to shifts in consumer demand.
- Describe how to measure and use elasticity to see the impact of price change and income fluctuation on a firm's sales and profits.
- Explain why it is difficult for agribusiness firms to raise the prices of their products.

Basics of Consumer Demand

For an agribusiness to succeed, its managers must understand how consumers make purchasing decisions and how they react to changes in price and other factors. As chapter 2 discussed, business managers draw on a number of academic disciplines to help them perform their job. In this case, economics helps explain what motivates consumer behavior.

Two Economic Principles That Drive Consumer Behavior

Although each consumer is unique, there are two universal economic principles of consumer behavior. These principles give managers a framework that increases their understanding of consumer behavior.

Utility (Satisfaction) Maximization—The first principle is that when given a choice, consumers will always select the item that gives them the highest level of utility (satisfaction). When asked to choose between a bowl of spinach and a bowl of ice cream, most will select the ice cream. Although the choice seems obvious, it should be remembered that some would choose the spinach. Thus, generalizations of what satisfies all consumers should be done cautiously.

Diminishing Marginal Utility—The second principle of consumer behavior is that the satisfaction obtained from consuming each additional unit of a good or service will diminish as more of it is consumed. For example, if you have been on a diet for a long time, the satisfaction you get from consuming a candy bar will be very high. After you have eaten your eighth candy bar in the last hour, the additional satisfaction from consuming another one would be lower. In fact, you might even be willing to pay someone not to have to eat it.

The principle of **diminishing marginal utility** explains why people consume a variety of goods and services in their pursuit of maximum total utility. If utility did not decline with additional consumption, consumers would buy only the single good or service that gives them the greatest utility. Since utility does decline with additional consumption, consumers eventually reach the point where they will choose spinach over ice cream.

The Role of Scarcity

If the world had unlimited resources, the discussion of consumer demand would end here. However, limits on time, money, labor, land, and so on prevent the consumption of everything that consumers want. Consumers are forced to make choices. Economics explains how people make good decisions when faced with choices. The combination of consumer desire for maximum total utility with the scarcity of resources available to fulfill them is what creates competition in the market. Producers' desire for the highest profits causes them to seek the lowest-cost methods of meeting consumer demand, and competition between producers leads to the lowest price for the consumer. Given a free-market setting and the fact that each producer is also a consumer of other goods and services, this situation leads to the best of all worlds—efficient production and high consumer utility.

How Price Allocates Scarce Resources

One of the secrets to achieving an optimal economic situation is to devise an efficient way to allocate scarce resources that limit the level of consumer satisfaction. In a free-enterprise system, this is done through price. Resources go to the highest bidder. For example, if the demand for a product increases, this is a signal to a producer to increase output. To achieve this, the producer must allocate the scarce resources needed to increase output of the product in demand by taking them away from other uses. The producer does this by paying a higher price for the resource than other users, which leads to their reallocation to his or her product.

Similarly, if the demand for the product falls, this signals the producer to reduce output. This reduction in output reduces his or her demand for the limited resources he or she uses. As a result, the prices of these resources should fall. The decline in price may reach the point where other users of the limited resource may outbid the original user for their use. When this happens, the scarce resources are reallocated to another user.

In each instance, the highest bidder obtains the use of the scarce resource. Each user's bid price reflects the value of that resource in his or her production process. Those who bid the highest price do so because the resource has higher value to them in their production process than anybody else. This way, scarce resources are always put to their highest and best use, and production remains efficient.

The driving force behind the allocation of all resources in a free-enterprise system is the profitable satisfaction of consumer demand. Successful producers in such a system are those that best fill consumer needs and do it at the lowest cost. Changes in consumer demand are reflected in the price changes of products. This leads to changes in the demand (allocation) of the scarce resources needed to produce it. The result is that consumer satisfaction is maximized, production is efficient, and society's welfare is maximized.

FACTORS INFLUENCING CONSUMER DEMAND

Identifying and profitably meeting consumer demand is at the center of our economic system. Because of its importance, economists and business managers have devoted a great deal of time to understanding and predicting consumer behavior.

Demand

From these efforts, some general ideas have been developed about what drives consumer demand. Let's start with a definition of demand. Economists define **demand** as a schedule of how much consumers are willing and able to buy at various prices. Note that the definition includes the phrase "willing and able to buy." This is an important distinction, since merely being willing to buy is different from actually being able to make a purchase. Sellers are interested only in *effective demand*, which involves those who are willing and able to buy the product.

Figure 5-1 is a graph of a demand schedule for coffee. One can make several observations about the demand. First, the higher the price, the lower the quantity of coffee demanded; price and demand are inversely related. This makes sense, since the consumption of coffee gives us positive utility (satisfaction) and we would consume more of it if limited pocketbooks did not restrict us. This inverse relationship between price and quantity demanded is called the **law of demand**. When economists put this relationship on a graph, price is on the vertical axis and quantity is on the horizontal axis.

Figure 5-1 A Demand Schedule for Coffee

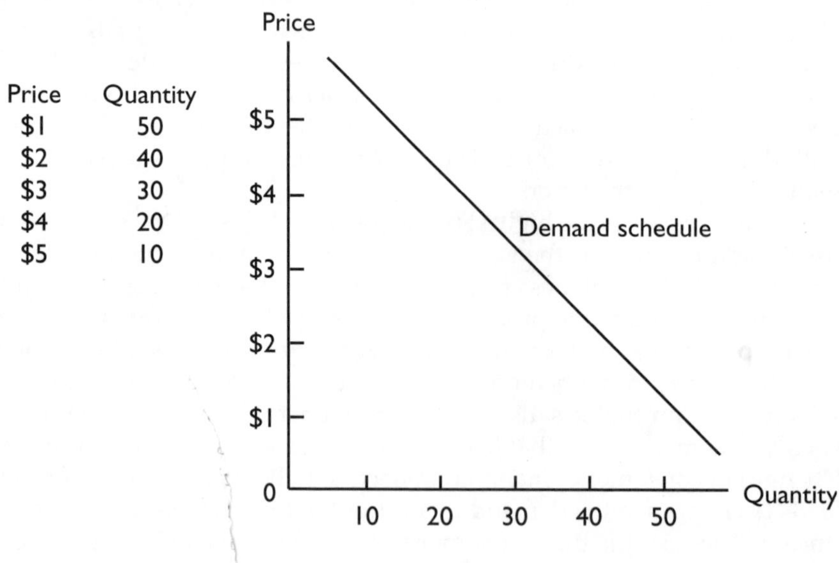

There are seven factors that affect the demand for a product:

1. ***Price of the product (own price).***
   The factor that is most likely to influence the demand of a product is its own price. In figure 5-1 we see that as the price of coffee rose from $1 to $5, the quantity demanded declined from 50 to 10 units—illustrating the law of demand (price and quantity are inversely related).
2. ***Seasonality.***
   The demand for many products follows a seasonal pattern. Christmas trees are in greater demand on December 15 than on July 15. Milk demand declines when school is not in session.
3. ***Price of competitors' products (substitute products).***
   The demand for coffee in the example is also influenced by changes in the price of competitors' beverages that could be substituted for coffee. An increase in the price of tea, for example, could lead some people to substitute coffee for tea. A decrease in tea prices could have the opposite effect. In the same way, the price of Folgers coffee can affect the quantity demanded of Maxwell House coffee.
4. ***Price of complement goods.***
   It is important to know the impact of changes in the price of goods whose use complements the use of your good. If the price of sugar was to shift significantly, it could affect the demand for coffee. Sugar could become so expensive that people who cannot drink their coffee without it would drink less coffee because of the high cost of sugar.
5. ***Income.***
   A direct relationship exists between income and the demand for most goods. The higher the income, the higher is the demand for the product. This follows the principle that consumer demand is endless. Consumers always want more.
6. ***Population.***
   A direct relationship exists between population and the demand for goods. If every consumer demands the same quantity at any given price, increasing the number of consumers will increase product demand.
7. ***Taste and preferences.***
   Consumer demand rarely stands still; desires are constantly changing. A positive trend in the demand for a product can quickly become a negative one. Red meat demand has been falling for many years, but is now again on the rise as eating red meat has become fashionable again.

Factors That Shift Demand

An important concept in understanding consumer demand is the difference between movement along the demand schedule and a **shift in demand**. When the quantity demanded changes in response to a raising or lowering of the price of the good, it generally indicates the normal response of the market to changes in price as explained in the law of demand. This is movement along the demand schedule. When the demand schedule shifts to the right (an increase in demand) or to the left (a decrease in demand) a serious change in the market for the product may have occurred that can affect the long-term profits of the firm. Such shifts may require major action by management, such as reevaluating its marketing plan and marketing mix. The factors that can cause a demand shift strike at the heart of the demand for your products. It is important to be able to separate them from movements along the demand schedule.

To use the coffee example again, if a firm sells 40 units of its brand of coffee at a price of $2.00 and then sells 30 units when the price rises to $3.00, the firm can feel comfortable that the change in its sales merely reflects movement along the demand line (figure 5-2). The rise in price brought a decline in quantity demanded. However, if it was selling 40 units at $2.00 and now finds it is selling 50 units at that price, a shift in demand (from Q_1 to Q_2) has occurred.

Figure 5-2 Shift in the Demand Schedule from Q_1 to Q_2

Price	Quantity 1	Quantity 2
$1	50	60
$2	40	50
$3	30	40
$4	20	30
$5	10	20

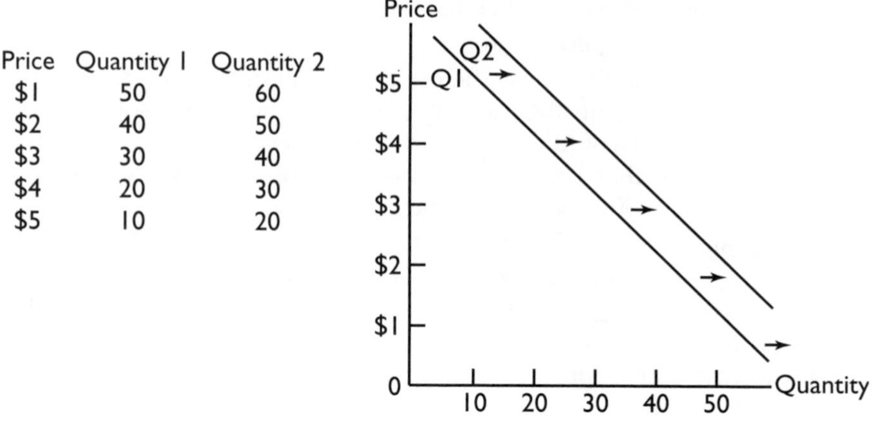

The factors that cause a shift from one demand schedule to another come from the list of things that affect demand (except the product's own price and seasonality). These factors are called demand shifters and include changes in the price of competitors' products, the price of complementary products, income, population, and consumer tastes and preferences.

Derived Demand

It is important that agribusiness firms throughout the agri-food system pay close attention to changes in consumer demand for food and fiber. Consumers help determine the demand for barns, tractors, processing plants, fertilizer, dairy cows, manufacturing plants, and most other resources used in the agri-food system. The demand for each of these resources is derived in part from consumers' demand for food in restaurants and supermarkets.

For example, farmers' demand for fertilizer is derived partially from consumers' demand for turkey dinners. If consumers demand more turkey dinners the price rises, which encourages turkey processors and producers to enlarge the size of their flocks. Increased flock size leads to greater demand for feed corn, which leads to greater demand for the fertilizer to grow it. The turkey producer, processor, feed company, and fertilizer company are all linked. The demand for each of their products is partially derived from the consumers' demand for turkey dinners. So the turkey grower, the turkey processor, the corn farmer, and the fertilizer company all need to pay close attention to shifts in the demand for turkey dinners and anything else that could affect the demand for their product. This also is another example of why it is important to think of all these firms as part of an agri-food system.

Demand Elasticity: The Impact of Price Changes on Sales

One of the major concerns of agribusiness managers is the effect of price changes on sales. Economics has a way to measure this response, it is called elasticity. Elasticity measures the percentage change in sales (quantity demanded) for a 1 percent change in price or income. Knowing the **elasticity of demand** can assist agribusiness managers in setting prices that will maximize their long-term profits.

Classifying the Sales Response

The level of response in sales to changes in price or income is classified into three categories: elastic, inelastic, and unitary. When a 1 percent change in price or income brings a response of more than 1 percent in sales (quantity demanded), then the response is classified as elastic. If the response is less than 1 percent, it is considered inelastic. A response of exactly 1 percent is unitary. It is important for agribusiness managers to know the market situation for their products because the correct pricing decision in an elastic market situation is exactly the opposite of that in an inelastic situation.

Price Elasticity. Price elasticity is the most commonly used measure of quantity response (sales). Price elasticity (E_p) is the percentage **change in quantity demanded** of a product, given a 1 percent change in its *own price:*

$$E_p = \frac{\%\text{ change in quantity}}{\%\text{ change in price}}$$

For example, if the price of caviar increases from \$20 to \$25 per pound (a 25 percent increase) and the quantity demand declines from 100 pounds to 50 pounds (a 50 percent decrease), the price elasticity of caviar would be –2:

$$\begin{aligned} E_p &= \frac{\%\text{ change in sales of caviar}}{\%\text{ change in price of caviar}} \\ &= \frac{-50\%}{+25\%} \\ &= -2 \end{aligned}$$

This tells us three things. First, the demand for caviar is elastic—the sales response to a change in the price of caviar will be greater than the percentage change in its price. (The impact of this finding will be examined in detail in the next section.) Second, caviar is a normal good because an inverse relation between price and quantity exists for this product. Third, for each 1 percent increase in the price of caviar, sales would decline by 2 percent. Armed with this information, a caviar processor could forecast next year's sales if he or she knew the expected change in the price of caviar.

Cross-Price Elasticity

Similar calculations are possible for changes in the prices of competitors' products and complement goods. **Cross-price elasticity** (E_{cp}) is the percentage change in quantity demanded, given a 1 percent change in the price of a competitors' product or a complement good.

$$E_{cp} = \frac{\text{\% change in quantity}}{\text{\% change in the price of a competitor's or complementary product}}$$

Continuing the caviar example, if people eat caviar on a cracker, crackers would be a complement to caviar. Caviar producers may wish to know how a change in the price of crackers influences the sales of their product.

If the price of crackers increases from $0.50 to $1.00 (a 100 percent increase) and caviar sales decrease from 100 pounds to 80 pounds (a 20 percent decrease), the cross-price elasticity of crackers on caviar is:

$$\begin{aligned} E_{cp} &= \frac{\text{\% change in sales of caviar}}{\text{\% change in the price of crackers}} \\ &= \frac{-20\%}{+100\%} \\ &= -0.2 \end{aligned}$$

This tells us three things. First, the cross-price elasticity of crackers on caviar is inelastic—the sales response to a change of the price of crackers will be less than the size of the price change in crackers. Second, for each 1 percent increase in the price of crackers, caviar sales will *decrease* 0.2 percent. Third, crackers are a complement good to caviar. The negative sign indicates an inverse relationship exists between changes in cracker prices and caviar sales. This is the same relationship that the sale of caviar has with its own price. Thus, it is a complement good to caviar.

Now let's look at the impact of a change in the price of cheese on sales of caviar, using the same cross-price elasticity formula. If the price of cheese increases from $0.40 to $0.50 (a 25 percent increase) and caviar sales increase from 100 to 110 pounds (a 10 percent increase), the cross-price elasticity of cheese on caviar is:

$$E_{cp} = \frac{\text{\% change in sales of caviar}}{\text{\% change in price of cheese}}$$
$$= \frac{+10\%}{+25\%}$$
$$= +0.40$$

Again, this tells us three things. First, the cross-price elasticity of cheese on caviar is inelastic—the sales response of caviar to a change in the price of cheese will be less than the change in the price of cheese. Second, for each 1 percent increase in the price of cheese, caviar sales will *increase* 0.4 percent. Third, cheese is a **substitute good** for caviar. The positive sign of the cross-price elasticity indicates that an increase in the price of cheese leads to greater caviar sales. The only logical conclusion is that people are substituting caviar for cheese as cheese prices rise.

Income Elasticity

Elasticity also can be calculated to determine the effect of changing incomes on the sales of products. **Income elasticity** (E_Y) is the percentage change in sales given a 1 percent change in income.

$$E_Y = \frac{\text{\% change in quantity}}{\text{\% change in income}}$$

For example, if consumers' incomes increased from $30,000 to $33,000 (a 10 percent increase) and caviar sales increased from 100 to 120 pounds (a 20 percent increase), the income elasticity of caviar is:

$$E_Y = \frac{\text{\% change in sales of caviar}}{\text{\% change in income}}$$
$$= \frac{+20\%}{+10\%}$$
$$= +2$$

This tells us four things. First, the income elasticity of caviar is elastic—the sales response of caviar to a rise in income will be greater than the rise of income. Second, the positive sign on the income elasticity indicates that caviar is a normal good; as income rises people will buy more caviar. Third, for every 1 percent increase in income caviar sales will increase by 2 percent. Four, caviar purchases will be a bigger part of consumers' spending as income rises.

Goods with an income elasticity of more than one are called *luxury goods* because people spend a larger portion of their income on them as their incomes increase. Goods with income elasticities between zero and one are called *necessities*. The income elasticity of most food items is positive but less than one. This means that as income rises, food purchases increase but the increase is less than the increase in income. The result is that food purchases comprise a smaller percentage of consumer spending.

The Impact of Price Elasticities on Total Sales

Price and cross-price elasticities are most important to an agribusiness manager when he or she is setting prices (table 5-1). If a manager knew that he or she faced an **inelastic demand** for a product, he or she might seek to raise the price of that item because it would lead to a rise in total sales and more profit. For example, if a firm sold 20 units at a price of $6.00, while sales fell to 18 at a price of $8.00, the price elasticity is:

$$E_p = \frac{\%\text{ change in sales}}{\%\text{ change in price}}$$
$$= \frac{-10\%}{+33\frac{1}{3}\%}$$
$$= -0.3\ (\text{elastic})$$

The change in total revenue and profit from this adjustment is

(Before) $6.00 × 20 units =	$120
(After) $8.00 × 18 units =	$144
Additional sales revenue and profit	$ 24

Table 5-1 Relationship between Price, Total Revenue, and Elasticity

E_p	Elasticity	Effect on Total Revenue
< 1	Inelastic	Price rise = total revenue up Price decline = total revenue down
= 1	Unitary	Price rise = total revenue unchanged Price decline = total revenue unchanged
> 1	Elastic	Price rise = total revenue down Price decline = total revenue up

If demand is inelastic, both dollar sales and profits can be increased by merely raising prices and, conversely, can be lowered by reducing prices. Unfortunately, few products have an inelastic demand. They are usually limited to necessities with few substitutes, such as petroleum products.

Goods with **elastic demand** (elasticity greater than one) have opposite effects on total revenue and profits. A rise in price leads to lower dollar sales and profits. For example, at a price of $6.00, 20 units were sold, but at a price of $8.00, only 12 units were sold. The price elasticity is:

$$E_p = \frac{\%\text{ change in sales}}{\%\text{ change in price}}$$
$$= \frac{-40\%}{+33\frac{1}{3}\%}$$
$$= -1.2\ (\text{elastic})$$

The change in dollar sales and profits is:

(Before) $6.00 × 20 units =	$120
(After) $8.00 × 12 units =	$ 96
Decline in total sales and profit	$–24

When demand is elastic, raising prices decrease dollar sales and profits because consumers find substitutes for the higher priced item. Unfortunately, the demand for most food products is elastic, so the best way to raise profits and sales is to lower prices.

Since food has few substitutes why is its demand not inelastic? The general category of food does have an inelastic demand. A graph of its demand curve would show a nearly vertical line (figure 5-3). However, many substitutes exist within the general food category and demand becomes more elastic (the demand curve is more horizontal).

Let's take a closer look at figure 5-3. Assume demand line A represents all food items. This line is the most inelastic. The next line (line B) could represent the demand for all dairy products. Line C could be the demand for all ice cream, while line D may be for all vanilla-flavored ice cream. The last line, E (the most elastic demand), could be for Häagen-Dazs vanilla ice cream. As a food product is more narrowly defined the demand becomes more elastic because the list of substitutes grows longer.

For example, you may have a craving for vanilla ice cream. Nothing else will do. But on your way to Häagen-Dazs you notice a sign that says that Baskin-Robbins is having a half-price promotional sale on vanilla ice cream. The lower price on the Baskin-Robbins ice cream causes you to substitute it for the Häagen-Dazs.

Figure 5-3 Shapes of Demand Schedules

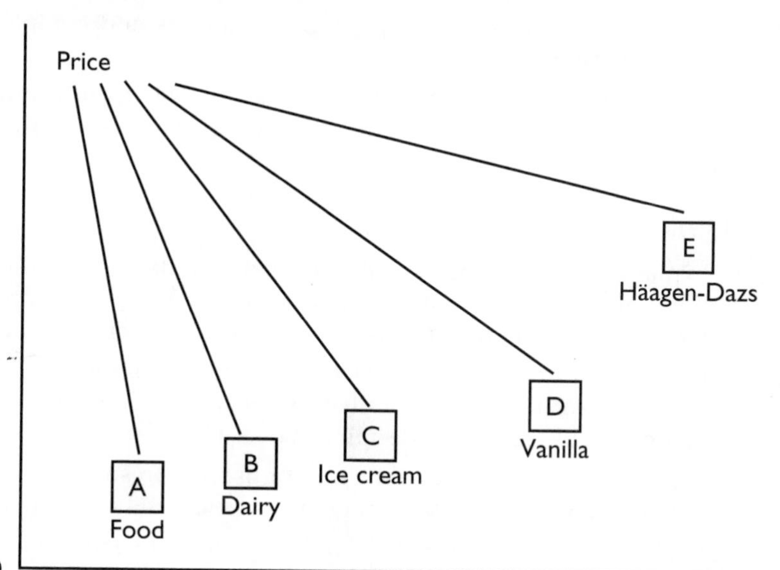

In this example, few substitutes exist for food. For dessert dairy products there are many substitutes, such as candy, baked goods, and fresh fruit. By the time that demand is refined all the way down to Häagen-Dazs vanilla ice cream the number of substitutes is large. Thus, the general level of food prices is easy to pass along to consumers, while the producer of a single food item such as Häagen-Dazs vanilla ice cream has a harder time raising prices.

Chapter Highlights

1. Consumers always select purchases that give them the highest level of utility (satisfaction) and each additional unit of consumption gives them less satisfaction than the previous one (the principle of diminishing marginal utility).
2. Knowledge of economics helps managers make good decisions because they are faced with limits on time, money, land, and so on.
3. In a free market, price is the best allocator of scare resources because it leads to resources being used most effectively.
4. Factors that affect the demand for a product include price of the product, seasonality, price of competitors' goods, price of complement goods, income, population, and taste and preferences.
5. Each of these factors, except a product's own price and seasonality, can lead to a shift in demand for the product. Demand shifts can signal a major change in consumer demand, which requires changes in the firm's marketing plan and marketing mix.
6. Elasticity is the best way to evaluate changes in sales and profits from a change in price or income.
7. The three types of elasticity are: elasticity on the product's own price, cross-price elasticity on the price of substitutes and complement goods, and income elasticity.
8. When demand is inelastic the best way to maximize profits is to raise prices. When demand is elastic (the most common case) the best way to maximize profits is to lower prices.

Chapter Quiz

1. Explain how the combination of consumers' desire for utility maximization with the scarcity of available resources leads to competition in the marketplace and greater satisfaction for all members of society.
2. Define the terms *utility, marginal utility,* and *the principle of declining marginal utility* as used by economists. Explain how these concepts show that people can be led to choose spinach over ice cream.
3. Explain why price is the best allocator of scarce resources in a free market. Explain how price allocates nonscarce resources in a free market.
4. Explain why economists make a distinction between consumers who are *willing* and those who are *able* to buy a product when they talk about effective demand.

5. Explain why the law of demand makes sense for consumers who are always seeking to maximize their total utility from the products they consume. When is consumer demand fully satisfied?
6. Identify and explain the factors that influence consumer demand. Which indicate a shift in consumer demand? Explain why shifts in consumer demand are important to agribusiness managers. What should a manager do if a shift in consumer demand for his or her product is found?
7. Explain why a manager of a fertilizer company needs to pay attention to changes in consumers' demand for chicken dinners with mashed potatoes and the value of the dollar in foreign currency exchanges.
8. Explain why an agribusiness manager should know if the demand for his or her products is elastic or inelastic. How does it help the firm achieve higher profits?
9. What does it mean to an agribusiness firm to find out that the income elasticity of its products is positive but less than one? How does this influence the formulation of the firm's marketing plan and marketing mix?
10. Since few substitute goods exist for food, why don't farmers simply raise prices in order to earn themselves a decent income? Explain your answer.
11. In agribusiness, many feel a discussion of the factors that affect demand is incomplete without including foreign exchange rates. Should they be included? Explain your answer.
12. Explain the concept of elasticity of demand, and how it helps agribusiness managers achieve their goal of maximizing their long-run profits.
13. Explain the concept of income elasticity and the implications for agribusiness of having an income elasticity between zero and one.
14. Explain the concept of cross-price elasticity of demand and how it should be used to help agribusiness managers make pricing decisions.
15. Explain how an advertising agency should use the concept of elasticity of demand to prove the value of their efforts.
16. Rank the seven factors plus foreign exchange rates that affect demand for a product from the most volatile to the least volatile. Explain why you chose the factors that were most and least volatile.
17. Explain how economics helps agribusiness managers maximize their long-run profits.
18. Give an example of how seasonality can affect the demand for an agricultural commodity or product. Draw a graph to illustrate your point.
19. Give an example of a food product that you expect to have a negative income elasticity (consumption goes down as income rises). Why does this happen?
20. Is income or price elasticity more important to the long-run success of an agribusiness? Explain your choice.

Case 5
Tom's Terrific Ice Cream

With his last ounce of energy, Tom clicked the lock shut on the door of the college's ice cream shop. It was after 11 o'clock on Sunday evening. He had been there since 7 AM, and today had been a carbon copy of Saturday. Even though homecoming weekend was the biggest sales week of the year, he was glad it was over. He was sure they had surpassed last year's record of dipping over 17,000 cones and selling 5,000 half-gallons during the past two days. Things were moving so fast he did not have time to count. They could figure it all out next week. All he wanted to do was to go home and sleep.

Things had run pretty smoothly all weekend. They had this down to a science. Customers came in one door, ordered and paid for their ice cream, and went straight out the other door. The new student employees had been carefully trained for several weeks and could dip the proper-sized cone in less than 20 seconds all day long. It seemed that everyone going to the game must have bought at least one cone.

Vanilla was still the number one choice. However, more people were asking for the other ten flavors they offered even though they charged 25 cents more per dip for them. Surprisingly, mocha marshmallow and raspberry swirl were the biggest sellers this weekend. They ran out of both of them before noon on Sunday. Yet his traditional hot sellers, peachy surprise and marvelous chocolate mint, did not sell nearly as well as he expected. Tom thought the cool, rainy weather might have affected people's choices.

Tom still looked tired when he got to Monday afternoon's staff meeting, where he slid into a chair next to Jennifer, who taught the agribusiness program's course in consumer food demand. When she asked Tom how the weekend had gone, he told her how pleased he was with everyone's effort, but said things would be a lot easier if they could better anticipate what their customers wanted. Jennifer said she was looking for a project for her class and offered to help.

Identify at least three things that Tom would like to know about the demand for the ice cream the creamery sold. Explain why you think each piece of information is important to ice cream sales.

Identify at least three things economics can tell Tom that will help him do a better job of meeting customer demand. Explain how the value of each item is important to a business manager.

Chapter 6

Staying Competitive

Chapter Learning Objectives

- Explain what strategic management is and why it is important to the long-run success of an agribusiness.
- Explain why a sustainable competitive advantage is important to the long-run success of an agribusiness today.
- Identify the two interrelated key elements in a firm's competitive advantage.
- Identify the three generic building blocks of competitive advantage.
- Describe how a firm goes about developing its competitive advantage.
- Explain Porter's Five Forces Model.
- Describe the context in which competitive strategy is formulated.

Introduction

Throughout most of our history poor communication and transportation limited the market area of most businesses. Towns were small, isolated, self-contained units that met all the needs of their citizens. Since the market area was small, towns could support no more than one or two of each type of business. As a result, firms faced limited competition, and consumers had little choice when they went to buy. The advent of interstate highways, better information technology (especially the Internet), and cable/satellite television changed all that.

Agribusinesses that were once their customers' sole supplier now find themselves engaged in fierce battles for that same business with scores of competitors who are located not only around the corner but also around the world. Today, customers find it just as easy to buy products off the Web from a distant supplier who has better prices and a bigger selection as it is to deal locally. Agribusinesses are adapting quickly to this new business model in order to survive.

The economic landscape is littered with once prosperous independent agribusiness firms (such as Monsanto, Agway, BASF, Pillsbury, Armour, and Green Giant) that were merged, taken over, or went out of business because they could no longer compete in this new business environment. Size no longer guarantees long-run success. An article on the Fortune 500 (a list of the largest firms in the United States) reported that over its 50-year history, 1,877 businesses have made this list, but only 71 have appeared every year. Some of the agribusinesses that have made this Hall of Fame are Campbell Soup, Archer Daniels Midland, John Deere, Coca-Cola, Pepsi-Cola, H.J. Heinz, and Hershey Foods.

Because of the speed of business today the need to establish and maintain a sustainable competitive advantage has never been greater. Agribusiness managers need to be thinking about their competitive situation and how to strengthen it every day. By understanding what the agribusinesses in *Fortune*'s Hall of Fame did to be successful, it will become easier to avoid the things that caused the others to fail. This is why a chapter on keeping a firm competitive is an important part of a book on agribusiness management. It is why Bill Gates, one of the richest men in the world who leads one of the United States' most successful businesses, reminds his employees every day that Microsoft is just two years away from bankruptcy. This is not the time for complacency. The proper outlook comes from the title of a famous business book by Andrew Grove, former head of Intel, *Only the Paranoid Survive.*

The goal of every agribusiness manager who wants to stay in business must be, *"How do I enhance my firm's edge* today *in this larger, faster moving, much more competitive market environment?"* Understanding how you strengthen your firm's competitive edge over the long run is a vital part of your success today, and has spawned a new area of business management called *strategic management*.

How Strategic Management Fits In

To understand how firms remain successful it is important to put strategic management into the context of what we have already learned about business management. Let's turn to the perspective of potential agribusiness investors.

1. If they decide to invest in an agribusiness, they will only do so if they can get a **return on invested capital (ROIC)** that is *at least equal* to the industry's average. However, when given a choice they should choose the agribusiness that gives the highest return above the industry's average value since this is what will maximize the long-run value of their investment.
2. Those with the highest ROIC are those that are accomplishing this book's unifying theme of maximizing long-run profits by profitably satisfying customers' needs. By maximizing long-run profits they are using the firm's resources **efficiently** (doing things well). By profitably satisfying customers' needs they are using the firm's resources **effectively** (doing the right things).
3. To efficiently and effectively employ the firm's resources the agribusiness must develop a **sustainable competitive advantage**. This comes from being either the *low-cost provider* in the market or offering a **differentiated product**.
   - Low-cost providers generate a higher ROIC from being able to offer the same products at prices below what their competitors charge and remain profitable.
   - Providers of differentiated products benefit from being able to charge higher prices due to their ability to fulfill consumers' needs better than anyone else in the market.

   Each can be the source of a sustainable competitive advantage, and lead to a higher ROIC. Successful firms do both. Managers must be constantly searching for bigger, better, faster, and different ways to satisfy their customers' needs. At the same time they must be relentlessly seeking ways to meet consumer needs at lower costs.
4. A strategic plan is valuable to an agribusiness only when it is efficiently and effectively implemented. A great plan with poor execution is the same as having no plan. Great execution of a carefully crafted plan can be the

basis of a firm's sustainable competitive advantage. The quality of a strategic plan and its execution can be evaluated by checking to see if the business is the first choice of their customers, employees, and investors.

5. Agribusinesses become the first choice of their customers, employees, and investors when they develop and maintain a sustainable competitive advantage by focusing on providing
   - ***superior efficiency,***
   - ***superior quality,***
   - ***superior innovation***, and
   - ***superior customer responsiveness***.

By being the lowest-cost provider of the most innovative, highest quality products that can be found that are sold with the highest levels of customer service, the firm makes it difficult for any of its competitors to survive. To accomplish this is no easy task. It takes daily adherence to the items listed above. It is why of the 1,877 firms that have made the Fortune 500 list in the last 50 years only 71 were able to do it every year.

WHAT IS STRATEGIC MANAGEMENT?

Strategic management is the process by which managers choose a set of strategies (broad approaches) that will allow their firm to be the first choice of their customers and employees so they can achieve the superior financial performance—the highest ROIC and stock price in the industry—their investors require. Strategic management is composed of three parts—the business vision statement, the strategic plan, and the implementation of the strategic plan.

The Business Vision Statement

Before a business can undertake strategic planning its senior managers must develop their business vision statement where they define (or reaffirm) the values, missions, and objectives for their firm.

The vision statement begins by stating what the firm aspires to be. It includes a values statement that explains how the business and all its employees are going to conduct themselves. Will it be honest and truthful in all its dealings with customers, employees, investors, suppliers, and the communities where they operate? Will it seek to offer its customers the best value possible? Will it always do what is right for the long-run success of its customers, investors, and employees rather than its own short-run profits? Will it be a good corporate citizen that is sensitive to the economic and environmental needs of the communities in which it operates? People like to be proud of where they work and what they do. They will seek out employers who share their personal values and worker harder for them because they see the value in what they do.

The **mission statement** defines the business's **purpose** by providing clear-cut answers to two questions.

- What group of customers is this business's product going to satisfy?
- What is the unmet need of this group of customers that this business is going to meet?

For the answer to the second question to have any value it must be given from a marketing approach perspective. This means it defines the unmet need in customer satisfaction terms—costs less, saves money, less time and effort—rather than technical product terms—made of steel, comes in a corrugated cardboard box, has digital controls. Customers seek satisfaction from the things they buy, not just the products. Having well-thought-out answers to these two questions is important because they define the firm in the eyes of its customers, employees, and investors.

The mission statement must also define the business's objective. The objective tells how the firm is going to accomplish its purpose by defining its *sustainable competitive advantage*—what this business is going to do better, faster, quicker, and cheaper than anyone else and how they are going to protect this advantage from being lost to competitors.

Tractor Supply Company (www.mytscstore.com) is an excellent example of a great business vision statement. They have a concise, clear listing of their values. The mission statement proclaims that its customer base is anyone living the rural lifestyle. This includes full-time and part-time producers, as well as hobby farmers. They sum this up in the phrase "the stuff you need out here." They realize their competitive advantage (objective) by providing the best assortment of high-quality goods at the best prices, and they stand behind everything they sell. Tractor Supply Company is your trusted friend who understands your needs, who will treat you right, and won't let you down. This approach has made Tractor Supply Company one of the fastest growing companies in the United States.

The Strategic Plan

The next step is to take the business vision statement and subject it to the realities of the market and the firm, then develop a strategic plan that will give the investors the best chance to achieve the superior performance (a high ROIC and stock price) they desire.

The *external environment* is analyzed first to identify *the market opportunities* (the things that could increase the business's ROIC and profits) and *the market threats* (the things that could reduce the firm's ROIC and profits). Many firms use scenario planning to accomplish this. Managers are given a set of possible future market situations—the best, worst, and most likely—the firm might face, where each imagined scenario is evaluated as either a threat or an opportunity to the firm's long-run competitive advantage. The scenarios must be realistic and comprehensive to be valuable.

Once the external environment is understood it is time to examine the firm's internal environment. The *internal environment* is analyzed to identify the *firm's strengths* (the things that will enable it to realize its objectives) and *weaknesses* (the things that will prevent it from realizing its objectives). This means looking at the firm's *current resources—human, physical, and financial, plus its distinctive competencies and capabilities*—to see if they are capable of accomplishing the business's vision statement in each of the potential external market environment scenarios identified above. The internal analysis must be comprehensive to be valuable. Each of the firm's current resources must be classified as either strengthening or weakening the firm's ability to do this. When a weakness is found, a plan must be devised that describes what will be done to make it a strength so the agribusiness will realize the ROIC and stock price objectives under each scenario.

The last part of this step is to develop a strategic plan that is compatible with the firm's values and accomplishes the firm's mission (purpose) and objectives. It should also give the investors the best chance to achieve the highest ROIC in the industry by building on the firm's strengths and reducing the firm's weaknesses so it can take full advantage of external opportunities and counter external threats.

In short, a strategic plan should put the firm in the best possible long-run position relative to its market situation and internal resources so it can achieve the highest ROIC in the industry.

The Implementation of the Strategic Plan

Writing the strategic plan is the easy part. Implementing the strategic plan is the real test of the quality of a firm's management and its commitment to keeping the firm competitive in the long run. Both must be done well for this planning effort to have any value.

Financial performance (ROIC) is how an agribusiness measures the strength of its long-run sustainable competitive advantage. ROIC is like the North Star. It never changes and always points managers and investors in the right direction. A high ROIC comes only from having a well-defined, continually updated sustainable competitive advantage in combination with the flawless execution of a well-written strategic plan. The implementation part of the plan includes all the details—who is going to do what, when, how, and for how much—so the firm can measure its progress toward achieving the sustainable competitive advantage explained in the strategic plan.

Strategic planning is an ongoing process that takes years to master, yet is never done. Reviewing, updating, and recommitting to the strategic values, missions, and objectives, plus constant reassessment of the external and internal environments, must be a regular part of every firm's standard operating procedures. Strategic planning is a task without end because all of its components—the external and internal environments, technology, consumer and employee needs—are constantly changing. The time and energy involved in strategic planning is well-spent because it helps the firm earn its future. Agribusinesses, such as those who have appeared yearly in the Fortune 500, endure and prosper because they do this. Firms that focus on only the urgent problems of today while ignoring the important ones (such as a deteriorating competitive advantage) will soon find themselves swept away by the winds of market change.

Porter's Five Forces Model

During the 1970s most American industries found that the approach they had used to succeed in business for the past 20 years was no longer working. Competitors from around the world were entering the U.S. market and consumers were showing a growing preference for all that they offered. A number of economists began to study the question of what keeps a business competitive.

The best known and most enduring of these efforts came from Michael Porter, who developed the Five Forces Model. This model identified and organized the forces that affect a firm's competitive position as:

1. The threat of new businesses entering a firm's existing market.
2. The threat of new products entering the firm's existing market that could replace the firm's current products.
3. The growing bargaining power of its suppliers.
4. The growing bargaining power of its buyers.
5. The level of rivalry among the existing firms in the industry.

Porter recognized that businesses develop their competitive strategy in a complicated and changing context, and separated them into two groups. The first set of forces is made up of the factors that are internal to the company. They include the prevailing personal values of the key implementers and the firm's current internal strengths and weaknesses. The second set of forces is composed of the factors that are external to the company. They include the industry's economic and technical opportunities and threats, and the broader societal expectations for businesses. Porter described how these two sets of constantly changing forces form the building blocks of a business's competitive strategy.

After conducting a *SWOT (Strengths-Weaknesses-Opportunities-Threats) analysis*, an agribusiness will be able to create the best business model that will match the firm's internal resources and capabilities to its external market opportunities and threats so it has the best chance to realize its sustainable competitive advantage and achieve its financial objectives of highest ROIC and stock price.

While focusing on the competitiveness of individual businesses, Porter developed a generalizable method for analyzing the competitiveness of any organization that can be applied successfully to nonprofit organizations, entire industries, whole sectors of the economy, countries, as well as regions of the world. His work has endured for more than 20 years and may be more valuable today than ever before. Thomas Friedman's 2005 best-seller, *The World Is Flat: A Brief History of the Twenty-First Century*, shows that those organizations that followed the procedures explained by Porter in the early 1980s have prospered, while those that ignored them are no longer the leaders in their markets. This all serves to remind us that strategic management must be a vital part of every manager's plan.

Chapter Highlights

1. Beginning in the 1960s, the supply of most products (including food) began to exceed demand, and improvements in transportation, information technology, and communications expanded the market area of businesses. As a result, agribusinesses found themselves facing greater competition, plus more rapid changes in technology and consumer tastes.

2. In order to survive in this faster-paced, more competitive market situation firms must continually reexamine the sources of their competitive advantage. This area of business management is called strategic management.
3. Strategic management is how a business analyzes its competitive situation and then develops a plan so that it can take advantage of external market opportunities and counter any threats to its existence so that it has the best chance of achieving its ROIC.
4. Firms have the best chance to realize their financial goals by developing a sustainable competitive advantage.
5. A sustainable competitive advantage can come from being either the low-cost provider of a product or by offering a differentiated product. Successful firms do both.
6. Firms maintain their competitive advantage by operating with superior efficiency and by giving their customers superior quality, innovation, and responsiveness.
7. Strategic management has three parts: the business vision statement, the strategic plan, and the implementation of the strategic plan.
8. Porter's Five Forces Model is the best-known explanation of the strategic management process.

Chapter Questions

1. Why have agribusiness managers recently become interested in studying what makes firms competitive?
2. Explain how Andrew Grove's book title *Only the Paranoid Survive* fits into the material in this chapter.
3. Explain how a strategic plan can result in a firm's investors obtaining the highest return on invested capital in the industry.
4. Explain what a sustainable competitive advantage is and why it is important in strategic management.
5. Explain how the efficient and effective use of the firm's resources leads to a high return on invested capital.
6. Which is more important to the firm over the long run, being the low-cost provider of a product or offering differentiated products? Explain your choice.
7. Explain why a firm wants to be the first choice of its employees and customers.
8. Identify and explain the three parts of strategic management, how they relate to each other, and how they help the firm to reach its financial goals.
9. Explain how analyses of the external and internal environment interact in the development of a successful strategic plan.
10. What are the five forces in Porter's model and explain how they describe the competitive process.

11. Identify and describe the five resources that define a business's internal strengths and weaknesses.
12. Explain the role that implementation plays in the development of a sustainable competitive advantage.
13. Explain why so few businesses have consistently remained in the Fortune 500 for the past 50 years.
14. American agriculture is immune from the forces of globalization so there is no need to be paranoid about being replaced as the world's bread basket by countries like Brazil. Do you agree or disagree? Explain.
15. Explain the difference between the vision and values statements, and the purposes of each.
16. Why do agribusiness investors refer to the ROIC as their North Star?
17. Explain why Porter's Five Forces Model also can be used to assess the competitive situation of nations.
18. Explain what a sustainable competitive advantage for an agribusiness is.
19. It is easier to maintain a sustainable competitive edge today in agribusiness because of the huge financial investment needed in technology. Agree or disagree? Explain.
20. Discuss how technology has changed the way people get music. Why were people so quick to give up their CDs for MP3s?

CASE 6
Steamer's Burgers

It was the day Larry thought would never come. Here he was, staring out across a nearly empty dining room during what used to be the lunch rush. Things had not always been this way. When he first opened Steamer's Burgers seven years ago he worried about whether the business would succeed. Things got off to a slow start, but within a year business was booming.

The students at the college, just across the street from his place, loved his special burgers. They were not like anybody else's in the area. They were steamed rather than fried or broiled and had lots of a special blend of Italian cheeses that made them incredibly juicy and full of flavor. (Students often rated his burgers by the number of napkins they needed to finish one off.) Larry patterned the business after a place he used to go to after school in his hometown in Nebraska. People used to wait in line just to pick up take-out orders since there was never an open table. He was sure the idea would be a hit here, too.

He kept his menu simple—just burgers, fries, and soft drinks sold in a 1950s decor. He did not take credit cards or checks, which he reminded his customers of with a big "In God We Trust, All Others Pay Cash" sign that hung on the wall next to the cash register. The volume of business was so good he never felt the need to advertise to the students. Larry's steamer burgers were usually sold with fries and a drink that ran about 20 percent more than everyone else charged in town for this type of meal. The price difference did not seem to matter since he had more people at lunch than he could handle. His dinner trade was steady and usually kept the place filled until they closed at midnight. Customers were always asking if they did catering and deliveries, but Larry felt he had all he could handle just keeping his customers happy in the store.

Two years ago Larry got the chance to move to a bigger building that more than doubled his seating capacity, plus it had decent free parking. The new location had essentially the same rent but it was five blocks away from the campus near a number of buildings full of commercial and professional businesses that were part of the school's high-tech park, and a half-mile from the school's public golf course. The student trade seemed to dry up as soon as he moved. He did a small but steady business with the people who stopped in after playing golf. They often came back for lunch with coworkers from the high-tech park, and later brought their families for dinner. These were the same people who were asking about catering and delivery. But it was not enough to be very profitable. He could not afford to hire any extra help; especially since the student business was so low. His old downtown location was now a new, big outlet for a national fast food pizza buffet place that appealed to budget-conscious consumers.

What should Larry do to make his business a success?

Chapter 7

Forecasting

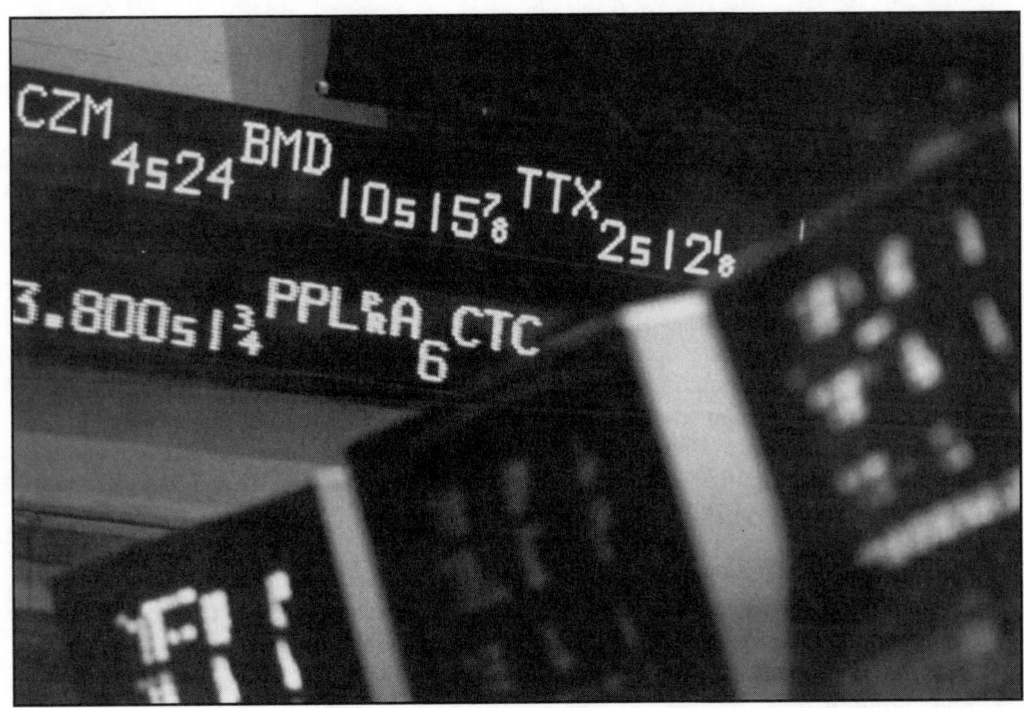

Chapter Learning Objectives

- Explain the value of forecasting in the successful operation of an agribusiness.
- Identify where to locate forecasts of major economic variables and those specific to a single industry.
- Demonstrate the use of the following forecasting procedures—extrapolation, graphical analysis, adjustment for inflation and population, and seasonal price and quantity indexes.
- Explain how futures markets work and how an agribusiness firm would use them to maximize its long-run profits.
- Describe how to successfully use forecasts in business planning.

Introduction

The globalization of the U.S. economy and the agri-food system has changed the way the world does business. Advances in logistics and telecommunications allow managers to effectively control and direct large and widely separated business activities. While these changes have permitted businesses to take advantage of the economies created by specialization and trade, they have made all of us more interdependent. The result is that U.S. agribusiness is no longer immune to changes in other parts of the economy, the country, and the world.

As agribusiness firms grow, they must constantly fight the tendency to move more slowly. This is particularly true now, since consumer tastes and preferences worldwide have become more sophisticated and change more quickly. Businesses strive to see and plan for the future in order to get there first. The ability to correctly forecast future business conditions and consumer preferences is vital to a firm's ability to achieve its purpose and objective.

Forecasting reduces the **uncertainty** surrounding business decisions and increases profits. For example, a firm would not seek to expand production if an economic downturn is forecasted for the next several years. However, if a vigorous expansion is expected next year, it might be wise today to devise ways to meet tomorrow's expected increase in demand. In both cases, the firm can put itself in the best possible position for the future if it has a reliable forecast to guide its planning.

Wise agribusiness managers use forecasts in decision making. They know what forecasts can do, how to use them, and how to recognize good forecasts. Forecasting pays. Forecasting is an important part of business success, but it is important to remember the old saying: half of all forecasts are useless, but we do not know which half until it's too late!

THE BASICS OF FORECASTING

Agribusiness managers utilize a variety of forecasts when making decisions. Some forecasts predict future levels of major economic variables such as the GDP, interest rates, inflation, income, unemployment, consumption rates, exports, currency exchange rates, and consumer confidence. However, to be useful these forecasts must relate the impact of these general variables to the individual firm's sales, profits, production levels, inventories, prices, input costs, and so on. For example, a farm-equipment manufacturer needs to know how a forecasted increase in next year's interest rates will affect farmers' decisions to buy new equipment from this company. An accurate forecast of the effect on sales will help the manufacturer determine how much to produce, how many workers to hire, and how many tires to order.

Forecasts study explanations of past customer buying habits to predict future customer buying habits; they also determine the impact of new technology on markets and glean information about other factors that affect the markets in which firms sell products or buy inputs. Failure to accurately predict changes is a leading cause of business failure. It is important to forecast frequently and to look at anything that could affect the future of your business.

Forecast methods range from unsophisticated approaches such as throwing darts to large, complex computer models. It is important to use forecasting techniques that are appropriate to the situation. The selection of a forecasting procedure depends on the relative importance of five factors: accuracy desired, time permitted to develop the forecast, complexity of the situation, the time period being forecasted, and level of resources available. Unfortunately, if the time permitted to develop the forecast is short, accuracy could suffer. On the other hand, if the time allowed is expanded, accuracy should increase, but so will the cost. The secret is to determine the proper mix of these factors and to integrate the forecast into the decision-making process. Generally, the best forecasts are those involving the most straightforward, uncomplicated methods.

Sources of Forecasts

Forecasts of future business conditions can be obtained from a variety of public and private sources. The growing recognition of the need and value of business forecasts has led to a surge in the number of private forecasting firms. These firms normally use large, sophisticated, mathematically based computer models to make their projections and sell them to other firms. Nearly all of them provide forecasting for agribusiness firms. A few large agribusiness firms operate their own in-house economic forecasting units to perform many of these functions.

Independent forecasting services often are priced beyond the financial reach of many smaller businesses. However, these firms can access such advice through membership in industry trade associations (such as the Cattlemen's Association or the Farm Bureau), major agribusiness publications, and university publications. A large number of high-quality economic forecasts are readily available free of charge from federal, state, and local government agencies. For example, it is possible to forecast local competition by keeping abreast of zoning changes and construction permits being granted by the local planning and zoning board.

Federal and state agencies maintain large amounts of economic data on a town, county, state, or zip code basis, and on a variety of items such as farm income, retail sales, income, population, number of households, and types of businesses. Many of these publications are available online. For example, if you wanted to open a farm-implement store in your county it would be wise to look at *The Census of Retail Trade*, available from the U.S. Department of Commerce (http://www.census.gov/mrts/www/mrts.html). If the census shows that several farm-implement dealers are already operating in the county, the number of outlets has been declining for the past few years, and the average annual sales are 30 percent below the state average, you may wish to reconsider your decision. A look at data from your state department of agriculture or the USDA for your county would also be helpful to determine the agricultural trends in your area.

Business and trade association publications are other sources of low-cost business forecasts. These include general business publications such as *Fortune*, *Forbes*, *Business Week*, and the *Wall Street Journal*. The agri-food system has a number of specialized industry publications such as *The Farm Journal*, *Grain Miller's News*, *The Drover*, *Hoard's Dairyman*, *Poultry Times*, and *Supermarket News*. General business publications keep up to date on major trends in the economy, while trade journals give specialized forecasts and analyses of events that are of particular interest to agribusiness. Each is designed to provide information that a business needs to place it in the best possible position relative to expected future conditions.

Two Ways to Look at Data

Forecast data can be arranged in two ways. The first is cross-sectional data. **Cross-sectional data** are collected from different groups or locations at the same time. The cross-sectional approach is used to understand a phenomenon at a single point in time. An example would be to collect this year's data on chicken consumption in each major city of the United States. This could be paired with other cross-sectional data in each city—such as the price of chicken, the price of barbecue sauce, and people's income—to see the impact of these variables on current chicken consumption. Cross-sectional economic analysis helps a poultry processor identify and understand the impact of these variables on current sales.

Time-series data are collected from one or more groups or locations over time. Time-series data are more frequently used in forecasting. An example would be to use monthly national data on the same variables used in the cross-sectional example to analyze 20 years of monthly observations. The goal of time-series economic analysis is to help a poultry processor predict future chicken prices and sales levels. This type of analysis also can identify recurring patterns in the price of chickens and feed that could be helpful in making selling and buying decisions.

FORECASTING PROCEDURES

Extrapolation

The simplest forecasting method is extrapolation. **Extrapolation** uses the idea that whatever happened in the past will happen again in the future. For example, if the price of fertilizer rose 6 percent last year, the extrapolation method would project a 6 percent rise again this year. Although this method is naïve and lacks an economic base, it often is effective in the short term (one year or less) since many economic variables are slow to change. The absence of an economic base, however, limits its long-term use and may cause a manager to miss abrupt changes in an economic environment. However, its ease makes extrapolation an attractive first-cut forecasting procedure.

Graphical Analysis

The forecasting power of extrapolation is increased when it is combined with graphical analysis. **Graphical analysis** is the plotting of data on a graph so that a manager can see what patterns are present in the data. This procedure normally uses time-series data with the data values on the vertical axis and a time period covered on the horizontal axis (figure 7-1). To get a better picture of the long-term directions of change, a trend line is fitted to the plotted data points. The **trend line** should move through the center of the plot and change direction when necessary. The slope of the trend line gives the average change for each period and can provide a general forecast of the expected future direction of change in the variable studied.

Figure 7-1 Farm-Level Price of Corn per Bushel

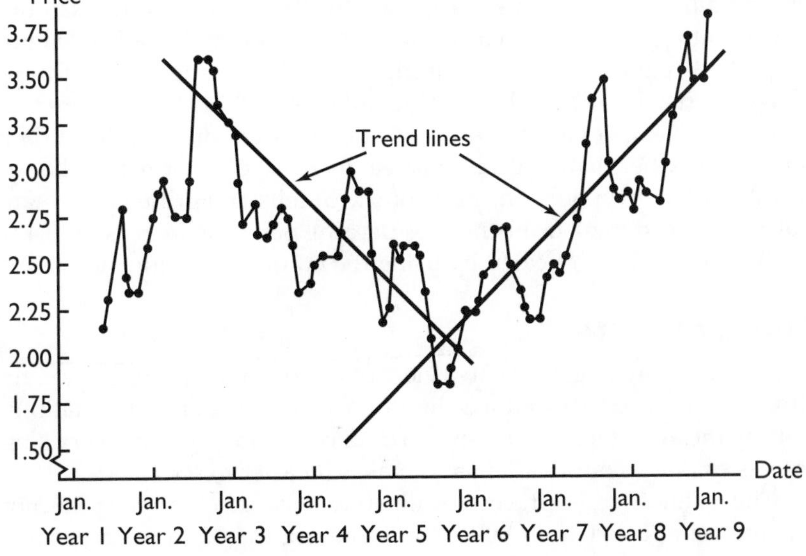

In figure 7-1, several trend lines can be fitted to this data. A trend line from December of year 5 to December of year 8 shows a price rise of approximately $1.26 per bushel (from approximately $2.24 to $3.50 per bushel) over the three-year period, or an average increase of $0.42 per bushel per year. If all else stays the same, the forecast for next year's price would be $0.42 higher than this year's price.

Like extrapolation, graphical analysis should be used cautiously and for short-term forecasting since it is without a strong economic foundation. However, it can help forecasters see the big picture by pointing out potential shifts in trends, even if it cannot explain them. For this reason, graphical analysis should always be a part of whatever forecasting procedures are used.

Adjusting for Inflation

To gain the full benefits of graphical analysis, it is important to get a clear picture of the data. A clear picture of price data is hard to obtain when inflation (a general rise in prices) is present. For example, we need to know if the projected annual price increase of $0.42 per bushel reflects a real increase in the price of corn or merely the rise in overall prices resulting from inflation. A real (inflation-adjusted) increase in price could signal an increase in demand, a decrease in supply, or both. Regardless, such an occurrence would be of interest to a forecaster. If it just reflects the influence of inflation, nothing has changed. It is important for managers to know the difference because it affects their marketing plans and marketing mix.

To adjust for the impact of inflation, it is necessary to deflate or remove the effect of inflation from corn prices. This is accomplished by dividing the corn prices by an appropriate general price index calculated for the same period, such as the Index of Prices Received by Farmers, the Index of Prices Paid by Farmers, the Consumer Price Index, or the Producer Price Index. In this example, the most appropriate deflator is the Index of Prices Received by Farmers.

Dividing each month's corn price by the deflator's index number for that same month gives the real corn price for that month (table 7-1). Figure 7-2 shows the plotted real price of corn. Fitting a new trend line for the three-year period shows the rise in price to be considerably less ($0.24) than before the adjustment ($1.26). The year-to-year trend in corn prices after adjusting for inflation is +$0.08 per bushel rather than +$0.42. This real increase of approximately 3.5 percent per year ($0.08/an average corn price of $2.25) tells an agribusiness manager a story that is very different from the +14 percent per year increase ($0.42/an average corn price of $3.00) indicated by using the noninflation-adjusted rate.

Moving Averages

Another way to get a clearer view of trends in data is to use moving averages. Moving averages help reduce the impact of short-term fluctuations in data by plotting the average value of several data points rather than every single one. This process smoothes out the data and makes it easier to see trends.

The value of this process is illustrated by calculating a 12-month moving average using the data in table 7-1. Summing the 12 most recent months' prices

Figure 7-2 Real Farm-Level Price of Corn per Bushel

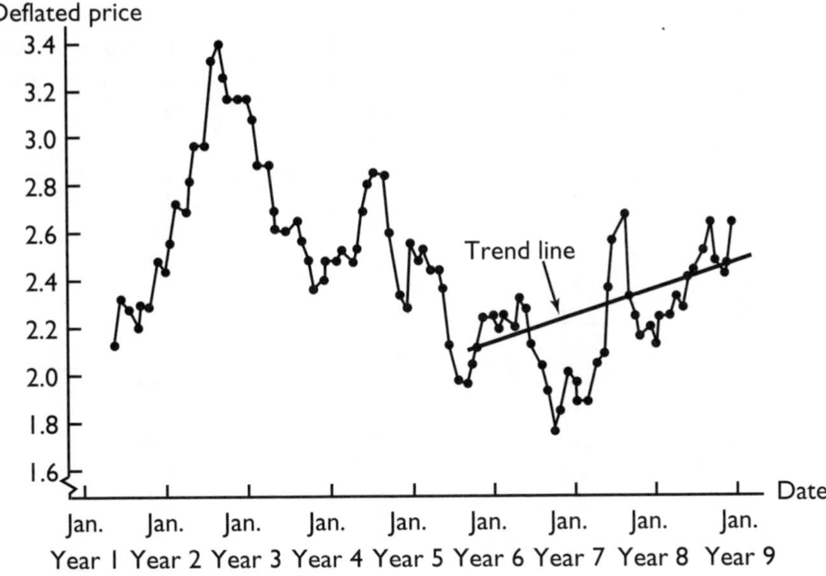

Table 7-1 Farm-Level Average Corn Prices, the Index of Prices Received by Farms, and Real Prices

	(1) Date	(2) Price per Bushel	(3) Index of Prices Received	(4) Real Price per Bushel	(5) Moving Average Price per Bushel
Year 1	Dec.	$2.23	99	$2.25	
Year 2	Jan.	2.27	102	2.22	
	Feb.	2.29	105	2.18	
	Mar.	2.43	109	2.23	
	Apr.	2.51	114	2.20	
	May	2.72	118	2.30	$2.11
	June	2.68	118	2.27	2.09
	July	2.49	117	2.13	2.07
	Aug.	2.35	116	2.03	2.04
	Sept.	2.27	118	1.92	2.01
	Oct.	2.20	125	1.76	2.00
	Nov.	2.20	119	1.85	1.98
	Dec.	2.45	122	2.01	1.99
Year 3	Jan.	2.48	127	1.95	2.03
	Feb.	2.46	132	1.86	2.08
	Mar.	2.54	134	1.90	2.11

(continued)

Table 7-1 *(continued)*

	(1) Date	(2) Price per Bushel	(3) Index of Prices Received	(4) Real Price per Bushel	(5) Moving Average Price per Bushel
	Apr.	2.74	134	2.04	2.15
	May	2.83	135	2.10	2.18
	June	3.14	134	2.34	2.20
	July	3.41	134	2.54	2.21
	Aug.	3.49	130	2.68	2.24
	Sept.	3.04	132	2.30	2.27
	Oct.	2.88	129	2.23	2.29
	Nov.	2.83	130	2.18	2.31
	Dec.	2.90	131	2.24	2.29
Year 4	Jan.	2.78	130	2.14	2.30
	Feb.	2.93	131	2.24	2.29
	Mar.	2.88	128	2.25	2.32
	Apr.	2.83	123	2.30	2.34
	May	2.85	125	2.28	2.36
	June	3.04	127	2.39	2.40
	July	3.30	135	2.44	
	Aug.	2.56	141	2.52	
	Sept.	3.75	142	2.64	
	Oct.	3.51	142	2.47	
	Nov.	3.52	144	2.44	
	Dec.	3.84	145	2.65	

To calculate a 12-month moving average:

1. First month: May Year 2
   a. Sum col. (4) Dec. Year 1 to Nov. Year 2:
      $2.25 + 2.22 + . . . + 1.76 + 1.85 = 25.34
   b. Divide by 12 to find col. (5):
      25.34 ÷ 12 = $2.112
2. Second month: June Year 2
   a. Sum col. (4) Jan. Year 2 to Dec. Year 2
      $2.22 + 2.18 + . . . + 1.85 + 2.01 = 25.10
   b. Divide by 12 to find col. (5):
      25.10 ÷ 12 = $2.092

Source: Pennsylvania Crop Reporting Service, *Annual Data.*

and dividing the total by 12 gives the first point of a 12-month moving average. This procedure is repeated each subsequent month with the oldest month's value being dropped and replaced by the next month's price. Plotting the moving average for these prices against the monthly prices shows the smoothing effect of this procedure (figure 7-3). For example, the new upward trend in the real price of corn is easier to find when moving averages are used.

Figure 7-3 Real Farm-Level Price and 12-Month Moving Average Real Price of Corn per Bushel

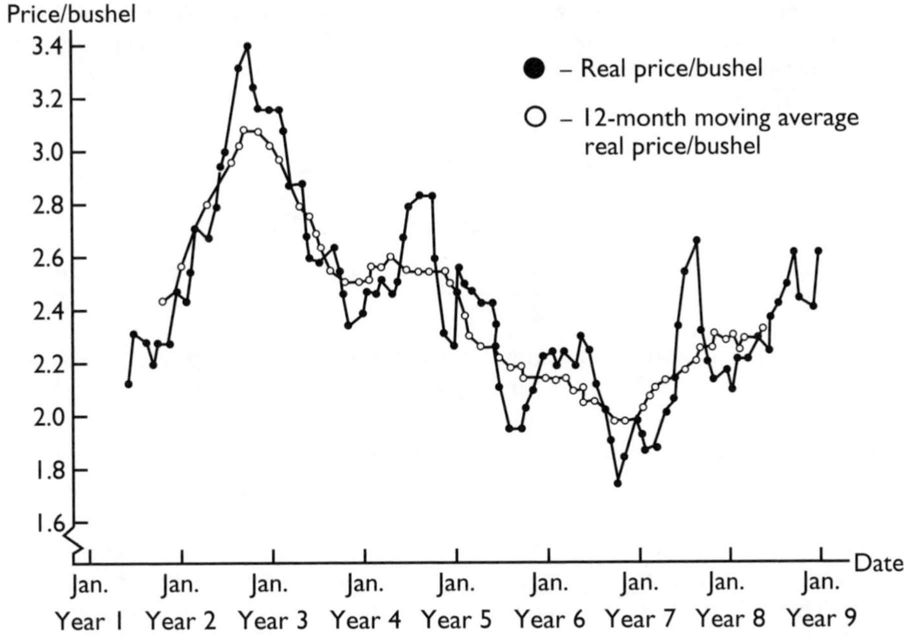

Adjusting for Population

Distortion of data is not limited to price. The effects of population often cloud a clear picture of the demand of some products. It is possible to remove the impact of changes in population by measuring sales on a per person (per capita) basis. This is done by dividing sales by population. Changes in per capita sales can indicate a shift in the demand for a product that requires a firm to reevaluate its marketing plan and marketing mix. In other cases, such as most food products, total annual sales increase, but only at the rate of population growth (approximately 1 percent per year). Thus, real sales are constant.

Consider, for example, the consumption of red meat (beef, veal, pork). The total consumption of red meat has remained nearly level since 1971 (table 7-2). However, when consumption is considered on a per capita basis, we find that it has declined over 22 percent. The per capita change shows the changing tastes and preferences of consumers that would have otherwise remained hidden. Such information has a profound effect on the future of firms in the meat industry.

Identifying Seasonal Patterns

Production agriculture has recurring patterns of prices and quantities that are rooted in the biology of agricultural production. While the production of many

Table 7-2 Total and Per Capita Consumption of Red Meat—Selected Years 1971 to 2005

Year	Red Meat Consumption (Million Pounds)	Percent Change Since 1971	Population (Millions)	Percent Change Since 1971	Per Capita Consumption (Pounds)	Percent Change Since 1971
1971	31,062	—	207,661	—	149.6	—
1981	30,901	–0.5	229,966	+10.7	134.4	–10.2
1991	30,056	–3.2	253,493	+22.1	118.6	–20.7
2001	33,595	+8.2	285,335	+37.4	117.7	–21.3
2005	34,493	+11.0	296,639	+42.8	116.3	–22.3

Source: The Economic Research Service, U.S. Department of Agriculture. Retrieved February 15, 2007.

commodities is limited to a single crop each year, consumption occurs throughout the year. This results in recurring **seasonal patterns** of prices and quantities. Graphical analysis of monthly prices for most commodities shows the lowest price at harvest time, followed by a slow rise each month throughout the rest of the year, followed by a decline just before the next harvest. This pattern normally repeats itself year after year. Agribusiness firms use this information to make buying and selling decisions that will enhance their profitability. The rise in prices after harvest induces producers and processors to store part of the annual crop.

This annual pattern is seen when monthly corn prices are plotted (figure 7-2). Prices are lowest at harvest (October to December) and reach their peak prior to harvest (July to September). Agribusiness managers can use this knowledge to develop a monthly **price (or production) index** (table 7-3) that can increase the effectiveness of their commodity buying and selling decisions.

To calculate a monthly price index:

1. Plot prices for the last several years on a graph and fit a trend line to the data. (Since the goal is to forecast the future price of corn, no inflation adjustment will be made in the data.)
2. Determine the average change in price per month by measuring the slope of the trend line and then subtracting it from each price to get the determined price.
3. Calculate the average determined price for each month of the year—the average price for all the Januarys, all the Februarys, and so on.
4. Calculate the overall average of all the determined prices in the data.
5. Divide each month's average price by the overall average price to obtain the monthly index of prices.

Each month's price index gives the average price in that month as a percentage of the year's average price. For example, according to the data in table 7-3, the January price index is 93.5. This means the price in January is 93.5 percent of the average price of corn for the year. The monthly price index tells managers that the lowest price for corn comes in November and the highest price comes in

Table 7-3 Corn Price* and Monthly Price Index

	Year 1	Year 2	Year 3	Monthly Average	Monthly Price Index
Jan.	$2.24	$2.02	$1.90	$2.053	93.5
Feb.	2.22	1.97	2.02	2.070	94.2
Mar.	2.32	2.02	1.94	2.093	95.3
Apr.	2.37	2.18	1.85	2.133	97.1
May	2.54	2.24	1.84	2.207	100.5
June	2.47	2.51	1.99	2.323	105.7
July	2.24	2.74	2.22	2.400	109.2
Aug.	2.07	2.79	2.44	2.433	110.7
Sept.	1.96	2.31	2.60	2.290	104.2
Oct.	1.85	2.11	2.32	2.093	95.3
Nov.	1.82	2.02	2.30	2.047	93.2
Dec.	2.03	2.06	2.58	2.223	101.2
Overall average price				$2.197	100.0

To calculate monthly price index:

1. Determine trend.
2. Remove trend and round to next full cent:
   a. Jan. Year 1 $2.27 – (1)($0.035) = $2.24
   b. Feb. Year 1 $2.29 – (2)($0.035) = $2.22
   c. Mar. Year 1 $2.43 – (3)($0.035) = $2.33
3. Calculate average price for all Jan., Feb., etc.:
   a. Jan. ($2.24 + $2.02 + $1.90) ÷ 3 = $2.053
   b. Feb. ($2.22 + $1.97 + $2.02) ÷ 3 = $2.070
   c. Mar. ($2.32 + $2.02 + $1.94) ÷ 3 = $2.093
4. Calculate overall average price:
   ($2.24 + $2.02 + . . . + $2.06 + $2.58) ÷ 36 = $2.197
5. Calculate monthly price index by dividing each monthly average price by overall average and multiply by 100 to get the monthly price index:
   Jan. 2.053 ÷ 2.197 × 100 = 93.5

*A trend variable of $0.035 per month ($0.42 per year) has been removed from these prices.

August. They can use this information to better time their buying, selling, and storage activities.

Managers also can use this knowledge to forecast future prices. For example, if corn sells for $3.00 a bushel in January, the expected average price for the year would be $3.21 ($3.00/0.935). It is also possible to forecast the price in any other month of the year by multiplying the January price by the ratio of price indices. The predicted December price would be $3.25 [$3.00 × (101.2/93.5)].

This procedure can also be applied to forecast future production, consumption, and slaughter levels. For example, if the slaughter of cattle in January is 200,000 head and the monthly index number is 95.4, the average monthly slaughter can be forecasted to be 209,644 head (200,000/0.954) for that year and the expected total slaughter for the year would be 2,515,728 (209,644 × 12).

The identification of seasonal price and quantity patterns and the calculation of monthly price and quantity indices go a long way to helping agribusiness managers make better buying, selling, and storage decisions.

Identifying Cyclical Patterns

Similar patterns in prices and quantities can extend beyond one year. These are called **cyclical patterns**. In production agriculture, cyclical patterns also come from biological factors and are more prevalent in livestock, especially hogs and cattle. Unlike annual crops such as grain, where output can be radically adjusted each season, changes in livestock production require a longer period of adjustment. In addition, crop producers can store their product at little cost if they find prices unfavorable, while livestock producers have little leeway since they must pay for feed, housing, veterinary expenses, and so on if animals are held past maturity. These constraints to production are reflected in the length of the price and production cycles for these commodities. For hogs, the full cycle of expansion and contraction takes approximately 3.5 to 4 years; for cattle it can last as long as 12 years.

For any industry, it is important to know which stage of a cycle the industry is in. For example, you do not want to expand your herd if you are near the top of the price cycle since it could be many years before prices get any higher. However, you might consider such a move if the industry is at the bottom or climbing an upward leg of the cycle. Understanding this phenomenon can guide agribusiness managers as well as bankers, feed salespeople, and processors to make better decisions.

Combining Adjustments

It is possible to combine several of the forecasting procedures just discussed when making a projection. For example, the most recent average yearly price for corn is \$3.21 per bushel, the trend in prices is \$0.42 per bushel per year, and there are no cyclical patterns in corn prices; therefore, it is possible to predict the average yearly price for corn two years into the future. To do this, take the most recent price and add the trend variable for the number of years being forecasted (in this case, two):

$$\$3.21 + (2)(\$0.42) = \$4.05$$

If all else stays the same, the annual average price for corn in two years will be \$4.05.

To determine the price in any particular month of that year, multiply the forecasted annual average price (\$4.05) by the appropriate monthly price index number. For example, if the goal is the harvest price (October), whose index number is 95.3, the forecasted price that month is \$3.86 (\$4.05 × 0.953).

Words of Caution

It would be unfair to end the discussion of forecasting without putting out some words of warning for all of these procedures. A forecast is just that—a best guess of the future. In our examples, the prices and quantities predicted would be accurate only if no change occurs in the underlying trends and cycles; that is, if it is a normal year in terms of weather for seasonal crops, no changes occur in consumer tastes and preferences, or no other demand shifters change.

In the long run, forecasts can be valuable even though predictions for individual years may miss the mark by a considerable margin. The value of forecasts rests in two areas. First, forecasts help agribusiness managers better understand the forces and changes affecting their markets; this makes them better able to adjust to these changes. Second, just knowing the direction and timing of such changes can reduce the uncertainty surrounding planning and decision making.

USING FORECASTS

The development of a forecast is only the first step in the effective use of these projections. Like other business procedures, they require careful application if they are to be of value.

1. ***Understand the assumptions behind the forecast.***
   Forecasting methods normally rely heavily on the assumption that what influenced things in the past will continue to influence them in the same way in the future, that is, no changes will occur in the fundamentals of the situation, such as new technology, changes in consumer tastes and preferences, changes in government policies, world events, and so on. Wise agribusiness managers know that this is not always true and can successfully anticipate changes in the fundamentals. They take the time to look behind the data. Their goal is to see the changes in the fundamentals before their competitors so they can be the first firm to take maximum advantage of these changes. A good example is the food industry's recognition of the change in consumer preferences toward organic foods.
2. ***Update forecasts.***
   Agricultural forecasts (especially production forecasts) are continually updated since much of the business is heavily influenced by uncontrollable events such as weather, disease, currency exchange rates, and the like. Forecasts need to be reviewed often to see if they still accurately represent the current situation or if new elements need to be incorporated. For example, the USDA updates its crop production forecasts throughout the growing season as it gathers new information on acreage, yields, weather, and other variables that influence crop size.
3. ***Use alternative outcomes.***
   One helpful approach to using forecasts is alternative outcomes. An example of alternative outcomes is to forecast the best outcome (where everything goes right), the most likely outcome (where things all result in their expected outcomes), and the worst case (where everything that could go wrong does). This approach gives the manager a range of possible outcomes and some notion of the risk the firm faces. It also keeps the manager's eyes open to the possible impact of changes on the firm and allows for contingency planning. Many agribusiness executives take com-

fort in knowing that if the worst-case situation does arise, it will not wipe out the firm.

Additionally, use of alternatives helps a manager determine which items going into the forecast have the greatest effect on the fortunes of the business. For example, if a company makes a sugar-coated breakfast cereal, and corn and sugar are the most important and expensive ingredients, forecasts of corn and sugar prices are important to the firm's profitability and should be monitored and forecasted often.

If a forecast fails to predict the actual situation, it should be cause for investigation. If the deviation arose from an unexpected event (such as an embargo), one can still feel confident of the forecasting procedures used; however, this information should be used to update remaining forecasts. If the deviations were the result of a change in a fundamental item (such as a change in technology or consumer tastes), it needs to be incorporated in future forecasts. Constant updating and use of alternative outcomes helps to reduce the impact of such mistakes and will improve forecasting skills.

The ultimate reason for forecasting is to put firms in the best possible position relative to future business conditions. An accurate estimation of future sales, prices, and so forth enables an agribusiness to do a better job of purchasing raw materials, scheduling production, deciding on inventory levels, introducing new products and services, and so on. Done correctly, forecasts should lead to lower costs and higher sales and profits—the final test of every forecast.

Use of Futures Markets to Forecast Future Prices

Unlike other businesses managers, most agribusiness managers deal with the buying and selling of raw agricultural commodities whose production is affected by uncontrollable forces such as weather, government policies, and the adoption of new technologies. When this is combined with the inelastic nature of the supply and demand for most commodities, even small changes in production can lead to big swings in commodity prices. It is very unsettling for an agribusiness to have such little control over such a major portion of its revenues or costs. Futures markets were developed to reduce this price risk. In a **futures contract**, buyers and sellers agree on a price, quantity, and quality of a commodity to be transferred some time in the future.

Futures markets exist because they fulfill several important needs for their users. First, for storable commodities (corn, soybeans, wheat, and so on), the futures contract makes it easier to carry inventories. It does this by spreading out demand throughout the year for commodities whose supply is generally limited to one harvest each year.

As was seen earlier in the chapter commodity prices are usually lowest around harvest time and rise throughout the rest of the year. The difference between the harvest price and a price a few months out is derived from what the market is willing to pay someone to store the commodity over a determined period until it is needed. Those that can store it for less than that amount will do it. Those that cannot should sell at harvest.

For example, if the cash price of corn on October 15 is $3.00 per bushel and the following May's futures price is $3.14 per bushel, there is a $0.14/bushel incentive—$0.02/month return to storage—for producers not to sell at harvest and to hold their corn until May. Those who can store for less than $0.02/bushel/month should do so since they can make money by not selling at harvest. Those whose storage cost is more than $0.02/bushel/month are better off selling at harvest. This price relationship between periods of time is how futures markets help allocate a storable crop when there is year-round demand and a fixed supply throughout the year.

The second major function of the futures markets, and why they are discussed in a chapter on forecasting, is that they provide users with information on prices in the future. This feature makes futures prices great forecasts that can assist producers in their input and production decisions. Processors and producers use futures markets to protect themselves from major shifts in product prices.

In the eyes of many people, the futures price is the best current forecast of the future price of a commodity. It embodies the judgment of everyone who has an interest in a commodity about what is the right price some time in the future. In a minute that price will change as new information becomes available. A minute after that it will change again. It is this ability to immediately assess the impact of new information such as the occurrence of showers in a production area, another day of drought, spread of a crop disease, or changing energy costs on a commodity's future price that makes futures prices great forecasting tools. Producers would be wise to look at the futures prices nearest their next harvest to get a good estimate of what harvest prices might be in order to guide their production decisions.

The third major function of futures markets is forward contracting and price risk reduction. If a producer or processor sees a futures price that looks appealing for an input or product, he can forward contract at that price and remove the price risk. A more likely procedure is to use **hedging**, where one takes equal and opposite positions in the cash and futures market. Hedging gives the producer all the price protection of using the futures markets without having to endure all the problems of actually shipping to or receiving the commodity at some distant location. Only a small portion of traders actually buy and sell commodities through the commodity exchanges. They do this by netting out their position by taking equal but opposite buy and sell positions in the market for the commodity.

Hedging works because the futures and cash prices for a commodity are affected by the same events. The difference in prices should reflect only the cost of storage over the remaining life of the futures contract. This is why they should move together and get closer as the maturity date of the futures contract approaches.

For example, on July 1, a buyer for a breakfast food company sees that the harvest price of wheat is $3.90/bushel. The buyer estimates that it will cost the firm $0.16/bushel to store the wheat until it is needed on March 1.

July 1	Cost of wheat	$3.90/bushel
	Storage cost	+ $0.16/bushel
	Total cost	$4.06/bushel

If the futures price next March is $4.10/bushel. A positive margin of $0.04/bushel ($4.10 – $4.06) can be made by buying wheat now and holding it until it is needed on March 1. To protect the firm against adverse price changes, a futures contract is *sold* to deliver wheat in March at $4.10/bushel.

On March 1, if both the futures and cash price are $4.30, the return in the cash market would be a savings of $0.24/bushel ($4.30 – $4.06) from purchasing at harvest and storing. The return in the futures market after *buying* a contract and netting out of the market would be a loss of $0.20/bushel ($4.10 – $4.30). Combining the two transactions yields a positive margin of $0.04/bushel ($0.24 – $0.20). The positive margin that was available in July is still locked in and the firm makes $0.04/bushel despite the adverse movement of prices.

On March 1, if the futures and cash prices are both $3.90/bushel, the return in the cash market would be a loss of $0.16/bushel ($3.90 – $4.06) from purchasing at harvest and storing. The return in the futures market after *buying* a contract and netting out of the market would be a gain of $0.20/bushel (–$0.16 + $0.20). When the two transactions are combined, the margin that was available in July is locked in, and the firm still makes the $0.04/bushel from purchasing in July at harvest despite the favorable price movement.[1]

Hedging helps firms reduce their price risk for many commodities. It means they also miss the advantages and disadvantages of playing the market. However, the firm must remember that its primary purpose is to sell breakfast cereal, not to be a price speculator. The goal of the hedge was to reduce price risk so the firm could better manage its costs and maximize its long-run profits. In this case, it accomplished that.

Futures markets can benefit both produces and processors. It allows producers to be sure of the selling price of their products. It assures processors of adequate supplies of inputs at predetermined prices so they can operate their plants more efficiently. Futures markets benefit the entire agri-food system by giving it good forecasts of future price levels that should lead to better production decisions.

Note

[1] This is a very simple example to illustrate the basics of hedging. All other costs, including **basis**, are ignored. If you wish to go deeper into this topic, please go to the Chicago Board of Trade's Web site. They have an excellent tutorial covering both futures and options markets.

Chapter Highlights

1. Globalization has made all businesses more interdependent.
2. Customer tastes and preferences have grown more sophisticated and volatile.
3. As agribusinesses grow larger, they must constantly fight the tendency to respond more slowly to changes in market situations.
4. Forecasting helps an agribusiness accomplish its planning goal of putting the firm in the best possible position relative to future business conditions.
5. Forecasts of future levels of major economic variables such as the GDP are valuable to an agribusiness if they can be related to the firm's sales and costs.

6. Forecasts are available from a variety of public and private sources, with many available online.
7. Forecasts are just a best guess, not a sure thing. It is important to understand the assumptions behind a forecast, update forecasts as needed, and use alternative outcomes (best case, most likely case, and worst case).
8. Futures markets provide the agri-food system with ways to reduce price risk as well as good price forecasts that should lead to better production decisions.
9. The ultimate reasons for forecasting are to understand the forces that have the greatest impact on the future success of a business and to give the business sufficient time to take maximum advantage of them.

CHAPTER QUIZ

1. Discuss why a huge global agribusiness firm such as Coca-Cola has a greater need for good forecasting than a local, independent, farm-supply store. Which firm is exposed to greater risk from changes in the market?
2. Explain how forecasting is related to the planning management function.
3. Explain how knowing next year's projected GDP can help an agribusiness decide how much inventory to buy.
4. Discuss the idea that forecasting is too complicated and expensive for small agribusinesses to afford. Explain why you agree or disagree with this statement.
5. Explain why graphical analysis should be a part of all forecasting efforts. Develop an example that proves your point.
6. Explain why it is important to be able to remove the effect of inflation, population changes, and other items from a forecast.
7. What is the difference between seasonal and cyclical patterns? Why are these things more important to agribusiness than other industries?
8. Discuss how a poultry processor can use a monthly price to his or her advantage to make buying, selling, and storage decisions.
9. Evaluate the statement that the best forecasts are those that you can directly apply to business planning. Explain your answer.
10. Evaluate the statement that the use of alternative outcomes in forecasting helps agribusiness managers sleep better at night. Explain your answer.
11. Explain why cash and futures prices move together, and why they converge at the end of a futures contract.
12. Discuss how hedging is different from forward contracting.
13. Why would a firm use hedging when it means missing out on advantageous price movements?
14. Describe how a producer could hedge both his inputs and products to lock in a positive margin before production begins.
15. Explain why very few people who use futures markets ever take or make delivery of a commodity.

CASE 7
Joe's Foray in Forecasting

From the big window near his desk, Joe could see for miles across the prairie. He was now an assistant grain buyer for a major feed processor with the responsibility for buying and transporting corn to company-run processing facilities such as the one in Kankakee, Illinois. This meant constantly searching the region's 100+ corn storage facilities for the best price so the processing plant could operate efficiently. Once he found the corn, he had to arrange for its shipment by truck, rail, or barge to the plant.

Joe was still wondering how a New Jersey kid like him ever ended up working in the Midwest, and in agriculture, of all things. When he went to college he knew that he had a strong interest in business, but had never given much thought to a specialty area. In his sophomore year, he took a course in business logistics and knew he had found his area. His internship with the feed processor last summer had gone well. Kankakee was a good place to live and it was just 90 minutes from Chicago.

The transportation part of the job was easy for him to master because of his background. The agricultural part was taking a lot longer. Joe was surprised by how much the price of corn changed throughout the year. During the orientation program he heard people talk about monthly price indices as a way to understand this phenomenon.

The next time he had a few moments, he called up an old, three-year set of monthly corn prices and put them into the spreadsheet (which is given below) so he could learn how to generate a monthly price index. Develop a monthly price index using the procedures in this chapter and the information below.

Month	Year 1	Year 2	Year 3	Average Monthly Index
January	4.48	4.04	3.80	
February	4.44	3.94	4.04	
March	4.64	4.04	3.88	
April	4.74	4.36	3.70	
May	5.08	4.48	3.68	
June	4.94	5.02	3.98	
July	4.48	5.48	4.44	
August	4.14	5.58	4.88	
September	3.92	4.62	5.20	
October	3.70	4.22	4.64	
November	3.64	4.04	4.60	
December	4.06	4.12	5.16	
Average	4.33			

When Joe was finished he was not sure what he had. If Joe asked you what the value of a monthly price index is, what would you tell him? What causes the values to change each month? Why does the overall average value of the index have to be 100?

Joe needs to use this to forecast a price, such as the average price in year six, if the price trend line is +$0.50 per year. Explain how you would do this.

Next, he needs to get a more precise forecast, such as the price for October in year six. Explain how you would do this.

What words of caution should you give Joe about using this method for all his buys in the future?

Chapter 8

Budgeting

Chapter Learning Objectives

- Recognize the role that budgets play in the successful operation of an agribusiness.
- Recognize the power of written goals.
- Identify the three types of budgets needed in an agribusiness.
- Describe the relationship between operating, cash flow, and capital expenditure budgets.
- Explain the benefits of budgeting.
- Explain the limitations of budgets.

The Purpose of Budgets

Once an agribusiness firm has identified its customers' needs and developed ways to keep abreast of changes through forecasting, it needs to complete the planning process by assessing how the accomplishment of its marketing plan's purpose and objective will allow the firm to achieve its financial objectives (see figure 4-1, p. 59). To do this, agribusiness managers must prepare financial plans, or **budgets**.

Some managers do their **budgeting** completely in their heads and have only a general idea of whether their businesses are profitable or have the potential to be profitable. Others have carefully prepared, written financial plans with clear measures of financial performance. A budget is a blueprint for action for a specific period (usually one year) that is based on sales, cost, and productivity estimates developed in the marketing plan.

Most managers make some informal estimates of **revenues** and costs for their business. To make purchases, a manager must have some estimate of future sales. To borrow money, some estimate of future profits needs to be made. Many agribusiness managers, however, do not undertake the detailed analysis of markets or production required to develop reliable estimates of revenues and costs. This kind of analysis cannot be done in your head or on the back of an envelope. Instead, it requires sitting down and carefully dissecting the business with paper, pencil, and a computer spreadsheet. The dissection is one of the biggest benefits of budgeting. It makes managers ask, for example, why labor costs or delivery costs are as high as they are and what can be done to lower them. It makes management ask why the firm is losing money in one part of its business and how it can change that. The budget process forces managers to ask not only what can be achieved, but also whether the marketing plan will meet the firm's financial objectives. The manager cannot just wish for higher sales, lower costs, and higher profits, but must make these things happen through the efficient and effective execution of the marketing plan.

The Power of Written Goals

The best argument for budgeting is that the act of thinking a plan through and writing it down gives managers the best chance of achieving their financial objectives. Forecasting sales, making the decisions needed to reach goals, estimating the time and materials needed, and putting dollar values on each of these keeps management's attention centered on the achievement of financial objectives. Written goals have the power to keep people focused and increase the chance that a firm's financial objectives will be realized.

A budget is the financial plan of management's expectations for the business in the future. It is a model of what management realistically thinks the future holds for the firm. As such, it represents a realistic assessment of what each part of the business can accomplish during the coming period.

Suppose a business is a combined farm-supply store and grain elevator. Management needs to develop separate budgets for each part of the business. In this case, it may mean that separate budgets are prepared by the feed division, the fertilizer division, the other supply divisions, the grain division, the storage division, and any other major parts of the business. These are all different business enterprises and need to be evaluated separately. Separate division budgets can be combined once they are completed to give one master budget for the firm. The process of developing budgets for each division helps managers and employees better understand their part of the business and what is expected of them in the coming year.

THREE TYPES OF BUDGETS

Well-managed businesses operate with three major types of budgets—an operating budget, a cash flow budget, and a capital expenditure budget.

Operating Budgets

The operating budget summarizes the expected sales, production activities, and related costs for the budgetary period. It is an estimate of sales and income plus the fixed and variable expenses the firm must incur in order to support the expected sales during a specified time (usually one year).

The starting point for an operating budget is sales, since income is the lifeblood of the business. The process of developing sales estimates begins with the marketing plan. Sales figures can be adjusted to reflect changes in competition, the addition of new products, or changes in economic climate.

The next step is to prepare an estimate of the costs of providing the products for sale for that period. This requires forecasting (1) the **cost of goods sold** and (2) fixed expenses. The cost of goods required to achieve the sales objectives can be forecasted using the procedures outlined in chapter 7. The accounting department can provide a good estimate of **fixed costs**.

The operating budget is more than a financial forecast. A forecast merely indicates what is likely to happen under a specific set of conditions. An operating budget, however, is a positive financial statement of what management expects to accomplish in the coming period (such as increasing sales 10 percent by spending more on advertising, introducing a new product that will make the firm more profitable, or reducing operating costs by decreasing the size of the sales force, and so on) in order to achieve its goal of maximizing long-term profits. An operating budget is a critical financial planning document that states the manager's goals in financial terms for the next period. The most successful operating budgets are those that result from having a clear business purpose, concise objectives, a well-defined marketing plan, and a strong marketing mix.

Cash Flow Budgets

Cash flow budgets summarize the amount and timing of cash that is expected to flow in and out of the business during the budgetary period. The timing of these flows may be very different from what is shown in the operating budget and can bring severe hardship to a business that is unprepared for this difference. Many managers forget that it often takes a long time for cash invested in a business to reappear as cash (figure 8-1). Cash can be tied up in inventory, goods in process, and accounts receivable. As a result, even a profitable firm can find itself without enough cash on hand to meet its daily obligations such as payroll, utilities, and rent. Cash inflow comes from sales of goods and services, borrowings, sale of capital goods, collections from accounts receivable, sales of stock, and so forth. Cash outflow comes from payments for goods and services, loan payments, purchases of capital goods, payment of **accounts payable**, and related expenses.

A cash flow budget shows when cash will be available to the business (cash receipts) during the budgetary period, and when cash payments need to be made by the business (cash disbursements) during the budgetary period. The purpose of the cash flow budget is to ensure that the business has enough cash at the right times to meet its obligations. A cash flow budget also helps managers identify when surplus cash is available so it can be put to work earning extra income in a

Figure 8-1 The Cash Cycle

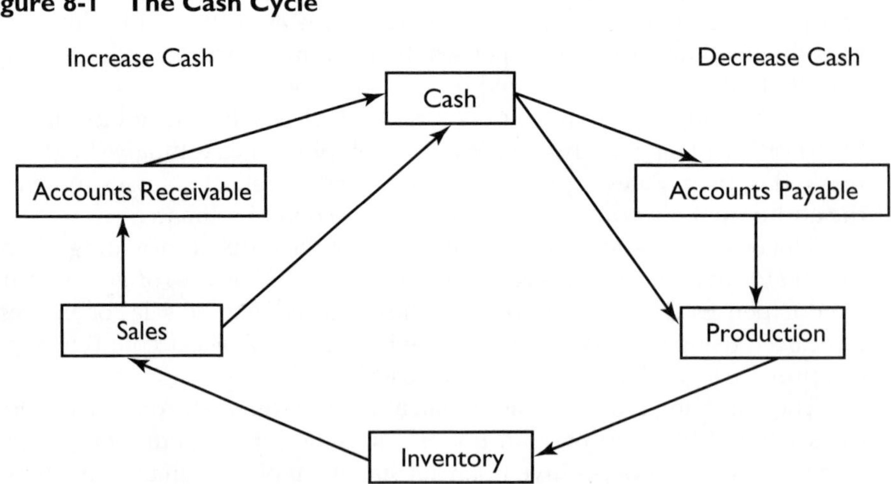

savings account or an investment or used to reduce debt. It can also be used to identify periods of cash deficits so borrowings and loan repayments can be anticipated.

A cash flow budget is prepared after the operating budget. Sales and other cash receipts are recorded according to the month when the firm expects to receive the cash from each sale, regardless of when the actual sale took place. The same is done for cash disbursements. Cash payments are put into the month when they are paid, regardless of when they are incurred. The beginning cash balance is combined with monthly cash receipts to give an amount of the total cash available. Cash disbursements are subtracted from this total to give the **net cash flow** position for the month. If a cash surplus is found, it becomes the beginning cash balance for the next month. The same process is conducted for each month. If the net cash flow position is negative, borrowing is needed. In many ways the cash flow budget resembles the way a checkbook is kept.

The cash flow budget tells the manager little about the profitability of the business. That is the job of the operating budget. The cash flow budget's purpose is to help manage the firm's cash balances so that sufficient cash is available to meet obligations as they come due. If cash is predicted to be insufficient at certain times of the year, plans can be made in advance to borrow the needed funds. Conversely, when surplus cash is projected, it can be invested or used to pay off loans taken out to cover cash deficits in other months. Wise cash management often has made the difference between the success and failure of many agribusinesses.

Capital Expenditure Budgets

Every business must make regular investments in its plant, property, and equipment or else wear and tear will eventually leave the business unable to perform efficiently. Capital expenditure budgets show how the money budgeted for capital expenditures is to be allocated among competing projects. The capital expenditure budget lists major capital expenditure items such as new trucks, computing systems, and buildings along with their estimated costs and expected payment plans. Capital expenditures also can be applied to the maintenance of existing plant and equipment; expansion of the plant, property, and equipment or product lines; cost-saving improvements such as energy conservation and information technology systems; and health and safety items.

It is common to arrange items in the capital expenditure budget by priority to enable managers to use their money on the most important items first. Changes in market conditions can force management to change the size of the **capital budget** and the priorities within it. By having priorities, management is more likely to use its limited investment funds in the most profitable ways possible.

Relating the Operating, Cash Flow, and Capital Expenditure Budgets

All three budgets are tied to the marketing plan through sales estimates. Sales estimates drive the formation of the operating budget because the level of sales determines most costs (figure 8-2). The marketing plan gives not only the level of sales but also a good indication of the timing of those sales. This information drives the formation of the cash flow budget. The sales estimate also gives infor-

Figure 8-2 Relating All Three Types of Budgets

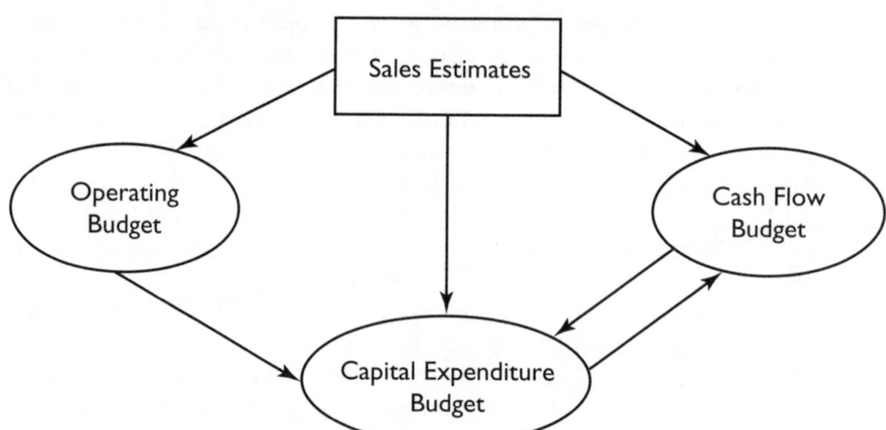

mation that influences the level of capital expenditures, while the operating budget and the cash flow budget typically impose constraints on the amount of money that can be spent for capital items. This leads to some give and take on the size of the capital expenditure budget.

Two important points should be taken from this discussion of budgeting. First, while the marketing plan is vital to success, it should still be remembered that the firm must meet its financial objectives and earn the highest return on invested capital (ROIC) that investors can get from the use of their funds. Second, financial success comes solely from the profitable sale of goods and services that satisfy a consumer need. This combination of effectively meeting a consumer need and doing so efficiently must both be present for the long-term success of the business. This reflects the unifying theme of this book, that every manager's goal is the maximization of the long-term profits of the firm by profitably satisfying consumer needs.

An Application of Budgeting

Suppose you are the manager of the AgBiz Corporation. Your firm has its own feed mill and specializes in merchandising feed and selling bulk, bagged, and liquid fertilizer. You offer custom fertilizer application with your own trucks and you rent fertilizer applicators to farmers so they can do the job themselves. The store also sells herbicides, but does not custom spray the herbicides.

Now suppose the board of directors wants to consider offering custom herbicide-application services. They want to know how this service will affect the profits of the business. They ask you to prepare an operating budget, a cash flow budget, and a capital expenditure budget for the following year to show the impact of this new service.

The board expects that AgBiz will have 20 percent of the custom herbicide application business in your trade territory within three years. They expect you to capture 5 percent of the market in the first year, 12 percent the second year, and 20 percent the third year. They also believe that total herbicide sales will increase because of the custom application service. Your analysis verifies that these assumptions are on the conservative side.

The Operating Budget

Two operating budgets for next year are shown in figure 8-3. The first (option A) is for the continuation of the business without the new service, and the second

Figure 8-3 Sample Operating Budgets

Operating Budget
AgBiz Corporation
for the Year 20__

	Option A: No Custom Herbicide	Option B:* Custom Herbicide Application
Sales:		
Feed	$ 829,500	$ 829,500
Seed	168,000	168,000
Fertilizer	647,600	647,600
Chemicals	343,400	369,150
Petroleum	87,700	87,700
Building materials	8,000	8,000
Supplies and hardware	77,800	77,800
Custom herbicide application	—	18,000
	2,162,000	2,205,750
Variable expenses:		
Materials	1,261,200	1,280,000
Labor	200,000	220,000
Office expenses	33,800	33,800
Advertising and selling	102,000	106,000
Miscellaneous	10,000	12,000
	1,607,000	1,651,800
Fixed expenses:		
Taxes and licenses	21,700	22,800
Depreciation and rent	305,000	327,000
Insurance	9,900	11,500
Utilities	52,500	53,000
Payroll taxes	16,000	17,600
	405,100	431,900
Total expenses:	$2,012,100	$2,083,700
Estimated net income	$ 149,900	$ 122,050

*First year of expansion into custom herbicide application.

(option B) is with the new service. Adding the herbicide-application service will require an additional employee, the purchasing of two trucks (one large and one small) with application units, and additional facilities for chemical handling. Notice that the budget separates sales by division. Expenses are separated into variable expenses (operating costs) and fixed expenses.

It would have been possible to summarize variable expenses by division. This was not done here in the interest of saving space. However, the operating budget normally has separate back-up budgets that compare projected sales and expenses for each division.

After seeing the operating budget for the first year with the new service, the board of directors may want to change its mind about adopting the new service. Total sales increased $43,750, including a 7.5 percent increase ($25,750) in herbicide sales, but the rise in costs is greater ($71,600) and profits are less ($27,850). The board will want to look at succeeding years (with added operating budgets) to see what the results may be over a longer planning period.

The Cash Flow Budget

After developing AgBiz's operating budget, it is time to translate it into cash receipts and disbursements. A cash flow budget will tell managers how to plan cash and financing needs.

Cash receipts will follow sales from the operating budget closely for most items because most farmers in the area pay their input suppliers' bills promptly from operating loan funds. The challenge will be estimating the actual inflow from store credit sales made the prior year to those new operators who could not get operating loans and may not repay all they owe to AgBiz.

The cash disbursements will differ from the operating budget because the firm acquired two trucks for the new herbicide work with a loan that will require a cash down payment and monthly payments. Additional cash disbursements need to be made the following year to repay debt incurred in prior years to purchase inventory, equipment, and additions to the plant.

The cash flow budget for AgBiz for option A (no herbicide application division being added) is presented in figure 8-4. Large cash outflows occur in the second and fourth quarters when large payments on old loans are due. Without the new herbicide service, the company expects to have a cash surplus of $80,000 in the first quarter of the year. The loan payment of $61,000 in the second quarter cuts the cash surplus nearly in half. Seasonal sales patterns show a decline in third-quarter sales, which forces the company to draw out the $80,000 cash surplus from the first quarter and to borrow an additional $188,900 to meet expenses. Business picks up in the fourth quarter sufficiently to meet the loan payment of $60,200 and also to repay the third-quarter loan. The year ends with a cash balance of $18,300.

The cash flow budget gives the managers much important information. First, it shows that the $80,000 cash surplus generated in the first quarter needs to be put aside so it can be used to meet the third quarter's cash needs. Second, the firm has enough money to repay its old loan obligations. Third, AgBiz will need to borrow money ($188,900) in the third quarter to overcome a temporary cash flow def-

Figure 8-4 Sample Cash Flow Budget for Option A

Cash Flow Budget for Option A
AgBiz Corporation
for the Fiscal Year Ending December 31, 20__

	Quarter			
	1	2	3	4
Cash balance, beginning of quarter	$ 2,200	$ 32,400	$ 62,200	0
Add: Cash inflows				
Feed	260,000	191,000	142,000	$236,500
Seed	30,000	60,000	10,000	68,000
Fertilizers	188,500	254,800	30,000	174,300
Chemicals	110,000	155,000	—	78,400
Petroleum	28,500	21,500	14,500	22,700
Miscellaneous	2,000	2,500	2,300	2,000
Supplies	24,000	21,000	16,500	16,000
Total inflows	643,000	705,800	215,300	597,900
Total cash available	645,200	738,200	277,500	597,900
Less: Cash outflows				
Materials	380,000	462,000	350,000	160,000
Labor	80,000	80,000	80,000	80,000
Overhead	12,000	8,000	6,000	12,000
Selling and administration	40,000	36,000	30,000	38,000
Income taxes	8,000	8,000	8,000	8,000
Equipment purchases	7,300	15,500	62,450	27,000
Debt payments	0	61,000	0	60,200
Dividends	5,500	5,500	5,500	5,500
Total outflows	532,800	676,000	541,950	390,700
Surplus (deficit)	112,400	62,200	(264,450)	207,200
Savings (to) from	(80,000)	0	80,000	0
Additional borrowings	0	0	188,900	0
Repayments of borrowings	0	0	0	(188,900)
Interest payments	0	0	4,450	0
Cash balance, end of quarter	$ 32,400	$ 62,200	0	$ 18,300

icit. Fourth, they can repay this loan from business receipts in the fourth quarter and end the year with a reasonable cash balance ($18,300). Fifth, they now have a cash flow budget to present to a bank for the loan needed to cover the cash needed in the third quarter. To do this, they must achieve the sales and cost levels set in the operating budget.

A cash flow budget is a critical part of every business's financial planning. None of this cash flow planning is found in the operating budget. If the managers fail to consider annual cash flow fluctuations during their financial planning, they might be unaware of the need for a loan in the third quarter and spend the $80,000 cash surplus, which could have disastrous results on the business. To see the impact of the new line of business on the firm, a cash flow budget needs to be constructed that considers the impact of the new herbicide-application business over the next three years.

The Capital Expenditure Budget

Major capital purchases should not be done on a whim. They should be planned because they involve large sums of money that cannot be reversed easily and subsequently can impact the financial position of the firm for many years. The capital expenditure budget for the coming year is presented in figure 8-5. It includes the items needed to undertake the new herbicide-application business as well as other capital items needed to maintain AgBiz's plant, property, and equipment.

Figure 8-5 Sample Capital Expenditures Budget

Capital Budget
AgBiz Corporation
for Year Ending December 31, 20__

Capital Item	Priority	Estimated Cost	Estimated Cash Outlay
Feed mill and controls	2	$130,000	$57,000
Trucks (two) for new herbicide operation	1	80,000	9,500
Pickup truck for manager	4	7,300	7,300
Bagging machine for feed mill	3	67,000	15,500
Replacement truck for petroleum division	6	20,500	5,450
Expand herbicide warehouse	8	16,900	6,000
Replacement 60-hp tractor for yard	5	15,000	7,500
Remodel manager and assistant manager offices	7	25,000	10,000
Semitrailer grain truck	9	32,000	8,000

The capital budget includes more items than funds allow. The decision of which items to buy and which items to defer is made by placing a priority ranking on each capital item. The rankings ensure that the money spent on capital items is allocated in an efficient manner.

Benefits of Budgeting

Budgeting has several functions, one of which is organization. The proper organization of information can give managers a focused view of financial decisions and expectations.

1. ***Budgets provide a way to measure business performance.***
   Performance is measured in two ways. First, the firm's performance is measured against the goals it set for itself in its budgets and its initial financial objectives. Second, the firm's performance is measured against that of its competition. In both instances, clear financial yardsticks exist to decide

how well the business is operating. In the first case, the measure is between the firm's actual performance and its expectations. In the second case, the measure is between the firm and its peers. Firms whose financial performance is below that of its peers and consistently below its own expectations have a harder time attracting and keeping capital in their businesses.

2. ***Budgets keep managers focused on the financial implications of their business decisions.***
   Managers often point with pride to their organizations' sales growth. However, when asked why the volume is growing at the rate it is or whether it is the maximum rate of increase consistent with maximizing long-term profits, they often find the questions hard to answer. Many companies have experienced large sales growth but failed to realize that profits actually have declined because the increase in costs has exceeded the increase in incoming revenue. Good budgeting with clear financial objectives reduces the chances of this happening.
3. ***Budgets help managers communicate expectations and quickly spot deviations.***
   When a business takes an unfavorable turn from the goals set in a budget, it can be detected quickly and corrective measures can be undertaken. Written budgets should be circulated widely among members of a business so that everyone knows what is expected of him or her and the overall organization, and how well things are going. Written goals and feedback (in the form of budget progress reports) focus people's attention and increase the likelihood that they will be achieved. This is true between all levels of management and between management and the board of directors.

LIMITATIONS OF BUDGETS

Budgets are merely pieces of paper, and paper is unable to do anything by itself. Budgets are managers' attempts to provide a financial plan for an agribusiness. The plan may be good or bad depending on the care and planning taken in its preparation. And, of course, budgets have to be used to be of value.

When implementing a budget, a manager should remember:

1. ***Budgets are estimates, not sure things.***
   Deviations are to be expected. As a business year progresses you may discover better ways to do things. Wise managers adjust their procedures and budgets in light of new information. Budgets are living documents. They are not chiseled in stone, and should be changed. Such changes are not signs of failure, but indications of learning. The result will be better business planning and greater success.
2. ***The execution of a budget is not automatic.***
   Managers must learn how to use budgets. They may learn that a different set-up or a combination of budgets from the three suggested in this chapter is the most proficient at achieving the organization's goals.

3. ***Budgets cannot take the place of good management.***
   Budgets are simply tools that can help management be more effective.
4. ***Good budgeting requires time and patience.***
   Once installed, it is estimated that three years are required to perfect a budgeting system within a medium-sized corporation. Initial difficulties and disappointments should not be allowed to discourage the budgeting effort. Thinking through the total business operation department by department will yield such insights that any reasonable amount of time and effort can be justified in mastering the basics of budgeting.

BUDGET TIME FRAMES

Under ideal circumstances, operating budgets are prepared on both a yearly and monthly basis. The yearly forecast gives an overall view of expected income from all sources and the anticipated expenditures needed to support this income. The difference between expected income and expenses gives expected profit.

Monthly budgets supplement the yearly budget. To be effective, they must provide as much detail as the manager needs to make decisions. Monthly budgets also incorporate anticipated seasonal and monthly patterns in sales and expenses. As deviations from the forecasted results occur, reexamine previous estimates for possible revisions. If the estimates remain valid, corrective action is called for.

CHAPTER HIGHLIGHTS

1. Managers assess the financial viability of the marketing plan through budgeting.
2. A detailed, written analysis of revenues, costs, and production is needed to develop reliable budgets.
3. Written goals have the greatest chance for success.
4. A budget is a financial plan of management's expectations for the business in the future. It is more than just a forecast. It is a positive statement of business goals.
5. The three major types of budgets are the operating budget, the cash flow budget, and the capital expenditure budget.
6. The operating budget summarizes the expected sales, production levels, and related costs for the budgetary period.
7. The best operating budgets come from firms that have a clear business purpose and objective, a well-defined marketing plan, and a strong marketing mix.
8. Cash flow budgets summarize the amount and timing of cash that is expected to flow in and out of the business during the budgetary period. The timing of these flows may be very different from what is shown in the operating budget.

9. The cash flow budget's purpose is to help manage a firm's cash balances so that sufficient cash is available to meet obligations as they come due.
10. The capital expenditure budget shows how money is to be spent for major capital items such as plant maintenance, property, and equipment.
11. Budgets provide a way to measure business performance.
12. Budgets keep managers focused on the financial implications of their business decisions.
13. Budgets help managers communicate expectations and quickly spot deviations from expectations.
14. Good budgeting takes time and patience to be effective.

Chapter Quiz

1. Explain how financial objectives influence the development of the marketing plan.
2. Written goals have the power to keep people focused and increase the chance that they will be achieved. Agree or disagree? Explain your answer.
3. Identify and define the three major types of budgets. How do they relate to each other?
4. A budget is just a forecast of the future. Agree or disagree? Explain your answer.
5. Some say that the cash flow budget is more important than the operating budget. Do you agree or disagree? Explain your answer.
6. If you are making a budget, explain why the operating budget and cash flow budget are likely to give you a different perspective for the same period.
7. Discuss why a budget is a great motivational tool for inspiring better performance by employees.
8. If business success rests on meeting customer needs, why is so much concern focused on meeting financial objectives?
9. Evaluate the idea that once a budget is set for the year it should be followed to the letter.
10. Evaluate the idea that good budgeting procedures are powerful business tools that are quickly learned.
11. A new approach to budgeting is to break out individual or groups of customers and develop a profit and loss statement for each. Explain what you would gain from this exercise. How would this affect the overall budgeting process?
12. Explain the business adage that budgets are useless but budgeting is invaluable. Give an example that supports your answer.
13. Evaluate the statement that good budgets do not take the place of good management.

14. Explain what is happening at each step in the cash cycle given in figure 8-1. Start and end your explanation with cash.
15. Explain the relationship between the four factors found in figure 8-2.
16. How does good budgeting help a firm achieve its goal of maximizing its long-run profitability by profitably satisfying its customers' needs?
17. Explain why the best operating budgets come from firms that have a clear business purpose and objective, a well-defined marketing plan, and an effective marketing mix.
18. Identify something other than a financial budget that a firm can use to measure its business performance.
19. Explain how a manager can use the budgeting process to gain personal commitments from employees for their achievement.
20. Does budgeting work best as a top-down (firm's goals to individual worker's goals) or a bottom-up (vice versa) process?

Case 8
Going Broke While Making a Profit

The sound of a clanging bell in the lobby had become familiar to nearly everyone who worked in the headquarters of Super Snacks. Sales this month had broken another record for the tenth month in a row. The firm owed it all to its new Super Potato Chips. Ever since they were introduced last fall in time for football season, they could barely keep up with demand.

Super Snacks is a long-time producer of snack foods. Its brand of Harvest Delight Snacks has enjoyed reasonable success in the region primarily by selling to small chains of convenience stores and supermarkets, sandwich shops, and alternative food stores. Sales increases had been steady but small before they started selling Super Potato Chips. The purpose outlined in their business plan called for them to shift to all-natural ingredients so they could give their customers the healthiest way to eat snack foods. Their products were designed to appeal especially to aging baby boomers that did not want to give up their comfort foods but still sought a healthy diet—as much as one could achieve while eating snack food.

One day a small biotechnology firm in the area came to talk about a new super vegetable oil they had invented. When used to deep-fry things like potato chips the food had a wonderful full-body flavor but the consumer did not absorb any of the fat. The result was a great-tasting, low-fat potato chip. Market testing by Super Snacks proved they were right. They quickly bought the exclusive world rights to the product.

Sales were brisk right away. However, the big break came when a national TV talk show host mentioned on the air that he ate some of the chips while on vacation and enjoyed them immensely. He even held up the bag. Sales skyrocketed after that.

Super Snacks' president, Warren Wheeler, had always been more of an entrepreneur than a conventional businessman. He quickly saw the market potential in these new chips and felt he had to move quickly to get them to market so his firm could stake out its claim to this market segment before anyone else did. As a result buildings were built, machinery was purchased, people were hired, and everything was focused on meeting the demand for the chips. Despite a period of tremendous growth, the managers did a good job of controlling costs, managing their growing need for potatoes, keeping their cost per bag on target, and getting their rapidly expanding list of customers to pay on time.

When Mr. Wheeler saw the firm's financials each month, he was delighted. By July, sales, costs, capital expenditures, and profits were so far off the chart he never even compared the results to what they had budgeted for this year back in December. The only number that disturbed him was the declining amount of cash, but Wheeler was a bottom line kind of guy. Sales and profits are all that matters so he did not worry about it.

On July 12, the vice president for finance came to Wheeler's office to tell him that Super Snacks was broke and could not meet this week's payroll.

How did this happen? What can they do to save the company? What are the lessons to be learned from this situation?

PART III

The Organizing Function

Once a firm has completed its planning function by determining how it is going to profitably satisfy its customers' needs, its managers need to devise an organizational structure that will permit it to efficiently and effectively accomplish its purpose and objectives. The organizing activities dealt with in this section are the organizational scheme and legal structure.

- *Chapter 9—Organizing for Success* The way a business is organized has a great deal to do with its performance. The decisions surrounding who is responsible to whom and who makes what type of decisions also can affect the long-term success of an agribusiness.
- *Chapter 10—Choosing a Legal Structure* The legal structure a firm selects can have profound effects on its profits and long-term success. In addition to the common alternative legal forms—sole proprietorship, partnership, and corporation—business owners have a number of new hybrid legal structures such as limited liability partnerships and corporations that may better serve their needs.

Chapter 9

Organizing for Success

Chapter Learning Objectives

- Explain the role that an effective and efficient organizational structure plays in the success of an agribusiness, especially in meeting the business objective.
- Explain why it is necessary to place special emphasis on identifying and giving prominence to critical tasks.
- Describe the principles of effective organizational design.
- Discuss the major ways to organize an agribusiness.
- Explain the difference between line and staff positions in a firm.
- Discuss the advantages and disadvantages of centralized versus decentralized decision making.
- Describe the importance of making decisions at the lowest levels possible in a firm.
- Identify the criteria for selecting the best organizational structure.

Introduction

Once an agribusiness has developed its plans for success, it is time to develop an organizational structure that will enable it to achieve its purpose and objectives efficiently and effectively. Developing the right organizational structure has a big impact on business performance. Determining the organizational structure involves more than just deciding who reports to whom. It requires deciding how to handle the flow of work through the organization, resolving differences in corporate goals, and deciding where business decisions should be made. These may seem to be trivial matters, but they strongly impact how employees view their work and the level of their performance. Each heavily influences how well the agribusiness meets the needs of its customers, and ultimately its long-term profitability.

The organizational scheme is a critical step in transforming a business plan into a profitable, operating agribusiness. The organizational plan assures that the firm's goals are accomplished as specified in the business's strategic plan. This is particularly important when implementing the business objectives, since this is what gives the firm its sustainable competitive advantage. Without strong management emphasis in this area, firms find themselves more focused on other things that diminish their competitive edge and profits.

Identifying Critical Tasks

Managers begin the development of organizational structure by identifying the firm's **critical tasks**. Critical tasks are the activities that must be done well if the business is to achieve its purpose and objectives. If the managers decided in the marketing plan that the business's purpose is to repair and service farm equipment and its objective is to do this faster, better, and cheaper than anyone else in the area, the central focus of the business is repair and service—not sales of new equipment or anything else. When these issues are clearly defined, managers have an easier time identifying critical tasks and developing an effective organizational structure in which these tasks are given prominence and will function smoothly.

In the example mentioned above, the critical tasks might be maintaining a proper parts inventory to ensure that all the parts needed for fast service are always in stock; establishing and maintaining a highly trained, certified, efficient group of mechanics who can provide fast service; and developing an effective program for monitoring costs to keep them low for the customer yet still profitable for the owners.

Failure to achieve any of these three critical tasks will cause this particular firm to lose its competitive edge and fail. Thus, the managers must see that all three critical tasks are given prominence, function smoothly, and are not subordinated by any other activity of the business. This type of decision is difficult to maintain, especially if the firm has the opportunity to enter other lines of business that appear profitable, such as selling new and used farm equipment. Changes in the business purpose, objectives, and organizational structure must be approached cautiously. Managers and owners must always remember what they do best and rarely stray from it without careful analysis.

Four Principles of Organizational Design

Now that the importance of an effective organizational structure is understood, let us turn our attention to designing one. As with other areas of business management, several general principles can be applied that help with this task.

1. ***Keep the organizational structure simple.***
   Have as few layers of management and interrelationships as possible to get the job done. Simplicity ensures that everyone in the organization has a clear understanding of what he or she is supposed to do and how his or her work contributes to the accomplishment of the overall corporate purpose and objectives.
2. ***Give critical tasks prominence and allow them to function without restriction.***
   Because of their importance to the success of the business, the performance of critical tasks must never be unduly restricted. In the equipment repair and servicing example, if the purchasing department has the opportunity to save money on some parts but it means not always having key parts in stock, they should pass it up. While keeping costs low is a critical task, this decision would reduce the firm's competitive advantage, which comes from providing fast service.
3. ***Keep support staff to a minimum.***
   Support staff working in the human resource, legal, and engineering departments are necessary but do not directly contribute to the profits of

the firm. They are not central tasks and should be kept to the minimum size necessary to do the job. Many firms keep their costs low by retaining these services from outside firms only as needed.

4. *Keep working units small.*
   Each group should be kept small enough to give its members a feeling of belonging, accomplishment, and influence. The group also should be just large enough to challenge itself and its manager to get the work done.

Strict adherence to these four principles will keep management ranks thin and keep everyone close to the action and focused on accomplishing the firm's purpose and objectives.

Ways to Organize

There are several ways to organize an organization. Each offers advantages and disadvantages.

By Business Function

Under this approach, departments are established around the basic functions of the business—such as sales, advertising, manufacturing, warehousing, inventory, accounting, and so on. Regardless of the number of products the firm handles, all business activities related to each business function are performed in one place. This gives management the advantage of greater control. If a problem arises in any function, such as warehousing, it is easy to identify those involved.

Because each business unit specializes in a single business function, it is expected to operate efficiently. The implicit assumption is that each product the firm sells can be handled the same way, so the firm can gain **economies of scale** by centralizing basic business functions. The disadvantage of this approach is that centralization can reduce the firm's ability to respond quickly to unique or rapidly changing market conditions.

By Product

Under this approach a business unit is established for each product, such as feed, seed, fertilizer, herbicides, and pesticides. Within each unit all the business functions associated with a particular product (sales, production, warehousing, accounting, and so on) are found. If each unit is given a high level of autonomy, it operates as an independent, separate business with a full range of business functions under its direct control.

Because of its smaller size, the product-specific business can operate in unique markets and can respond quickly to changes in the market. This approach assumes that each product faces a unique market situation that requires a different marketing plan and marketing mix in order to maximize its competitive advantage. The downside is that central management exerts less control over each business unit and the firm gives up some operating efficiencies that are possible under the functional approach.

By Geographic Area

Under this approach, each business unit handles the sales of all the firm's products sold in a specific geographic area; for example, the Hong Kong office handles the sales of all the company's products in China. It puts the manager that is closest to the market in charge.

This works best when the entire market for the firm's products in a specific geographic area is unique and changes quickly. When customers in a specific market area are different from what the company normally faces for all of its products, a flexible, unique marketing plan and marketing mix are needed to achieve the firm's purpose and objectives. The downside is that this approach reduces central management's control over the unit, and the firm gives up some operating efficiencies that are possible under the functional approach.

The obvious question at this point is, "Which of these approaches is best?" The answer is the one that does the most to help the business maximize its long-run profits and profitably satisfy its customers' needs.

Since organizational structure has a great deal to do with business performance, many firms use a mixture of approaches to fit a variety of situations. However, this can result in a manager reporting to two bosses, each with different organizational objectives. For example, to provide a special variety of seed corn in time for Ohio farmers to plant by April 15, a seed packaging plant must run overtime for several weeks. From the viewpoint of the head of Ohio operations, this makes sense. However, the financial analysts at headquarters in Missouri may complain about the high cost of labor during this period. Because of situations like this, some companies use a **matrix approach**, where the two bosses are brought together with higher-level management to resolve the conflict in organizational goals. Their solutions should always lead to the greatest overall long-term profits.

Line and Staff Activities

Another important distinction in organizational structure is the difference between line and staff activities. Line activities include things such as sales, production, and purchasing, which directly affect profits and the accomplishment of the firm's purpose and objectives. Staff activities include things such as human resources, legal issues, and the mail room, which indirectly support the accomplishment of the firm's purpose and objectives. Usually line people have the authority to make decisions, while **staff people** only advise line personnel.

APPROACHES TO DECISION MAKING

When formulating the organizational structure, it is important to determine the firm's approach to decision making. In a **centralized decision-making** system, all the decision-making authority is held by a few top executives who become involved in every decision, regardless of its importance. In a **decentralized decision-making** system, decision-making authority for routine matters is delegated to lower levels of management while top management time is used for decisions that affect strategic matters, such as changes in the firm's purpose and objectives. Decentralized decision making gives lower-level managers an opportunity to develop their decision-making skills and frees top management to work on strategic issues that affect the long-term profitability of the firm, such as anticipating the influence of the next technological change on the demand for their products.

Deciding Where Decisions Are Made

The level in the organization at which a decision is made depends largely on the type of decision being made. The decisions that are best made at the *lowest levels* of the organization are those that affect the firm for a short period of time, involve small amounts of money, and do not affect the business's purpose and objectives. Decisions about ongoing, routine matters that affect only a single unit of the business are best left to the person at the scene. This gives the person at this level the opportunity to develop his or her decision-making skills.

Decisions that are best made at the *highest level* of the organization are those that affect the firm for a long period of time, involve large amounts of money, and dramatically affect the business's purpose and objectives. Decisions about building a new plant or entering a new line of business will have a long-term impact on the organization's profits and deserve the full attention of the highest levels of management. When top management has freed itself from dealing with routine daily decisions, it can devote the time needed to address these important long-term issues.

Two criteria should guide the selection of the appropriate level for a decision. First, the decision maker should be high enough in the organization so that the major impact of the decision falls within units under his or her control. Second, the decision maker should be low enough to have firsthand knowledge of the situation. In short, the best decisions are made at the lowest levels of management possible. Managers at this level usually have the best understanding of the problem as well as a few ideas for a good solution and can implement the decision quickly. These factors diminish as the decision is passed to higher levels in the organization and this reduces the firm's performance of its financial and marketing objectives.

Although in general the principle of making decisions at the lowest levels of management is sound, only top management should handle certain decisions. These include:

- Setting the broad policies or guidelines that concisely define and carry out the firm's purpose and objectives (such as guidelines for achieving the fastest service and the lowest prices in the market).
- Determining what constitutes progress toward the purpose and objectives (such as increasing sales or market share).
- Establishing the standards that measure individuals' and work units' performance (such as setting time standards for carrying out particular jobs).
- Being present where prestige is important (such as having the president of the firm hand out employee achievement awards or receiving important clients).

Selecting the Best Organizational Structure

Deciding which organizational structure is best for a particular firm is difficult. The best structure depends on the size and type of business, the people involved, and where the people are located. However, the success of delegating decisions to the lowest levels of management possible, the need to give managers an entrepreneurial sense of involvement, and the need to provide a training ground for future top management leads many firms to prefer a decentralized decision-making system.

With a decentralized decision-making system, business units are autonomous and managers are given broad guidelines within which to work. Their success or failure is measured by the performance of their unit. This system provides an excellent training ground for new managers to develop their skills. As these individuals demonstrate that they can handle more responsibility, they advance through the system to larger work units. At each step, managers are given greater freedom to encourage their entrepreneurial spirit. This system frees top management from supervising day-to-day activities so they can focus on broader longer-term strategic issues. It also helps to develop future managers and improves the firm's overall decision making by keeping the decisions and the decision makers close together.

Although it may not be best for all forms of agribusinesses, autonomous profit centers have much to offer. They put people in charge of their own destiny. They offer fast feedback on performance. They keep work units small enough to provide a sense of involvement and achievement for their workers. And they can be accomplished with a minimum number of management levels regardless of the size of the firm. In short, the organization of autonomous profit centers can be an effective way to accomplish a business's purpose and objectives without slowing its response time as the firm grows larger. In the end, the best organizational structure is the one that does the best job of helping the firm maximize its long-run profits and profitably satisfy its customers' needs.

Chapter Highlights

1. Developing an effective organizational structure is important because it has a large impact on the financial and marketing performance of an agribusiness.
2. Organizational structure heavily impacts how employees view their work and their level of performance.
3. An effective business structure is important to accomplishing the business objectives of an agribusiness.
4. Critical tasks are activities that must be done well if the business is to achieve its purpose and financial and marketing objectives.
5. In the organizational structure, critical tasks must be allowed to function smoothly and without restriction.
6. Keep the organizational structure simple, keep support staff to a minimum, and keep work units small.

7. The best way to organize is to select the most effective and efficient ways to meet the firm's purpose and objectives.
8. Line employees have the authority to make decisions, while staff people usually only advise line personnel.
9. Decisions should be made at the lowest organizational levels possible.
10. Autonomous business units are an efficient and effective way to accomplish a business's purpose and objectives.

CHAPTER QUIZ

1. Identify and explain the role that organizing plays in the successful operation of an agribusiness. Develop an example to illustrate your argument.
2. What defines a critical task in a business? How does a manager go about finding them? What part do they play in the organizational structure of the firm?
3. Identify and define the four principles of effective organizational design. Describe how they relate to one another and to the success of an agribusiness.
4. Compare and contrast three ways to organize a business. Describe two advantages and disadvantages of each. Describe a selection procedure and criteria for selecting the best one.
5. Describe the differences between line and staff activities. Give an example of each. In an era where firms seek to be "lean and mean," would you rather be in a line or staff position?
6. Describe a situation in which you would want to use centralized decision making. How would you classify the decision-making system of the U.S. Army? Your university? A group you belong to? Would you change the system used in any of these cases? Explain the reasons for your answer.
7. Explain how the level at which decisions are made has important implications for the long-term performance of an agribusiness.
8. Identify and explain the types of decisions that must be made by top management for an agribusiness to flourish.
9. Identify and develop a program to develop the decision-making skills of agribusiness managers. Give reasons for each part of your program.
10. Explain why agribusinesses need autonomous profit centers to have good managers ten years from now.
11. Explain how organizational structure affects the financial performance of an agribusiness.
12. How do you determine which organizational structure is best for your business?
13. Explain how each of the four principles of organizational design helps an agribusiness accomplish its goal of maximizing long-run profits by profitably satisfying customers' needs.

14. Explain how the organizing management function works with the planning management function to make a business successful.
15. How do you identify a critical task in a business and then organize around it?
16. Explain why profitable firms have an externally focused organizational scheme.
17. Explain why profitable firms give broad authority to employees who deal directly with customers. Describe at least two long-run benefits to the firm.
18. Identify at least two situations where a decision needs to be made solely by the top executives. Explain why this is necessary.
19. Can a fast-growing business, such as the one in the case for this chapter, outgrow a successful organizational scheme? What does Sam need to do to put his business back on track?
20. If a business wants to make its decisions at the lowest levels possible, what must top management do to see that this decision is implemented effectively?

CASE 9
Sam's Success Story

Everyone within two blocks heard the sound of the big diesel engine in Sam's bright red truck come to life. Without even looking at their watches, they knew it was 3 PM. You would think a guy who keeps country club hours would want to be a little discrete about sneaking out early, but not Sam. He enjoyed the role of prominent businessman. Besides, he felt he had earned it after building a successful business for the past 20 years.

As he headed to the country club for a round of golf, he thought how things had changed since the auto assembly plant opened two years ago. Before the plant opened, Onarga had been a quiet farming community that had been saved about 20 years ago by the construction of an interchange off Interstate 98. The development of the truck stop, motels, gas stations, and restaurants had given just about anyone who wanted to stay in town a chance to find a decent job. It had sure helped Sam's farm-equipment dealership, because the people who stayed in town bought lawn and garden equipment from him. He never enjoyed selling these toys, but they made up almost 20 percent of his annual sales and compensated for the decline in sales of the big pieces of farm equipment that he really wanted to sell. Sales and profits grew slowly but steadily. Sam boasted he could run the whole operation from the little date book he carried in his shirt pocket. This all changed once the plant was built.

It did not seem as if they hired anybody local to work at the plant. Before long there were houses going up everywhere. The school board was talking about raising taxes so they could accommodate all the new students that were coming, and a new shopping center was planned. Because he was the only equipment dealer within 30 miles, Sam's sales tripled in less than two years. He finally made enough to buy his new truck and join the country club.

The growth at the dealership had not been painless. Although sales were way up, profits did not grow nearly as fast. His days seemed to be starting earlier and ending later. It seemed to Sam that nobody could make a decision about anything without running to him and he was tired of it. Part of the reason he started playing golf every afternoon was to have an excuse to get away from the business. Besides, it was not the same business anymore.

Twice as many people worked for him now, and he wasn't sure he knew all their names. The lawn mowers and tractors were pushing 90 percent of his sales. His big-equipment mechanics hardly had enough work to keep them busy, while the ones who serviced the little stuff could not keep up. Sam had difficulty scheduling their time. His long-time service manager was threatening to quit if he did not solve these problems. Sherry, his long-time office manager, was constantly stacking papers on his desk that needed either his signature or an OK. Some of these things were easy, she said, like selecting the company that would supply their copier paper. As Sam was heading to his truck this afternoon, the last words he heard were Sherry yelling, "Don't blame me if we don't have electricity tomorrow! I've been after you for weeks to sign the checks I left on your desk." How would he ever get out of this mess?

Chapter 10

Choosing a Legal Structure

Chapter Learning Objectives

- Recognize the legal, income, and tax implications of selecting a legal structure for an agribusiness.
- Explain the reasons to involve a tax attorney, tax accountant, or other experienced, competent experts when deciding on a legal structure for a business.
- Explain the three primary types of legal structure, which are sole proprietorship, partnership, and corporation.
- Summarize the advantages and disadvantages of using a sole proprietor legal structure.
- Summarize the three types of partnerships and the advantages and disadvantages of each.
- Explain the five types of corporations and the advantages and disadvantages of each.
- Describe the characteristics of limited liability companies (LLCs) as a legal structure.
- Explain the factors to consider when evaluating various legal structures.

Introduction

The selection of a legal structure can have long-term financial implications for a firm's owners, their heirs, and the existence of the business. In order to make a good decision in this area, managers must seek professional advice from a tax accountant and a lawyer before deciding which legal structure the firm will employ.

Unlike other parts of agribusiness management, where the principles of successful management endure over time, the changing legal environment, particularly tax laws, makes it impossible to offer these kinds of general recommendations. Managers making decisions in this area need to assemble a team of experts who can provide the best information for the current legal situation. The goal for this chapter is to point out the major considerations associated with choosing from the business legal structures available.

Sole Proprietorships

A **sole (or individual) proprietorship** is owned and managed by a single individual, who thereby assumes all the risk and derives all the profits. Most businesses in the United States (including agribusinesses) are sole proprietorships. A sole proprietor holds all the rights in the business, except those reserved for society, and is subject to all laws and regulations.

Creating a Sole Proprietorship

Sole proprietorship is popular in part because it is the most flexible legal structure and the easiest to start and end. Generally, it requires no government approval to start, but some licenses and certificates may be needed for activities such as applying agricultural chemicals. Fewer government regulations and restrictions apply to sole proprietorships than any other form of business. If a business operates under a name other than that of the owner, for example AAA Trucking rather than Mary J. Smith Trucking, the owner normally must register the business name with the state as a business operating under a fictitious name. This puts the relationship on public record. Ownership of a sole proprietorship does not mean the owner actually owns all the business's assets. Operators can rent property, buildings, and equipment, and hire employees.

Sole proprietorship is the oldest and most widespread legal structure. As a result, the laws regulating its legal rights and obligations are clear. Similarly, the rules regulating the relationships between a sole proprietor and his or her agents, creditors, and others with whom he or she has business dealings also are well-established.

Advantages

In an individual proprietorship, the business owner is the boss. All decisions, operations, policies, and goals rest with that one person. Concentration of management avoids the problems of disagreements among owners. The owner gets all the rewards of good management directly. The sole proprietor can employ assistants to operate parts of the business. The owner can hire professional and outside services such as lawyers, tax accountants, farm managers, or agricultural chemical applicators to perform services for the business.

One of the biggest advantages of sole proprietorship is flexibility. A private citizen working in Ohio can own a sole proprietorship business in Colorado without being taxed differently on his or her federal income tax return from a sole proprietor who lives and works in Florida. The owner can quickly and easily expand or contract the size of the business, add or eliminate business activities, and increase or decrease inventory as he or she sees fit. As the sole decision maker, the owner is the only one who must be satisfied with each management decision. This means that decisions can be made more quickly than when more than one person is involved. Unfortunately, this does not always work to the advantage of the sole proprietor because he or she does not have the advantage of hearing helpful ideas from others; this can lead to putting off difficult decisions.

Disadvantages

The biggest disadvantage is that all losses are the exclusive responsibility of the owner. When profits do exist in a sole proprietorship, they are taxed at individual rates that may be higher than the corporate tax rate. Although no legal time limit exists for a sole proprietorship, it is not perpetual. The business ends with the death of the owner.

The owner is responsible for acquiring all the capital the firm needs to operate. He or she is also responsible for repaying all its debts. This can come from personal assets, since no distinction exists between personal assets and those of the business in a sole proprietorship. If the owner is sued as an individual for something not related to the business, his or her business assets can be used to meet the claim if his or her personal assets are not sufficient to meet it, and vice versa.

The owner can hire family members if the family member is paid a reasonable wage for the service rendered. This usually happens when the owner plans to bring younger family members into the business while retaining control of the operation. A family with these intentions should consider partnership or corporate structures to better meet their needs.

PARTNERSHIPS

A **partnership** is a voluntary association of two or more people as co-owners of a business for profit. Each partner can be a person, corporation, or partnership. This does not mean that the partnership must own all the assets it uses; it may own some, none, or all of them. What is important is the shared ownership of the business. The rules governing the operation of partnerships are clearly specified in the **Uniform Partnership Act**, but can be superseded by any rules the partners may adopt on their own in their partnership agreement.

General Characteristics of a Partnership

In most partnerships:

- Each person involved participates in management decisions.
- Assets are jointly owned.
- Profits are shared.
- Losses are shared.
- The parties operate under the firm's name.
- The parties have a joint bank account for their business.
- The parties keep a single set of business records.

If an alternative arrangement exists for one or more of these characteristics, a partnership may not exist. No one factor is controlling.

The Importance of a Written Partnership Agreement

If the partners do not have a written partnership agreement, their partnership will be governed under the rules established in the Uniform Partnership Act. While a written agreement is not necessary, experience shows the best partnerships have well-defined written agreements and a convergence of interests. Partnerships work when all parties have faith and confidence in their partners' abilities and appreciate how combining resources enables each partner to gain more than would be possible on their own.

The written partnership agreement needs to address:

- *How much control does each partner have in business decisions?* Unless specified, each partner legally has an equal voice in management control, and a voting majority of the partners controls business decisions.
- *How much control does each partner have over real and personal property used by the partnership?* Both real and personal property may be owned by the partnership. Unless specified, each partner has an equal partnership interest and an equal right to possession and control of partnership property for carrying out the partnership's business. Individual partners often agree to contribute the use of their personally owned property to the business. In such cases, title to such property remains with the person contributing it. The partnership may **lease** real and personal property.
- *How are profits and losses distributed among the partners?* Partners do not normally draw compensation for their services. When they do, they are treated as advances on their share of the profits. Profits and losses do not have to be distributed on the basis of the amount of capital contributed by each partner.
- *How does the partnership plan to keep records?* Although a partnership pays no income taxes, a return is filed reporting its tax information. All partners should have access to the partnership's financial records on a regular basis. The partners pay income taxes on their share of the partnership income as specified in the partnership agreement.

Three Types of Partnerships

The following is a brief description of the functions of three types of partnerships and the general roles of those who participate in them.

1. *General partnerships.*
   In a general partnership, each of the partners is involved in the operation and decision making of the partnership. Each **general partner** is personally responsible for the payment of partnership debts and obligations, and such payment may be taken from their personal assets.
2. *Limited partnerships.*
   In a limited partnership, two classes of partners exist—general partners and **limited partners**. General partners have managerial decision-making authority. They are personally liable for all debts and obligations incurred by the partnership business. Limited partners do not have managerial decision-making authority. Because of this, they are not responsible for the payment of partnership debts and obligations beyond their financial investment in the partnership. In this way, limited partners are like investors in a corporation.
3. *Registered limited liability partnerships (LLPs).*
   This third type of partnership is a variation of the partnership legal structure. In a registered limited liability partnership the partners are not liable for debts or obligations charged to the partnership from the negligence, wrongful acts, or misconduct by another partner or other lawful represen-

tative of the partnership. In order to qualify for this partnership, the firm must carry a high level of liability insurance or other financial security. This protection does not extend to any liability arising from the acts of others who are acting on behalf of the partnership.

The Family Partnership

The family partnership is an important part of agribusiness. The combination of the wisdom and experience of parents and relatives with the energy and labor of a son, daughter, niece, or nephew potentially makes a good team. A partnership is a convenient way for a younger family member to gradually assume managerial responsibilities. Although this has obvious advantages over thrusting someone into a decision-making position with no experience, the decision to form a family partnership should be based on careful consideration of family circumstances and goals, as well as the factors discussed above for all partnerships.

In a family partnership, the senior member (usually a parent) may be making a considerable sacrifice. For example, the parent may have accumulated sufficient resources to take life easier and still have a satisfactory income. Forming a partnership with children or other relatives often necessitates expanding the business, borrowing more money, and taking on additional risk, which can keep the original owners working full time for more years than planned. In other cases, a daughter who works for her parents may find she is still treated like a kid at age forty.

A family partnership works best when it involves one child. The chances of family disagreements multiply when more than one child is involved, particularly if they work elsewhere. A family partnership should be adopted only if it does a better job of meeting personal and family objectives than the alternatives (a sole proprietorship or corporation).

Terminating a Partnership

A partnership may be terminated by agreement among the partners or by operation of the law. Dissolution under a partnership agreement generally occurs when the term of business in the agreement is finished. If the duration is not fixed in the partnership agreement, any partner may terminate the partnership at any time. Dissolution by operation of law occurs in the event of bankruptcy, the death or incapacitation of any partner, or by any event that makes continuation of the business unlawful.

Although a partnership is easy to terminate, careful thought should be given to this topic at the time the partnership is formed. Looking ahead will allow a high degree of continuity of management and ownership at the death of a partner, if continuation is desired. Planning will help to minimize hard feelings should one party wish to leave the partnership.

CORPORATIONS

The **corporation** is a legal entity that is separate and distinct from the shareholders who own it, from the individuals who manage it, and from its employees.

It is created by state law and organized to carry on a business for profit or nonprofit. The corporation is a legal "person" in the eyes of the law that is separate from its shareholders and has most of the legal rights and duties of an individual. A corporation has a life of its own that can go on in perpetuity. It can enter into contracts, transact business, own property, sue, and be sued.

The concept of legal separateness is what distinguishes a corporation from partnerships and sole proprietorships. Some credit the invention of the corporation for the growth of the free-enterprise system. The corporate legal structure encourages investors to take greater risks because a person's liability is limited to only their investment in the corporation; no other personal assets are at risk.

Five Types of Corporations

While corporations may be similar in form in terms of liability, each of the five different types of corporations is structured based on how its stockholders wish to operate their business.

1. *Business corporations.*
   This is the most common corporate legal structure. It is formed to conduct a commercial activity for profit. The Internal Revenue Service calls this a **Subchapter C corporation**.
2. *Nonprofit corporations.*
   This is used by nonprofit organizations that wish to obtain the limited liability protection offered by a corporation.
3. *Close (or closely held) corporations.*
   These are small business corporations with 35 or fewer stockholders that wish to simplify the management of the corporation and restrict ownership to a defined class of people, such as family members of present shareholders. All shareholders must agree to accept this tax status. The Internal Revenue Service calls this a **Subchapter S corporation** or **S-corporation**.

   An S-corporation is not taxed directly, but serves as a conduit to transfer income to the individual shareholders. The shareholders are then taxed at their individual rates, much like the partners in a partnership. Income is transferred to the shareholders in the same form that the corporation receives it. Thus, long-term capital gains for the corporation are proportionally allocated to the shareholders and are treated as long-term gains on their individual income tax returns.
4. *Professional corporations (PCs).*
   These are business corporations created to provide professional services that require a license, such as medical, dental, legal, or accounting services.
5. *Cooperatives.*
   These nonprofit corporations exist to benefit their owner-users by allowing them to band together to buy and sell so they can lower their costs and increase their revenues. For this reason they seek to break even on their sales and distribute all revenues above costs back to their owners in accordance with their volume of business with the cooperative.

Creating a Corporation

The steps of incorporation vary from state to state but generally include:

1. The organization of responsible people to become officials of the new corporation. In most agribusiness corporations, the interested parties are family members or close friends.
2. The filing of a special document (called the articles of incorporation) with the designated state official. These articles, together with the bylaws, make up the charter governing the relationships between the corporation, its owners/shareholders, the officers, and the board of directors.
3. Payment of an initial tax and certain filing fees is normally required.
4. In order to establish the business for which the corporation was formed, certain official meetings must be conducted to deal with specific details of organization and operation.

The following steps are normally followed in setting up a corporation:

1. List the goals of the corporation, which can come from the business plan's purpose and objectives.
2. Retain the services of an attorney who is experienced in corporate law.
3. Engage a certified public accountant to set up the accounts and records.
4. Obtain a state corporate charter.
5. Divide stock in accordance with the corporate charter.
6. Issue stock certificates.
7. Hold the first stockholders' meeting, elect a board of directors, and adopt the bylaws of the corporation.
8. Elect corporate officers.
9. Set wages and salaries and establish remunerations for assets leased to the corporation.
10. Define the corporation's fiscal year.

If the organization of a corporation is properly planned, the transfer of property or money to the corporation and the receipt of stock by the shareholders are not taxable. The basic requirement is that the incorporators receive at least 80 percent of the corporation's stock. The income tax basis the corporation takes in assets transferred to it is the same as the shareholder had in assets. Each shareholder's basis in stock is the same as the assets each shareholder contributed to the corporation. This arrangement defers taxes until a shareholder sells stock.

Unlike the organization of a partnership, the termination of a corporation is generally a taxable event. With careful planning, it is possible to plan the termination so the gain is taxed at a favorable long-term capital gain rate. This type of planning is very technical and will require consultation with competent tax counsel; however, any expense for this advice will likely be repaid in tax savings.

Anyone considering incorporation should contact a qualified lawyer, accountant, or other professional familiar with specific state requirements. A corporation is the most complex, formal, and expensive method of organization to form. Organizational costs for a corporation may be several thousand dollars.

Timing may be important in incorporation. Selection of the right time depends on both the circumstance and the purpose for incorporating. A person with substantial personal assets besides an agribusiness might want to incorporate as soon as possible if he or she is interested in separating business ventures and limiting personal liability. Practical reasons may exist for delaying incorporation, such as using up old tax losses, letting inventories reach a low level, or waiting until the end of a fiscal year.

Advantages of Incorporation

The corporate legal structure offers advantages that are not found in other legal structures. The benefits include limited personal liability, continuity of management, income tax minimization, estate planning, and specialization of management decision making. In a corporate structure, employee health benefits and retirement plans are often tax deductible. The benefits of incorporation are attractive to many interested parties.

Limited Liability. An important characteristic of the corporation is the limitation of liability of the shareholders for the actions and obligations of the corporation. If the business fails or is sued for negligent acts of its officers or employees, the shareholder is only risking the amount he or she has invested. Personal assets not invested in the corporation cannot be used to satisfy this obligation. This is not true for firms that are sole proprietorships or partnerships.

The corporation also is not liable for its shareholders' personal obligations. Suppose that a shareholder is sued for something unrelated to the corporation. The creditors may be awarded the shareholder's stock to meet that obligation, but the corporation as a separate legal entity will continue and they will not be able to confiscate the corporation's assets.

Continuity of Operation. A corporation exists as long as shareholders support it and it fulfills the requirements of the law; i.e., the corporation operates in perpetuity. Shareholders can come and go, but the firm lives on. Shareholders can give, will, or sell their shares to others subject to the articles of incorporation or bylaws. However, a corporation also must fulfill the requirements of the law to be allowed to continue. If the corporation fails to meet these requirements, it will be terminated by the state and its articles of incorporation will be forfeited.

Estate Planning. Estate planning has been the major factor in the development of small agribusiness corporations. The corporate structure, if done correctly, tends to allow a shareholder to minimize estate taxes and facilitates the transfer of a business to others. It is easier to transfer shares of stock by gift or sale than to transfer bulk assets such as land, property, and equipment.

LIMITED LIABILITY COMPANIES

Limited liability companies (LLCs) are a hybrid between corporations and partnerships and are designed to give owners the advantages of each legal structure. They do this by offering the owners limited liability for debts and expenses that come from the corporate structure while allowing the firm to be treated as a partnership for most other operational purposes. In terms of federal taxes, a limited liability company has the option of being taxed as either a partnership or corporation, although most are taxed as a partnership.

COMPARING LEGAL STRUCTURES

The preceding sections have pointed out the special characteristics of the three primary legal structures—sole proprietorship, partnership, and corporation. (The limited liability form will not be part of the comparison because it is a hybrid of the corporate and partnership structures. However, it will be listed as an alternative solution for some situations.) Choosing a business structure on the basis of a single advantage such as estate planning can lead to a faulty decision. The idea is to apply good decision-making procedures, which means looking at a number of criteria: resource acquisition, continuity of existence, liability of the owners, participation in management, compensation of management, ability to transfer ownership, record keeping, and tax planning.

Resource Acquisition

All businesses must be concerned with having adequate resources to accomplish their purpose and objectives. The three legal structures vary in their ability to obtain capital. The sole proprietorship is the most limited. The only sources of capital for a proprietor are personal funds, prior earnings, and loans. The amount a creditor will loan to a business depends on the business's potential future earnings and personal wealth of the owner. This normally greatly limits its chances to obtain outside capital.

Because of the need to gain economy of size, capital requirements outstrip the potential future earnings of most agribusinesses. Thus, they rely on external capital to grow. The result is a rise in the use of partnerships. Partnerships often can raise funds more easily than sole proprietors because several individuals are liable for the firm's debt. In fact, some partnerships can borrow on better terms than some corporations.

Like the partnership, a corporation allows and facilitates the pooling of capital by two or more individuals. In addition, during the estate transfer process, the corporate structure may encourage nonbusiness heirs to maintain their ownership in the business and to keep their inherited capital in the firm. Most likely, the nonbusiness heir will expect to be paid a return on inherited capital if the equity is to be left in the business.

The corporate form of business organization also provides a longer planning horizon for an agribusiness firm. When a sole proprietor dies, often the business is dissolved and divided among the heirs. On the other hand, a properly organized corporation will allow the firm to continue even after the death of a major shareholder. This awareness may encourage lenders to loan larger amounts of money to a corporation.

The opportunity for labor and management specialization in multi-owner firms is a benefit since only larger partnerships and corporations can afford to hire the best qualified managers. The axiom that two heads are better than one still holds true. It is difficult for a sole proprietor to be competent in all areas such as production, marketing, labor management, and so on.

Continuity of Existence

As indicated above, continuity of existence increases the ability of a firm to acquire capital. Although sole proprietorships are under no legal time limit, they are not perpetual; they are limited to the lifetime of the proprietor. Multi-owner structures have a big advantage in this area. The death of an owner in a multi-owner business does not mean the death of the firm. However, to maintain continuity in the case of death may be more costly to a partnership than a corporation, because it may be necessary to purchase the deceased partner's interest.

Continuity of existence is particularly important to consider when estate planning and when arranging for the transfer of a business from one generation to another. Multi-owner organizations facilitate the transfer of property between generations without destroying the firm.

Liability of Owners

The degree to which the owners of an agribusiness risk legal liability for the debts of the firm is a major consideration. A single proprietor is liable for all business debts; this liability extends to personally owned property. Similarly, each general partner is fully responsible for all debts owed by the partnership regardless of the amount of his or her own investment unless specified otherwise in the partnership agreement. Limited partners are liable only for the amount of their investment. To protect partners from the negligent acts of a single partner, a partnership can become a registered LLP. Increasing numbers of partnerships have adopted this structure to gain the benefits of limited liability while retaining all the other benefits of a partnership.

Corporations have a real advantage over other legal structures in this regard. Creditors can force payments of their claims on the corporation only to the level of the agribusiness's assets. The only exception occurs when the shareholder is also a director or manager. In this case, he or she may be personally liable as well. Personal liability of corporate directors and officers most often occurs in small corporations that require the managers' personal signatures for loans and agreements. In these instances, both the signers and the cosigners lose the advantage of limited liability.

Participation in Management

The extent that the owners will participate in management decisions also should be considered when selecting a business organization. When more than one person is involved in management and each specializes in one area of the business, the overall quality of management normally improves. On the other hand, as the number of managers increases, so does the potential for conflict, and disagreements may be serious enough to lead to the dissolution of the organization. The sole proprietor has no such problem with conflict but also offers fewer opportunities to specialize. Many single proprietors overcome this by forming an informal board of directors made up of advisers such as attorneys, accountants, and management consultants.

Compensation of Management

The sole proprietor is the sole recipient of the profits of a business. He or she gets all the money that is left after all the bills are paid. A strong incentive exists for sole proprietors to make the profit as large as possible.

General partnerships are much like sole proprietorships with regard to compensation. The potential for higher profits from specialized management may be a major factor in favoring a partnership over a sole proprietorship. When considering this organizational option, it is important to carefully determine the distribution of profits and losses before beginning the business.

The advantage of the corporate structure is that profit sharing and fringe-benefit programs such as health care and retirement programs can be used to compensate employees, even in a family corporation. Most fringe benefits can be treated as ordinary, tax-deductible expenses in the corporate structure but not in sole proprietorships and partnerships, which must pay for such items from after-tax income. Furthermore, a constant salary for management and employees can be established and bonuses paid in exceptionally profitably years.

Transferability of Ownership

The ability to easily transfer ownership includes not only the transfer of property but also the transfer of the management responsibility associated with it. Owners of small firms need to think only about how to transfer their assets to their children or heirs. However, to make sure those assets are productive, the owners need to be sure the recipients learn how to properly manage them.

Because a sole proprietorship is dissolved when the owner dies, it provides little help in transferring managerial responsibility to the next generation. In contrast, corporations and partnerships facilitate the transfer of the business as an ongoing entity. Multi-owner structures facilitate not only the transfer of assets but also the transfer of management and financial responsibility to heirs by allowing them to grow into the management role under the supervision of a more experienced owner.

Record Keeping

All businesses need to keep complete, concise records, but record keeping has different implications for each of the legal structures. A sole proprietor must have records sufficient to prepare defensible income-tax returns. A partnership also must file an annual tax form. It requires financial records that will allow any partner to know the status of the business at any moment. Complete financial records will minimize opportunities for disagreements among partners. Sole proprietors and partnerships can perform this function in-house by using a standard computer bookkeeping system or hire an outside firm to do it.

Doing business as a corporation requires a more comprehensive set of records than either a sole proprietorship or partnership. In addition to regular accounting records, it must keep minutes of at least the annual meeting of shareholders and the board of directors. Some states also require corporations to publish annual reports.

Tax Planning

Regulations regarding income, estate, and gift taxes for the different business structures are an important concern for all agribusiness owners. It is important to obtain the counsel of a competent, experienced attorney and tax accountant before beginning. Tax laws and tax rates across the United States are different and change constantly, so it is difficult to state that one particular structure is best.

In the case of income taxes, a sole proprietor is taxed at personal rates. In a partnership, taxable income is transferred to each partner, who then pays taxes at personal rates. The same is true for the owners of S-corporations. In other corporations the profits are taxed twice. First, the firm's profits are taxed. Second, the **dividends** received by each shareholder are taxed again at personal income-tax rates.

For those concerned about being able to pass their businesses on to their heirs, a small corporation may provide the best liquidity and flexibility by lowering taxes that must be paid when ownership is transferred from one generation to the next. The corporate organizational structure makes changing the ownership structure of the business easier without affecting the asset structure by transferring shares of stock as gifts to heirs.

Chapter Highlights

1. The selection of a legal structure is a major decision for an agribusiness and can have long-term implications for its owners, their heirs, and the existence of the business.
2. A changing legal environment makes the recommendation of a single best legal form impossible. However, it is possible to explain the advantages and disadvantages of each legal structure. The selection of the best structure should consider the needs and goals of the business owners and enlist the help of an experienced tax attorney and tax accountant.
3. The three primary types of legal structure are sole proprietorships, partnerships, and corporations.
4. The sole proprietorship is the most popular structure because it is the easiest to form, but it does little to limit owners' personal liability and ends with the death of the owner.
5. A partnership gives a firm the benefits of multi-ownership and strengthens the firm's management.

6. The rules for operating a partnership are given in the Uniform Partnership Act, unless specified in a written partnership agreement drawn up by the partners.
7. Three types of partnerships exist—general, limited, and registered limited liability.
8. The corporation is the most complex but enduring legal structure and has the greatest ability to provide limited personal liability for its investors.
9. Limited liability companies are a hybrid between corporations and partnerships, which gives the owners the benefits of limited liability and the operational functions of a partnership.
10. The selection of the most appropriate legal structure for an agribusiness should be based on an assessment of several factors, including continuity of existence, taxes, and liability of the owners, among others.

Chapter Quiz

1. Explain why the selection of a legal structure is an important decision for an agribusiness and its owners.
2. Identify and describe at least four factors that need to be considered when deciding a business's legal structure.
3. Develop a chart that defines sole proprietorship and lists the advantages and disadvantages of this legal structure.
4. Develop a chart that defines the three types of partnerships and give the advantages and disadvantages of each.
5. Develop a chart that defines the five types of corporate legal forms and give the advantages and disadvantages of each.
6. Evaluate the statement that family partnerships are the best way to involve a family in a business.
7. What is a limited liability company and how does it differ from a registered limited liability partnership?
8. Compare and contrast what happens to a business when the owner dies if the business is organized as a sole proprietorship, a partnership, or a corporation.
9. Explain the difference between a general partner and a limited partner. Give an example of why someone would wish to be each.
10. What is the relationship between the Uniform Partnership Act and the written partnership agreement?
11. Why should the partnership agreement be in writing? Explain your answer.
12. Some argue that the corporate legal structure, which gives most corporate executives protection from personal liability for acts of their corporation, gives executives too much immunity from responsibility for their acts. How do you feel about this? Explain your answer.

13. It is argued that the limited liability of the corporation structure is responsible for the economic growth of Western civilization. Agree or disagree? Explain.
14. In the chapter it is said that the best partnerships are born when there is a convergence of interests. What does this mean?
15. Outline the process you would follow in deciding which of the legal structures covered in this chapter would be best for a family business.

Case 10
The End of Gene's Dream?

Martha knew something was bothering her husband, Gene, as soon as she saw him get out of his truck. She thought that sending him into town for supplies would raise his spirits a bit. Gene still had not recovered from the sudden death of his lifelong friend, Allen Hutchinson. They had grown up together in Paxton. Their fathers had farmed next to each other. They had shared equipment once they took over from their dads and always watched out for each other for all those years. Now Al was gone and the world just did not seem the same.

Once inside the farm office, Gene slid into the chair nearest his wife's desk and stared at the floor. When she asked him what was going on he told her that the word in town was that the Hutchinson farm was going up for sale. As far as Gene knew, Al's will gave everything to his wife Sally, but it seems that she does not want the responsibility for their 1,000-acre farm. The Hutchinsons' two sons, Steve and Tom, both left the area once they graduated from college and could not devote much time to managing the operation. Everyone had wanted the farm to stay in the family so their mother could remain in the farmhouse, and they planned to rent the land so she would have an income to live on.

The reality of their father's death had forced the two brothers to take a closer look at their family situation. Their mother's health had been failing and they were not sure she was able to live alone way out in the country. As they settled their father's estate, the family's lawyer told them they might face a considerable tax bill once their mother passes on. He suggested considering incorporating their farm as a way to limit their taxes. Once Steve and Tom weighed all the information, they convinced their mother that selling the farm would be best. It was good land and prices had been good.

Gene told Martha that it was time for them to think about their situation. Their three daughters, Emily, Jamie, and Casey, had all graduated from college and had families of their own. Only Emily's husband Rick worked on their farm and had a long-term commitment to farming. "I just don't want to see our farm end up like the Hutchinson place. Gone from the family after all these years," Gene said sadly.

What can they do to make Gene's dream come true?

PART IV

The Controlling Function

Once an agribusiness manager has developed her business plan and devised an organizational scheme to carry it out, the next step is to develop ways to measure the firm's progress toward the accomplishment of the goals set in the planning function. The chapters in this section focus on evaluating the production process, measuring the firm's financial performance, and evaluating capital expenditures.

- ***Chapter 11—Organizing Production Using Economic Principles*** In order to manage production a manager must understand the production process. Managers need to recognize that it takes both technical know-how and economic analysis to find the point where long-term profits are maximized.
- ***Chapter 12—Production and Inventory Management*** This chapter continues the financial analysis of the production process by using its most important concepts to measure and evaluate the financial performance of the firm's production activities. This includes deciding which costs are relevant for decision making, determining when a plant should be shut down, determining the break-even points in sales, understanding the role of management information systems and supply chains, and knowing how to effectively manage the firm's inventory.
- ***Chapter 13—Basic Accounting Documents*** Agribusiness managers need to understand a firm's basic accounting documents in order to assess the business's financial performance. The starting point for this understanding is the balance sheet and the profit-and-loss statement. How these documents are developed and organized and what they measure is the focus of this chapter.
- ***Chapter 14—Using Accounting Information for Business Control and Planning*** This chapter builds on the learning begun in the previous chapter. The emphasis is on using the information in the basic accounting documents to evaluate past business financial performance and to make decisions affecting the firm's future.
- ***Chapter 15—Capital Budgeting I: Principles and Procedures*** The discussion of business management up to this point has assumed no change in a firm's plant, property, and equipment. Eventually all managers will face the job of investing in these items. This chapter builds the framework for making this type of decision.

- ***Chapter 16—Capital Budgeting II: Applications*** This chapter builds on the previous chapter. The emphasis is on applying capital budgeting procedures to decisions such as whether to lease, borrow, or buy equipment. The chapter includes a short worked case study to show how the material presented can lead to better financial decisions by agribusiness managers.

Chapter 11

Organizing Production Using Economic Principles

Chapter Learning Objectives

- Explain the role that production management plays in the profitability of an agribusiness.
- Explain why technical efficiency is a prerequisite to economic efficiency.
- Summarize how the production process works and the role of the principle of diminishing marginal returns.
- Describe how to calculate the proper level of input use that will maximize long-run profits by evaluating its efficiency and contribution in the production process.
- Define the profit-maximizing production area.
- Describe how to use incremental analysis to reach economic efficiency.
- Explain the principle of equimarginal allocation.

Introduction

All agribusinesses produce something. In some cases that something is a product such as wheat, flour, or a breakfast cereal. In other cases, it may be a service such as grain storage, food warehousing, or banking. Regardless of the situation, it is the manager's job to take a set of **inputs,** such as land, fertilizer, people and machinery, and transform them through the **production process** into an **output** (either a product or service) that the firm can sell at a profit.

Tying long-run profit maximization to the production process is a fairly simple task that requires both technical and economic know-how. First, the production process must be made *technically efficient*—production managers must get the maximum output from each unit of input. Second, the production process can then be made *economically efficient*—business managers must determine the level of output that will generate the greatest profits. This process is easier when managers know how to apply economics to the problem.

The Production Process

Agribusiness managers face three big decisions when they undertake production:

- ***What to produce?*** What products can the business profitably offer? This question is answered in the business plan.
- ***How to produce?*** What is the most efficient combination of inputs to produce the desired products? This is a technical question that is answered by production people.
- ***How much to produce?*** What amount of output will maximize long-run profits? The answer to this question comes from economics.

The answers to these production decisions are also influenced by the demand for the firm's products. As was seen in chapter 5, demand is affected by the price of the product, the price of substitutes and complements, income, and consumer tastes and preferences.

In order to provide a product at a profit, producers must also understand the production process and how it affects their costs. Firms must sell their products for more than they cost or they will go out of business. It is the same as producing cattle feed that sells for $400 per ton when cattle feeders can not afford to pay more than $300.

THE PRODUCTION FUNCTION

All business managers need to understand the **production function** and the economic analysis needed to decide how much to produce to maximize long-run profits. A production function describes the technical relationship between inputs and outputs by summarizing the output possible from different levels of input use. For example, a production function might describe the relationship between grain output and fertilizer use on an acre of land. For a nitrogen fertilizer plant, the production function might show the quantity of nitrogen fertilizer that can be produced from using various quantities of natural gas.

A representative production function for a nitrogen fertilizer plant is shown in figure 11-1. The amount of nitrogen fertilizer (the output) possible from each level of natural gas use (the input) is recorded in the production function, labeled *TP* for **total product**. The shape of the production function depends on the technology. How high the *TP* line is on the graph depends on the technical efficiency of the plant and its managers. As technical efficiency increases, the *TP* line rises. As it decreases, the *TP* line falls.

The production function *(TP)* starts at zero. If no natural gas is used, no fertilizer is produced. A production function does not have to begin at zero. A production function for a crop may show some production even when fertilizer application is zero, since some production would be possible even without the application of fertilizer.

Measuring the Contribution and Efficiency of Inputs

The shape of the *TP* curve in figure 11-1 shows how output increases as more input is applied to the production process. Three interesting points are found on the production function—*A*, *B*, and *C*. In the production function shown, output increases rapidly for the first few units of natural gas until reaching point *A*. After point *A*, output continues to increase, but at a decreasing rate, until maximum production is reached at point *C*. Point *B* is the place where a line from the origin to the *TP* line has the greatest angle. Points *B* and *C* define the **profit-maximizing production area.**

The *TP* curve defines the maximum output that can be obtained from various levels of input use. The *TP* curve also provides information about the contribution and efficiency of each unit of variable input.

Economists call the **contribution** of each unit of input to output **marginal product (*MP*).** Marginal product is calculated by dividing the change in output by the change in input needed to generate it, with all other inputs held constant. They define the **efficiency** of input use as **average product (*AP*).** Average product is calculated by dividing output by the corresponding level of input. The points of maximum contribution, efficiency, and production are found at points *A*, *B*, and *C* respectively in figure 11-1.

Point *A* is the inflection point on the *TP* curve—the slope of the output line reaches its maximum. After point *A* the slope of the line begins to decrease because the increase in output for each new unit of input begins to decline. Point *A* corresponds to the point of maximum contribution. All additional units of input bring progressively smaller contributions (lower *MP*) to output, which eventually becomes zero at maximum output (point *C*).

Figure 11-1 The Production Function for a Nitrogen Fertilizer Plant

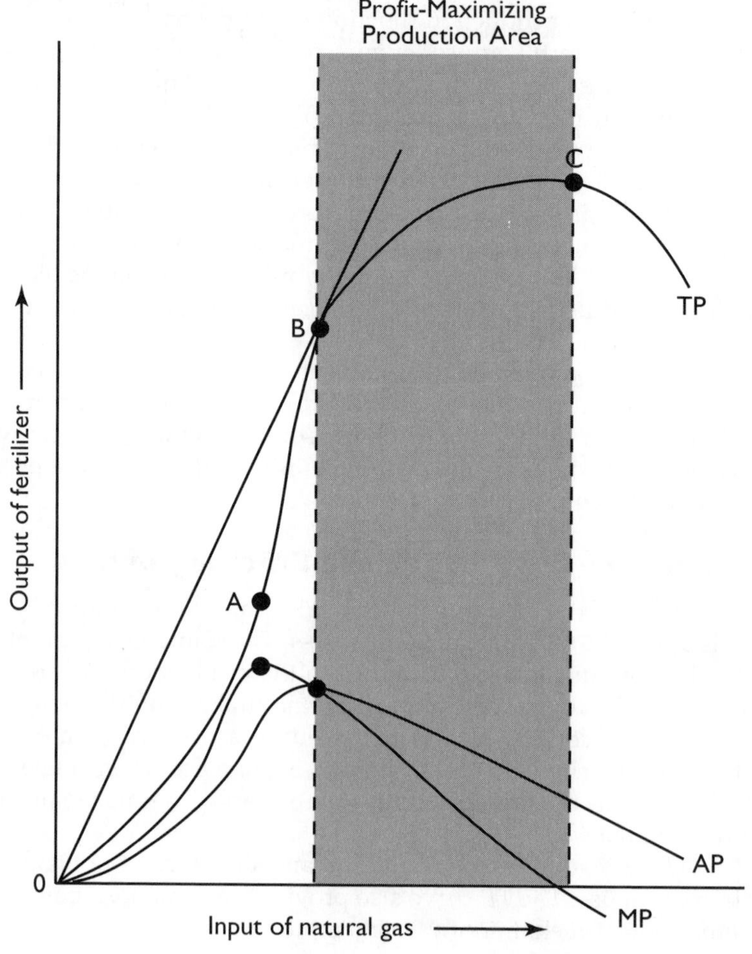

Point *B* is the point of maximum efficiency (maximum average product) on the *TP* line. If a straight line is extended from the origin to the *TP* line its slope would be the ratio of output/input—or the efficiency of input use (average product). This point defines the lower end of the profit-maximizing production area, because it marks the start of the stage where the contribution of additional units of input begins to lower the efficiency of production. *The amount of input used at point B is the minimum needed to maximize profits.* Since producers are assumed to be interested in maximizing their profit, each additional unit of input used up to point *B* brings greater efficiency than the last unit of input. This means the firm's output and profits are rising, so naturally producers would like to continue to expand output. After point *B*, efficiency falls with each additional unit of input and the interest in further production increases begins to decline.

Point *C* is the point of maximum output, at which the slope of the *TP* line is zero. This defines the upper end of the profit-maximizing production area. *The amount of input used at point C is the maximum needed to maximize profit.* At this point, the contribution of the last unit of input to output (marginal product) is zero. The use of additional units of input beyond this point causes output to fall; this would add to costs but lower output and profits.

To determine the amount of input needed to reach economic efficiency (maximum profit) requires the addition of input and output prices. However, it is possible to define the profit-maximizing production area as the area between maximum efficiency (maximum average product) and maximum output (maximum total product).

Determining the Profit-Maximizing Production Area

The shape of the production function illustrates the principle of diminishing marginal returns. The **principle of diminishing marginal returns** states that as more units of a variable input (such as natural gas) are used in production, when at least one other production input (such as plant size) is held constant, total product will increase at an increasing rate (up to point *A*), then increase at a decreasing rate (points *A* to *C*), reach a maximum (point *C*), and then decline. Many people are astonished to learn that production is not a continually upward-sloping straight line, that it declines at high levels of input use. The principle of marginal diminishing returns teaches managers that just making your operation bigger is not always the way to make it more profitable.

Table 11-1 shows a production function for a feed manufacturing plant that illustrates this principle. According to the table, two workers can do more than twice the work of one worker and three workers can do more than one and a half times as much work as two workers. Up to three workers, *TP* increases at an increasing rate. This is seen in two ways. First, the *efficiency* of labor use increases with each new worker from 20 to 25 to 28 tons per worker. Second, the rise in efficiency comes from the increasing *contribution* of each additional worker to output, which rises from 20 to 30 to 34 tons per new worker.

Beyond three workers there is a change in the situation. The efficiency of labor use declines with the addition of workers four, five, six, and seven because

Table 11-1 Production Function for Labor in Feed Production

Amount of Variable Input (Labor)	Amount of Output (Tons of Feed)	Average Product (Output/Input)	Marginal Product (Δ Output/Δ Input)	
0	0	—	20	
1	20	20.0	30	
2	50	25.0	34	
3	84	28.0	26	Profit max-
4	110	27.5	10	production
5	120	24.0	6	area
6	126	21.0		
7	122	17.4	–4	

the contribution of each of these workers declines. In fact, the addition of the seventh worker causes output to go down. Because the manager seeks to maximize profits, a seventh worker should never be hired even if the worker is free.

Efficiency and contribution of input use help managers define the profit-maximizing production area before any price information is included. In the example, a manager would know that his most profitable range for production is between three workers (the point of maximum labor efficiency) and six workers (the point of maximum output). With the addition of prices of labor and feed the point of maximum profit could be determined.

Using Prices to Find Economic Efficiency

Total product, average product, and marginal product are all physical measures of the production process. They must be combined with price to determine the point of economic efficiency (maximum profit).

Let's continue the feed manufacturing example. Suppose that manufactured bulk feed sells for $200 per ton, labor costs are $600 per worker, and the feed ingredients cost $150 per ton. Assume all other costs are fixed. Table 11-2 summarizes the technical and economic data needed to determine where profits are maximized.

For these prices and technical conditions, the most profitable option is to employ four workers. Each of the first four workers adds more to returns than to costs ($1,000 versus $600, $1,500 versus $600, $1,700 versus $600, $1,300 versus $600). The fifth worker, however, adds $500 to returns but costs $600 to employ. For this set of conditions, employing four workers maximizes profit (economic efficiency).

The technique of comparing added costs to added returns to find the most profitable production levels is called **incremental analysis**. Incremental refers to the additional returns and costs from producing the next unit of output. As a rule, as long as incremental revenue is greater than incremental cost, expansion should continue until they are equal. When this occurs, economic efficiency (maximum profit) has been achieved. Agribusiness managers who regularly use incremental analysis when making decisions are more likely to make correct decisions.

Table 11-2 Determining the Profit-Maximizing Point for Labor Use

Amount of Output (Tons of Feed)	Net Revenue*	Marginal Revenue (Δ Revenue/ Δ Output)	Amount of Variable Input (Labor)	Total Cost of Labor (At $600/ Worker)	Marginal Cost (Δ Cost/ Δ Labor)
0	0		0	0	
20	$1,000	$1,000	1	$ 600	$600
50	2,500	1,500	2	1,200	600
84	4,200	1,700	3	1,800	600
110	5,500	1,300	4	2,400	600
120	6,000	500	5	3,000	600
126	6,300	300	6	3,600	600
122	6,100	–200	7	4,200	600

*Each ton of feed sells for $200 and ingredients cost $150. "Net revenue" exclusive of labor is $50/ton ($200 – $150).

Another decision-making tool that is useful when considering expansion is the **equimarginal allocation principle**. It compares the change in profit from using an additional input to produce one product versus another. The principle is stated as follows: any limited input should be allocated between two or more products so that the total profit cannot be increased by taking one unit away from one product and using it to produce another. In short, always use inputs where they give the greatest return.

For example, a firm's manager decides to use a unit of input to produce product Y, which had previously been used to produce product X. This reduces the revenue from product X by $10, but increases the revenue from product Y by $12. This makes good economic sense, since overall profits increase by $2. If another unit of input is transferred from X to Y and it only increases Y's revenue by $10 while still reducing X's revenue by $10, the manager should decide not to transfer the input. In this case, profits are already maximized.

Chapter Highlights

1. How an agribusiness manager combines inputs to produce a product has a great deal to do with the level of profits the firm generates.
2. Profit maximization of a production process involves two steps. First, technical production specialists must achieve technical efficiency. Second, once technical efficiency is realized, the manager needs to apply incremental analysis to achieve economic efficiency.
3. Production occurs when inputs are used to produce an output (product).
4. The production function describes the technical relationship between inputs and output over a range of input use.
5. The profit-maximization production area is between maximum efficiency (maximum of average product) and maximum output (marginal product of zero).

6. The economic principle of diminishing marginal returns shows that production does not increase in a straight line forever as input is increased. When at least one other input is held constant, production will increase at an increasing rate, increase at a decreasing rate, reach a maximum, and then decline as more input is added.

Chapter Quiz

1. Explain why production does not increase in a straight line forever as more input is applied. Give an example of a situation that supports your argument.
2. Define and explain the relationship between economic efficiency and technical efficiency and show how managers would use them to achieve their objective of maximizing long-term profits.
3. Agribusiness managers face three major production decisions—what to produce, how to produce, and how much to produce. Where does a manager find the answers to these three questions? Why are these answers important?
4. Define and explain the difference between the average product and marginal product and explain how to use them in production management decisions.
5. What is the profit-maximizing production area? Explain what the lower and upper bounds of this area are and why they exist where they do.
6. Explain how to locate economic efficiency within the profit-maximizing production area.
7. Explain the principle of diminishing marginal returns.
8. Explain why the production function increases at an increasing rate, increases at a decreasing rate, reaches a maximum, and then declines as more input is added. Give an example to illustrate this principle.
9. Explain the principle of equimarginal allocation. How does it relate to the concept of marginal product discussed in the chapter? Give an example to illustrate the use of this principle.
10. Explain how an agribusiness manager combines the production management decisions given in this chapter with consumer demand to operate a profitable business.
11. Why is technical efficiency a prerequisite to economic efficiency?
12. Explain how economics helps agribusiness managers accomplish their goal of maximizing long-run profit.
13. Who is more important to the long-run success of an agribusiness, the production manager or the business manager? Explain.
14. What is incremental analysis, and how can it help business managers make good decisions?
15. Rank your choices of the three big production decisions in order of importance. Explain the reasons for your ranking.

CASE 11
Donna's Dilemma

The flicker of the computer screen filled the darkness in Donna's cluttered office as she pored over her hog unit's spreadsheets one more time. She was sure something was wrong with the numbers. Hog and feed prices had been stable for much of the year. The high unemployment rate in the area had allowed her to keep wages unchanged and hire all the new help she needed during this year's expansion. What really confused her was how she could increase production by nearly 25 percent and see profits fall.

When she took over the operation a year ago, Donna was sure she could increase sales and profits. The facility was in pretty good shape, but was running at only 80 to 85 percent of capacity. Donna extrapolated her costs and revenues per unit to higher production levels and calculated the extra profits that should be there. This was easy, since she could do this without investing in any new equipment or buildings.

If Donna asked you what happened what would you tell her? If Donna is interested in maximizing the total profit of her operation what should she do?

Chapter 12

Production and Inventory Management

Chapter Learning Objectives

- Recognize how understanding production cost relations and procedures can lead to better business production processes and more effective production decisions.
- Explain how management information systems assist agribusiness managers in carrying out the controlling management function.
- Describe the meanings of the term *cost*, and recognize which ones are relevant for business decision making.
- Explain the contribution concept and break-even analysis.
- Demonstrate how to evaluate various business decisions such as pricing, evaluating the return on advertising, and meeting profit objectives using break-even analysis.
- Explain the cost relationships that surround holding inventory and demonstrate how to use them to minimize costs.
- Explain the importance of good inventory management on the long-term profits of an agribusiness.

Introduction

In chapter 11, the relationship between production, costs, prices, and profits was developed with the help of economics. This chapter refines that information and applies it to production and inventory management. The discussion includes how to define and manage costs and determine the most profitable levels of production and inventory. These cost concepts also can be employed to assess a firm's chances for success in a market by first determining the combinations of sales, costs, and selling prices needed to break even; then this information can be compared to sales estimates from the marketing plan. Agribusiness managers need to understand cost relationships and procedures so they can better manage their business's production processes and make more effective production decisions.

The term *cost* has many meanings. It is possible for two people discussing cost to have different things in mind. When a business manager says that it costs $500 to produce a product, he or she might be referring to the total production cost, the **average cost** per unit, the historical cost, or an estimate of what costs will be if things go according to plan. It is important to know what comprises a definition of cost.

Management Information Systems

Managers need timely and accurate information on costs and production in order to make good business decisions. They need to know which costs will vary with sales volume and how they will respond. They need to know which costs they can affect and which are beyond their control. To do this, a firm needs a **management information system (MIS)** that provides accurate and timely production and cost information on all phases of the business; data in the proper form for decision making; accounting information that allows accurate and quick assessment of the financial situation; and a means for efficiently and effectively monitoring and controlling business production costs and revenues.

Accounting records summarize the financial transactions of a business and are the primary source of information about costs. However, they typically do not provide management with the information they need for decision making. An effective MIS overcomes this problem by supplementing financial records with information on costs, usage rates, and so on. An MIS also can be used to provide information in a variety of areas beyond accounting, production, and cost management (such as sales, health and safety, equal employment, and wage and salary reporting) that are required for decisions.

Agribusinesses use MIS to carry out the third management function—control. Generating efficient and effective feedback information about a firm's performance makes it possible to see how well actual performance matches what was proposed in the planning function. It also can be used to evaluate the effectiveness of the firm's organizational structure. An effective management information system is a key part of a business's control function that gives its managers timely feedback on business performance.

Defining Costs

Managers are responsible for developing a management information system that provides them with all the data needed to make decisions. In particular, managers must be sure that costs are allocated properly and that all relevant costs are considered in each decision. Accounting personnel often provide the information that is required but they need management's direction and assistance to be sure that all necessary information for decision making is made available.

Before looking at general cost concepts and the use of cost in management analysis, it is necessary to understand the basic cost vocabulary. Cost as it is used in general conversation can mean many things. The best definition of cost is that which is given up to acquire a good or service. When someone pays $25 for a shirt or $75 for a tire, the cost is very clear. An amount, $25 or $75, was given up to obtain the specific good purchased.

However, cost is not always so obvious. Suppose a business buys a new seed cleaner for $25,000, plus the trade-in of a 10-year-old cleaner. How much did the new cleaner cost the business? One person might feel that the old cleaner was worthless and so the new cleaner cost $25,000. Another person might reason that the old cleaner was worth $5,000, making the cost of the new cleaner $30,000. According to the Internal Revenue Service, the true cost of the new machine would be $25,000 plus the **book value** of the old machine. However, its book value can vary depending on the **depreciation** procedure used by the accountant who determined it. It is possible to get different but perfectly legal estimates of the machine's book value, and thus the cost of the new machine. An accountant may view costs differently than an economist, and a manager may view costs differently than either of them. The reason that necessitates developing cost information often determines how a cost is defined.

GENERAL COST CONCEPTS

Some light can be thrown on the concept of cost by looking at different types of costs. In the business world, the context of cost defines the term and indicates whether anything can be done about it or if it is relevant. If an accountant determines that the cost of an activity is $5,000, this is a historical cost and a manager can do nothing about it. On the other hand, if a person says that the cost of a planned project is $20,000, a number of things may be done about that. The term cost conveys a different meaning in each example.

Opportunity, Implicit, and Explicit Costs

For an economist, the relevant cost concept is opportunity cost. **Opportunity cost** is the return that is given up by not selecting the highest-valued alternative among several projects. Because inputs can be used to produce a variety of products and they are purchased in an open market, the opportunity cost of an input is normally equal to its market price. Inputs go to those willing to pay the highest prices for them, if resources are used efficiently.

In another case, let's assume that a business chooses to make product X, which makes a profit of $10 per unit, rather than producing product Y, which yields a profit of $25 per unit. In terms of accounting, the business is making a profit by producing product X. However, from an economist's standpoint, the business is losing $15 per unit. The difference is that the economist is including the opportunity cost ($25 per unit) of the business not producing the product with the highest profit. The economist would argue that society is losing $15 per unit from this misallocation of resources.

The costs directly traceable to an end product are called **explicit costs**. For example, suppose that a feed store purchases corn, soybean meal, vitamins, and antibiotics to prepare a special animal feed. The inputs are purchased on the open market at specific prices. These prices multiplied by the quantities will equal the explicit cost of the feed.

A business may incur costs that do not involve explicit payments. These are called **implicit costs**. Implicit costs are costs that do not include cash payments but need to be included in the calculation of the **total cost** of a product. In the feed example above, management should include the costs of using buildings, equipment, and labor in determining the final cost of the feed even though they have taken delivery of the items and have paid for them. If these implicit costs are not included, the true cost of the feed will be understated.

The implicit costs of a product can be considerable. In addition to the items stated in the example above, implicit costs include depreciation of the firm's plant, property, and equipment and the return on the owner's capital investment if it were invested elsewhere (i.e., the opportunity cost). This should include income the owner could earn by working for someone else.

Accountants tend to regard costs as an outward flow of assets. Their sharpest focus is on dealing with historical costs incurred by the business. These figures can be added to the implicit costs to determine the full costs of manufacturing a product. Overlooking implicit costs leads to bad business decisions that can have adverse affects on the long-term profitability of the business.

Managers also are concerned with the proportion of explicit to implicit costs. If the bulk of costs are explicit and traceable to specific inputs, a manager is more likely to understand why the cost was incurred and has an easier time finding ways to control it. The manager can see the final product in the plant. He or she can see the employees working on the product and easily determine if they are producing it within the correct specifications. He can observe mistakes in the manufacturing process and correct them. On the other hand, most managers have a hard time with implicit costs that are imposed on the business because they cannot see or control them.

Controllable and Uncontrollable Costs

Business managers become agitated when they face situations where the majority of their costs are not controllable. If the business is producing a product where most of the costs are either implicit or uncontrollable, such as a labor contract that limits production to a specified number of units per hour regardless of product demand, managers have very limited control over the cost of their product and ultimately over the profit.

A **controllable cost** is one that can be regulated by managers. If most costs incurred by a department or unit are controllable, managers are in a better position to efficiently manage the use of those inputs and achieve greater profits. While it is possible to achieve a reasonable profit when most of the costs are uncontrollable, it is much more difficult.

Incremental, Avoidable, and Sunk Costs

One of the biggest dilemmas managers face is deciding which costs to pay attention to when making a decision. This leads to a continuation of the discussion of incremental analysis started in chapter 11, which stated that the relevant costs in decision making are those that change as a result of the decision. This idea brings two new types of costs into the discussion: avoidable costs and sunk costs.

Avoidable costs are those that cease because of a decision. As such, they are **incremental costs** and should be included in the decision analysis. In this case, they are reductions in costs, or savings.

Sunk costs have been incurred in the past and will not change regardless of what decisions are made. Since they cannot change, sunk costs are not included in decisions. This is consistent with the original proposition of incremental analysis: if the increase in return is greater than the increase in cost, do it; if the increase in return is less than the increase in cost, do not do it.

Fixed and Variable Costs

To control costs, a manager must have accurate data and understand how costs behave when production varies. Costs vary for two reasons: passage of time and level of production. All the costs of producing a product are separated into two categories based on these circumstances.

Fixed costs arise from the passage of time and remain the same each period regardless of the level of production. Insurance, property taxes, and mortgage or rent payments are examples of fixed costs.

Variable costs change with the level of production. Materials, labor, shipping, and packaging are examples of variable costs. The total cost (*TC*) of production is the sum of total variable cost (*TVC*) and total fixed cost (*TFC*).

These cost concepts often are better understood when graphed. Figure 12-1 shows that *TFC* is a horizontal straight line that remains the same over all levels of production. Figure 12-2 shows that *TVC* is an upward sloping straight line that goes higher as production is increased. Figure 12-3 shows that *TC* is the sum of the total variable cost and total fixed cost (*TC* = *TVC* + *TFC*). The *TC* line has the same slope as the *TVC* line with the vertical distance between them equal to the amount of the *TFC*.

Figure 12-1 Total Fixed Costs

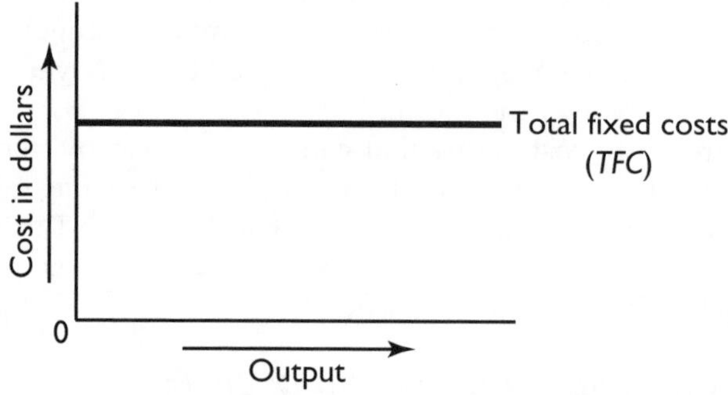

Figure 12-2 Total Variable Costs

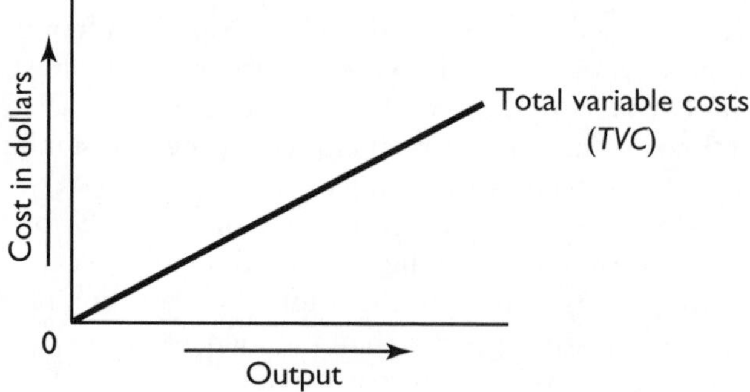

Figure 12-3 Total Cost

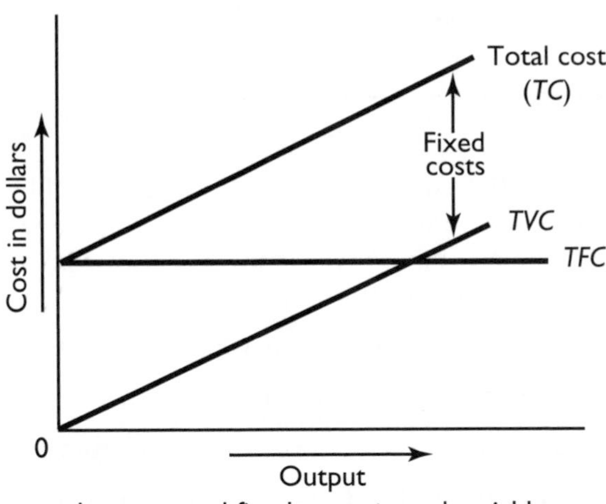

total cost = total fixed costs + total variable costs

Although it is convenient to define costs as either fixed or variable, some do not fit either category. Take the situation of an agribusiness that rents an extra truck for a month during its busy season. The company is charged a fixed monthly fee plus a surcharge for each mile the truck is driven. The cost of the truck is a mixture of fixed and variable costs. Some cost items may be a variable cost to one firm but a fixed cost to another. A good example is labor. It is normally thought of as a variable cost; however, if a firm has guaranteed the annual income for all of its workers regardless of the number of hours worked, it becomes a fixed cost.

Maintenance costs are another gray area when determining costs. The level of business activity at the firm does not generally affect the cost of upkeep on buildings and equipment. However, some maintenance costs do vary with production. If production is increased 20 percent using the same equipment, maintenance costs can be expected to increase. Once the variable part of the maintenance cost is defined, it can be effectively managed as a part of total variable cost.

The Use of Cost Standards

Managers should work at understanding how the costs of their businesses behave until they have a realistic expectation of what can be achieved. What can be realistically achieved depends on such factors as the type and volume of business, its size, the degree of automation, the quality of the workforce, and the age and condition of the plant and equipment. Managers also need to know how their costs compare with industry standards and those of their main competitors.

The balance between fixed and variable costs can affect the degree of control a manager can exert. If most of the costs are fixed, a manager may have few options except to expand volume to spread the fixed costs over more units and to buy more productive fixed assets. When more of the costs are variable, the producer can seek better, lower-cost inputs, and more efficient production processes. In either case, the manager constantly should be seeking ways to enhance the value and profits from the products being produced.

CONTRIBUTION

It is possible to determine a business's most profitable level of output in measurable units (pounds sold, acres sprayed, bags sold). To do this requires creating a formula for pricing that covers fixed and variable costs of production and includes some provision for profit:

selling price per unit = total costs per unit + profit per unit

Separating the costs according to the classification scheme gives:

selling price per unit = fixed costs per unit + variable costs per unit + profit per unit

Let's simplify and call the fixed costs *overhead*, since this is the term most businesses use. Finally, let's rearrange the terms into a more useful pricing equation:

selling price per unit – variable costs per unit = overhead per unit + profit per unit

By moving the variable costs per unit to the other side of the equal sign, the difference between the selling price and the variable costs per unit is equal to the overhead plus the profit per unit.

Suppose a seed company performed this analysis for one of its products and found the variable costs of producing that product to be:

Materials	$55/bag
Direct labor	+ $20/bag
Total variable costs	$75/bag

If each bag sells for $125, $50 will be left over to pay for overhead and profit:

Selling price	$125/bag
Total variable cost	– $ 75/bag
	$ 50/bag

This $50 per bag would be available to contribute to paying overhead and profit. **Contribution** is the difference between the selling price and variable costs per unit, and equals overhead plus profit per unit.

Establishing the Selling Price of a New Product

Contribution can be used to establish a selling price for a new product. In the seed example, 40 percent of the selling price per unit is available to pay overhead and profit:

Selling price/bag	$125		100%
Variable cost/bag	– $ 75	or	– 60%
Contribution/bag	$ 50		40%

If this **contribution margin** (40 percent) is typical for all the products sold by the firm, the selling price of any other product can be determined quickly once the variable costs per unit are known by using the following formula:

$$\text{total variable costs per unit} = [1 - \text{contribution margin}] \times \text{selling price per unit}$$

For example, if the firm sold another type of seed that had a total variable cost of $120 per bag, the formula would look like this:

$$\$120 = [1 - 0.40] \times \text{selling price per bag}$$

Therefore, its selling price should be:

$$\text{selling price per bag} = \frac{\$120}{\$0.60}$$
$$= \$200$$

By knowing and applying contribution, managers can simplify their pricing and cost analyses. Contribution is valuable when determining prices and performing break-even analysis.

Short-Term versus Long-Term Pricing: The Shutdown Point

Sometimes the best decision is to accept a price that does not permit the firm to make a profit. This may seem odd but it can make sense. Let's think about the definition of fixed costs. Fixed costs continue even when production stops; even if producers cease operation, they still have to pay their fixed costs. Losses are smaller if the price of the job allows them to recover all the variable costs and makes a contribution toward paying at least part of the fixed costs.

The concept of contribution can help make that decision, since contribution is selling price per unit minus variable cost per unit. When the contribution per unit is positive, even if it is not enough to pay all the fixed costs, it is better to accept the job because at least part of the total fixed costs are being paid.

This pricing decision works only in the **short term**. Over the **long term**, the firm must cover all its costs to continue to operate. When a business has idle capacity (such as during a slow season) it is better to take a job with a price that does not cover all its costs but does cover variable costs rather than to pass up the work. If the price of a job does not have a positive contribution, it is better to shut down than to take the job because losses will be smaller.

Break-Even Analysis

The objective of production management is to generate the largest profit at the selling price and sales level given in the marketing plan. **Break-even analysis** helps managers do this by finding the combination of costs, output, and selling price that will permit the firm to break even with no profits or losses. Break-even analysis is a first-stage management tool used to quickly determine the chances for success in a given production situation. For example, if break-even analysis shows that at the selling price given in the marketing plan output would have to be twice the estimated sales just to break even, little chance exists for success. On the other hand, if output has to be just 35 percent of what is estimated in the marketing plan to break even, the chances for success are much higher.

The Three Components of Break-Even Analysis

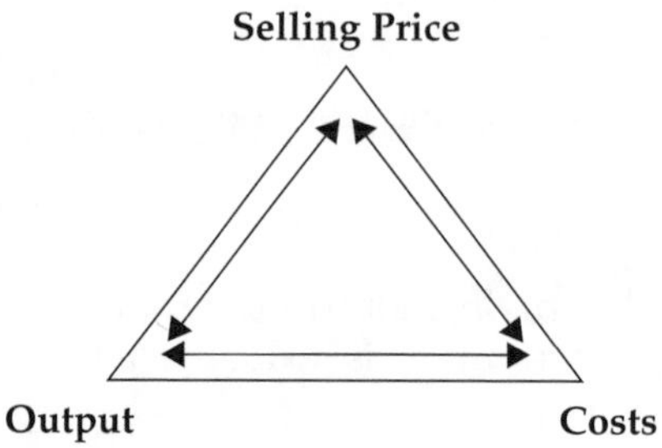

The **break-even point (BEP)** is calculated from a profit equation when profit equals zero.

$$\begin{aligned} \text{Profit} = 0 &= \text{total revenue} - \text{total costs} \\ &= \text{total revenue} - \text{total variable costs} - \text{total fixed costs} \\ &= (P \times Y) - (VC \times Y) - TFC \end{aligned}$$

Where P = selling price per unit
Y = quantity sold
VC = variable cost per unit
TFC = total fixed costs

Rearranging the terms and solving for the output (Y) when profit is zero gives

$$\begin{aligned} 0 &= (P \times Y) - (VC \times Y) - TFC \\ &= (P - VC)Y - TFC \\ TFC &= (P - VC)Y \\ Y &= \frac{TFC}{(P - VC)} \end{aligned}$$

Thus, the quantity (Y) needed to break even is given by dividing the total fixed costs (TFC) by the contribution ($P - VC$) per unit.

To illustrate the use of break-even analysis, let's draw on the seed example again. Assume the firm expects to sell 20,000 bags in the coming year at $125 per bag, when the variable costs equal $75 per bag. If the company has an overhead (total fixed costs) of $750,000, how many bags do they need to sell to break even? Another way to ask this same question is, how many bags of seed do they need to sell to break even when each bag is contributing $50 toward paying off total fixed costs of $750,000?

$$\begin{aligned} Y &= \frac{TFC}{(P - VC)} \\ &= \frac{\$750,000}{(\$125 - \$75)} \\ &= 15,000 \text{ bags} \end{aligned}$$

Therefore, the company would need to sell 15,000 bags in order to break even.

To see if the formula worked, let's rework the profit equation.

$$\begin{aligned} \text{Profit} &= PY - (VC)Y - TFC \\ &= (\$125)(15,000) - (\$75)(15,000) - \$750,000 \\ &= \$1,875,000 - \$1,125,000 - \$750,000 \\ \text{Profit} &= \$0 \end{aligned}$$

If the company sells the 20,000 bags estimated in its marketing plan, how will it do?

$$\begin{aligned} \text{Profit} &= PY - (VC)Y - TFC \\ &= (\$125)(20,000) - (\$75)(20,000) - \$750,000 \\ &= \$2,500,000 - \$1,500,000 - \$750,000 \\ \text{Profit} &= \$250,000 \end{aligned}$$

If the company sells the 20,000 bags anticipated in its marketing plan, its profit will be $250,000. By using break-even analysis, the managers of the seed company know that the firm's sales can be as much as 25 percent below expectations before they start losing money. This information makes it easier for managers to assess their chances for success.

Allocation of Contribution between Overhead and Profit

Another way to look at this example is to note that the profit level at the expected sales level (20,000 bags) is equal to the contribution per bag times the number of bags sold above the break-even point ($50 × 5,000 = $25,000). A graph can help explain this relationship (figure 12-4).

As output increases, so do the levels of total variable costs and total costs, with the difference being the total fixed costs. Contribution also grows with expanding output, as each additional bag sold pays off another $50 of fixed costs until they are completely paid off at the break-even point. Once past the 15,000-bag break-even point, all fixed costs have been paid and any additional contributions are made exclusively to profits. When sales are 20,000 bags, profit is equal to the contribution per bag times 5,000 (the number of bags over the break-even point).

Figure 12-4 Break-Even Chart Showing Contribution to Profit

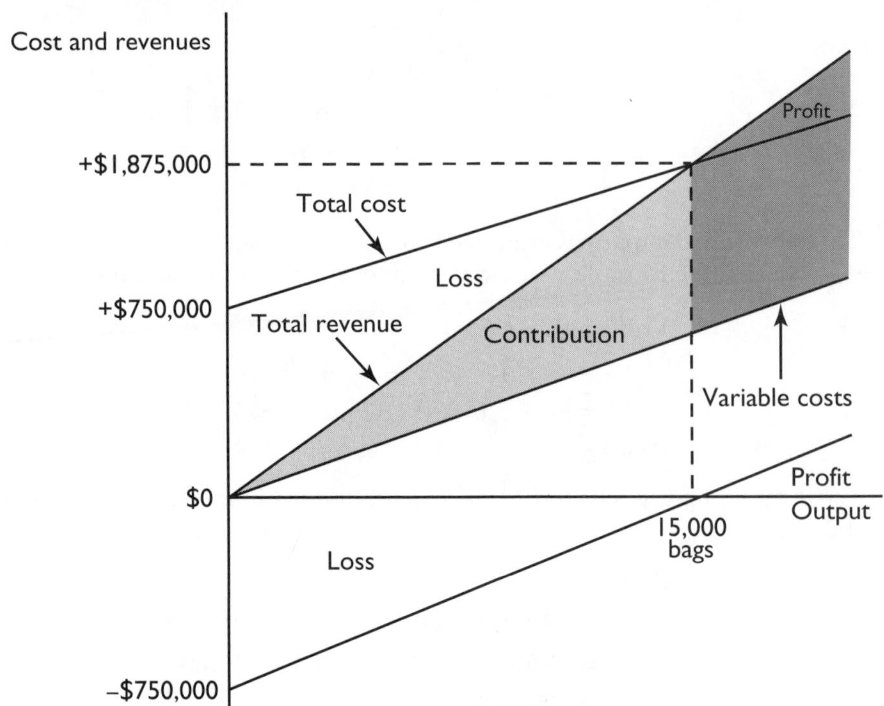

Calculating the Break-Even Point in Dollars

In some cases, it may be more useful to determine the break-even point in dollars rather than units. The formula is much the same, except the denominator is the **contribution margin percentage *(CMP)***. CMP is the percent of the selling price per unit that is contributed to paying off the overhead. The formula to break even in this case is

$$BEP\$ = \frac{TFC}{CMP}$$

Where TFC = total fixed costs
CMP = contribution margin percentage
$BEP\$$ = break-even point in dollars

Another perspective is to ask what level of dollar sales is necessary for the amount being contributed to fixed costs ($BEP\$ \times CMP$) to be equal to the fixed costs?

Applying this formula to the seed example gives

$$BEP\$ = \frac{\$750{,}000}{0.40}$$
$$= \$1{,}875{,}000$$

Therefore, the break-even point in dollars is $1,875,000.

Or, in order to achieve a break-even point in sales, we could ask the following question: 40 percent (or the *CMP*) of what level of dollar sales is equal to the amount of the company's total fixed costs ($750,000)? We can answer this question by multiplying the *CMP* by the *BEP$* (0.40 × $1,875,000 = $750,000).

If a manager wishes to convert this answer to bags, he or she should divide the *BEP$* by *P* (the selling price per unit):

$$\frac{\$1,875,000}{\$125/\text{bag}} = 15,000 \text{ bags}$$

Note that this gives the same answer as before. The break-even point can be calculated in units or dollars, depending on which form is most appropriate.

Meeting a Profit as a Percentage of Sales Objective

Sometimes a manager is provided with a profit objective that is defined as a percentage of sales. The break-even point can be calculated most easily in terms of sales percentage by adjusting the dollar-sales equation above.

For example, if the objective is to have a profit equal to 10 percent of sales before a firm enters a market, the minimum level of sales required to meet that objective can be calculated by subtracting the required profit percentage (*RPP*) from the denominator. The revised formula is

$$BEP\$ = \frac{TFC}{(CMP - RPP)}$$

Plugging in the values from the example gives

$$\begin{aligned} BEP\$ &= \frac{\$750,000}{(0.40 - 0.10)} \\ &= \$2,500,000 \end{aligned}$$

If a manager wished to convert this number to bags:

$$\frac{\$2,500,000}{\$125/\text{bag}} = 20,000 \text{ bags}$$

To double check the results, the profit formula is used again.

$$\begin{aligned} \text{Profit} &= PY - (VC)Y - TFC \\ &= (\$125)(20,000) - (\$75)(20,000) - \$750,000 \\ &= \$2,500,000 - \$1,500,000 - \$750,000 \\ \text{Profit} &= \$250,000 \end{aligned}$$

The profit of $250,000 is equal to 10 percent of dollar sales, so the profit objective is met. Annual sales for the firm must be at least $2,500,000 rather than $1,875,000 because of the imposition of the 10 percent profit objective. The managers must assess their chances for selling 20,000 units in this market. Since the sales estimate comes from the marketing plan, the firm is likely to accomplish this profit objective.

Evaluating Changes in Fixed Costs

Break-even analysis can help a manager evaluate changes in fixed costs. One approach is to determine the minimum increase in dollar sales needed to break even for each additional dollar spent on fixed costs. For example, if advertising is considered a fixed expense, a manager might want to know the minimum increase in dollar sales required to recover the costs of a new advertising campaign. This can be determined using the following variation of the break-even formula:

$$\frac{\text{change in fixed costs}}{\text{contribution margin percentage}} = \text{the minimum change in dollar sales needed to break even}$$

Using the seed example (with a contribution margin percentage of 0.40) and assuming a $1.00 increase in advertising costs, gives:

$$\frac{\$1.00}{0.40} = \$2.50$$

Each new dollar spent on advertising raises the break-even level of sales by $2.50. Thus, for advertising to be profitable, sales must increase by at least $2.50 for each dollar spent on advertising. This gives managers a way to objectively measure the effectiveness of the money spent on advertising or any other fixed cost.

This same approach can be applied to a situation in which the firm has a fixed profit objective. For example, if the seed company had decided that it would not enter a new market unless it could achieve a profit of at least $100,000, what is the minimum level of sales needed to realize this goal? If the profit goal is seen as a change in fixed costs, break-even analysis can find the answer.

Where

$$TFC = \$750{,}000$$
$$CMP = 0.40$$
$$\text{Profit goal } (PG) = \$100{,}000$$

$$\begin{aligned} BEP\$ &= \frac{TFC + PG}{CMP} \\ &= \frac{\$750{,}000 + \$100{,}000}{0.40} \\ &= \$2{,}125{,}000 \end{aligned}$$

To convert to bags:

$$\frac{\$2{,}125{,}000}{\$125} = 17{,}000 \text{ bags}$$

Testing this using the profit formula shows

$$\begin{aligned}\text{Profit} &= PY-(VC)Y-TFC\\ &= (\$125)(17{,}000)-(\$75)(17{,}000)-\$750{,}000\\ &= \$2{,}125{,}000-\$1{,}275{,}000-\$750{,}000\\ \text{Profit} &= \$100{,}000\end{aligned}$$

To meet the fixed profit objective of $100,000, it requires sales of at least $2,125,000, or 17,000 bags. This answer must be compared to the sales estimate and financial objectives given in the business plan to assess the chances for success.

Determining a Selling Price

Break-even analysis can be used to find a selling price that is consistent with a set of costs and expected sales. If any two of these values are known, it is possible to find the third.

Remember

$$\text{contribution} = \text{selling price per unit} - \text{variable costs per unit}$$

Rearranging the terms gives

$$\text{selling price per unit} = \text{contribution} + \text{variable costs per unit}$$

Hence, if the variable costs per unit are known, all that is needed to determine the corresponding selling price is the level of contribution.

Contribution can be determined by rearranging the terms of the break-even equation so

$$\text{contribution} = \frac{TFC}{Y}$$

Using the values from the seed example in the preceding section and applying them to the modified formula gives

$$\begin{aligned}\text{contribution per bag} &= \frac{TFC+PG}{Y}\\ &= \frac{\$750{,}000+\$100{,}000}{17{,}000}\\ &= \$50\\ \text{selling price per bag} &= \text{contribution per bag} + \text{variable costs per bag}\\ &= \$50+\$75\\ &= \$125\end{aligned}$$

A selling price of $125 per bag is needed for the firm to reach its $100,000 profit objective given the firm's costs and estimated sales.

If the business wishes to achieve its original sales objective of 20,000 bags, it will need a contribution of

$$\frac{\$750,000+\$100,000}{20,000}=\$42.50\,/\,\text{bag}$$

The selling price that corresponds to this level of contribution is

$$\begin{aligned}\text{selling price} &= \$42.50 + \$75\\ &= \$117.50 \text{ per bag}\end{aligned}$$

The managers need to compare this price with the one estimated in the marketing plan ($125). If the financial objective was a minimum profit of $100,000, they will be happy to see that they can achieve this at the lower price.

This procedure gives agribusiness managers a way to quickly test a variety of relationships between price, costs, profit, and quantity. It is possible to find any one of these values when the others are known. For example, if the selling price in the example had been above the selling price determined by marketing research, it is possible to test various changes in costs to determine a selling price that is consistent with the other values. In this instance, it means looking for ways to lower the total fixed costs or variable costs per unit. By using planning tools such as break-even analysis, managers have the ability to see the consequences of their decisions before they are implemented. Once a satisfactory solution is found, it also establishes cost standards managers can use to carry out their controlling function.

Inventory Management

Up to this point, the discussion has assumed that businesses produce just what they need to meet demand and then sell it immediately. This makes explaining concepts such as production management a good deal easier, but it hardly reflects the way most agribusinesses operate. Agribusinesses hold inventories for a number of good reasons.

Reasons to Hold Inventory

- ***Match Supply with Demand.*** In agribusiness, the supply of many commodities is seasonal (only one crop per year is produced for things such as corn and wheat), but demand is year-round. This mismatch forces someone, either producers or processors, to hold inventories. The reverse is also true. Demand can be seasonal but supply may be year-round. The best example is Christmas trees.
- ***Stockout Prevention.*** Businesses often hold inventory to ensure that they always have important parts for production or products on hand for sale. Not having these items can lead to plant shutdowns, lost customer sales, higher costs, and lower profits.
- ***Lower Purchasing Costs.*** Firms typically find that they can lower costs per unit by purchasing large quantities per order and holding inventory. This

reduces the number of orders placed each year and allows the firm to take advantage of quantity discounts and lower transportation costs (full truckload orders cost less to ship than partial truckloads). If an item is produced within the firm, large production runs lead to lower costs per unit.

Reasons Not to Hold Inventory

- *High Maintenance Costs.* If an inventory is held, a physical location must be found and an opportunity cost will be incurred. In addition, people must be found to count, weigh, transport, and maintain the inventory.
- *High Protection Costs.* Inventory requires security and insurance to protect the firm from loss due to weather damage, fire, flood, theft, and other hazards.
- *Depreciation and Obsolescence.* For agricultural commodities and food products that are perishable this means maintaining the quality of the product.
- *Taxes.* In some places, businesses pay a tax on the value of their inventories.

It is estimated that inventory **carrying costs** amount to 20 to 30 percent of the value of the inventory.

The Value of Good Inventory Management

Good inventory management is vital to every firm's bottom line. If an agribusiness firm has an inventory worth $100,000, a profit margin on sales of 5 percent, and inventory carrying costs of 25 percent, it costs $25,000 per year just to hold and maintain the inventory. Each $1,000 reduction in inventory adds $250 to profits. This is equivalent to increasing sales by $5,000 ($5,000 × 0.05 = $250). Cutting inventory in half would raise profits by $12,500 and would be equivalent to raising sales by $250,000. Thus, a real incentive exists to keep inventories low.

However, if inventories are kept too low, firms run the risk of losing sales because of stockouts and having lower profits from higher operating costs. The objective of good inventory management is to keep costs low while keeping customer satisfaction high. In an ideal world, this means holding only those items that are needed and just enough to meet demand.

Supply Chain Management

Inventory management has made great strides towards achieving this goal. Technological advances in information technology (IT) make it possible for managers to get the MIS data they need in time and in the form they need to make effective inventory management decisions. Armed with these facts, they can seek greater coordination and cooperation from all of the firms they do business with, from input suppliers to retailers. By working together and sharing expected consumer demand and production schedules, everyone in the global agri-food system can reduce the levels of their inventories. This process is called **supply chain management**.

Supply chain management started by employing just-in-time inventory management systems, in which suppliers guarantee delivery of needed inputs according to a precise schedule given by the user. In the food business, this means that supermarkets can devote less space to inventory and more space to selling. For many items, what is delivered goes right on the shelves. It is estimated that the entire inventory of a supermarket is replenished every 72 hours. However, this system led to suppliers holding larger inventories so they would not be subject to stockouts. To overcome this problem, suppliers needed the same customer demand information that retailers had. This need rippled back through the agri-food system. Information technology gives everyone, all the way back to the raw input suppliers, the opportunity to have access to the same information, in the same form, and at the same time as the retailer. Possession of this information allows everyone to reduce the uncertainty surrounding future demand so they can lower their costs by holding less inventory.

The Basic Inventory Management Model

To help managers better understand the cost relationships involved with inventory management, a basic inventory management model was developed. The total cost of inventory (*TC*) is the sum of **ordering costs (*OC*)** and carrying costs (*CC*). This is represented as

$$TC = CC + OC$$

The goal is to minimize total costs. To accomplish this, a manager needs to determine two things: the **economic order quantity (*EOQ*)**, or the number of items to buy in each order that will minimize total cost, and the **reorder point (*ROP*)**, or when to reorder to minimize the chances for stockouts.

Carrying costs are calculated as a fixed percentage of the dollar value of the average level of inventory.

carrying costs = average inventory level × price/unit × carrying cost percentage

or

$$CC = Q/2 \times P \times C$$

Ordering costs are calculated as the number of orders placed per year times the cost of placing an order. The number of orders placed each year is equal to annual use divided by the amount ordered each time.

ordering costs = annual use/Q × cost of placing an order

or

$$OC = R/Q \times S$$

Total costs of inventory (*TC*) equal the sum of carrying costs and ordering costs

$$\begin{aligned} TC &= CC + OC \\ &= (Q/2)\,PC + (R/Q)S \end{aligned}$$

Determining EOQ. Using this formula, it is possible, through trial and error, to determine the level of Q that keeps TC at a minimum. From table 12-1, it can be seen that TC is at a minimum when Q equals 80 units per order. Therefore, in this case the EOQ is 80. When this relationship it placed on a graph, it shows that the minimum point on the total costs line occurs when ordering costs are equal to carrying costs (figure 12-5). Table 12-1 also shows this.

Table 12-1 Determination of Total Inventory Cost under Various Levels of Quantity Purchased per Order*

	Q	Carrying Cost (Q/2) × P × C	+	Ordering Cost (R/Q) × S	=	Total Cost CC + OC
	10	$ 10.00		$640.00		$650.00
	20	20.00		320.00		340.00
	30	30.00		213.33		243.33
	40	40.00		160.00		200.00
	50	50.00		128.00		178.00
	60	60.00		106.67		166.67
	70	70.00		91.43		161.43
	79	79.00		81.01		160.01
EOQ	80	80.00		80.00		160.00
	81	81.00		79.01		160.01
	90	90.00		71.11		161.11
	100	100.00		64.00		164.00

*P = $10/unit; C = 20% per year; R = 320 units/year; S = $20/order.

Knowing this piece of information, it is possible to solve directly for Q (the EOQ) that will give the lowest total costs. Setting carrying costs equal to ordering costs and solving for Q does this.

$$CC = OC$$
$$(Q/2)PC = (R/Q)S$$
$$(QPC)/2 = (RS)/Q$$
$$Q^2PC = 2RS$$
$$Q^2 = 2RS/PC$$
$$Q = \sqrt{2RS/PC}$$

Q equals the EOQ and TC is minimized.

Reworking the example presented in table 12-1 and figure 12-5 yields

$$\begin{aligned} Q &= \sqrt{2RS/PC} \\ &= \sqrt{2(320)(20)/(10)(0.20)} \\ &= \sqrt{12,800/2} \\ &= 80 \text{ units per order} \end{aligned}$$

Determining ROP. Now that the question of how much to order each time has been answered, it is time to decide when to place an order so the costs of stockouts are minimized. This is done by determining the average use per day and combining it with how long it takes to get an order. The *ROP* is given by

$$ROP = (\text{annual use}/360 \text{ days}) \times (\text{number of days to get an order})$$

Figure 12-5 Total Cost, Ordering Costs, and Carrying Costs of Inventory at Various Levels of Quantity Requested per Order

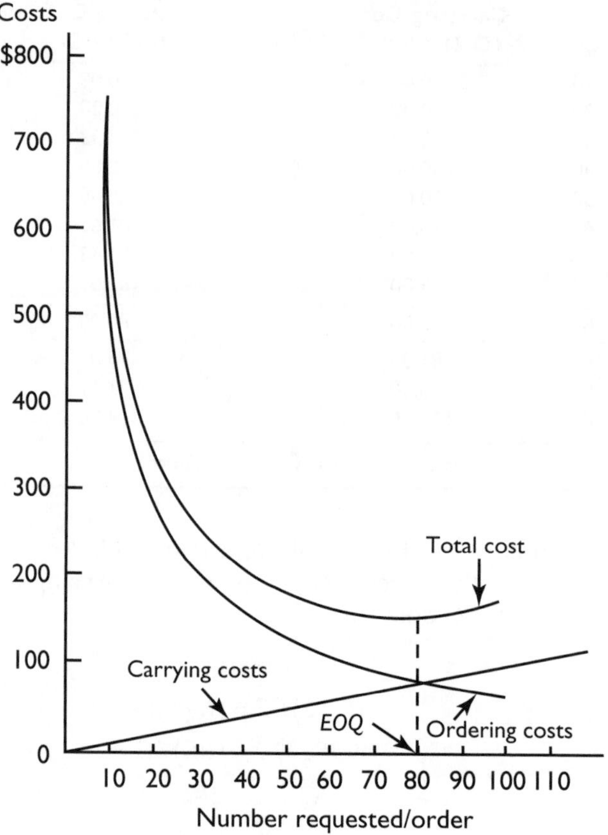

Continuing the previous example, in which annual use was 320 units, if it takes 21 days to get an order, the *ROP* is

$$\begin{aligned} ROP &= (320/360) \times 21 \\ &= 0.888 \times 21 \\ &= 18.7 \text{ units} \end{aligned}$$

When 19 units (18.7 rounded up to the next whole number) are left in inventory, the firm should place an order for 80 more units (its *EOQ*) to minimize its total cost of inventory.

Words of Caution. The inventory management model developed here includes a number of assumptions that are difficult to find outside of a textbook. These include the assumptions that all usage rates, lead times, and costs are known and never vary. This model is used here because of its simplicity and ability to show the trade-offs and relationships surrounding inventory management. Most firms' inventory management procedures are far more complex than what is presented here but are based on these principles. Because profit margins in agribusiness are small and inventory costs are large, managers must not overlook this area when seeking better production control.

Chapter Highlights

1. Agribusiness managers need to understand the cost relationships and procedures that surround production so they can better manage their business's production process and make more effective production decisions that will permit the firm to realize its financial objectives.
2. A management information system helps managers get accurate and timely production and cost information on all phases of the business. MIS enables agribusiness managers to carry out the controlling management function so they can get the feedback they need to monitor and evaluate the firm's progress toward the goals set in the planning function.
3. The term cost has many meanings. Managers need to know and understand the differences between opportunity, implicit, and explicit costs and how they can affect pricing.
4. Agribusiness managers need to know how to use incremental analysis in decision making. This includes understanding why avoidable costs are included in a decision and sunk costs are not.
5. To gain control of costs, a manager must have accurate data and understand how costs behave when production levels vary.
6. Production costs are separated into two categories: fixed and variable costs. Fixed costs do not vary with production levels; variable costs do.
7. Contribution is selling price per unit minus variable costs per unit. The contribution per unit is used to pay off fixed costs before being interpreted as profits.
8. In the short run, a firm with idle capacity can take a job whose price does not cover all costs, so long as the contribution is positive. If the contribution is negative, the firm is better off shutting down.
9. Break-even analysis helps managers find the combination of costs, output, and selling price that permits the firm to break even with no profits or losses.
10. Break-even analysis is a first-stage management tool that helps managers quickly assess their chances for success when the results are compared to those found in the business and marketing plans.
11. The basic inventory management model is a first-stage management tool that helps managers understand the cost relationships that surround holding inventories.
12. The basic inventory management model determines the amount to order each time (*EOQ*) that will minimize the total cost of holding inventory.
13. The reorder point determines when the manager should place an order for new inventory.

CHAPTER QUIZ

1. Explain why an agribusiness manager needs to understand production and inventory management. Give two examples of situations in which cost management makes a difference.
2. Describe the relationship between a firm's accounting system and its management information system. Give a definition for each. Explain which is most important to management.
3. What is opportunity cost? Is it relevant to business decision making? Explain your answer. Give an example that shows its impact.
4. Describe the relationship between implicit and explicit costs. Describe how they are measured. Explain their role in production and pricing decisions in an agribusiness. Use an example to describe how the failure to properly account for these costs can get an agribusiness into trouble.
5. Explain how agribusiness managers use avoidable and sunk costs in their decision making.
6. Why is the decision-making process called incremental analysis?
7. Define economic efficiency and give an example to show how incremental analysis helps firms increase their economic efficiency.
8. Draw a simple graph showing total costs, fixed costs, and variable costs as production increases. Explain why each line looks the way it does.
9. Define the term "contribution" as used in this chapter. Give an example of how it could be used to price a new product.
10. Explain why a firm would take a job that does not give it a chance to make a profit. Explain when it would make sense not to accept this opportunity. Use a numerical example to explain why it is important for a manager to know the difference.
11. Using the break-even equation describe and explain the relationship between costs, selling price, and output. Use a numerical example to make your points.
12. Describe and explain the importance of good inventory management to a firm's overall objective of maximizing its long-term profits.
13. What is the role of supply chain management and information technology in inventory management? Use a numerical example to support your answer.
14. Some feel that supply chain management is responsible for much of our recent economic prosperity. Do you agree? Explain.
15. How do effective managers use their management information systems to improve the profitability of their firms?
16. Explain why incremental analysis is a good decision-making tool when it does not look at all of the costs and income figures in the business in its evaluation.

CASE 12
What Price Progress?*

The lunch rush was finally beginning to let up. It had been a hectic day since opening at 5:30 this morning. Joe, the owner and operator of Joe's Diner for 36 years, was a local institution. Over the years he had been able to survive the many changes in the downtown area, from fast-food restaurants to specialty coffee shops.

As he was cleaning up behind the counter, Joe saw one of his customers who had recently started appearing nearly every day for lunch. He told Joe that he was an accounting efficiency expert who specialized in helping small businesses such as Joe's Diner. Last week he had offered to give the diner a quick once-over at no cost so Joe gave him some basic cost information. The expert said his analysis was done and asked Joe to pull up on the stool next to him.

Efficiency Expert: Joe, let's start with this peanut rack right here. You said you put in these peanuts because some people ask for them, but did you realize what this new rack of peanuts is costing you?

Joe: It ain't gonna cost much. It's *gonna* be pure profit. See, I had to pay $75 for the fancy rack to hold the bags, but the peanuts cost only 25 cents a bag and I sell 'em for 50 cents. The students, they love peanuts, and they'll love paying only 50 cents. I figure to sell 50 bags a week to start. It'll take six weeks to cover the cost of the rack. After that, I make a 25-cent profit on each bag. The more I sell, the more I make.

Efficiency Expert: Joe, I'm afraid that your thinking is old and simplistic. It's not 1965 anymore. Fortunately, modern accounting procedures permit a more accurate picture that reveals the complexities involved.

Joe: Huh?

Efficiency Expert: To be precise, those peanuts must be integrated into your entire operation and be allocated their appropriate share of business overhead. They must share a proportionate part of your expenditures for rent, heat, light, equipment depreciation, decorating, salaries for your waitresses and cook. . . .

Joe: The cook! What's *he* gotta do with the peanuts? He doesn't even know I got 'em!

Efficiency Expert: Joe, I know you've been in business for almost 40 years, which is probably a record around here. But look, the cook is in the kitchen, the kitchen prepares the food, the food is what brings people in here, and the people ask to buy the peanuts. That's why you must charge a portion of the cook's wages, as well as a part of your own salary, to the peanut sales. This spreadsheet I have here contains a carefully calculated cost analysis that indicates the peanut operation should pay exactly $6,390 per year toward these general overhead costs.

*This is an updated version of a case found in W. W. Haynes and W. R. Henry, *Managerial Economics*, Third Edition (1974), page 50. They reprinted it from *Lybrand Journal*, whose editors told them, "We have been unable to locate the source of this paper. If any of our readers can provide us with this information, we shall be delighted to acknowledge our indebtedness." We would be happy to do the same.

Joe: You're nuts! $6,390 a year for overhead? The peanuts?

Efficiency Expert: It's really a little more than that. You also spend money each week to have the windows washed, to have the place swept out in the morning, keep soap in the washroom, and provide free Cokes to the police. That raises the total to $6,550 per year.

Joe (thoughtfully): But the peanut salesman said I'd make money. . . . Put 'em on the counter, he said . . . and get 25 cents a bag profit. . . .

Efficiency Expert (with a smirk): He's not an accountant. Do you actually know what the portion of the counter occupied by the peanut rack is worth to you?

Joe: It ain't worth nothing . . . no stool there . . . just a dead spot at the end.

Efficiency Expert (with pity): Joe, Joe, Joe. The modern cost picture permits no dead spots. Your counter contains 60 square feet and your counter business grosses $75,000 a year. Consequently, the square foot of space occupied by the peanut rack is worth $1,250 per year. Since you have taken that area away from general counter use, you must charge the value of the space to the occupant.

Joe: You mean I gotta add $1,250 a year more to the peanuts?

Efficiency Expert: Right, now you're thinking. That raises the general operating costs to a grand total of $7,800 per year. Now then, if you sell 50 bags of peanuts per week, these allocated costs will amount to $3.00 per bag.

Joe: What?!?

Efficiency Expert: To that total, we must add the purchase price of 25 cents per bag, which brings the total to $3.25 per bag. So you see, by selling peanuts for 50 cents per bag, you're losing $2.75 on every sale.

Joe: Something's crazy! Either you or me, and I don't think it's me!

Efficiency Expert: Joe, it's all here in black and white. My figures prove your peanut operation cannot stand on its own feet.

Joe (brightening): Suppose I sell *lotsa* peanuts . . . a thousand bags a week instead of 50.

Efficiency Expert (tolerantly): Joe, you don't understand the problem. If the volume of peanut sales increases, our operating costs go up. No, I'm afraid increasing the volume of sales won't help.

Joe: Okay. You're so smart, you tell me what I gotta do.

Efficiency Expert (condescendingly): Well . . . you could first reduce operating expenses—move to a building with cheaper rent, cut staff salaries, wash windows only biweekly, decrease the square footage of your counter. That way, you'll reduce the amount allocated to the peanuts. If you cut operating costs by 50 percent, you can reduce the sale price of peanuts to $2.00 per bag.

Joe: That's nuts. Who's gonna buy 'em at that price?

Efficiency Expert: That's not the issue.

Joe: Look . . . I gotta better idea. Forget the peanuts. I'll put 'em in the trash can.

Efficiency Expert: Joe, it isn't that simple. You're in the peanut business now! Throwing the peanuts out adds to your overhead. You really can't afford to do that.

Joe: It's unbelievable. Last week I was making money. Now I'm in trouble . . . just because I think peanuts on the counter is gonna bring in some extra profit.

Efficiency Expert: Joe, my friend, that is the object of modern cost studies: to dispel the false illusion of financial success.

Is Joe making any money on the peanuts by selling them for 50 cents a bag? What is the incremental cost and revenue for each bag of peanuts?

If someone offered Joe the opportunity to sell gum at that same spot on the counter, how would he decide if he would make more money doing that than selling peanuts? If the counter area used for the peanut sales is a dead spot because there is no stool, how does this change the analysis?

Is Joe handling the cost of the peanut rack correctly? Will he really be making a profit of 25 cents on every bag once the rack is paid for?

Evaluate the expert's argument that each product sold must cover its fair share of the diner's overhead.

Chapter 13

Basic Accounting Documents

Chapter Learning Objectives

- Explain why managers must understand balance sheets and profit-and-loss statements in order to evaluate the financial performance of their businesses and to establish whether the business is meeting the financial objectives set in planning.
- Describe the functions of an accounting system.
- Explain the accounting equation (assets equal liabilities plus owners' equity).
- Explain how a balance sheet is organized.
- Explain how a profit-and-loss statement is organized.
- Identify when a business is solvent or insolvent, and when it might file for bankruptcy.
- Describe how profit-and-loss statements are related to balance sheets.

Introduction

Accounting records are the foundation of an agribusiness's controlling function because money is the common denominator for just about everything a firm does. If a business undertakes a new product or service or builds a new plant, the costs and returns from these decisions are measured in dollars. The two basic accounting documents discussed in this chapter are the primary ways an agribusiness measures its financial performance. In order to understand how well the firm is doing, a manager must understand balance sheets and profit-and-loss statements, which are the starting points for most other forms of financial analysis. The information found in these two documents enables owners and managers to determine if a business is meeting the financial objectives set in planning.

This task is made easier since accountants follow a uniform set of generally accepted accounting principles when developing these documents. Learning to read and understand one set of financial statements makes it fairly easy to follow those of any other firm. A good analogy is that accountants are like the official scorer in a baseball game. While they do not play, they know the rules of the game and how to keep score. In order to make comparisons easier, all the teams play by the same rules and keep score the same way. Thus, **accounting** is nothing more than the process of recording, classifying, and summarizing business transactions according to generally accepted accounting principles.

A firm's accounting system performs several functions:

- It must present an accurate picture of the firm's current profitability.
- It must give an estimate of the firm's current and future financial position.
- It must provide input to the firm's MIS, which gives managers the information they need for day-to-day decision making.

- It must provide an accurate record of past financial performance for owners and tax collectors, as well as other kinds of reporting required by local, state, and federal government officials.

Profits and losses are computed for a given period of time, whether for one month, six months, or one year. This time span is known as the **accounting period**. For tax purposes, the accounting period is normally one year. The fiscal year does not have to coincide with the calendar year; the fiscal year for the federal government, for example, is October 1 to September 30. Because of the seasonality of their work, many agribusinesses use July 1 to June 30 as their fiscal year because it represents the end of their seasonal business cycle.

THE BALANCE SHEET

The **balance sheet** is a statement of the financial condition of a business on a specific date. A number of metaphors have been used to explain the role of the balance sheet. Some have characterized it as a snapshot of how a business looks at one point in time. Others have referred to it as a physician's checkup. It tells something about the health of a business on a given day. However, its health can change quickly with the passage of time.

Basic Setup

A balance sheet for the AgBiz Corporation for December 31 is shown in figure 13-1. It represents AgBiz's financial condition on that date and only that date. A statement prepared one month later or earlier may show the financial health of AgBiz to be very different from what is shown on December 31. This can happen especially in an agribusiness in which sales and revenues are highly seasonal. A balance sheet should be prepared at least once a year, usually at the end of the fiscal year. Statements may be prepared more often depending on the size and complexity of the business and the needs of management.

A balance sheet is arranged to reflect what would happen if the business ended that day, sold all of its assets, paid off all of its debts, and gave what is left to its owners. To do this, the firm needs to separate things into two piles. The first pile includes all of the things the firm has and owns. The items in this pile are called **assets**. Each asset is assumed to sell for what it cost the firm to acquire it or for its current fair market value, whichever is lower. The second pile includes all the firm's debts. Items in this pile are called **liabilities**. It is assumed that all the liabilities are paid in full. What is left is given to the owners. The leftovers are called **owners' equity, net worth,** or **stockholders' equity**. If the assets are greater than the liabilities, owners' equity is positive and the business is **solvent**. If the assets are less than the liabilities, owners' equity is negative and the business is **insolvent**, and could file for bankruptcy.

Accountants have modified this idea (assets – liabilities = owners' equity) to create balance sheets. In the balance sheet, liabilities are moved to the other side of the equal sign, giving the **accounting equation**:

Assets = Liabilities + Owners' Equity

On a balance sheet, assets are found in the left-hand column and liabilities and owners' equity are found in the right-hand column, reflecting the accounting equation. The total of the left-hand column will always equal, or balance, the total of the right-hand column. Hence, this document is called the balance sheet. Let's take a closer look at the items that make up each of the three major categories.

Figure 13-1 Sample Balance Sheet

Balance Sheet
AgBiz Corporation
December 31, 20__

Assets		
Current assets:		
Cash	$ 17,000	
Accounts receivable	30,000	
Inventories	127,000	
Total current assets		$ 174,000
Fixed assets:		
Land	250,000	
Buildings and equipment	660,000	
Less allowance for depreciation	170,000	
Total fixed assets		740,000
Other investments:		
Cash value of life insurance	6,600	
Investment in stock in other companies	24,400	
Investment in subsidiary	75,000	
Total other investments		106,000
Total assets		1,020,000
Liabilities and Owners' Equity		
Current liabilities:		
Accounts and notes payable	$ 53,000	
Accrued taxes payable	1,750	
Installments due this year on long-term debt	35,200	
Total current liabilities		89,950
Long-term liabilities:		
Long-term notes payable		320,050
Total liabilities		410,000
Owners' equity:		
Capital stock	390,500	
Retained earnings, January 1	177,200	
Net income for the year	42,300	
Retained earnings, December 31	219,500	
Total owners' equity		610,000
Total liabilities and owners' equity		$1,020,000

Assets

An asset is something of value a firm owns or uses. It is expected to provide future benefits to the firm, usually by contributing to sales, and its value is measured in dollars. Assets can be tangible (inventory or equipment) or intangible (such as patents or goodwill associated with the firm's past performance).

Not all assets are equal. The value of an asset such as cash is very specific. The value of someone's debt to the firm may be harder to define because of the potential for default. Assets are divided into two classes based on their liquidity, or when they can be converted into cash. The most liquid assets, current assets, appear first on the balance sheet.

Current Assets. A **current asset** is either cash or an item that will become cash within the accounting period. Cash, accounts receivable, and inventories are typically part of this class of assets. The level of current assets is important to the business because it measures the amount of money the firm expects to have in the coming accounting period to pay its bills.

Cash is a current asset since it can be used immediately to pay debts. In the example, AgBiz cannot be 100 percent sure it has $17,000 available because this total may include some checks that could turn out to be worthless; thus, even the cash account is to some degree an estimate.

Accounts receivable is debts that others owe the business, usually arising from previous credit sales. They are listed as a current asset because it is expected that they will be paid within the next accounting period (usually one year). Most businesses have an adjustment for bad debts in its accounts receivable account to reflect sales for which it will never collect any money. Bad debts, while a reality of doing business, should be kept as small as possible because they can reduce profits dramatically.

Inventories are goods that are expected to be sold during the coming accounting period. Inventories include finished goods that are ready for sale but also can include goods in process, such as growing plants (in the case of a greenhouse) or grain in storage that will be made into feed (in the case of a feed mill). The actual value of items in inventory may not be known until they are sold. For example, AgBiz management hopes to sell the listed inventory for $127,000, but there is no way to tell the exact amount it will bring during the next year.

Fixed Assets. A **fixed asset** is something the firm owns or uses that will not turn into cash within the next accounting period. Fixed assets include things such as property, buildings, and equipment. These assets provide benefit to the firm for more than one accounting period. Except for land, which accountants assume never wears out, fixed assets are assumed to depreciate over many periods. Their value to the business diminishes over time.

The rules accountants work under lead them to be very conservative in placing a value on fixed assets. Because of this, fixed assets are placed on the balance sheet at their acquisition cost (less any depreciation) or current market value, whichever is lower. The $740,000 book value (the depreciated value shown in the balance sheet in figure 13-1) on fixed assets held by the corporation may or may not reflect their current market value if they are sold on December 31. The land may have tripled in value since it was acquired, but it goes on the balance sheet at the price paid by the firm or at the price it would bring today, whichever is less. Equipment, on the other hand, may be worth less than the book value shown on the balance sheet because of technological change.

Other Investments. The last category of assets is other investments. This section includes investments made outside the normal business of the firm. In the example, the other investments include the cash value of life insurance the firm maintains on some key employees, stock investments in other companies, and money invested in a subsidiary firm. These assets are grouped this way so they can be separated out for financial evaluations that concern only the firm's primary line of business.

Liabilities

A liability is an obligation to pay a debt. Just like assets, liabilities can be classified as either current or long term, based on when they must be paid.

Current Liabilities. A **current liability** is a debt that must be paid within the next accounting period. Examples of current liabilities are accounts payable, **principal** and interest payments on long-term debt that are payable during the next accounting period, and taxes.

Long-Term Liabilities. A **long-term liability** is a debt whose payments will be made after the next accounting period. Examples of long-term liabilities are mortgage payments, leases on equipment or machinery that extend beyond one year, and loans that extend beyond one year.

Owners' Equity

Owners' equity is also called net worth because it is the difference between a firm's assets and its liabilities. In a sole proprietorship or partnership it is called owners' equity because of the way the firm is structured. In a corporation it is referred to as stockholder equity. Owners' equity should include the value of the owners' investment in the firm plus net **retained earnings**.

The Profit-and-Loss Statement

The second major financial document is the **profit-and-loss statement**. It summarizes the revenue and expenses of a business over a given period of time. If revenues exceed expenses, the firm made a profit. If expenses are greater than revenues, the result is a loss. Profit is sometimes referred to as **net income**. Thus, a profit-and-loss statement (P&L statement) is also called an income statement. The choice of names is based on personal preference because the purpose and concept of the document is the same under either label. Just like balance sheets, the arrangement of the items on profit-and-loss statements follows a fixed format.

Revenue

Revenue, or sales, is the first item on a profit-and-loss statement. It represents the amount of money the firm earned from the sale of its goods and services during the current accounting period.

Cost of Goods Sold

The second item on a P&L statement is cost of goods sold. It is shown as "less: cost of goods sold" since it is deducted from revenue. Cost of goods sold represents the direct costs to the business of producing the goods that were sold to generate the revenue reported during that accounting period. It does not include all the production costs of the firm during this period. It includes only the cost of the items that were sold during this accounting period. (Items that were produced but not sold are accounted for in the inventory value found on the balance sheet.)

In most businesses the cost of goods sold is the largest expense item—one reason why cost of goods sold is reported separately. (Another reason is that it equals the total variable cost of production.) Since the cost of goods sold represents only the cost of the items that were actually sold during a particular accounting period, it can be determined indirectly. The cost of goods sold is the difference between what the firm had available for sale in inventory at the start of the period (plus any additions) and what was left in inventory at the end of the accounting period. Using the values from figure 13-2 as an example, the cost of goods sold for this period for AgBiz is:

Beginning inventory	$ 151,000
+ Inventory purchases this period	+ 1,105,000
Total goods available for sale this period	1,256,000
– Ending inventory	– 127,000
Cost of goods sold this period	$1,129,000

A wholesale or retail business such as a grocery or farm supply store buys its goods specifically for resale. The sum of these costs plus transportation charges constitutes the full cost of goods for their products. On the other hand, a manufacturing firm such as a feed mill should include the costs of raw materials, transportation costs, and labor costs for transforming the raw ingredients into feed ready for sale in its cost of goods sold.

Gross Margin

Gross margin, or gross profit, is what remains after subtracting cost of goods sold from revenues. Gross margin shows the income that remains to cover **operating expenses** (overhead). Gross margin is equivalent to contribution (see chapter 12).

Operating Expenses

The general costs of operating and administering the business outside of the direct costs of goods sold are included in the operating expenses. These costs also are referred to as overhead or fixed costs. It includes the manager's salary, rent,

Figure 13-2 Sample Profit-and-Loss Statement

Profit-and-Loss Statement
AgBiz Corporation
for the Year Ending December 31, 20__

Revenue from sales		$1,465,000
Less: Cost of goods sold		
Inventory, January 1	$ 151,000	
Plus: Goods purchased	1,105,000	
Cost of goods available for sale	1,256,000	
Less: Inventory, December 31	127,000	
Total cost of goods sold		1,129,000
Gross margin		336,000
Less: Operating expenses		
Salaries and wages	140,000	
Office expenses	3,400	
Selling and promotion	72,000	
Utilities and fuel	44,600	
Rent	5,000	
Depreciation	20,000	
Total operating expenses		285,000
Income before taxes		51,000
Allowances for income taxes		8,700
Net income (to retained earnings)		$ 42,300

salespersons' salaries, and anything else involved in operating the business that is not directly associated with the sale of particular products.

Profit and Net Profit

Profit is the famous bottom line that managers talk about. Profit is equal to gross margin minus operating expenses. **Net profit** is profit left after income taxes have been paid; in other words, what is actually available for the business. Net income can be returned to the owners as dividends or reinvested in the business. Reinvested funds are called **retained earnings**. They are added to owners' equity on the balance sheet. (In the AgBiz example, the $42,300 of retained earnings on the P&L statement in figure 13-2 is added to the owners' equity category of the balance sheet in figure 13-1.)

Chapter Highlights

1. Accounting records are the foundation of an agribusiness's controlling function.
2. Balance sheets and the profit-and-loss statements are the starting points of most financial analysis.

3. In order to understand a business's financial performance, a manager must understand its balance sheet and profit-and-loss statement.
4. Because these documents are constructed according to general accounting principles, managers who can read one set of these documents should find it easy to follow those of any other firm.
5. A business is solvent if the value of its assets minus the value of its liabilities (net worth or owners' equity) is positive. If net worth is negative, the business is insolvent and could file for bankruptcy.
6. Balance sheets utilize the accounting equation (assets = liabilities + owners' equity) so that the total of the left-hand column (assets) always equals the right-hand column (liabilities and owners' equity).
7. Current assets are either cash or items that will become cash within the next accounting period.
8. Current liabilities are debts that must be paid during the next accounting period.
9. Profit-and-loss statements summarize the revenue and expenses of a business over a given period of time. It records revenues earned and expenses incurred for the current accounting period.
10. The cost of goods sold is calculated indirectly by measuring total goods available for sale during the period and then subtracting ending inventory.
11. Categories on profit-and-loss statements generally follow the fixed and variable cost scheme developed in earlier chapters.
12. Retained earnings from the profit-and-loss statement are transferred onto the balance sheet in the owners' equity category.

Chapter Quiz

1. Explain why it is important for managers to understand financial management in order to be effective. Why does this process start with the balance sheet and the profit-and-loss statement?
2. Describe the balance sheet and what it tells managers. What does it not tell managers about their businesses?
3. Describe the profit-and-loss statement and what it tells managers about their businesses.
4. Explain why the accounting period and the fiscal year may not coincide with the calendar year.
5. Explain the difference between current and fixed assets on the balance sheet. Why are they arranged this way?
6. Describe the depreciation process used by accountants and why accountants use it.
7. Explain when a business is solvent and insolvent. Develop an example for an agribusiness when it might be solvent in one part of the year and

insolvent in another. Explain why an insolvent business may not need to file for bankruptcy.

8. Explain how to calculate the value of cost of goods sold on a profit-and-loss statement. Explain why this works. What would be an alternative way to calculate cost of goods sold?
9. Explain how you would decide if a cost should be allocated to cost of goods sold or operating expenses. Give an example of each.
10. Define and explain the difference between profit, net profit, and retained earnings. Why are retained earnings transferred to owners' equity on the balance sheet after they are calculated?
11. Which is more important to an agribusiness manager, the balance sheet, or the profit and loss statement? Explain.
12. Critics argue that accounting documents are worth little since they tell managers only about the past. Agree or disagree. Explain.
13. If you have a great accounting system you do not need a management information system. Agree or disagree. Explain.
14. Explain the term depreciation, and how it is accounted for on the balance sheet and profit-and-loss statement.
15. Explain how the accounting equation is formulated.

CASE 13
Fred's Financial Phobia: Part I

Fred Williams was beaming as he surveyed all that lay before him. Here he was, general manager of the newest Smitty's Supermarket—one of the nation's most innovative supermarket chains. The store was a high-tech marvel that employed nearly 500 people and was open 24/7. Things had turned out pretty well for a guy who majored in food science in college. Who would ever have thought that someone who felt nothing but science mattered would find himself as a big-time business manager? At least he was still working in the food business.

His first job out of college was in quality control for a small cheese company. In fact, he was the quality control department. Soon he was production manager for the company. When the cheese company was taken over by Smitty's, Fred was given jobs that moved him further and further from the laboratory. Managing operations turned out to be something he enjoyed. When he saw the job posting for manager of the new store he knew this was his chance to jump full-time into operations. Besides, if he wanted to go higher in the company, he would have to have a successful stint as a store manager on his record.

Smitty's takes an entrepreneurial approach to the operation of each of its 63 stores. Every store operates as a separate business with its own balance sheet and income statement. Managers are given general guidelines to follow by headquarters. Beyond that they are allowed to operate any way they want as long as their stores meet their financial goals each month. Accounting is one area of business where Fred feels unsure of himself. He turns to you to answer his questions in this area.

What is the difference between an income statement and a balance sheet? Which one is more important to a manager? Why?

What is the difference between the inventory on the balance sheet and the cost of goods sold on the profit-and-loss statement? Which one is more important to a manager? Why?

Chapter 14

Using Accounting Information for Business Control and Planning

Chapter Learning Objectives

- Demonstrate how to use balance sheets and profit-and-loss statements to evaluate the financial performance of an agribusiness.
- Explain how to analyze basic accounting documents using comparative statement analysis, net working capital analysis, and ratio analysis.
- Demonstrate how to develop and use a pro forma cash flow budget.
- Explain how to develop and use a sources and uses of net working capital statement.
- Summarize how to use the information in basic accounting documents to accomplish the controlling management function.

Introduction

The value of an accounting system does not rest solely on the accuracy of its record keeping. Although this is an important function, the greatest value of the accounting system to the managers and owners of an agribusiness comes from what the data in the balance sheet and profit-and-loss statement can tell them about the financial health and performance of their operation now and into the future.

This chapter is devoted to explaining how the controlling management function can be accomplished using the balance sheet and profit-and-loss statement. It focuses on three main areas of financial analysis: comparative statement analysis, net working capital analysis, and ratio analysis. These three forms of analysis can be performed quickly and easily using the basic accounting concepts developed in chapter 13.

Accounting data also can be used for business planning. The basic data found in balance sheets and profit-and-loss statements combined with the values developed in ratio analysis can be used to forecast future cash needs in a pro forma cash flow budget. Mastery of the four procedures covered in this chapter provides managers with a clearer picture of the financial condition of their firm and helps them chart a successful path for the future.

Comparative Statement Analysis

Comparative statement analysis involves doing just what the name says. Balance sheets and P&L statements from two periods (usually consecutive) are placed side by side and are examined for any significant changes that could affect the financial condition of the firm. Comparative statement analysis is much like a medical checkup. If your doctor finds you have a fever, this does not reveal what is wrong with you but does point out the need for further analysis. The same is true of comparative statement analysis. It generally does not tell managers what is wrong with the financial health of their business, but it does point out areas where further analysis is needed. Each time managers see a large increase or decrease in a value they should put a question mark next to it so they can examine the reasons for the changes in greater detail. This is a simple but very powerful financial analysis tool that helps pinpoint possible problems quickly.

Comparative Balance Sheet Analysis

Balance sheets for the past two years are given for the AgBiz Corporation in figure 14-1 on the following page. To make the analysis easier to follow, two types of comparisons have been made. First, a dollar difference is given for each value for year 2 versus year 1. Second, the difference is given as a percentage. This two-way analysis makes it easier to spot large differences that need further review.

Beginning with current assets, a decrease is found in cash and inventories as well as a 500 percent increase in accounts receivable. Such large shifts in both cash and inventories may signal a decline in the firm's liquidity. The decline may come from the large increase in accounts receivable: if others are not paying their bills to AgBiz, this reduces its available cash. While all three items are cause for concern, it might be wise to mark cash and accounts receivable for further investigation. The fixed assets subcategory (buildings and equipment) increased $160,000 (32 percent). How this expenditure was financed may also have had an impact on AgBiz's liquidity, so it also should be marked for a closer look. The change in the other asset categories is small. Although total assets increased 12 percent ($109,200), most of the increase came from the acquisition of buildings and equipment.

An examination of current liabilities shows an increase of $48,450 (116.7 percent) with most of that coming from the increase in accounts payable and payment on long-term debt. Both items should be marked for investigation since they can affect the firm's liquidity. Total liabilities have risen slightly since last year, and total owners' equity increased by the amount of net income ($42,300). As expected, the rise in total liabilities and owners' equity is exactly equal to the rise in total assets, and the accounting equation (assets = liabilities + owners' equity) holds.

Based on this quick look at comparative balance sheets, it appears that AgBiz is suffering from a liquidity problem. The increase in accounts receivable needs to be examined to determine if the problem is simply a higher level of receivables or if people are paying AgBiz more slowly, or not at all. In any case, this could be the cause of lower cash and inventory and the higher level of accounts payable. The way the firm paid for its new buildings and equipment also may be contributing to its lowered liquidity. Just by examining the comparative balance sheets, a manager can obtain a great deal of information about the financial health of the AgBiz Corporation.

Comparative Profit-and-Loss Statement Analysis

A similar analysis can be performed on the P&L statement found in figure 14-2. The AgBiz Corporation had a great year. It increased its profits 41 percent on a 17.2 percent increase in sales in year 2. This is partly explained by an increase of only 10 percent in cost of goods sold to meet the 17.2 percent rise in sales. However, the 51.6 percent increase in operating expenses absorbed part of these savings.

Figure 14-1 Comparative Balance Sheet

Comparative Balance Sheet
AgBiz Corporation

Account	December 31, Year 1	December 31, Year 2	Difference	Percent Difference
	Assets			
Current assets:				
Cash	$ 49,000	$ 17,000	$ –32,000	–65.3
Accounts receivable	5,000	30,000	+25,000	+500.0
Inventories	151,000	127,000	–24,000	–15.9
Total current assets	$205,000	$ 174,000	$ –31,000	–15.1
Fixed assets:				
Land	250,000	250,000	0	0
Buildings and equipment	500,000	660,000	+160,000	+32.0
Less: Depreciation	–150,000	–170,000	–20,000	–13.3
Total fixed assets	600,000	740,000	$+140,000	+23.3
Other investments:				
Cash value of life insurance	6,400	6,600	+200	+3.1
Investment in other firms	24,400	24,400	0	0.0
Investment in subsidiary	75,000	75,000	0	0.0
Total other	105,800	106,000	+200	+0.2
Total assets	$910,800	$1,020,000	$+109,200	+12.0
	Liabilities and Owners' Equity			
Current liabilities:				
Accounts payable	$ 20,000	$ 53,000	$ +33,000	+165.0
Taxes payable	1,500	1,750	+250	+16.7
Installment on long-term debt due this year	20,000	35,200	+15,200	+76.0
Total current liabilities	41,500	89,950	+48,450	+116.7
Long–term liabilities:				
Long–term notes payable	301,600	320,050	+18,450	+6.1
Total liabilities	$343,100	$ 410,000	$ +66,900	+19.5
Owners' equity:				
Capital stock	390,500	390,500	0	0.0
Retained earnings, January 1	147,200	177,200	+30,000	+20.4
Net income for year	30,000	42,300	+12,300	+41.0
Retained earnings, December 31	$567,700	$ 610,000	$ +42,300	+7.5
Total liabilities and owners' equity	$910,800	$1,020,000	$+109,200	+12.0

Figure 14-2 Comparative Profit-and-Loss Statement

Comparative Profit-and-Loss Statement
AgBiz Corporation

	Year 1	Percent of Sales	Year 2	Percent of Sales	Difference	Percent Difference
Revenue from sales	$1,250,000	100.0	$1,465,000	100.0	$+215,000	+17.2
Less: Cost of goods sold						
Inventory—Jan. 1	100,000		151,000		+51,000	+51.0
+ Goods purchased	+1,077,000		+1,105,000		+28,000	+2.6
Goods available for sale	1,177,000		1,256,000		+79,000	+6.7
– Inventory—Dec. 31	–151,000		–127,000		–24,000	–15.9
Cost of goods sold	1,026,000	82.1	1,129,000	77.1	+103,000	+10.0
Gross margin	224,000	17.9	336,000	22.9	+112,000	+50.0
Less: Operating expenses						
Salaries and wages	100,000	8.0	140,000	9.6	+40,000	+40.0
Office expenses	1,000	0.1	3,400	0.2	+2,400	+240.0
Selling and promotion	38,000	3.0	72,000	4.9	+34,000	+89.5
Utilities and fuel	30,000	2.4	44,600	3.0	+14,600	+48.7
Interest expenses	4,000	0.3	5,000	0.3	+1,000	+25.0
Depreciation	15,000	1.2	20,000	1.4	+5,000	+33.3
Total operating expenses	$ 188,000	15.0	$ 285,000	19.5	$ +97,000	+51.6
Income before taxes	36,000	2.9	51,000	3.5	+15,000	+41.7
Less: Allowance for income taxes	6,000	0.5	8,700	0.6	+2,700	+45.0
Net income (to retained earnings)	$ 30,000	2.4	$ 42,300	2.9	$ +12,300	+41.0

Calculating each item on the statement as a percentage of revenues before looking at year-to-year changes enhances the information derived from comparative P&L statement analysis. In year 1, for each dollar taken in, 82.1 cents was spent on the cost of goods sold ($1,026,000/$1,250,000). This left 17.9 cents to contribute to operating expenses and profits. In year 2, the amount spend on cost of goods sold was reduced to 77.1 cents, leaving a contribution of 22.9 cents for operating expenses and profits. This extra 5 cents per sales dollar may reflect good management.

During this same period, operating expenses rose to 19.5 percent of sales, with the largest portion coming from increases in salaries and wages, selling and promotion costs, utilities, fuel, and depreciation. Because of the size of the percentage and dollar amount of these changes, a second look is warranted for these items.

Moving down the sheet, it can be seen that income before taxes rose to 3.5 percent of sales from 2.9 percent. The extra operating expenses seem to have been well spent, as net income rose to 2.9 percent of sales from 2.4 percent.

A quick look at the comparative income statement shows that AgBiz managed its significant sales increase quite well. The increase in accounts receivable is large when measured from year to year, but it is still a very small part of total sales (0.4 percent in year 1 and 2 percent in year 2). Nevertheless, a review of accounts receivable policies is in order to be sure that efficient practices are being used. A review of the financing of the growth in buildings and equipment should also be performed to see if it is consuming a great deal of cash each year. Because of the growth of sales, the firm needs to closely manage its cash flow in order to have enough money on hand to meet its bills as they come due. Overall, AgBiz seems to be doing well.

Comparing to Industry Standards

Another way to measure a firm's financial condition and performance is to compare it to industry standards. A good place to obtain industry standard financial performance data is the Risk Management Association's (RMA) *Annual Statement Studies*. (For more information, visit http://www.rmahq.org.)

For example, if we were to compare AgBiz to its competitors using the comparative balance sheet (see figure 14-1), at the end of year 2 AgBiz's current assets were approximately 17 percent of its total assets ($174,000/$1,020,000), while average firms had 62.5 percent of their assets listed as current assets. AgBiz is less liquid than the typical firm in this industry.

At the end of year 2, AgBiz's current liabilities represented 8.8 percent of the total value of liabilities and owners' equity, while the typical firm had current liabilities of 43.3 percent. Thus, the lower liquidity reported for AgBiz for current assets is balanced by fewer obligations on the liability side.

Now, if we were to do a comparison using the comparative P&L statement (see figure 14-2), the gross profit margin for year 2 for AgBiz was 22.9 percent of sales versus a gross profit of 38.2 percent for a typical firm. However, despite this lower gross profit, the AgBiz Corporation had an income before tax of 3.5 percent of sales in year 2 versus a profit before tax for the typical firm in this industry of 2.1 percent. AgBiz's revenue and expenses are different from those found in this industry, but overall it manages them well, as evidenced by its higher profit percentage.

As this discussion illustrates, comparative statement analysis is an efficient and effective tool to evaluate the financial condition of a business, how it changes over time, and how it compares with others in its industry. Comparative statement analysis helps managers identify specific areas of financial performance, such as cash management, that may need improvement and monitoring.

Comparisons with industry standards should be part of the comparative statement process. It is important to know how and why your business differs from others in your industry. Lenders such as banks use references such as RMA's *Annual Statement Studies* in evaluating loan applications. Knowing in advance how your business compares with industry standards can help you anticipate lenders' questions. For those starting a business, such a reference can give entrepreneurs an idea of the levels of profits and sales that should be expected and what the financial requirements are for a particular type of business.

Net Working Capital Analysis

A major concern of agribusiness managers is liquidity—the availability of cash to meet bills as they come due. To ensure adequate liquidity, agribusiness managers monitor their firms' net working capital. **Net working capital (NWC)** is the difference between current assets and current liabilities as expressed on the balance sheet, that is, the amount of cash available to the firm to meet day-to-day and unexpected expenses. Inadequate **working capital** means the firm will have trouble paying its bills, taking advantage of unexpected business opportunities, and meeting emergencies.

To understand the value of net working capital analysis, let's look at the comparative balance sheet for AgBiz in figure 14-1. By using the following formula, we can determine the amount of NWC available for each year:

	current assets	–	current liabilities	=	net working capital
Year 1:	$205,000	–	$41,500	=	$163,500
Year 2:	$174,000	–	$89,950	=	$ 84,050

The NWC position is strong in both years, but it decreased in year 2 by $79,450 ($163,500 – $84,050).

In this case, AgBiz does not appear to be in any kind of danger of being unable to pay its bills since its current assets are nearly twice its current liabilities. However, it is important to know what influences a firm's net working capital so it can be better managed. Let's examine some hypothetical activities and see their impact on the balance sheet and the net working capital.

If inventory is purchased and paid for in cash, the value of the inventory rises by the same amount as the cash account declines. The value of current assets remains the same. Current liabilities are unchanged. Therefore, NWC is unchanged.

NWC = current assets – current liabilities
= (cash ↑ = inventory ↓) – (no change)
NWC is unchanged.

Let's assume the inventory purchase is charged. What happens then? The value of the inventory rises and so does the value of current assets. The amount of accounts payable rises by the amount of the charge, as does the value of current liabilities. Thus, NWC remains the same.

NWC = current assets − current liabilities
= inventory ↑ − accounts payable ↑
NWC is unchanged.

What if we borrow the money for the new inventory by taking out a long-term (more than one year) loan? The value of the inventory and current assets rise, but no change occurs in current liabilities since the loan increases long-term liabilities only. Therefore, NWC increases.

NWC = current assets − current liabilities
NWC = inventory ↑ − (no change)
NWC increases by the amount of the change in inventory.

When the loan is paid off, cash and total current assets will decrease. Current liabilities will remain unchanged since the reduction will occur in long-term liabilities. NWC will decrease by the amount of the cash payoff.

NWC = current assets − current liabilities
= cash ↓ − (no change)
NWC decreases by the amount of the cash payoff.

The only way to produce a change in NWC is for a current asset or current liability item to affect a noncurrent balance sheet item. Conversely, a change in a noncurrent part of the balance sheet can lead to a change in either current assets or current liabilities that changes NWC. This happens because the accounting equation (assets = liabilities + owners' equity) must always balance.

Sources and Uses of Net Working Capital Statements

Using the concept of net working capital, it is possible to develop the third major accounting document—the **sources and uses of net working capital statement**. This document is included along with a balance sheet and the P&L statement in many firms' annual reports. The sources and uses of net working capital statement tell managers and shareholders where the firm acquired its working capital and where it was spent. (A variation of this statement is called the sources and uses of cash statement. It focuses on determining the sources and uses of cash rather than working capital but provides managers with the same information.)

Sources and uses of NWC statements involve items from the noncurrent part of the balance sheet. The sources are items that increase NWC. The uses are items that reduce NWC. Each source of NWC in the list below has a corresponding use in the opposite column, except for depreciation.

Sources of Net Working Capital	**Uses of Net Working Capital**
Profits	Payment of dividends
Sale of fixed assets	Purchase of fixed assets
Sale of investments	Purchase of investments

Long-term loans taken out	Repayment of long term-loans
Sale of stock	Retirement of stock
Depreciation	

To build a sources and uses of NWC statement requires two consecutive balance sheets and the P&L statement for the period between the two balance sheets. Figure 14-3 shows the three-step process for developing a sources and uses statement for the AgBiz Corporation.

Step One. Calculate the NWC for each year from the balance sheets and determine the change in the NWC between the two periods. In year 1, the NWC was $163,500. In year 2, it was $84,050. The change in the NWC was a decline of $79,450.

Step Two. Using the list above, determine whether changes in value for each category are a source or use of NWC. If the value of fixed assets on the balance sheet declined, it is safe to assume that fixed assets were sold. If it rose, it can be assumed fixed assets were purchased. In the example, the value of buildings and equipment rose by $160,000, so this amount is entered in the table as a use of NWC for fixed assets. The total uses of NWC exceed the total sources of NWC by $79,450. The decline in NWC should match the value given in step one.

Figure 14-3 Developing the Sources and Uses of a Net Working Capital Statement

1. Determine the Change in the Net Working Capital

Year	*Current Assets*	–	*Current Liabilities*	=	*Net Working Capital*
1	$205,000	–	$41,500	=	$163,500
2	$174,000	–	$89,950	=	$ 84,050
			Change in Net Working Capital	=	$–79,450

2. Determine the Sources and Uses of Net Working Capital

Sources of NWC		*Uses of NWC*	
Profits (Retained Earnings)	$42,300	Dividends	0
Sale of Fixed Assets	0	Purchase of Fixed Assets	$160,000
Long-Term Borrowings	18,450	Repay Debt	0
Sale of Stock	0	Retirement of Stock	0
Depreciation	20,000	Other Investments	200
Total Sources	$80,750	Total Uses	$160,200

$80,750 – $160,200 = $–79,450

3. Determine the Changes within Current Assets and Current Liabilities

Change in Current Assets		–	Change in Current Liabilities		= Change in NWC
$–32,000	Cash		$+33,000	Accounts Payable	
+25,000	Acct. Rec.		+250	Taxes Payable	
–24,000	Inventories		+15,200	Current Part Long-Term Debt	
$–31,000	Net Change Current Assets		$+48,450	Net Change Current Liabilities	

$–79,450 = Change in NWC

Step Three. The changes that occurred within the current assets and liabilities also are important to the liquidity of the firm and need to be calculated. The same answer (a decline in NWC of $79,450) should be found.

The sources and uses statement shows where the firm acquired its working capital and where it was spent during the past year. In the example, profits and long-term borrowing provided three-fourths of the firm's working capital. The dominant use of working capital was to purchase fixed assets (buildings and equipment). To accomplish this, cash and inventories were reduced while accounts receivable, accounts payable, and the current portion of long-term debt all rose.

In this case the sources of NWC make sense. An ongoing, growing business should receive the bulk of its working capital from its business operation (profits), prudent use of borrowed funds, and the sale of stock. The use of NWC to finance the purchase of new buildings and equipment also makes sense when building a business. The statement shows that the firm financed nearly half its new investment out of NWC, which reduced its overall liquidity. Within the current assets, the two parts that are most liquid declined while accounts receivable increased.

The biggest growth in current liabilities came in accounts payable. This looks reasonable. If all this happened as part of a careful plan developed by management, it would be wonderful. If managers and owners are surprised by what they see in this statement, it is cause for alarm because it may indicate a lack of competence on their part.

If the sources and uses statement had shown all the sources of NWC to be bank borrowings and all the uses to be dividends, this also would be cause for concern. The business would not be making any money from its operation and is borrowing money to pay dividends! This is not a prudent use of money. The sources and uses of net working capital statement highlights the movement of funds so managers can quickly see what is going on and better monitor and manage the financial operation of their businesses.

RATIO ANALYSIS

Another valuable way to analyze financial performance is to look at the relationship among various components of the balance sheet and P&L statement. This approach is called ratio analysis. Financial ratios can be separated into four categories: **liquidity ratios, solvency ratios, activity ratios,** and profitability ratios. Each deals with an important aspect of the firm's financial health and is illustrated using an example from the AgBiz Corporation.

Liquidity Ratios

Liquidity, the ability to meet the day-to-day cash needs of the firm, is of paramount importance to a manager. To measure liquidity, three ratios are used.

Current Ratio. The **current ratio** is the relationship between current assets and current liabilities as listed on the balance sheet. Like net working capital, it shows the firm's ability to meet its bills during the next accounting period. Rather than being stated in terms of absolute dollars, the current ratio measures relative liquidity by dividing current assets by current liabilities.

$$\text{Year 1:} \frac{\text{current assets}}{\text{current liabilities}} = \frac{\$205,000}{\$41,500} = 4.94$$

$$\text{Year 2:} \frac{\text{current assets}}{\text{current liabilities}} = \frac{\$174,000}{\$89,950} = 1.93$$

In year 1, AgBiz had $4.94 of current assets to meet each $1.00 of current liabilities in the next accounting period. In year 2, it had $1.93 to do this. Although AgBiz is less liquid in year 2, the firm still has enough cash to meets its needs.

Quick Ratio. This ratio is calculated the same way as the current ratio except that the value of inventories is subtracted from the current assets. This is done to reflect the less liquid nature of inventories, especially if bills have to be paid quickly.

$$\text{Year 1:} \frac{\text{current assets} - \text{inventories}}{\text{current liabilities}} = \frac{\$205,000 - \$151,000}{\$41,500} = 1.30$$

$$\text{Year 2:} \frac{\text{current assets} - \text{inventories}}{\text{current liabilities}} = \frac{\$174,000 - \$127,000}{\$89,950} = 0.52$$

In year 1, the AgBiz Corporation had $1.30 in cash to meet each dollar of current liabilities. In year 2, it had fallen to 52 cents in cash to meet each dollar of indebtedness. Thus, if the firm had to pay its bills quickly and its inventories could not be sold in the next year to generate cash, the firm could not meet its obligations. The weight put on this ratio depends on the likelihood of this situation and how easy it would be to sell the inventory. If the inventory could be sold, there is little to worry about.

Acid Test Ratio. The ultimate test of liquidity is the acid test ratio. It assumes that all bills must be paid immediately and inventories and accounts receivable cannot be converted into cash. In the acid test ratio, the numerator includes only cash and marketable securities. In the example, AgBiz does not own marketable securities, so the ratio is calculated using cash only.

$$\text{Year 1:} \frac{\text{cash}}{\text{current liabilities}} = \frac{\$49,000}{\$41,500} = 1.18$$

$$\text{Year 2:} \frac{\text{cash}}{\text{current liabilities}} = \frac{\$17,000}{\$89,950} = 0.19$$

In year 1, AgBiz was extremely liquid. It had $1.18 in cash for each dollar it owed in the coming year. In year 2, AgBiz's liquidity was reduced drastically to 19 cents in cash for each dollar it owed. Although this is a large decline, it may not be bad, but it does signal a need for a closer look. Again, how much weight should be put on this ratio depends on the situation. It is rare for a firm to be placed in this situation.

Solvency Ratios

Lenders are concerned not only with whether a business has enough cash to meet the coming year's bills but also the bigger question of whether the firm could repay the money loaned if the firm stopped doing business today. Solvency ratios give lenders a relative measure of the chances the money they have invested in the AgBiz Corporation will be repaid and the likelihood that the firm will be able to meet the interest payments on its debts.

Debt to Equity Ratio. This ratio measures the relative size of claims on a firm's assets between its creditors and the owners.

$$\text{Year 1:} \frac{\text{total debt} = \text{total liabilities}}{\text{owners' equity}} = \frac{\$343{,}100}{\$567{,}700} = 0.60$$

$$\text{Year 2:} \frac{\text{total debt} = \text{total liabilities}}{\text{owners' equity}} = \frac{\$410{,}000}{\$610{,}000} = 0.67$$

This ratio shows some deterioration between years 1 and 2. In the first year, creditors had "invested" 60 cents in the AgBiz Corporation for each dollar put up by the owners. In the second year, creditors had increased their "relative investment" to 67 cents for each dollar from the owners. Another way to look at this is to say that the creditors (both bankers and those who have sold things to the firm on credit) have provided 37.7 percent ($343,100/$910,800) of the total capital investment in AgBiz in year 1. Their investment grew to 40.2 percent ($410,000/$1,020,000) in the second year.

Times Interest Earned Ratio. Lenders are always concerned about the level of risk they are taking when loaning money. One measure of risk is the size of the organization's pretax earnings relative to the loan interest due during the accounting period. These figures are from the P&L statement.

$$\text{Year 1:} \frac{\text{income before taxes} + \text{interest expense}}{\text{interest expense}} = \frac{\$36{,}000 + \$4{,}000}{\$4{,}000} = 10.0$$

$$\text{Year 2:} \frac{\text{income before taxes} + \text{interest expense}}{\text{interest expense}} = \frac{\$51{,}000 + \$5{,}000}{\$5{,}000} = 11.2$$

Although the interest expense rose between years 1 and 2, income increased more. In year 1, $10 of income was generated for each dollar of interest expense. In year 2, the amount of income was $11 for each dollar of interest due. It would take a considerable drop in pretax income to place the interest payments in jeopardy.

Activity Ratios

The third type of ratio deals with the level of activity of the business relative to its inventory levels, customer credit payments, and its own bill paying.

Inventory Turnover Ratio. As was seen in an earlier chapter, inventory management is an important managerial task that has a big impact on profits.

Another method of measuring the effectiveness of inventory management is to measure its activity—how often the inventory is used up and replaced each year. Dividing the cost of goods sold as listed on the P&L statement by the level of inventory found on the balance sheet determines the inventory turnover per year.

$$\text{Year 1:} \frac{\text{cost of goods sold}}{\text{inventory level}} = \frac{\$1{,}026{,}000}{\$151{,}000} = 6.79$$

$$\text{Year 2:} \frac{\text{cost of goods sold}}{\text{inventory level}} = \frac{\$1{,}129{,}000}{\$127{,}000} = 8.89$$

AgBiz's inventory turned over 6.79 times in year 1 and 8.89 times in year 2.

It is easier to grasp the meaning of the turnover numbers when they are converted to the average number of days it takes for the inventory to turn over. This is determined by dividing the number of days in a year (365) by the number of inventory turnovers per year. In year 1, the inventory turned over every 53.8 days (365/6.79). In year 2, the inventory turned over every 41.1 days (365/8.89). The inventory turned over more quickly in year 2 than in year 1.

Accounts Receivable Turnover Ratio. An important part of a firm's liquidity is how long it must wait to receive money from sales made on credit. While normal terms for credit sales require full payment in 30 days, some customers fail to meet this commitment. Because sales are the primary source of cash for business, any delay in receiving payment adversely affects the firm's own cash position and slows its bill payment. The accounts receivable turnover ratio is determined by dividing the credit sales during the accounting period (found on the P&L statement) by the amount of accounts receivable (found on the balance sheet). In the example, credit sales are assumed to be 10 percent of total sales.

$$\text{Year 1:} \frac{\text{credit sales (10\% of total sales)}}{\text{accounts receivable}} = \frac{\$125{,}000}{\$5{,}000} = 25$$

$$\text{Year 2:} \frac{\text{credit sales (10\% of total sales)}}{\text{accounts receivable}} = \frac{\$146{,}500}{\$30{,}000} = 4.88$$

AgBiz's accounts receivable turned over 25 times in year 1 and 4.88 times in year 2.

Just like the inventory turnover ratio, it is easier to grasp the meaning of the turnover numbers by converting them to the average number of days to receive payment from a credit sale. This is determined by dividing the number of days in a year (365) by the number of accounts receivable turnovers per year. In year 1, the average time the firm had to wait to receive payment on a credit sale was 14.6 days (365/25). In year 2, the average time grew to 74.8 days (365/4.88). This is a substantial increase in the time to receive payment for a credit sale and warrants an investigation as to why it is happening. One way to begin is to examine AgBiz's credit sales policies, which may be a source of the liquidity problem.

Accounts Payable Turnover Ratio. This ratio is similar to the accounts receivable turnover ratio. It measures how fast the firm pays its own bills. The ratio is calculated by dividing the value of credit purchases (found on the P&L

statement) by the amount of accounts payable (found on the balance sheet). In the example, it is assumed that credit sales are 25 percent of goods purchased.

$$\text{Year 1:} \frac{\text{purchases on credit (25\% of goods purchased)}}{\text{accounts payable}} = \frac{\$269{,}250}{\$20{,}000} = 13.5$$

$$\text{Year 2:} \frac{\text{purchases on credit (25\% of goods purchased)}}{\text{accounts payable}} = \frac{\$276{,}250}{\$53{,}000} = 5.21$$

AgBiz's accounts payable turned over 13.5 times in year 1 and 5.21 times in year 2.

It is easier to grasp the meaning of the turnover numbers when they are converted to number of days. This is determined by dividing the number of days in a year (365) by the number of times the accounts payable turned over per year. In year 1, it took AgBiz an average of 27 days (365/13.5) to pay its bills. In year 2, it took an average of 70 days (365/5.21) to pay its bills. This is a significant increase and deserves further investigation by management. The increase is likely to be tied to the similar increase in the accounts receivable turnover ratio.

Profitability Ratios

Profits are of constant interest to managers. Three ratios are used to assist them in assessing performance in this area.

Return on Invested Capital Ratio. The return on invested capital (ROIC) ratio measures profit before taxes as a percentage of the value of all the assets used by the firm to earn that profit. It is calculated by dividing the income before taxes (found on the P&L statement) by total assets (found on the balance sheet).

$$\text{Year 1:} \frac{\text{income before taxes}}{\text{total assets}} = \frac{\$36{,}000}{\$910{,}800} = 3.95\%$$

$$\text{Year 2:} \frac{\text{income before taxes}}{\text{total assets}} = \frac{\$51{,}000}{\$1{,}020{,}000} = 5.00\%$$

In year 1, the assets invested in the AgBiz Corporation had a return of 3.95 percent. In year 2, the ROIC in AgBiz had risen to 5 percent. Management used its resources more efficiently in year 2.

Return on Owners' Equity Ratio. The ROIC ratio discussed above can paint a misleading picture of financial returns if the firm leases or borrows a large portion of its assets. A more accurate assessment of the owners' return may emerge by measuring the return on owners' equity. It is calculated by dividing income before taxes (found on the P&L statement) by owners' equity (found on the balance sheet).

$$\text{Year 1:} \frac{\text{income before taxes}}{\text{owners' equity}} = \frac{\$36{,}000}{\$567{,}700} = 6.34\%$$

$$\text{Year 2:} \frac{\text{income before taxes}}{\text{owners' equity}} = \frac{\$51{,}000}{\$610{,}000} = 8.36\%$$

The return on owner-invested capital (owners' equity) improved to 8.36 percent in year 2 from 6.34 percent in the first year. The higher return may reflect better management in year 2.

Profit as a Percentage of Sales Ratio. This last profitability ratio measures profit as a percentage of each sales dollar. This is the same procedure used in analyzing comparative P&L statements. It is calculated by dividing income before taxes by the total revenue from sales as given on the P&L statement.

$$\text{Year 1}: \frac{\text{income before taxes}}{\text{total sales}} = \frac{\$36,000}{\$1,250,000} = 2.88\%$$

$$\text{Year 2}: \frac{\text{income before taxes}}{\text{total sales}} = \frac{\$51,000}{\$1,465,000} = 3.48\%$$

The profit per dollar of sales shows improvement, rising from 2.88 cents of each dollar to 3.48 cents per sales dollar. This may reflect good management.

Comparing Ratios to Industry Standards

The ratio analysis employed so far is a valuable way to detect trends and evaluate changes in the liquidity, solvency, activity, and profitability of a business. As shown in the section on comparative statement analysis, comparing a company's performance to industry standards can enhance the value of financial analysis of the business. Again, RMA's *Annual Statement Studies* is a convenient source of industry-standard data. Their data is given for the past three years and is also broken down by asset size. RMA reports a number of ratios highlighted in this chapter, plus several more, for each major industry group.

If we compare AgBiz to the industry standards given by RMA, the firm's accounts receivable turnover ratio in year 2 (74.8 days) compares poorly with the median value of the industry (29.6 days). In fact, the wait of nearly 75 days is very high by industry standards. Another example is the inventory turnover ratio. In year 2, AgBiz Corporation experienced a turnover once every 41.1 days versus a median value for the industry of every 76 days. This is much faster than is normal for firms like AgBiz. Just as they did for comparative statement analysis, comparisons with industry standards give managers and lenders a better feel for how a single firm's financial performance measures up to typical firms in their industry.

Developing Pro Forma Cash Flow Budgets

Accounting documents are useful in recounting past financial activity, but tell managers little about the future. Fortunately, they contain the ingredients needed for financial planning. One very useful document that can be built from them is the pro forma cash flow budget.

A cash flow budget operates the way most people keep their checkbooks. Income is not counted as received until a deposit is made. Expenses are not recorded until a check is written. This is very different from the P&L statement, in which income and expenses are recorded in the period they are earned and incurred regardless of when the money is received and paid. Net cash flow for any period is the difference between cash actually received and cash actually paid out during that period. Using information in the marketing plan, balance sheet, P&L statement, and several financial ratios, a pro forma cash flow budget can be developed that will help managers forecast their future cash needs. Again, let's use the AgBiz Corporation as an example and develop a pro forma cash flow budget for the six-month period from December to May.

Determining Cash Outflows

The process begins by estimating the cash outflows for this period (see figure 14-4). The driving force behind the firm's cash flow is sales, so it is appropriate to use the monthly sales estimates from the marketing plan for this period. These are entered on line A. The inventory turnover ratio for AgBiz Corporation is six. This means that the average item in their inventory stays there for two months before it is sold. For example, an item placed in inventory in December will not be sold until February. At the end of each month, the value of inventory is equal to the current month's and previous month's purchases (line F).

A look at AgBiz's P&L statement shows that the cost of goods sold (the purchases) is 75 percent of the selling price. This provides enough information to estimate the size and timing of the purchases needed to support the estimated sales each month. For example, to support estimated sales of $320,000 in February, the firm must purchase $240,000 (0.75 × $320,000) of inventory in December. To support the estimated $640,000 of sales in March, the firm must purchase $480,000 of inventory in January. And so on.

The accounts payable turnover ratio is 12. This means AgBiz pays for its purchases one month after receiving them. This gives the firm a cash flow problem because it must pay for goods before they are sold. For example, goods purchased in December are sold in February but paid for in January. This pattern repeats itself each month.

The total cash outflow for each month (line E) is the total of accounts payable (line C) and overhead (line D). The total outflow for December is $225,000, $285,000 for January, and so on.

Determining Cash Inflows

The same approach is used to estimate cash inflows (figure 14-5). Begin by using the same cash sales estimates from the marketing plan. If sales historically have been 50 percent cash and 50 percent credit, record the cash sales that way on line B. The accounts receivable turnover ratio is eight. This means that AgBiz waits an average of 45 days to collect the money from credit sales. This is equivalent to collecting half of the credit sales money 30 days after the sale and the other half 60 days after the sale. For example, of the $160,000 in sales in December, half are paid in cash that same month; the remaining $80,000 is paid half in January and half in February. It takes three months for AgBiz to receive all the cash from each month's sales. The total cash inflow for each month comes from three

Figure 14-4 Estimating Cash Outflows

AgBiz Corporation's Estimated Monthly Cash Outflows, December–May

Item	Dec.	Jan.	Feb.	Mar.	Apr.	May
A. Projected Sales	$160,000	$192,000	$320,000	$640,000	$800,000	$192,000
B. Purchases	240,000	480,000	600,000	144,000	144,000	144,000
C. Payment of Accounts Payable	180,000	240,000	480,000	600,000	144,000	144,000
D. Payment of Overhead	45,000	45,000	45,000	45,000	45,000	45,000
E. Total Cash Outflow (C + D)	225,000	285,000	525,000	645,000	189,000	189,000
F. Inventory Levels	384,000	720,000	1,080,000	744,000	288,000	288,000

Assumptions:
1. The inventory turnover ratio = 6. This means items stay in inventory for two months, and are purchased two months before sale.
2. Inventory = current month's purchases + previous month's purchases.
3. Cost of goods sold = 75% of sales.
4. Accounts payable turnover ratio = 12. This means bills are paid in 30 days (i.e., the next month).

Figure 14-5 Estimating Cash Inflows

AgBiz Corporation's Estimated Cash Inflows, December–May

Item	Dec.	Jan.	Feb.	Mar.	Apr.	May
A. Projected Sales	$160,000	$192,000	$320,000	$640,000	$800,000	$192,000
B. Cash Sales	80,000	96,000	160,000	320,000	400,000	96,000
C. Collect Accounts Receivable—1 month old	35,000	40,000	48,000	80,000	160,000	200,000
D. Collect Accounts Receivable—2 months old	30,000	35,000	40,000	48,000	80,000	160,000
E. Total Cash Inflows (B + C + D)	145,000	171,000	248,000	448,000	640,000	456,000

Assumptions:
1. Sales are one-half cash, one-half credit.
2. Accounts receivable ratio = 8 = average 45 days to be paid. This means half of sales are collected in the first 30 days and half in the second 30 days after the sale.

sources—cash from sales this month, receivables from last month's sales, and receivables from sales two months ago (lines B + C + D). The total cash inflows are $145,000 in December, $171,000 in January, and so on.

Developing the Pro Forma Cash Flow Budget

Combining cash inflows and outflows for the period will give the pro forma cash flow budget for the period (figure 14-6). Assume the firm begins with a cash balance of $200,000 and has decided that the minimum cash balance it needs to operate is $100,000. AgBiz will borrow money any time they go below the minimum cash balance and will use any money above the minimum end-of-the-month cash balance to repay loans.

The process of determining cash needs will be done month to month. It is easier to visualize this process by thinking of the cash inflows coming in throughout the month, with bills (cash outflows) paid the last night of the month after closing for the day.

In December, the firm starts with its opening cash balance of $200,000 and brings in $145,000 (the total cash inflow amount from line E of figure 14-5). On the night of December 31, when the managers sit down to pay their bills, they find a checkbook balance of $345,000. The bills for December are $225,000 (the total cash outflow from line E of figure 14-4). When they are finished paying bills the checkbook has a balance of $120,000. Since this is above the minimum cash balance, there is no need to borrow.

In January, the firm's beginning cash balance is equal to last month's ending cash balance ($120,000). During the month the firm brings in $171,000. On the night of January 31, when the managers sit down to pay their bills, they find a checkbook balance of $291,000. The bills for January are $285,000. When they are finished, the checkbook has a balance of $6,000. Based on the assumptions, AgBiz needs to borrow $94,000 in January in order keep their cash balance at the $100,000 minimum.

In February, the firm's beginning cash balance equals last month's ending cash balance ($100,000). During the month the firm brings in $248,000. On the night of February 28, when the managers sit down to pay bills, they find a checkbook balance of $348,000. The bills for February are $525,000. This will leave them with a deficit of $177,000. To remedy this they will need to borrow $277,000 in February. They will need $177,000 to cover their bills plus another $100,000 to restore the minimum cash balance.

In March, the firm faces the same type of cash shortfall. This month, AgBiz needs to borrow $197,000.

Things improve in April. The firm brings in $640,000 and has a checkbook balance of $740,000 when the managers sit down to pay bills on April 30. The bills for April are $189,000. This leaves a balance of $551,000. Based on the assumption about using the cash above the minimum cash balance amount ($100,000) to repay loans, AgBiz uses $451,000 to repay its loans. This reduces the size of its loan to $117,000 and still leaves an ending cash balance of $100,000.

In May, the firm takes in $456,000 and has a checkbook balance of $556,000 when the managers sit down to pay bills on May 31. The bills for May are $189,000. Again, using cash above the minimum amount to repay loans, AgBiz

Figure 14-6 Pro Forma Cash Flow Budget

AgBiz Corporation's Pro Forma Cash Flow Budget, December–May

Item	Dec.	Jan.	Feb.	Mar.	Apr.	May
A. Beginning cash balance	$200,000	$120,000	$100,000	$100,000	$100,000	$100,000
B. Cash inflow	+ 145,000	171,000	248,000	448,000	640,000	456,000
C. Total cash available (A + B)	345,000	291,000	348,000	548,000	740,000	556,000
D. Cash outflow	(225,000)	(285,000)	(525,000)	(645,000)	(189,000)	(189,000)
E. Net cash (C – D)	120,000	6,000	(177,000)	(97,000)	551,000	367,000
F. Needed borrowings	+ 0	94,000	277,000	197,000	(451,000)	(117,000)
G. Ending cash balance	120,000	100,000	100,000	100,000	100,000	250,000
H. Cumulative borrowings	0	94,000	371,000	568,000	117,000	0

Assumption: The minimum cash balance is $100,000.

uses $117,000 to pay off the last part of its loan. They end this six-month period with no loans and a cash balance of $250,000.

Value of the Pro Forma Cash Flow Budget

The cash flow budget gives managers and potential lenders answers to five important financial planning questions:

1. Does the business need to borrow money?
2. If so, how much money needs to be borrowed?
3. When does the money need to be borrowed?
4. How will the money be repaid?
5. When will the money be repaid?

These are important questions that lenders will ask and requires managers to have solid answers. To illustrate the value of this process, let's look at the answers that the managers of the AgBiz Corporation should be giving to these questions.

Does the business need to borrow money?

Yes. Two reasons exist for borrowing. First, a look at the historical sales figures shows that AgBiz's sales are highly seasonable. This is expected because AgBiz is a farm-supply business in which sales are highest in March and April, the height of the planting season in their market. Second, an examination of cash flows showed that they pay for their purchases one month before they sell their products. These two reasons should make the AgBiz Corporation a good candidate for a seasonal loan each year.

How much money needs to be borrowed?

The firm should request a line of credit of at least $600,000 because it expects its maximum indebtedness to be $568,000.

When does the money need to be borrowed?

A line of credit should be established in December but it will not be used until January, when the firm expects to borrow $94,000. It will draw another $277,000 in February and $197,000 in March.

How will the money be repaid?

This will be a self-liquidating loan. The money will be used to pay for products that will be sold. The proceeds from the sales will be used to repay the loan.

When will the loan be repaid?

The bulk of the loan ($451,000) will be repaid from sales in April. The remaining part ($117,000) will be repaid in May.

A lender can quickly and easily monitor the progress of AgBiz in repaying this loan by reviewing monthly balance sheets and P&L statements from the firm. From these documents, the loan officer can check to see if they are hitting their sales, cost of goods, accounts receivable, accounts payable, and overhead cost goals that are critical for generating the cash flows needed to repay the loan. The pro forma cash flow budget gives the lender clear answers to the five questions given above. This should give most of the information needed to assess the creditworthiness of AgBiz for a seasonal loan.

All of this information comes from the marketing plan's sales estimates and the ability to read and analyze basic accounting documents. This approach also can be used to develop pro forma balance sheets and profit-and-loss statements. **Pro forma statements** enable managers to use their accounting data to plan for the future as well as explain past financial performance.

Chapter Highlights

1. The accounting system does more than provide an accurate record of business performance. It helps managers understand, evaluate, and monitor the financial performance of their businesses.
2. A great deal of the controlling function of management can be accomplished using the data found in the balance sheet and profit-and-loss statement.
3. Accounting data also can be used for business planning. The data in the balance sheet and profit-and-loss statement can be combined with ratio analysis to create a pro forma cash flow budget to forecast future cash flows.
4. Managers should perform three forms of analysis of basic accounting documents: comparative statement analysis, net working capital analysis, and ratio analysis.
5. A regular part of financial analysis should include year-to-year changes as well as comparisons to industry standards.
6. Comparative statement analysis is an efficient and effective way to evaluate the financial condition of a business, how it is changing over time, and how it compares to industry standards.
7. The sources and uses of a net working capital statement gives managers a way to quickly see where the firm's working capital came from and how it was used.
8. Ratio analysis is another way to analyze the financial performance of the firm by looking at the relationship between various components of the balance sheet and profit-and-loss statement.
9. The pro forma cash flow budget gives managers a way to forecast and explain their future cash needs and cash flows.
10. The pro forma cash flow budget answers the five key questions of financial planning.

Chapter Quiz

1. Explain how the accounting system presents an accurate record of business financial dealings to managers, owners, and government regulators.
2. Explain how the controlling management function can be accomplished using the data found in the balance sheet and profit-and-loss statement. Give two examples of things it can do.
3. Compare and contrast how comparative statement analysis, net working capital analysis, and ratio analysis can help managers and owners evalu-

ate a firm's financial performance. Give an example of how each type of analysis can illuminate a different area of financial performance. Show how they can be combined to assist managers in accomplishing the controlling function.

4. Explain why a regular part of business financial analysis should be the use of industry standards and year-to-year comparisons.
5. Give an example to illustrate how a person interested in starting a new business could use industry-standard data to make a pro forma (estimated) profit-and-loss statement and balance sheet for the intended business.
6. Illustrate with an example why the only way to produce a change in net working capital is for the change in current assets or current liability to affect a noncurrent part of the balance sheet.
7. Explain why all three steps of the procedure to develop a sources and uses of net working capital statement have the same answer for the change in net working capital. What does a manager gain by having a sources and uses of net working capital statement?
8. Use an example to explain the difference between liquidity and solvency in a business. Explain the difference between how the current ratio and net working capital analyze liquidity. Which does a better job? Explain your choice.
9. How do you know if a ratio's value is good or bad? Is it possible for a ratio to be too high in one case and too low in another? Explain your answer with an example using one of the ratios given in the chapter.
10. Explain which of the four types of ratios—liquidity, solvency, activity, and profitability—is most important to the firm over the long term. Explain your answer using an example.
11. Use an example to explain how the profit-and-loss statement differs from a cash flow statement for a business. Which is more important to a business? Explain your answer.
12. What does the sources and uses of net working capital document tell you that you do not get from the other documents found in this chapter?
13. Why do you have to understand the balance sheet, profit-and-loss statement, and financial ratios before you can see the value of flow budgets?
14. How does a cash flow budget improve the financial management of a business?
15. What does the term pro forma mean?

CASE 14
Fred's Financial Phobia: Part II

Answer these questions from Fred based on what you learned about his situation in part I of this case.

1. What is the difference between the cash flow budget and the sources and uses of net working capital statement? Explain how managers use both to do a better job planning and controlling their businesses.
2. What analysis should Fred perform to gain some perspective on his store's financial performance?
3. The normal accounting data—balance sheets and income statements—measure a firm's past financial performance. So what good are they for financial planning?
4. It looks like if you have a good accounting system, you have everything you need to run a successful business. Do you agree or disagree? Explain your answer.

Chapter 15

Capital Budgeting I

Principles and Procedures

Chapter Learning Objectives

- Explain how capital budgeting decisions differ from other management decisions.
- Summarize the characteristics of a good capital investment.
- Recognize the correct data to use in making a capital budgeting decision.
- Explain the importance of using the time value of money when making a capital budgeting decision.
- Demonstrate the use of the four basic capital budgeting decision procedures that use the time value of money.

Introduction

Up to this point, emphasis has been placed on the control and operation of an ongoing agribusiness. However, sooner or later managers are faced with decisions regarding the acquisition of new fixed assets such as property, buildings, and equipment. These are different from other decisions managers face because (1) they involve long-term commitments of large amounts of money; (2) they are normally nonreversible; and (3) they have a large impact on the firm's financial position for many years. This special class of decisions is called **capital budgeting** decisions.

Capital budgeting decisions involve evaluating the profitability of the firm's potential investments in new property, plant, and equipment. Managers face two types of situations when they do this. The first situation occurs when managers are given two or more ways to achieve the same result. For example, this might involve deciding whether it is more profitable to replace a worn-out piece of equipment with a machine that has to be replaced every five years or to buy a higher-priced machine that will last ten years. The second situation occurs when managers have to evaluate the profitability of a potential investment. For example, this might involve evaluating the profitability of investing in a plant that will last 30 years in order to support an expected increase in sales.

Differences in the length of investments and the amount and timing of costs and benefits from each alternative solution make it difficult for managers to apply more conventional decision-making procedures to these types of situations. Managers need a decision procedure that (1) fully accounts for the timing and amount of capital required for the investment, (2) fully accounts for the timing and amount of added benefits likely to result over the life of the investment, and (3) can objectively evaluate capital budgeting decisions so management can maximize long-term profits. This chapter is devoted to filling this need so that managers can make capital budgeting decisions efficiently and effectively.

THE DECISION FRAMEWORK

Before a capital budgeting decision can be made, a decision framework must be developed that meets the needs described above. A good capital investment has four characteristics.

1. It provides a positive long-term net profit to the firm.
2. When selecting among alternative capital budgeting solutions, it is the investment alternative that provides the highest long-term net profit to the firm.
3. It provides benefits sooner rather than later.
4. It provides the lowest risk.

The proper data to use when making a capital budgeting decision are after-tax incremental cash flows. These data are used because:

- A good capital investment is one that gives benefits sooner rather than later. Thus, the timing of benefits and costs are important. Cash flow data adjusts for the timing of revenues and costs. Accounting data do not.
- Incremental analysis shows that the only relevant cash flows in decision making are those that change as a direct result of a decision.
- The best way to see clearly the net effect of a decision is to evaluate incremental cash flows after the payment of taxes.

Now that the manager knows the characteristics of a good capital investment and which cash flows to measure in evaluating alternatives, the third step is to identify which decision-making procedures are objective ways to evaluate capital budgeting alternatives. Two groups of popular capital budgeting decision procedures will be evaluated. The first group evaluates decision procedures that do not consider the time value of money. The second group considers the time value of money as part of its evaluation.

CAPITAL BUDGETING DECISION PROCEDURES THAT DO NOT USE THE TIME VALUE OF MONEY

Investments in capital items such as property, plant, and equipment have far-reaching implications for a firm's earning power, growth, and survival. This section evaluates two popular techniques—payback and the average rate of return—that do not use the time value of money in evaluating capital budgeting decisions.

The Payback Method

The payback method evaluates capital budgeting opportunities by determining the number of periods (months or years) required for the sum of the benefits to be equal to the investment. For example, a project that requires a $5,000 investment and yields a benefit of $1,000 per year has a payback of five years. In other words, it takes five years for the firm to recover its investment ($5,000) in this project ($1,000 × 5 years = $5,000). Managers normally determine the maximum time period that the business is willing to wait to recover its investment and accept all investment opportunities with **payback periods** less than or equal to that maximum. Any investment that requires more time than the maximum is not acceptable. When faced with two or more investment alternatives that solve the same problem, the one with the shorter payback period is preferred.

Although the payback method is widely used in making capital budget decisions, it has disadvantages that limit its ability to reveal the best investment for the firm. For example, assume two competing investment alternatives (A and B) each require an investment of $1,000. Investment A has a life of five years. Investment B has a life of six years. Assume further that management has set its maximum payback period to four years. The after-tax incremental cash flows for each year are given in table 15-1.

Table 15-1 Analysis of Investments A and B Using the Payback Method

	After-Tax Benefits		
Year	A	B	
1	$500	$100	
2	400	200	
3	300*	300	
4	200	400*	
			Maximum payback allowed
5	100	500	
6	—	600	
Total benefits	$1,500	$2,100	
Payback in years	2.3	4.0	

*Indicates year when initial outlay ($1,000) is paid back.

Investment A returns $900 of its initial outlay of $1,000 in the first two years. In the third year it returns $300, but only $100 (one-third) of this amount is required to complete the recovery of the initial investment of $1,000. Thus, investment A has a payback of 2 years. Investment B returns the full value of its investment by the end of year four. Since the firm's maximum payback period is four years, both investments are acceptable. However, if only one can be chosen, the firm should choose investment A because it recovers its investment more quickly (2 years) than investment B (4 years).

Disadvantages. What about benefits from investment B in years 5 and 6? Under the rules of the payback method, they are ignored. However, the total benefits from investment B are $600 greater than those from investment A. Thus, the payback method violates the second criterion of a good investment that when faced with alternative solutions, always select the one that gives the firm the highest long-term net benefit. The payback method also violates the third criterion of a good investment—early benefits are preferred to later benefits—because a benefit received in the first year is given the same weight as one received in the last period. A method needs to be devised to compensate the investor for having to wait to receive those distant benefits. The payback method, though quick and easy, does not always give managers a way to consistently select the alternative that gives the highest net benefit to the firm, and it makes no adjustment for the timing of benefits and costs.

The Average Rate of Return Method

The average rate of return method evaluates capital budgeting opportunities by measuring the annual percentage return on the capital invested in a project. When faced with alternative investment opportunities for the same money, the manager should select the option with the highest rate of return. When faced with a potential investment, a manager should choose only those opportunities whose average rate of return equals or exceeds the minimum rate set by the firm.

Table 15-2 shows how to calculate the average rate of return for the same two investment alternatives studied earlier. The investment in each alternative is equal to the average amount invested per year over the life of the project. The yearly benefit is calculated as a simple average. Dividing the average yearly return by the average yearly investment gives the average rate of return.

Table 15-2 Analysis of Investments A and B by Average Rate of Return Method

	Year						
	1	2	3	4	5	6	Average
				Investment A			
After-tax benefits	$500	$400	$300	$200	$100	—	$300
Value of investment*							
Jan. 1	1,000	800	600	400	200	—	
Dec. 31	800	600	400	200	0		
Average	900	700	500	300	100	—	$500

$$\text{Average rate of return} = \frac{\$300}{\$500} \times 100 = 60\%$$

	1	2	3	4	5	6	Average
				Investment B			
After-tax benefits	$100	$200	$300	$400	$500	$600	$350
Value of investment*							
Jan. 1	1,000	833	666	499	332	166	
Dec. 31	833	666	499	332	166	0	
Average	917	750	583	416	249	83	$500

$$\text{Average rate of return} = \frac{\$350}{\$500} \times 100 = 70\%$$

*Using straight-line depreciation with no expected salvage value.

If the firm has a policy of accepting investment opportunities with an average rate of return of 20 percent or more, both projects are acceptable. If only one can be chosen, investment B is better according to the average rate of return method because it gives a 70 percent return, versus a 60 percent return from investment A. This result is the opposite of that obtained using the payback method, in which the investment in project A should be chosen because it is recovered in a shorter period of time.

Disadvantages. The average rate of return method has the advantage of using all of an investment's returns in its analysis. Nevertheless, it still has the problem of giving the same weight to benefits received in early years as those received in later years, and no compensation is given for waiting. In addition, investments are ranked by their percentage return, so a manager cannot tell which project is most profitable. This is called a size-disparity problem. The best way to define this problem is to ask, "Would you rather make 70 percent on an investment of $1 or 60 percent on an investment of $1,000?" The average rate of return method cannot tell a manager that the lower rate of return (60 percent) on a $1,000 investment will give the firm a larger net benefit than the higher rate of return (70 percent) on a $1 investment. Thus, the average rate of return method, while better than the payback method, still has its drawbacks.

THE TIME VALUE OF MONEY

The biggest drawback to evaluating investment alternatives using either the payback method or the average rate of return method is their failure to compensate investors for waiting to receive benefits that occur later in a project. Let's take the example of investment A. The firm invests $1,000 today and realizes a string of profits from that investment for five years. If all those benefits occurred today, the evaluation of this investment would be easy. A $1,000 investment returns $1,500. The business makes a profit of $500. The economic principle of opportunity cost provides a way to overcome this oversimplification.

Opportunity cost considers the return given up by investing in a particular project rather than doing something else with the money. For example, let's introduce the option that the firm could put its $1,000 in a savings account paying 5 percent in interest per year rather than investing in project A.

If the firm makes a profit of $40 this year on its $1,000 investment, but could have earned a profit of $50 by putting that same money in a savings account, the best thing to do with the money is put it in the bank and not invest in project A. The only investments that make sense to a business are those that give them a return greater than 5 percent (its opportunity cost). Otherwise, they can make more by putting their money in the bank.

In the capital budgeting arena, **the opportunity cost of money** is called the **time value of money**. Considering the time value of money is the proper way to compensate investors for waiting to receive the delayed benefits of a capital investment. This can be done two ways. The first is **compounding**—calculating how much a dollar put into a savings account today will be worth years from now. The second process is called **discounting**, and is the reverse of compounding. Managers can calculate how much money they need to put into a savings account today so it can grow to a specified amount at a certain time in the future.

Compounding

Compounding is the process of determining how much an investment will be worth some time in the future. This value can be calculated because interest payments are made at regular intervals. For example, suppose that $1.00 is placed in a savings account for one year at 12 percent, which is paid at maturity. One year later, the owner of the account would have $1.00 (the principal) plus 12 cents interest for a total of $1.12. If the $1.12 were left in the account for one more year, there would be $1.25 (rather than $1.24) at the end of the second year. The extra penny of interest comes about because the interest earned during the second year is figured using the new starting value of the principal, $1.12 ($1.12 \times 0.12 = 13$ cents). This illustrates the power of **compound interest**: if money is left intact in an account, interest is earned on interest paid previously.

This relationship can be expressed mathematically as follows:

$$FV = VN\,(1 + i)^N$$

Where FV = future value
VN = value now
i = interest rate per period
N = number of times interest is paid

In the example, the calculations for the first year are

$$\begin{aligned} FV &= VN\,(1 + i)^N \\ &= (\$1.00)(1 + 0.12)^{N=1} \\ &= (\$1.00)\,(1.12) \\ &= \$1.12 \end{aligned}$$

The value of the account at the end of two years would be

$$\begin{aligned} FV &= VN\,(1 + i)^N \\ &= (\$1.00)(1 + 0.12)^{N=2} \\ &= (\$1.00)(1.12)^2 \\ &= (\$1.00)(1.25) \\ &= \$1.25 \end{aligned}$$

How often interest is paid makes a great deal of difference in the future value of an investment. Using the same example, if interest is paid twice a year rather than once a year, the interest rate per period is halved but the number of times it is paid is doubled. As a result, the value of the account is higher at the end of the period.

$$\begin{aligned} FV &= VN\,(1 + i/2)^N \\ &= (\$1.00)(1 + 0.12/2)^{N=4} \\ &= (\$1.00)(1.06)^4 \\ &= (\$1.00)(1.26) \\ &= \$1.26 \end{aligned}$$

If interest were paid four times a year, the value of the account would be

$$
\begin{aligned}
FV &= VN\,(1 + i/4)^{N} \\
&= (\$1.00)(1 + 0.12/4)^{N=8} \\
&= (\$1.00)(1.03)^{8} \\
&= (\$1.00)(1.27) \\
&= \$1.27
\end{aligned}
$$

Thus, the more often interest is paid, the higher the value of the savings account at the end of the period because there are more opportunities to earn interest on interest payments already received.

Discounting

Discounting is the reverse of compounding. Compounding asks how much a dollar will be worth at some time in the future if it is compounded at some interest rate for so many years. Discounting reverses that question and asks how much money needs to be put into a savings account today earning a certain amount of interest in order to have a dollar so many years from now. The amount of money needed to be put into the account today (called the **present value**) is less than (discounted) one dollar because the investment will grow to equal one dollar by the time it is needed because of interest payments.

To show this relationship mathematically, the equation that was used for determining compounding is rearranged and solved for the value now (*VN*):

$$
\begin{aligned}
FV &= VN(1+i)^{N} \\
\frac{FV}{(1+i)^{N}} &= VN \\
VN &= \frac{FV}{(1+i)^{N}}
\end{aligned}
$$

Using the previous example but looking at it from the point of view of discounting, the question becomes how much money needs to be put into a saving account today in order to have $1.25 in two years if the account earns 12 percent interest per year. The present value (*VN*) of $1.25 to be received in two years discounted at 12 percent is:

$$
\begin{aligned}
VN &= \frac{\$1.25}{(1+0.12)^{2}} \\
&= \frac{\$1.25}{\$1.25} \\
&= \$1.00
\end{aligned}
$$

Receiving $1.25 in two years is the same as having $1.00 today if the **discount rate** (the opportunity cost) is 12 percent per year.

To simplify things, tables have been developed that give the present value for a dollar. For example, the table would show the present value of $1.00 received in two years discounted at 12 percent per year to be

$$VN = \frac{\$1.00}{\$1.25}$$
$$= 0.80$$

Since the amount to be received in two years in the example is $1.25 rather than $1.00, it is necessary to multiply $1.25 by 0.80 to get the appropriate value of $1.00.

Compounding Tables. Appendix table 1 provides the future values of $1.00 compounded for various interest rates and time periods. To use the table, it is necessary to find the intersection of the desired interest rate and time period. For example, to locate the future value of $1.00 invested today at 5 percent in one year, look at the intersection of 5 percent and one year ($1.05).

What is the value of $250 placed in a savings account at 10 percent interest per year for 10 years? The compounding table shows that $1.00 increases in value to $2.5937 in ten years when it can earn 10 percent interest per year. Therefore, $250 compounded at 10 percent per year for ten years would be worth $648.425 ($250 × 2.5937).

Discounting Tables. Appendix table 2 gives the discounted or present value of $1.00 for various interest rates and time periods. This table works the same way as table 1. It is necessary to find the intersection of the desired interest rate and time period. For example, to find the present value (discounted value) of $1.00 to be received 10 years from now, look at the intersection of 10 years and 10 percent (0.3855). This says that if 38.55 cents are put into a savings account today that pays 10 percent interest per year, the value of the account will grow to $1.00 in 10 years. The present value of that investment is 38.55 cents.

The present value of $648.425 received in ten years discounted at 10 percent per year (its opportunity cost) is equal to $648.425 times the discount factor found in table 2 (0.3855), or $249.97. Although the sum does not exactly equal $250.00 due to rounding, it does show that compounding and discounting are opposite sides of the same concept. The discount factors found in appendix table 2 are the reciprocals of the compounding factors found in table 1. (For example, for investment A they are 1/2.5937 = 0.3855.)

Annuities

A common occurrence when evaluating future benefits and costs in a project is to determine the present value of a series of equal-sized cash flows made over a number of periods. These types of benefits and payments are called annuities (see table 15-3). Examples of annuities are mortgage and car payments, student loans, and lottery winnings, where the same amount of money is paid or received each month for so many years.

For example, what is the present value of receiving $100 per year for each of the next five years when discounted at 12 percent? (An alternative way to look at

Table 15-3 An Illustration of an Annuity

Year	Beginning Balance	+	Interest Earned	=	Money Available	–	Net Withdrawal	=	Amount
1	$360.48	+	$43.26	=	$403.74	–	$100	=	$303.74
2	303.74	+	36.45	=	340.19	–	100	=	240.19
3	240.19	+	28.82	=	269.01	–	100	=	169.01
4	169.01	+	20.28	=	189.29	–	100	=	89.29
5	89.29	+	10.71	=	100.00	–	100	=	0.00

Interest of 12 percent per year is paid at the end of each year.

this is how much money needs to be put into a savings account today in order to take out $100 each year for the next five years if the account earns 12 percent per year?) The solution to this problem is found by multiplying $100 by the present value factors given for 12 percent, found in appendix table 2, for years 1 through 5. The present value is $360.48.

Year 1: $100 × 0.8929 = $ 89.29
Year 2: $100 × 0.7972 = 79.72
Year 3: $100 × 0.7118 = 71.18
Year 4: $100 × 0.6355 = 63.55
Year 5: $100 × 0.5674 = 56.74
$500 × 3.6048 = $360.48

This same answer could have been derived more quickly by multiplying $100 by the sum of the present value factors (3.6048). In fact, this is exactly what an **annuity** factor is—the sum of the present value factors over the number of periods desired. These values also have been summarized in tables and appear in appendix table 3. The tabular value for this example (3.6048) is found at the intersection of 12 percent and five years.

The annuity is represented mathematically in the following way:

$$VN = XA_{5,\,12\%}$$

Where X = amount paid or received each period
$A_{5,\,12\%}$ = annuity factor, or present value of a dollar received each period for five periods discounted at 12 percent per period
VN = value now (present value)

Using the example,

$$\begin{aligned} VN &= XA_{5,\,12\%} \\ &= \$100 \times 3.6048 \\ &= \$360.48 \end{aligned}$$

Thus, if you put $360.48 in the bank today, you could take out $100 the first day of each year for the next five years before running out of money in the account. To see if this annuity formula really works, look at table 15-3.

CAPITAL BUDGETING DECISION PROCEDURES THAT USE THE TIME VALUE OF MONEY

With a foundation now in place, it is possible to examine the capital budgeting procedures that use the time value of money in their evaluation. Each procedure is performed slightly differently but all rely heavily on measuring incremental after-tax cash flows. These are the best procedures to follow when making capital budgeting decisions.

The Net Present Value Method

An investment's **net present value (NPV)** is the difference between the present value of its benefits and the present value of its costs. A firm should invest in projects with a positive net present value (that is, the present value of the benefits is greater than the present value of the costs). As can be seen in table 15-4, the after-tax present value of the benefits in the continuing example of investments A and B exceeds the present value of their cost of $1,000. Both are acceptable based on the results of the NPV method. If only one project can be undertaken, investment B provides the largest net benefit ($514.70) and should be selected.

The net present value method meets all the investment criteria stated earlier in this chapter. In addition, it avoids the size disparity problem of other evaluation procedures by giving the net return from each investment in dollars so managers can obtain the greatest long-term net benefit from its capital expenditures.

Table 15-4 After-Tax Net Present Value for Investments A and B

	Investment A					Investment B				
Year	Yearly After-Tax Benefit	×	Present Value Factor*	=	After-Tax Present Value of Benefits	Yearly After-Tax Benefit	×	Present Value Factor*	=	After-Tax Present Value of Benefits
1	$ 500		0.926		$ 463.00	$ 100		0.926		$ 92.60
2	400		0.857		342.80	200		0.857		171.40
3	300		0.794		238.20	300		0.794		238.20
4	200		0.735		147.00	400		0.735		294.00
5	100		0.681		68.10	500		0.681		340.50
6	—		—		—	600		0.630		378.00
Total	$1,500		3.993		$1,259.10	$2,100		4.623		$1,514.70
Less: Initial cost					1,000.00					1,000.00
Net present value					$ 259.10					$ 514.70
Benefit/cost ratio					1.26					1.51

*Discounted at 8%.

The Benefit/Cost Ratio Method

A variation of the net present value technique is the **benefit/cost (B/C) ratio**. When using this method, the present value of an investment's benefits is divided by the present value of its costs. An investment should have a ratio value greater than 1.0 for a project to be acceptable.

Using the B/C ratio to determine the profitability of any given investment generally will give the same results as those found using the NPV method. However, different rankings can be obtained when the B/C method is used because it measures relative profitability rather than total net benefits. Because of this, the B/C method often is preferred over the net present value method when all acceptable investment opportunities cannot be undertaken because it gives a measure of the benefits generated for each dollar invested.

To illustrate how different results in rankings can occur between net present value and benefit/cost, assume that investments C and D are under consideration. Investment C has an initial cost of $5,000. Associated with this investment is a present value of benefits of $6,000. Dividing $6,000 by $5,000 yields a B/C ratio of 1.2. If investment D has an initial cost of $10,000 and the present value of its benefits are $11,000, its B/C ratio is 1.1. The B/C ratios indicate that both investments are acceptable, but if a choice must be made, investment C should be selected because of its higher ratio (1.2 versus 1.1). Under the net present value method, both would have the same NPV ($1,000) and the investor would be indifferent.

The Internal Rate of Return Method

The **internal rate of return (IRR)** method is a variation of the NPV method. The IRR is the discount rate that makes the present value of an investment's benefits equal to the present value of its costs. Rather than applying a known discount rate, the goal is to solve for the discount rate that makes the NPV equal to zero. That discount rate is the rate of return in the project. The decision rule for many firms is to accept projects with a rate of return greater than or equal to the opportunity cost of investment for the firm. Investment projects that do this also have a positive net present value.

The internal rate of return computation for investments A and B requires finding the rate of return that discounts the present value of the returns to $1,000 (the initial outlay). The internal rate of return for investment A is 20–21 percent (table 15-5). At a discount rate of 20 percent, the present value of the benefits still exceeds the costs by $4.67. However, at a discount rate of 21 percent, the net present value is –$11.64. The IRR for investment A is between 20 and 21 percent.

The Amortization Method

The amortization method evaluates capital budgeting alternatives by putting everything on a yearly basis rather than comparing total benefits and total costs. Costs and benefits are converted to a yearly basis using the annuity formula. This sometimes makes it easier to evaluate alternatives.

For example, let's look at investment A again with its initial cost of $1,000. Further, assume the required minimum rate of return (the opportunity cost) is 8 percent

Table 15-5 Determining the Internal Rate of Return for Project A

	Discounted at 20%					Discounted at 21%				
Year	Yearly After-Tax Benefit	×	Present Value Factor	=	After-Tax Present Value of Benefits	Yearly After-Tax Benefit	×	Present Value Factor	=	After-Tax Present Value of Benefits
1	$ 500		0.8333		$ 416.65	$ 500		0.8266		$ 413.30
2	400		0.6944		277.76	400		0.6834		273.36
3	300		0.5787		173.61	300		0.5651		169.53
4	200		0.4823		96.46	200		0.4675		93.50
5	100		0.4019		40.19	100		0.3867		38.67
Total	$1,500		2.9906		$1,004.67	$1,500		2.9293		$ 988.36
Less: Initial cost					1,000.00					1,000.00
Net present value					$ 4.67					$ -11.64

and the investment has a life of five years. What is the **equivalent annual cost (EAC)** of the $1,000 initial cost under these assumptions? To convert the $1,000 to an annual cost, find the intersection of five years and 8 percent on appendix table 3 (3.993). Place this value into the annuity equation and solve for *X*, the amount paid per period.

$$VN = XA_{5,\,8\%}$$

$$\$1{,}000 = X \times 3.993$$

$$X = \frac{\$1{,}000}{3.993}$$

$$X = \$250.44$$

In other words, the EAC of investing $1,000 at the start of a project when the discount rate is 8 percent is $250.44 per year for the next 5 years. If the investment has expected after-tax benefits of $300 per year for each of the next five years, the net present value per year is $49.56 to the firm and the project is acceptable. The B/C ratio is found by dividing $300 by $250.44, which yields a ratio of 1.2 per year. This makes it possible to conduct all the same types of capital budgeting decision evaluations as before. The only difference is that everything is done on an average yearly basis.

The real value of the amortization method is in situations in which benefits and costs vary from year to year. Investment A is an example of this situation. Discounting the returns of investment A at 8 percent gives a total present value $1,259.10 (table 15-4). To convert these total returns to an average annual benefit, divide the total present value of the benefits by the annuity value for that period (3.993). Thus, receiving an average annual benefit of $315.33 per year is equivalent to total benefits over the five-year period of $1,259.10. The same procedure can be applied to costs. The average annual cost of this investment is $250.44. This gives an annual net benefit to the firm of $64.89 and a B/C ratio of 1.26. The project is still acceptable whether the analysis is done on the present value of total benefits and costs or annual benefits and costs.

Chapter Highlights

1. Financial decisions regarding the acquisition of property, plant, and equipment are in a special class of decisions called capital budgeting decisions.
2. Capital budgeting decision-making procedures require compensation to investors for the delay in receiving benefits. The economic principle of opportunity cost is used to overcome this problem.
3. A good capital investment provides the largest long-term net profit to the firm, provides benefits sooner rather than later, and has the lowest risk.
4. The proper data for capital budgeting decisions are after-tax incremental cash flows.
5. The payback and average rate of return methods of evaluating capital budgeting decisions are flawed because they do not consider the time value of money.
6. The time value of money is its opportunity cost. This means including the cost of what you are giving up when calculating the total cost of an investment.
7. Compounding is the opposite of discounting. Compounding is about finding the value of something in the future. Discounting is about finding the value of something today that will be received in the future.
8. The best capital budgeting evaluation methods are those that incorporate the time value of money in their calculations. They include the net present value, benefit/cost ratio, internal rate of return, and amortization methods.

Chapter Quiz

1. Explain why capital budgeting decisions are different from other management decisions. Use an example.
2. Identify and explain the four characteristics of a good investment and show how each helps the firm accomplish its objective of maximizing long-term profits.
3. What are the best data for making capital budgeting decisions?
4. Describe the advantages and disadvantages of the payback and average rate of return methods for evaluating capital budgeting decisions.
5. Explain how the time value of money is the same as the economic principle of opportunity cost. Show how it should be included in the evaluation of an investment.
6. Define the terms compounding and discounting as they are used in capital budgeting decisions. Compare and contrast the two terms.
7. Why has compound interest been called the miracle of the modern world? Develop an example that shows its impact over a 40-year period.
8. Convert the savings account example found in table 15-3 into a loan. Using a table, determine the amount of the payments, show how the payments exactly pay off the loan, and give the lender the interest that is expected.

9. Explain how the net present value of a project is the profit from an investment. How does the time value of money make this true?
10. Create a table comparing and contrasting the evaluation procedures that use the time value of money. Give an example of a situation in which each would be the best to use.
11. Define and explain the term equivalent annual cost.
12. Explain why net present value is the preferred capital budgeting tool by agribusinesses.
13. Explain why projects with internal rates of return greater than their opportunity cost have positive net present values.
14. Explain why firms that make investments in projects only with a positive net present value are said to be generating capital.
15. Explain why firms that make investments in projects only with a positive net present value become the first choice of investors.

CASE 15
Nick's Financial Future: Part I

Nick was starting to feel at home with his new job. He thought his boss was finally beginning to have some confidence in him. During most of the past six months since Nick started this job, Mr. Raymond had always gone back to carefully scrutinize every calculation and decision that Nick had made. So far, everything checked out.

Nick's latest assignment was to evaluate whether it was worthwhile to purchase a new grinding machine for the feed plant. This assignment seemed different. All Mr. Raymond did was to send him an e-mail with some suggestions about where he could find all the information he needed and a date to get it back. In all his previous assignments, Nick had to sit through a 30-minute meeting where Mr. Raymond gave him detailed, step-by-step instructions about what to do and how to do it. Since he was coming up on his first six-month performance review, he took this as a good sign. Nick finished his analysis, wrote a nice report, and got back to Mr. Raymond three days before the deadline.

When he got back from lunch on Friday, he had a voice mail message from Mr. Raymond that said, "Come see me NOW!" Nick hurried off to Mr. Raymond's office.

Mr. Raymond ushered him right into to his office saying, "I gave you a simple assignment, and all I wanted was a simple answer, not a lot of gobbledy gook. You recommend buying the grinding machine but I don't have a clue why. If I don't understand how you did it, we won't be doing it. In the past we have made these decisions by going with everything with a payback period of three years or less. What we do isn't good enough for you?"

It was clear Mr. Raymond had never heard of opportunity cost, the time value of money, and the net present value method of evaluating capital expenditures. Nick had 10 minutes to explain what he did.

If you were Nick, what would you say?

Chapter 16

Capital Budgeting II

Applications

Chapter Learning Objectives

- Explain the importance of using the right discount rate in capital budgeting analysis and how it can affect a firm's long-term financial survival.
- Describe how changes in the discount rate affect capital budgeting decisions.
- Explain how to calculate a firm's cost of capital.
- Explain how to adjust cash flow for taxes.
- Summarize why depreciation is a noncash expense and how it affects capital budgeting decisions.
- Explain how to evaluate capital budgeting alternatives with unequal physical lives.
- Show how to handle uncertainty and risk in capital budgeting analysis.
- Explain how to decide whether it is better to pay cash, take out a loan, or lease a capital good.

Introduction

The principles and procedures of capital budgeting were explained in chapter 15. A large part of that chapter was devoted to understanding the time value of money and how it enables managers to make objective capital budgeting decisions. This chapter refines these principles and procedures so managers can effectively apply them when making capital investment decisions.

Discount Rates

The Importance of Selecting the Right Discount Rate

The discount rate an agribusiness uses in its capital budgeting analysis plays a major role in its long-term financial survival. It can be as important to the acceptance or rejection of an investment as cash flows. Since capital budgeting decisions deal with projects that have major impacts on firms' long-term revenues, costs, and profits, it is important for managers to use the right discount rate when evaluating capital expenditures. But managers need to know more than just where to insert the discount rate into a formula to make good capital budgeting decisions. They need to understand what the discount rate represents, how it is determined, and how changes can influence the firm's capital budgeting decisions.

To attract investment capital, a firm must generate a return on capital at least equal to the average ROIC in that industry. If a firm cannot do this, little incentive exists for investors to put their money into it. Thus, an appropriate starting point for a discount rate on the firm's capital is the industry's average ROIC. This can be found in places such as RMA's *Annual Statement Studies*, mentioned in chapter 14, and *Fortune* magazine's annual list of the 500 largest businesses.

The positive dollar value found at the end of a net present value calculation is the profit from the investment after adjusting for the time value of money (the opportunity cost on the firm's capital). The net present value (NPV) is how much this capital project will add to the value of the firm. Dividing NPV by the number of shares of stock in the business tells how much the price per share should rise. Conversely, if the firm accepts investments with negative net present values (returns below its opportunity cost) the value of the firm and its stock will decline. If the firm accepts only projects with the highest positive NPV, it will always get an ROIC that is above the industry average and the firm will become the first choice of investors.

Potential shareholders are aware of the opportunity cost for capital in an industry and evaluate a firm's financial performance using that discount rate. They will invest in those firms that consistently provide the highest returns on capital. It is important for managers to know what discount rate investors are using and how they calculate it so they can apply the same rate when evaluating their business's capital budgeting opportunities.

The Effect of Changes in Discount Rates on Capital Budgeting Decisions

Table 16-1 shows the effect of changes in discount rates on the present value of benefits, the net present value, and the benefit/cost ratio of investment A from chapter 15. As the discount rate on capital increases, the present value of the benefits decreases—less money needs to be invested today in order for it to grow to the anticipated benefit to be paid each year of the project.

To obtain the expected $500 of after-tax benefits in year one, an investor with an 8 percent opportunity cost would need to invest $463.00 today. Investors with a 15 percent opportunity cost would need to deposit $435.00; those with a 24 percent opportunity cost would need to invest only $403.50 today.

Table 16-1 Discounted Cash Flow for Investment A

Year	Yearly After-Tax Benefit	Present Value of Benefits Discounted at: 8%	15%	24%
1	$ 500	$ 463.00	$ 435.00	$ 403.50
2	400	342.80	302.40	260.00
3	300	238.20	197.40	157.50
4	200	147.00	114.20	84.60
5	100	68.10	49.70	34.10
Total	$1,500	$1,259.10	$1,098.70	$ 939.70
Less: Initial cost		1,000.00	1,000.00	1,000.00
Net present value		$ 259.10	$ 98.70	$(60.30)
Benefit/cost ratio		1.26	1.10	0.94

The result is that businesses with opportunity costs of 8 and 15 percent would find investment A acceptable. The value of those firms would increase by $259.10 and $98.70 respectively. If the firms had 100 shares of stock, the value of each share would increase $2.5910 and $0.9870. For a business with a 24 percent opportunity cost, the value of the firm would decline by $60.30 or $0.603 per share if they had 100 shares of stock.

By selecting capital investments with the highest positive net present values, a company becomes more valuable because its ROIC is increasing. This leads to a higher price for the stock. Profit-maximizing investors typically gravitate to those firms in an industry whose investments offer the greatest financial returns to their shareholders.

Investors select an industry for investment based on its return on invested capital and the variation in the return. Normally these two items have an inverse relationship. Those investors seeking stability may prefer an industry that generates a regular payment of 8 percent per year to one currently paying 25 percent but varies dramatically from year to year. Once an industry decision is made, investors should always seek firms within that industry that consistently give the best returns.

Determining Cost of Capital

If agribusinesses were financed solely by stock, no more would need to be said about discount rates. But like most other businesses, agribusinesses also use borrowed money and retained earnings for financing. A business's operation is supported by all the capital employed, so the best way to reflect this is to use a **weighted average cost of capital,** where the weights are the proportion of total capital coming from each source.

Determining the Cost of Borrowed Capital. Methods for determining reliable interest rates on borrowed capital vary among firms, since different agribusinesses use different proportions of long-term and short-term debt. Financial institutions offer a variety of fixed and variable rates for borrowed capital and these rates often change. Predicting interest rates for the future is imprecise, but the task is easier when an agribusiness has considerable long-term borrowing at fixed rates.

For simplicity, assume that a firm has a real estate debt with an insurance company of $50,000 at an 8.25 percent interest rate. In addition, it has short-term bank loans that over the past few years have averaged $10,000 per year at an average interest rate of 6.75 percent.

The weighted average interest rate on the borrowed money in this example would be:

	(1) amount of borrowed capital	(2) interest rate (%)	(3) interest charge [(1) × (2)]
	$50,000	8.25	$4,125
	$10,000	6.75	675
Total	$60,000		$4,800

The weighted average = ($4,800 / $60,000) × 100 = 8%

Dividing the total interest paid ($4,800) by the total capital borrowed ($60,000) gives a weighted average cost for borrowed capital of 8 percent.

Determining the Cost of Ownership Capital. Determining the cost of ownership/equity/retained-earnings capital is difficult. Theoretically, the cost of ownership capital is the investor's opportunity cost. For the firm to retain owners' funds in the business it must provide a return to them that is greater than what they can obtain by investing elsewhere. The fact that they have invested in the firm indicates the business offers at least a satisfactory rate of return. The procedure used here assigns the average industry rate of return on capital to ownership capital. This can be adjusted to meet different situations.

Determining the Firm's Weighted Average Total Cost of Capital. Using the right-hand side of a balance sheet, it is possible to calculate the percentage of total capital derived from each source. The example shown in table 16-2 assumes that the owner supplies 50 percent of the capital (both as direct investment and retained earnings) with the remainder being borrowed. The weighted average cost of capital is the sum of the weighted costs of the individual sources of capital, or 9.4 percent.

Table 16-2 Determining the Average Cost of Capital

	(1) Percent of Total Capital	(2) Interest Cost	(3) Weighted Cost [(1) × (2)]
Equity capital	50	0.10	5.00
Borrowed capital			
Bank	40	0.09	3.60
Insurance company	10	0.08	0.80
	100		9.40

In this case, the cost of borrowed capital is less than the equity capital and the weighted cost of capital for the firm is less than the long-term return on capital in this industry. This is not always the case. When the cost of borrowed money is greater than the equity capital, the weighted average cost of capital can exceed the opportunity cost on equity, so the discount rate for capital budgeting projects needs to be adjusted upward.

The goal is to find projects where the internal rate of return (IRR) is greater than the **cost of capital** used to finance them—the weighted average cost of capital. By minimizing the weighted average cost of capital, managers maximize the potential benefit to their shareholders because more investment projects will have an IRR that exceeds its cost of the capital. When this happens a business is creating new capital and value for its shareholders. This is reflected in bigger dividends and higher stock prices. Agribusinesses whose investments do not meet this test are consuming their investment capital and will see a decline in the price of their stock.

THE EFFECT OF TAXES

So far, the discussion of investment analysis has been limited to profitability analysis in its simplest form. The effect of taxes on investment decisions has been deliberately omitted to simplify the computations. However, taxes are an important part of investment analysis because they influence the size of the cash flows in an investment.

Effect of Taxes on Discount Rates

Income taxes only affect discount rates if 100 percent of the investment in a company is borrowed. Otherwise, the right discount rate is the firm's weighted average cost of capital. To the outside world—investors and lenders—a business is supported by its entire **capital structure**. They do not separate out each piece or project to see how that one project was financed. Every project is financed by the firm's total capital structure as reflected in its weighted average cost of capital. This is why it is cash flows rather than discount rates that are adjusted for taxes.

Depreciation: A Noncash Expense

Although it is usually best to keep costs as low as possible, it is important to remember that expenses have an impact on the amount of income tax paid by a firm. When revenues are held constant, each additional dollar of cost reduces taxes by the amount of the applicable tax rate.

For example, if the tax rate is 20 percent, the net cost to the firm of each additional dollar of expense is only 80 cents. Each added dollar of cost drops before-tax profits by $1.00, but taxes subsequently decline by 20 cents. One way to think of it is that for each dollar of expense the firm pays, the government gives them a 20 percent "refund" in the form of lower taxes. This relationship is illustrated in the example below. (This affect also can be seen by taxing revenues and costs first, and then subtracting the after-tax values from each other.)

	Before	After	Difference
Revenues	$100.00	$100.00	$ 0
Less expenses	– 60.00	– 61.00	–1.00
Profits before tax	40.00	39.00	–1.00
Less taxes @ 20%	– 8.00	– 7.80	–(0.20)
Profits after tax	$ 32.00	$ 31.20	($0.80)

Depreciation was created by accountants to reflect the annual "consumption" of a fixed asset, such as a building or piece of equipment. For example, if a business buys a building for $100,000 and expects it to last 20 years, it is assumed that $5,000 worth of the building is "consumed" each year. Every year for the next 20 years, the business will have a $5,000 tax-deductible depreciation expense.

When a firm buys a fixed asset, it pays the seller the full amount of the purchase price upon delivery. From a cash flow perspective, the purchase is recorded as a single cash outflow equal to the purchase price. How the business got the money to pay for the item is not important. Regardless of whether the firm pays cash or borrows the funds to make the purchase, the accountant will enter a depreciation expense each year for the item. Were it not for income tax, depreciation expense entries on balance sheets and income statements would be of little interest to a manager thinking of making a capital investment.

As mentioned earlier, unlike other tax-deductible business expenses, depreciation expenses do not involve a payment or cash outflow. However, they do reduce firms' income taxes because of the "tax refund" on each expense dollar. For example, with a 20 percent tax rate, each $1.00 of depreciation lowers the firm's tax bill by 20 cents, as in the example above. The value of the depreciation tax shield is equal to the tax rate times the depreciation expense for the period. This often provides a firm with a substantial reduction in its tax bill, which can greatly increase the likelihood that a capital budgeting project will yield a positive net present value.

Tax Incentives to Encourage Business Investment

To encourage capital investment by businesses, the federal government has from time to time provided tax incentives. The accelerated cost recovery program in the 1980s was designed to increase the likelihood that a net present value calculation will show positive results. It increases the after-tax present value of the depreciation tax shield by reducing the amount of time needed to fully depreciate a fixed asset. A faster depreciation rate on fixed assets generates higher annual depreciation expenses, a higher present values of depreciation tax shield, and lower tax bills. For example, if an asset that was being depreciated over 10 years is now allowed to be fully depreciated in five years, this doubles the size of the annual depreciation expense and substantially increases the present value of the depreciation tax shield in a net present value analysis.

Another extra tax incentive often used to encourage business investment is an **investment tax credit**. Although the details of this program vary, investment tax credits generally permit a firm to deduct what they spend on certain capital goods directly from their tax bills, up to a specified percentage (often 10 percent). If, for example, a firm were to undertake an investment of $10,000 on a qualified capital good, it could deduct 10 percent of the investment ($1,000) directly from its tax bill. The effect is to reduce the initial cost of the investment by 10 percent. In this example, the effective cost to the firm for this investment is now $9,000 rather than $10,000.

Both of these tax investment incentives have been used to increase business investment during economic downturns. They are typically put into effect for limited periods until the economy resumes its growth. The exact procedures and where they apply change regularly, so it is important to consult with a tax preparer to get the most current regulations.

Mutually Exclusive Investments

In the previous discussion of investments A and B, the analysis operated under the implied assumption that the projects are mutually exclusive; that is, only one investment will be selected from all of the alternatives. Generally, when mutually exclusive investment opportunities exist, a manager is presented with several ways to solve the same problem, such as which new machine provides the lowest cost solution. In this situation, the manager simply needs to select the one with the largest positive net present value. However, if the projects have different physical lives, an adjustment must be made so that all investment options cover the same amount of time before net present values can be properly compared.

Adjusting for Unequal Physical Lives

One way to account for unequal durations is to give all alternatives a common termination date regardless of how long the capital investment lasts. For example, if the shortest life for one investment alternative is five years, it can be assumed that all other investments will last that long and their investment is terminated at that time. Alternatively, a replacement cycle of investment can be assumed until all alternatives have a common ending date. For example, if one investment gives benefits for four years while the other gives eight years of benefits, assume the first investment is replaced at the end of the fourth year so both options can be evaluated over an 8-year period.

Let's look at investments E and F. They are mutually exclusive and have physical lives of five and ten years, respectively. Each requires an investment of $5,000. After-tax annual net cash flows are $2,500 for E and $2,000 for F. The net present values and benefit/cost ratios for each option using an 8 percent discount rate are:

Investment E:

1. Present value of benefits $= \$2{,}500 \times A_{5,\,8\%}$
   $= \$2{,}500 \times 3.993$
   $= \$9{,}982.50$
2. Net present value $= PV$ of benefits $- PV$ of costs
   $= \$9{,}982.50 - \$5{,}000$
   $= \$4{,}982.50$
3. Benefit/cost ratio $= PV$ of benefits $/\ PV$ of costs
   $= \$9{,}982.50\ /\ \$5{,}000$
   $= 1.9965$

Investment F:

1. Present value of benefits $= \$2{,}000 \times A_{10,\,8\%}$
   $= \$2{,}000 \times 6.710$
   $= \$13{,}420$
2. Net present value $= PV$ of benefits $- PV$ of costs
   $= \$13{,}420 - \$5{,}000$
   $= \$8{,}420$
3. Benefit/cost ratio $= PV$ of benefits $/\ PV$ of costs
   $= \$13{,}420\ /\ \$5{,}000$
   $= 2.684$

The decision-making rules discussed to this point indicate that the best investment is F, because both the NPV and the B/C ratio are higher. But is this correct? A more complete analysis requires that after the end of the fifth year, when the physical life of investment E ends, other investments that yield at least 8 percent are available for the next five years so both alternatives can be compared over the same period.

The Common Termination Period Method. The common termination period method assumes that both investments stop at the end of year 5, when the physical life of investment E (the investment option with the shortest physical life) expires. If the capital investment in investment F can be sold for $2,000 at the end of year 5, the present value of the benefits from investing in F is now $9,348 (see below). This reduces its NPV to $4,348 and its B/C ratio to 1.870. Investment E becomes the best investment when they are compared using a common termination period.

Investment F:

1. Present value of benefits
   a. Cash inflow years 1–5 $= \$2,000 \times A_{5,\,8\%}$
   $= \$2,000 \times 3.993$
   $= \$7,986$
   b. Salvage value end of year 5 $= \$2,000 \times PV$ at 8%
   $= \$2,000 \times 0.681$
   $= \$1,362$
   c. Total (a + b) $= \$9,348$
2. Net present value $= PV$ of benefits – PV of costs
   $= \$9,348 - \$5,000$
   $= \$4,348$
3. Benefit/cost ratio $= PV$ of benefits / PV of costs
   $= \$9,348 / \$5,000$
   $= 1.870$

The Replacement Cycle Method. Under the replacement cycle method, investments are assumed to continue until a common terminal period is reached. This procedure might be used when, for example, alternative machines are available to perform a job that is likely to continue for a long time, such as a milling machine in a flour mill.

Investments E and F, although they differ in terms of the value of their annual cash flow, can be configured for a common terminal date of 10 years. In this situation, it is assumed that the firm would purchase another machine at the end of year 5. As a result, both E and F would wear out at the same time (at the end of year 10).

Assume that a replacement machine for investment E can be purchased for $6,000 at the end of the fifth year. (The $1,000 increase in the initial cost is the expected price increase in investment E.) Computations of the net present value and benefit/cost ratio when E is replaced at the end of the fifth year are:

Investment E:

1. PV of benefits 1–10 years = $2,500 × $A_{10,\,8\%}$
   = $2,500 × 6.710
   = $16,775
2. Present value of costs = *PV* of initial purchase + *PV* of second purchase
   = $5,000 + ($6,000 × 0.681)
   = $9,086
3. Net present value = *PV* of benefits – *PV* of costs
   = $16,775 – $9,086
   = $7,689
4. Benefit/cost ratio = *PV* of benefits / *PV* of costs
   = $16,775 / $9,086
   = 1.846

Under this method, investment F is the best alternative because of its higher NPV ($8,420 versus $7,689) and B/C ratio (2.684 versus 1.846).

The selection of method depends largely on the planning horizon of the firm and the rate of technological change. In situations where technology or costs change rapidly, the shortest common terminal period may be best to use. In more settled situations, where continuous replacement of a settled technology is more likely, the replacement cycle method may be best. The selection is left to the judgment of the manager.

Dealing with Uncertainty and Risk

Risk and uncertainty in investments are very different things. Risk implies sufficient knowledge about a situation so that probabilities can be attached to various outcomes. Risk assessment is the basis of insurance. For example, an insurance company can evaluate the likelihood that a given firm will experience an accident or a fire that damages its buildings or equipment. It uses this information to set a price that will yield a profit.

Uncertainty implies the lack of sufficient knowledge about possible outcomes to assign any probabilities. Changing government farm programs and regulations, the introduction of new technologies, and other activities that influence food production and marketing generate investment uncertainty. Let's look at a situation where a peanut farmer has the opportunity to buy another farm that also comes with a peanut allotment. Uncertainty results if the farmer is unable to objectively evaluate whether the peanut program will be continued.

From an individual manager's point of view, deviations arising from either risk or uncertainty are very similar. Agribusinesses use insurance as a way to protect themselves from physical risks such as fire, weather, and crop damage. However, insurance cannot cover all risks. Several means exist to help agribusinesses assess and cover those risks they cannot insure against.

Developing Alternative Outcomes

The discussion of cash flow budgets in chapter 8 highlights the advantage of alternative budgets. They show the impact of changes in key financial variables on the profitability of the business. The most widely used method is to develop budgets and cash flow projections using three scenarios: the most optimistic, the most likely, and the worst case. This procedure provides the decision maker with a crude measure of the risks associated with a given circumstance.

Consider a case where two investments with the same costs and durations have: (1) the same B/C ratio under the most likely case, (2) B/C ratios that differ slightly under the most optimistic outcome, and (3) B/C ratios of 0.5 and 1.0 when the worst-case outcome is evaluated. The right decision would be to select the investment whose B/C ratio remains profitable regardless of the situation.

Break-Even Cash Flows

Just as break-even calculations can help an agribusiness make good pricing and production decisions, the same approach can be applied to measure the sensitivity of capital-budgeting decisions to changes in cash flows. A break-even cash flow occurs when the discounted cash flows over the economic life of a project result in a net present value of zero or a B/C ratio of 1.0. It is different from the internal rate of return (IRR) procedure. In IRR the goal is to adjust the discount rate until the NPV is equal to zero. In break-even cash flows, the discount rate is left unchanged but the timing and sizes of revenues or costs are adjusted until the NPV is zero.

Comparing break-even cash flow estimates with the most likely outcomes provides a measure of the uncertainty associated with an investment. The usual procedure is to compute the percentage decline in revenue or increase in cost needed to reach a zero NPV.

For example, suppose a new machine is introduced. It costs $10,000 and is expected to last 10 years. The manufacturer agrees to remove it at the end of its life for $1,000. The machine is expected to increase after-tax net cash flow by $2,000 per year. Given a discount rate of 10 percent, the calculation of the break-even after-tax net cash flow can be done using the amortization technique, that is, by dividing the present value of costs by the annuity factor for the appropriate time period and interest rate. The annuity factor for 10 years at 10 percent is 6.145.

The break-even cash flow is determined as follows:

PV of initial outlay	$10,000
PV of removal cost ($1,000 × 0.386)	+$ 386
PV of total costs	$10,386

$$NPV = 0 = PV \text{ revenue} - PV \text{ costs}$$

$$0 = XA_{10,10\%} - PV \text{ costs}$$

$$0 = (X)6.145 - 10,386$$

$$X = \frac{\$10,386}{6.145}$$

$$X = \$1,690.15 \text{ per year}$$

Thus, the annual after-tax net income could fall as low as $1,690 (the break-even value) and still provide the firm with a 10 percent return on its investment. Another way to look at the break-even cash flow is to determine the percentage decline in return needed. In this case, the break-even point is approximately 15 percent below the expected increase in net cash flow ($2,000). In other words, the annual after-tax net cash flow would have to be more than 15 percent below what is expected before the investment starts losing money.

Suppose that a special promotional deal is available that gives a 20 percent discount off the selling price for a purchase made this month. This lowers the PV of the cost to $8,386. In this case, the break-even savings figure falls to $1,365 ($8,386 / 6.145). Now the break-even increase in revenue would have to fall by more than 32 percent before the investment starts losing money. Such computations for different investment alternatives provide the decision maker with a measure of the sensitivity of their investments to changes in the value of key variables.

A Case Study: Evaluating the Financial Feasibility of Adding a Liquid Fertilizer Line to a Farm Supply Business

The owner of AgBiz Corporation has been approached by a fertilizer distributor to see if he is interested in taking on a liquid fertilizer line. He has adequate space and storage facilities to handle the new business. However, he will need to purchase a new spray truck for $80,000. The truck will be used for five years and could be sold for $20,000.

The manager has been considering this option for some time and has done some research on it as part of his marketing plan. He estimates that he would be able to sell 80,000 pounds of product each year at 22 cents per pound and make a gross margin (selling price – cost of goods sold) of 4 cents per pound. Because there is little competition in the area, he feels that the addition of the liquid fertilizer also will allow him to custom-spread 10,000 acres per year with an application fee of $3.50 per acre.

One part-time worker to drive the spray truck will need to be hired at a cost of $8,000 per year. Additional operating costs for custom work are expected to run around 50 cents per acre. The firm uses 12 percent as its opportunity cost (discount rate) and has a tax rate of 20 percent. Because of his excellent credit rating, he is able to borrow the full price of the spray truck.

Using partial budgeting to determine the costs and benefits, he estimates a change in net income before depreciation and taxes of $25,200. To complete the analysis, the manager takes into consideration the impact this decision will have on cash flows and performs a net present value calculation on the investment.

The cash flow feasibility analysis (table 16-3) shows negative cash flows in years one, two, and three if the operation is financed with a three-year loan. The cash flow remains positive in all five years if the loan is repaid in five years (table 16-4). The negative cash flows in the three-year loan arise because the length of the loan is less than the life of the asset (five years). The most feasible option from a cash flow perspective is to use a five-year loan.

Table 16-3 Cash Flow Feasibility Analysis for Starting a Line of Liquid Fertilizer Financed with a Three-Year $80,000 Loan at 15 Percent

	Year 1	Year 2	Year 3	Year 4	Year 5
Change in cash income after operating expenses	$25,200	$ 25,200	$ 25,200	$ 25,200	$25,200
Less: Loan payment	−35,038	−35,038	−35,038	0	0
New cash income	−9,838	−9,838	−9,838	+25,200	+25,200
Less: Change in taxes*	−560	+211	+926	+1,840	+1,840
Net cash flow	$-9,278	$−10,049	$−10,764	$+23,360	$23,360

Depreciation is a straight line: $80,000 / 5 years = $16,000/year.
Loan interest is paid on the unpaid balance for years 1–3: $12,000, $8,545, and $4,570.

*Calculated as new cash income less depreciation and loan interest = before-tax income, which is taxed at 20 percent.

Table 16-4 Cash Flow Feasibility Analysis for Starting a Line of Liquid Fertilizer Financed with a Five-Year $80,000 Loan at 15 Percent

	Year 1	Year 2	Year 3	Year 4	Year 5
Change in cash income after operating expenses	$25,200	$25,200	$25,200	$25,200	$25,200
Less: Loan payment	−23,865	−23,865	−23,865	−23,865	−23,865
New cash income	+1,335	+1,335	+1,335	+1,335	+1,335
Less: Change in taxes*	−560	−200	+205	+676	+1,217
Net cash flow	$+1,895	$+1,535	$+1,130	$ +659	$ +118

Depreciation is a straight line: $80,000 / 5 years = $16,000/year.
Loan interest is paid on the unpaid balance for years 1–5: $12,000, $10,220, $8,174, $5,820, and $3,114.

*Calculated as new cash income less depreciation and loan interest = before-tax income, which is taxed at 20 percent.

The net present value of the investment and its B/C ratio show the project is worthwhile (table 16-5).

It is important to note that the decision to adopt a new product line required a marketing assessment, cash flow analysis, and capital budgeting analysis. In this case they gave favorable results. The company should add the liquid fertilizer line and finance it with a five-year loan.

Table 16-5 Net Present Value Analysis of Adding a Liquid Fertilizer Line Discounted at 12 Percent with a 20 Percent Tax Rate

Year	Item	Amount	×	Annuity or PV Factor	×	Tax Effect	=	After-Tax Present Value
0	Buy spray truck	$80,000		1				$-80,000.00
1–5	Increase in operating earnings/year	25,200		3.6048		(1 – 0.2)		+72,672.77
1–5	Depreciation expense/year	16,000		3.6048		0.2		+11,535.36
5	Sell spray truck	20,000		0.5674		—		+11,348.00
							NPV =	$ 15,556.13

$$\text{B/C ratio} = \frac{\$95,556.13}{\$80,000} = 1.19$$

Deciding Whether to Lease, Borrow, or Buy

Leasing of machinery, buildings, equipment, and even livestock provides agribusinesses an option to ownership of assets. Leasing gives operators a way to gain the use of assets without a major capital investment. An agribusiness manager needs to understand the advantages and disadvantages of leasing and must know how to evaluate a lease-or-buy decision. A lease is a contract between someone who owns an asset but sells the right to use it to someone else. The **lessor** is the one that owns the asset. The **lessee** is the user of the leased asset.

Three Types of Leases

Three general types of leases are commonly used in agribusiness. Each offers the lessee and lessor a set of advantages and disadvantages that both parties must weigh when selecting the best type of lease and whether leasing is the right choice.

Operating Leases. An **operating lease** is a contract, generally written for short periods, that is based on a set charge per hour, week, or month. Typically, the lessor pays the cost of maintenance and taxes. This type of lease is most commonly used with machinery and equipment rentals.

Financial Leases. A **financial lease** is a long-term contract where the lessee acquires sole use of the equipment or machinery in return for lease payments. Typically, the lessee pays the cost of maintenance, insurance, and taxes, while the lessor retains ownership of the item and takes the depreciation and any other tax deductions that are available. Lease payments are a tax-deductible business expense for the lessee in most situations.

Lease-Purchase Options. In most cases, a lease with a purchase option is similar to a financial lease. The major difference is that the lease agreement contains a provision for the lessee to buy the equipment at the end of the lease period for a prearranged price. This type of lease may not be tax deductible.

The IRS has three sets of leasing rules to evaluate whether a transaction qualifies as a true lease. Those that qualify as true leases are termed *regular, safe harbor,* or *finance* leases. A transaction needs to qualify under only one set of rules to be treated as a true lease.

Advantages of Leasing

Leasing can provide an agribusiness a number of advantages over buying. A lease agreement may call for the lessor to periodically upgrade the item at the lessor's expense so a piece of machinery or equipment remains on the cutting edge of technology and efficiency. This may be important in areas of rapid technological change because it removes this risk from the lessee. Also, lease payments are often lower than loan payments. This is especially true in the early years of a lease because the payments normally cover a longer period than loan payments.

Many leases require a down payment that is less than what would be required to purchase the item with a loan. Leasing can reduce the capital investment needed to acquire an asset, keep its technology up to date, and reduce the monthly cash outflows needed to acquire it. These are important considerations to a business, especially one just starting.

Advantages of Ownership

In a true lease, the lessor retains ownership of the item. Many leasing companies seek only to recover 10 to 30 percent of the original value of the item by the end of the contract. The ability to anticipate and evaluate what will happen at the expiration of the lease can be the most important consideration when deciding whether to lease or buy.

If the residual value of the equipment is low because it is worn out or obsolete, there is no advantage to taking ownership at the end of the lease. However, if the equipment has a physical life that is longer than the leasing period and the end-of-lease purchase price is reasonable, having a lease with a purchase clause can be worthwhile.

Lease Details

Lease Rates and Terms. Leasing firms typically figure lease payments on a percentage basis, like loans. The lease payment can vary between leasing firms depending on their costs, taxes, and profit goals. The length of the lease also can affect the lease payment. It pays to shop for the best rates and terms.

Insurance. The lessee is responsible for damage to leased equipment. When damage occurs, the lessee is responsible for repairs and is still liable for the remaining lease payments. Many leasing firms insist that the lessee have insurance to cover this possibility.

Repairs and Taxes. Usually a financial lease requires the costs of repairs and sales taxes to be paid by the lessee. Be sure to check. New equipment usually comes with warranties to cover repair costs in the early years of a lease. Dealers may be more interested than an outside leasing firm in including a warranty and repair service in a lease.

Terminating the Lease. Most leases obligate the lessee to make lease payments for the entire life of the lease. Circumstances can develop where the lessee would want to terminate the lease before its scheduled date. The lease agreement should specify the conditions and procedures for early lease termination. Some lessors are willing to sell the equipment before the end of the lease. In this case, the lessee is often obligated to reimburse the lessor for any unrecovered cost lost by the sale and early termination. It is important to understand the procedure and cost of quitting a lease before entering a lease agreement.

Expiration of the Lease. Many things take place at the end of a lease that could affect a leasing decision. A manager needs to anticipate and evaluate those costs prior to entering into a lease. For example, who pays for dismantling and removing leased property when the lease expires? If the lease states that the lessee is responsible, this will be an added expense. It also puts the lessee in a weaker bargaining position for negotiating the purchase of the equipment when the lease ends.

How to Decide between Leasing, Buying, or Borrowing

The decision between leasing, buying, and borrowing is a capital budgeting decision because it often involves large amounts of money, can affect the long-term profitability of the firm, and is nonreversible once it is made. The net present value procedure is the most appropriate decision-making method. This is best illustrated by an example.

You have the opportunity to buy a much-needed piece of equipment for $50,000. The purchase can be financed by either: (a) paying cash, (b) putting $9,500 down and financing the rest with a five-year loan at 12 percent, or (c) taking a financial lease for five years with annual payments of $12,000. If you decide to lease, the first lease payment is due on delivery. You are in the 30 percent tax bracket and typically you earn 10 percent after taxes on your investments. The dealer offers you a purchase option at the end of the lease to buy the machinery for $10,000.

Tables 16-6 through 16-8 show the results of the net present value analysis associated with a cash purchase, a purchase with borrowing, and a financial lease with a purchase option of the machinery. In this situation, the cash purchase is the lowest-cost way to pay for the equipment (NPV = –$38,627.60), followed by purchasing with borrowing (–$40,717.24), and the financial lease (–$41,236.16).

Table 16-6 Net Present Value Analysis for a Machine—Cash Purchase Option

Year	Item	Amount	×	Annuity or PV Factor	×	Tax Effect	=	After-Tax Present Value
0	Buy equipment	$50,000		1		—		$-50,000.00
1–5	Depreciation tax shield	10,000		3.7908		0.30		+11,372.40
							NPV =	$-38,627.60

Discounted at 10%.

Table 16-7 Net Present Value Analysis for a Machine—Purchase/Borrow Option

Year	Item	Amount	×	Annuity or PV Factor	×	Tax Effect	=	After-Tax Present Value
0	Down payment	$9,500		1		—		$ -9,500.00
1–5	Loan payments	11,235		3.7908		—		-42,589.64
1–5	Depreciation tax shield	10,000		3.7908		0.3		+11,372.40
							NPV =	$-40,717.24

Discounted at 10%.

Table 16-8 Net Present Value Analysis for a Machine—Financial Lease Option

Year	Item	Amount	×	Annuity or PV Factor	×	Tax Effect	=	After-Tax Present Value
0	Lease payment	$12,000		1		(1 – 0.3)		$ -8,400.00
1–4	Annual lease payment	12,000		3.1699		(1 – 0.3)		-26,627.16
5	Buy machine	10,000		0.6209		—		-6,209.00
							NPV =	$-41,236.16

Discounted at 10%.

CHAPTER HIGHLIGHTS

1. The determination of the proper discount rate is as important to a capital budgeting decision as cash flows.
2. The discount rate represents the opportunity cost that investors place on a firm's investment decisions. The firm must have a rate of return on its investments at least equal to the industry's rate.
3. The proper discount rate is the weighted average cost of capital for the firm, in which the weights reflect the relative proportions of capital coming from debt, equity, and retained earnings.

4. The depreciation tax shield comes about because depreciation is a noncash, tax-deductible expense on a profit-and-loss statement. Its existence can affect capital budgeting decisions.
5. Accelerated cost recovery and investment tax credits are two programs used by the federal government to spur business capital investment.
6. Mutually exclusive capital investment projects need to be evaluated over the same period of time. Having a common termination date or a replacement cycle with a common ending date can accomplish this.
7. Managers can test the sensitivity of their capital budgeting decisions against changes in the timing and size of cash flows by using alternative outcomes and break-even cash flow analysis.
8. Leasing of machinery, buildings, equipment, and even livestock is an increasingly popular way for businesses to obtain needed assets. This enables agribusinesses to gain access to needed assets without a major capital investment. Net present value is the best way to analyze the decision of whether to buy, borrow, or lease assets.

CHAPTER QUIZ

1. Explain why a firm's investments must generate a return on capital at least equal to the average return on capital for that industry.
2. Explain why an inverse relationship exists between the present value of an investment and its discount rate.
3. Explain how a firm's cost of capital is determined. In your answer describe how the cost of each part is determined.
4. Explain why depreciation is a noncash expense and how the depreciation tax shield affects a firm's capital budgeting decisions.
5. Develop a simple capital budgeting example using the NPV procedure that shows how the accelerated cost recovery program increases the likelihood of greater capital investment by an agribusiness. Do the same for investment tax credits.
6. Give your reaction to the statement that programs like accelerated cost recovery and investment tax credits distort financial markets and lead to overinvestment in capital goods.
7. Explain how you would decide whether to use the common termination period method or the replacement cycle method when evaluating mutually exclusive capital budgeting projects.
8. Define risk and uncertainty. Explain how a manager can best deal with each.
9. Describe the procedures for developing alternative outcomes and break-even cash flows. Explain how an agribusiness manager would use them in making capital budgeting decisions.
10. Give three advantages of owning assets rather than leasing them. Give three advantages of leasing for an agribusiness.

11. Explain the financial procedures used to evaluate whether to acquire assets by leasing, buying with cash, or buying with borrowed money. What financial calculations and other factors would you use to decide what was best?
12. What is an agribusiness's board of directors saying about the opportunity cost of money when they keep the profits rather than giving them back to the shareholders as dividends?
13. Explain why a firm would want to calculate break-even cash flows on a capital budgeting project.
14. Explain why depreciation expenses, unlike other tax deductible expenses, generate just a tax shield, and how this affects the cash flow in a capital budgeting decision.
15. Explain the difference between an operating lease, a financial lease, and a lease/purchase agreement.

CASE 16
Nick's Financial Future: Part II

Nick did such a great job of explaining the concepts given in the previous case that Mr. Raymond gave him a new assignment. In this case, it was to decide how to acquire a new diesel truck for the business. The dealer was trying to sell him on the idea of paying cash. His banker told him the best thing to do was to get a loan from his bank. One of his golfing buddies said that modern corporations lease things like this. He asked Nick to look into it and give him a full report on Monday about how to make this kind of decision.

Write a short report for Nick about how to do this using a realistic worked example that you feel will make your point.

PART V

The Directing Function

The directing business management function is vital but often overlooked, partly because it is the soft side of business management. The first three management functions—planning, organizing, and controlling—deal with *things that can be managed* using well-defined procedures. The directing function is about *leading people,* where the proper procedures are less defined. This is why business management is still an art supported by science.

The success of a business may depend more on how well the directing function is done than on any other management function. Good directing can overcome poor planning, organizing, and controlling. However, poor directing can sink even the best planning, organizing, and controlling. A business can never be better than the people who work there. Happy workers are productive workers; happy workers make for happy customers; happy customers make for happy managers and bigger profits.

- ***Chapter 17—Human Resource Leadership*** The importance of leading people, as opposed to managing things, is the focus of this chapter. The goal is to recognize the elements of a work environment where everyone seeks to excel. One of management's primary objectives is to help all employees reach their full potential. This starts with understanding what motivates human behavior and how work can fulfill these needs. In order to be a great manager you must first be a good leader.
- ***Chapter 18—Human Resource Management*** This chapter builds on the previous chapter. It focuses on defining the technical or supporting procedural activities of human resource management (staffing)—determining personnel needs, recruiting, setting pay levels, and so on. While these activities need to be done well in order for a firm to succeed, they are still subordinate to leading people and establishing an environment where everyone seeks to excel.
- ***Chapter 19—Personal Selling*** The ultimate directing function is selling. Without selling nothing happens. A good business plan with an effective marketing mix is a good first step, but ultimately someone has to bring the firm's products to the attention of the customer and make the sale. Selling is easier when businesses follow the planning procedures described in this

book. External and internal selling are critical activities that contribute to a firm's success and need to be a part of every manager's skills.

- ***Chapter 20—Developing a Workable Approach to Agribusiness Management*** Directing is the art of agribusiness management. It is what normally separates great managers from the rest. Managers practice business management just like physicians practice medicine and lawyers practice law. It is a combination of technical know-how and judgment. Good managers have mastered the technical skills of management and know-how to lead people to accomplish a common goal—the firm's purpose and objective.

Chapter 17

Human Resource Leadership

Chapter Learning Objectives

- Explain how the directing function is different from the other three management functions.
- Explain why managers must be good leaders before they can be great managers.
- Explain why the directing function is the most important of the four management functions.
- Summarize why business management is an art supported by science.
- Discuss how happy workers make happy customers and how this leads to greater profits.
- Summarize how to establish a work environment in which everyone seeks to excel.
- Explain why the business plan is the starting point of a good work environment.

Introduction

One person could do everything that has been covered in this book up to now. Working alone, she could develop the marketing and financial plans, the organizational scheme, and the feedback mechanisms needed for a good business plan. However, unless the proposed business is very simple, bringing it to life will involve working with other people. Effective managers understand this and realize they also must be good leaders. This is why management is defined as the accomplishment of work through people. Great managers who have mastered the directing function are those who know:

- what motivates human behavior;
- how to effectively and efficiently organize the individual talents and needs of employees in order to maximize the collective value of their efforts; and
- how to lead employees to accomplish the firm's goal and purpose.

Great managers seek to understand what motivates human behavior because they know that happy workers are more productive and they in turn are more likely to lead to happy customers. This generates greater sales and profits, and makes it easier for the firm to accomplish its central objective of maximizing long-term profits by profitably satisfying customers' needs.

In order to achieve the greatest net benefit from the collective effort of their employees, managers need to recognize that everyone is not alike. Each worker has strengths and weaknesses and is motivated by different needs. The manager's job is to utilize this information to build the most effective and efficient organization possible.

DIRECTING MEANS LEADING PEOPLE, NOT MANAGING THINGS

The first three management functions focus on managing things such as marketing plans, organizational charts, and feedback forms. The directing function is different—it is about leading people to accomplish the purpose and objective found in the firm's business plan. It is true that you need great plans, efficient organizational structures, and good feedback mechanisms. However, without great leadership in implementing those things, the firm will never achieve true greatness. This is why you must be a good leader and a good follower before you can be a great manager.

Directing is the most important thing that managers do. It occupies about 90 percent of their time. It is what separates good managers from the rest. Good leadership (directing) can transform a poor business plan into a success. Poor leadership can sink even the best business plan. Although directing is closely related to the other management functions, the skills needed to successfully perform the directing function are very different. They are more qualitative than quantitative, and more peopled oriented. This is why business management will always be an art supported by science. While directing is a vital part of any business's success, it is still important to remember that the most successful firms are those that consistently perform all four management functions well.

UNDERSTANDING HUMAN MOTIVATION

Until the development of modern management theory, many managers looked at their employees in the same light as machinery, buildings, and other physical inputs to the production process. They were to be used and then replaced. Workers were considered little more than lazy, self-centered beings that would work only when required to do so.

The early scientific investigations of work in the late nineteenth century reflected this orientation and used an engineering perspective, in which labor was managed like any other input to a production process. Good examples are the studies by Frederick W. Taylor and others that concentrated on mechanical relationships, such as what size shovel a worker should use to move the maximum amount of coal in a day. It was not until the 1920s at the Western Electric Company's Hawthorne Plant outside of Chicago that Elton Mayo recognized that workers can be more than self-centered, disposable inputs.

Mayo and his associates carried out a series of experiments, the most famous being the determination of the level of light that maximizes worker productivity. A number of people who worked in relative obscurity in the large plant were selected to be studied. They were divided into two groups: a test group and a control group. The level of lighting for the control group was held constant, while the level of the light in the test group was progressively increased.

The level of output in the test group increased with the level of the lighting. However, to the surprise of the researchers, the level of the output for the control group also showed an almost equal increase. The same kind of increase occurred for both groups when the level of lighting was reduced.

Similar experiments in other parts of the plant gave the same results and indicated the presence of other variables that overcame the effects of physical changes in the workplace. These included a changed perception of workers by their superiors and, more important, a change in workers' attitudes towards themselves and their jobs. The conclusion was that the way employees are treated by their supervisors affects their productivity. In this case, all the workers selected for the study received special recognition from the researchers and their bosses and became celebrities within the plant. What they did was no longer unrecognized but carefully reviewed by the researchers. This increased the esteem that others had for them and raised their self-esteem as well. The outcome was greater productivity. Mayo and his associates' study marked the beginning of human resources as an area of business management.

Since Mayo's work, others have attempted to identify the specific motivational factors that make workers more productive. As a result of these investigations, the traditional view of workers as lazy, irresponsible individuals has faded. Researchers increasingly have found evidence that given the right environment, workers take initiative, seek responsibility, and set high quality and quantity standards for themselves. Such environments allow both managers and workers to enjoy a better life by increasing workers' pay and company profits.

How Work Can Fulfill Human Needs

Human beings are complex organisms that are driven by many physiological and psychological needs. These basic needs can serve as powerful motivators of human activity. They have been identified and classified by psychologists in various ways.

A widely quoted classification scheme is A. H. Maslow's pyramid of human needs (figure 17-1). The pyramid is divided into five levels, with more basic needs at the base. Humans concern themselves primarily with the satisfaction of the lowest level of basic needs before they turn their attention to those above it. Once a level of need has been fulfilled, it is taken for granted and ceases to be a strong motivator of human behavior. A person then turns her attention to fulfilling the needs of the next highest level. However, if a previously fulfilled need is suddenly not met, it becomes a source of great anxiety and the person's attention returns to meeting that need.

At the base of the pyramid are *physiological needs*—the need for food, water, shelter, and so on. Next are *safety needs*—the need for protection from pain, danger, and other forms of privation. Third are *belonging needs*—the need for love, affection, and acceptance by others. *Esteem needs* come fourth—the need for self-respect and the respect of others. On the highest level are *self-fulfillment needs*—the need to become all that one is capable of.

According to Maslow, successful attainment of a particular level of needs should lead to a feeling of satisfaction and increased desire to strive for the next level. On the other hand, failure to reach the higher level can become a source of frustration and result in decreased interest in reaching that level. The level of frus-

Figure 17-1 Maslow's Pyramid of Human Needs

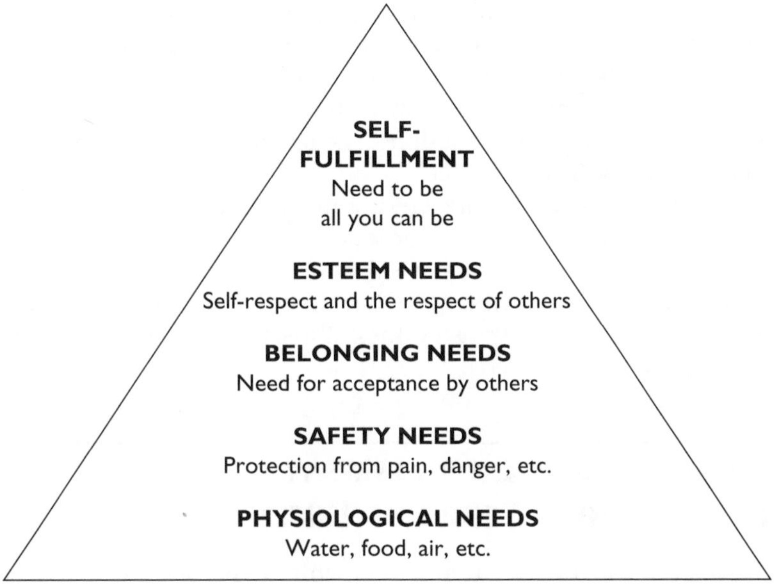

SELF-FULFILLMENT
Need to be all you can be

ESTEEM NEEDS
Self-respect and the respect of others

BELONGING NEEDS
Need for acceptance by others

SAFETY NEEDS
Protection from pain, danger, etc.

PHYSIOLOGICAL NEEDS
Water, food, air, etc.

tration can be reduced with patience and a realistic assessment of one's own abilities and circumstances.

Work is a common way for people to meet these needs. It is capable of fulfilling any of the five levels of human needs described by Maslow. Work can meet a person's physiological needs by providing the means for workers to buy the food, shelter, and clothing that they and their families need to survive. The safety needs of people can be met through a job when workers are assured that their jobs will continue, pay a steady wage, protect them from disasters, and provide for their retirement. The first two levels of human needs are satisfied by most jobs, so people are concerned with these items only when they are threatened with their loss. Thus, individuals become concerned primarily with the satisfaction of the remaining three levels of needs from their work.

Work provides individuals with opportunities to fulfill their belonging needs through relationships with fellow workers. These social contacts meet their need for community and provide strong social bonds. Typically this is formally accomplished when groups of workers transform themselves into teams in order to complete their work. Firms do this on an informal level through company-sponsored sports teams and social events.

Work also can be thought of as an extension of one's personality and as a way to measure self-worth. It can provide a way for people to satisfy their self-esteem needs and to gather the esteem of others. Self-esteem comes from the satisfaction of doing well at a worthwhile job. The esteem of others comes from the recognition and respect from others for the quality of one's work and its value in others' eyes.

When the first four levels of needs are fulfilled, the most pressing concern becomes finding a job that provides continuing challenges and room for growth so that a person can reach his or her full potential—meeting their self-fulfillment needs. Attainment of this top level of human needs is difficult because few jobs allow sufficient flexibility for this to happen. It is important for everyone to have a strong sense of self-awareness that includes a realistic assessment of his or her abilities, expectations, and situation so he or she does not suffer unnecessary frustrations when this is not possible.

Developing jobs and work environments that meet these human needs not only leads to happier and more productive workers; it can also result in higher customer satisfaction and greater sales for the firm. Employees who are happy about who they are, see value in what they do, and see a chance for future job growth are more likely to transfer this enthusiasm to their customers and do a better job of meeting their needs.

Developing a Work Environment in Which Everyone Seeks to Excel

Developing a work environment in which everyone seeks to excel is a difficult task, with each situation calling for unique handling. It is another reason why the directing function is considered to be more of an art than a science. Nevertheless, some general principles can be applied to guide managers through this process.

The Starting Point: The Values, Purpose, and Objective Found in the Business Plan

The proper starting point to develop the right work environment is the values, purpose, and objective found in the firm's business plan. They give the firm its identity and should separate it from their competitors in the eyes of their customers. The values tell everyone—customers, employees, investors, and the community—what the firm stands for and how it is going to conduct its business. This statement covers things like honesty, integrity, and responsibility. The purpose is a clear, concise statement of *what* the firm is going to do. The purpose may be to fulfill the world's unmet need for pizza. It could be to provide a full line of farm chemicals in a particular two-county area of Indiana. It might be to meet farmers' need for grain storage and shipping in the Pacific Northwest. Detailed statements of the firm's purpose give everyone (owners, managers, employees, customers, and suppliers) a clear idea of what the organization is to do.

The firm's objective is a clear, concise statement of *how* the firm is going to gain its competitive edge in the market. How is it going to accomplish its purpose better, faster, or cheaper than its competitors so a potential customer will buy this firm's product rather than someone else's? Examples of objectives could be fastest service, lowest price, largest selection, or best products. Each of these statements classifies the firm in the eyes of customers, managers, and employees.

Communication and Personal Acceptance. Once the firm's values, purpose, and objective have been defined, they must be widely and relentlessly communicated to everyone inside and outside the organization. They must be more than words on a plaque, coffee cup, or T-shirt. Employees and customers must see them put into action every day in every transaction. This takes leadership by example on the part of management. If honesty is a part of the firm's values, employees cannot see the boss taking cash out of the register every day to pay for his lunch or see customers being cheated. Quite the contrary, they need to see managers being unscrupulously fair and honest in all their dealings both in and out of the firm and all cases of dishonesty being dealt with decisively. When employees see this type of behavior by managers they will quickly know how to handle any situation they might encounter.

All employees must understand and accept as worthwhile what the firm does and how it does it. Even more important, they must see and accept their role in the accomplishment of these good things. Personal identification with the firm's values, purpose, and objective helps create a sense of pride and feeling of self-esteem that provide the starting point for building a productive work environment. It is much like the adage about two stonecutters in a quarry who were asked what they did for a living. The first said sadly that all he did was cut little rocks from big ones. The second, with a big smile, said he was building a cathedral. The feeling that what you do makes the world a better place makes all the difference.

Defining Tasks and Developing Jobs

The next step in building a good work environment is to define the specific individual tasks that need to be done to accomplish the purpose and objective. These can be simple things, like opening the mail, mixing the feed ingredients, or sending out the bills. Once all the needed tasks have been defined, compatible tasks should be combined into jobs and the jobs organized into an interrelated network that effectively and efficiently accomplishes the firm's purpose and objective. This approach to job development ensures that all tasks needed to do the work are included, each job contributes to the overall work of the firm, and only those jobs that perform necessary work are developed.

When constructing jobs in this way, care must be taken to ensure that each job includes room for growth in skills and responsibility plus a clear definition of successful performance, as well as where the job leads if the incumbent does well. These elements are many times more important than pay.

Development of Job Descriptions and Quantitative Performance Measures

Once jobs have been developed, the next step is to establish written job descriptions for each position. Descriptions come from all the tasks combined to form that job and define as quantitatively as possible the types and levels of performance needed to do it successfully. A good example is a cone dipper in an ice cream shop, whose job description includes a performance requirement of being able to dip at least three cones per minute to a tolerance of ± ½ oz. of the prescribed amount of ice cream within a week of starting the job. In this type of work, speed and consistent portion size are critical performance criteria. New cone dippers are hired at minimum wage and then given either a raise of $2.00 per hour or are fired after their first week on the job. These two physical performance measures are critical to meeting the firm's purpose (satisfying peoples' desire for ice cream) and objective (providing customers with good value and quick service), so they are important parts of a cone dipper's job description and pay.

The Manager's Technical Responsibilities to Their Employees

Managers have a number of important responsibilities for the technical aspects of the jobs their employees do so that the firm will be successful. They must:

- Develop a set of clear, concise, written instructions of how to perform each job, including job descriptions and the expected performance standards. This helps employees define the skills, experience, and education needed to do the job successfully.
- Establish a fair pay level for each position. The salary or wage should be commensurate with the job and reflect the market value of the skills and education required to perform it.
- Specify the equipment necessary to do the work and see to it that these items are available to workers.
- Define and give workers access to the additional training they will need in the future in order to keep their skills up to date.
- Define clear lines of authority between all levels of management so everyone knows what is expected and how his or her job helps the firm to accomplish its purpose and objective.
- Give job specifications in terms of job/product outcomes and leave considerable latitude in how the group carries out its work once they have mastered their jobs.
- Apply all rules, regulations, and evaluations evenly to everyone regardless of their position and be sure they are consistent with the firm's values. Penalties should fit the crime and be understood by all employees, including those who are fired for failing to comply with them.

The Manager's Leadership Responsibilities to Their Employees

In addition to the technical aspects of a good motivational environment, successful implementation takes a strong dose of leadership. The leadership needed here is different from the items covered earlier in this chapter. Here the emphasis is on mentoring—helping others realize their full potential.

The most obvious form of mentoring is formal mentoring. This happens at the annual performance review. At this meeting a boss reviews the past year with a worker. The boss's assessment of the worker's performance should be based heavily on two criteria: how well the worker fulfilled the performance measures found in his or her job description and whatever new performance goals were set at last year's performance review session. At the end of the review, they should jointly set new performance goals for the coming year. Whatever pay increases the worker receives as a result of this review should be tied heavily to his or her performance on these items.

The most important form of mentoring is informal mentoring. Managers can show their leadership skills by helping their employees develop their own human potential and satisfy the higher levels of their human needs as found in Maslow's pyramid. Informal feedback often is no more than a "well done," "thank you," or "I appreciate what you did" given to workers just as they finish a job. It also can be a quiet "we need to talk" or "could you stop by my office." For this type of feedback to be worthwhile it must be given in a timely, consistent, constructive manner that helps the employee understand and gauge her performance in the eyes of the boss. Positive feedback should be given in public. Negative feedback should be given in private.

To make this work, the boss must constantly watch what her employees are doing. This does not mean being an active part of what is happening. Quite the contrary, it means not interfering, just observing. In some cases it may be letting an employee endure a "controlled failure." This means letting a worker's decision lead to failure so that it can be used as a learning experience. A manager should only intervene when the decision could lead to a major loss.

Kenneth Blanchard, a highly successful management consultant, has developed a whole series of books called *The One-Minute Manager.* An important concept is the need for one-minute reprimands when things have gone badly. More important is the one-minute complement given when people do things well. Both need to be given often, especially when a manager sees people doing well. They need to be given as soon as possible after the act so workers can connect the feedback with the act and improve their future performance. If the boss waits several months to deliver this type of feedback at the annual review the message will be lost. Developing better workers and future managers is always the job of the current managers. To do this takes leadership.

Managers show good leadership in how they supervise. Once those responsible for a job show they have mastered it, leave the details of how the work is done to them. Good leaders become concerned primarily with the outcome rather than the process. This participatory approach permits those performing the work to apply their own special firsthand knowledge, experience, and education to the process. This often results in better methods and completion rates that exceed the most optimistic hopes of the managers who developed the business plan.

By leaving these decisions in the hands of those who do the work, the manager shows respect for their skills, abilities, and decision-making prowess. Those who work in such an environment gain a greater sense of control over their work and are able to better fulfill their esteem needs from their work. The result is happier workers that are more productive and efficient. This leads to greater company profits.

An implicit assumption behind the success of this approach to directing is mutual trust and respect between managers and their workers, and an understanding of their interdependency in accomplishing their common goals and objectives. Each party brings unique skills to the situation that if properly combined will yield results far in excess of what any one person could do alone. None of us is as smart as all of us. The size of a business's success depends in large part on the success of its employees. It is hard for a business to be better than its weakest employee.

Understanding this concept is a key ingredient in developing a good motivational environment. It is easier to meet this prerequisite when there is wide-open, honest communication between all parties and solid agreement on the corporate values, purpose, and objective.

Building and maintaining a good motivational environment takes time, commitment, and the right people. Adherence to correct principles, as well-known management expert Stephen Covey points out in his popular book *Principle-Centered Leadership*, is the way to always keep going in the right direction. These principles apply at all times and places, and never change. When agribusinesses fail it is often because they strayed from the principles explained here.

To succeed all levels of management, especially senior management, must honestly and genuinely believe and follow all the elements presented here every day. Good leadership means never asking others to do things you are not willing to do. Employees can quickly spot those just going through the motions and will respond accordingly. The development of a positive work environment requires considerable effort and can be maintained only through daily adherence and personal contacts.

It also takes hiring the right people. This means people who come to the business already sharing the firm's values, and believing their purpose and objective are worthwhile. It always pays to hire for attitude and then train for skills. While more demanding than other styles, the payoff from the participatory management style is higher customer satisfaction and higher profits. This point is summarized in the management phrase hire hard so you can manage easy.

The procedures and elements of the proper motivational environment outlined above are only the basic elements of job development and motivation. The art of management's directing function comes from skillfully mixing all the elements with a strong dose of good leadership. When sorted down to its basics, directing is about leading a group of people to accomplish a common goal: the business's purpose and objective.

Management Styles

Managers use a variety of methods to get the job done. Some use the same management approach regardless of the situation, while others never use the same one twice. There are almost as many approaches as there are managers. Despite this diversity, it is possible to separate these approaches into several broad groupings called management styles.

The Autocratic Style

The earliest management style was the autocratic approach. It grew out of the need to motivate a large number of people, mainly factory workers, to coordinate their efforts to produce a product. In this approach, a leader maintains strict control over his or her followers by directly regulating policy, procedures, and behavior. Due to the belief that employees will not function effectively without direct supervision, they generally feel that people left to complete work on their own will be unproductive. This type of leader dominates interactions, resulting in infrequent positive feedback and a lack of creative opportunities. As a result, distance is created between leaders and their followers as a means of emphasizing role distinctions. With this type of management, a manager can expect high productivity from his or her employees, as well as increased discontent and decreased commitment among followers. Highly structured or simple tasks based on a routine are often effectively accomplished under autocratic leadership. It also can be beneficial when a manager is much more knowledgeable about a product or procedure than his or her employees, when groups of workers are extremely large, or when time constraints restrict a more participatory style of communication.

The Participatory Style and Theory X & Y

The autocratic management style prevailed until Mayo's work at the Hawthorne Plant in the 1920s showed workers to be more enlightened and their productivity responsive to better treatment by their superiors. This evidence spawned a new branch of business management called human resource management. One of the best-known proponents of this new approach was Douglas MacGregor. He referred to the traditional (autocratic) style as Theory X, and the new participatory style as Theory Y. A manager's style, MacGregor said, can be defined by where she would fit on an X:Y graph such as that given in figure 17-2.

According to Theory Y, workers have a psychological need to work and actively seek achievement and responsibility. In addition, workers should be encouraged to participate in the planning of their work objectives because they

Figure 17-2 MacGregor's Theory X + Y

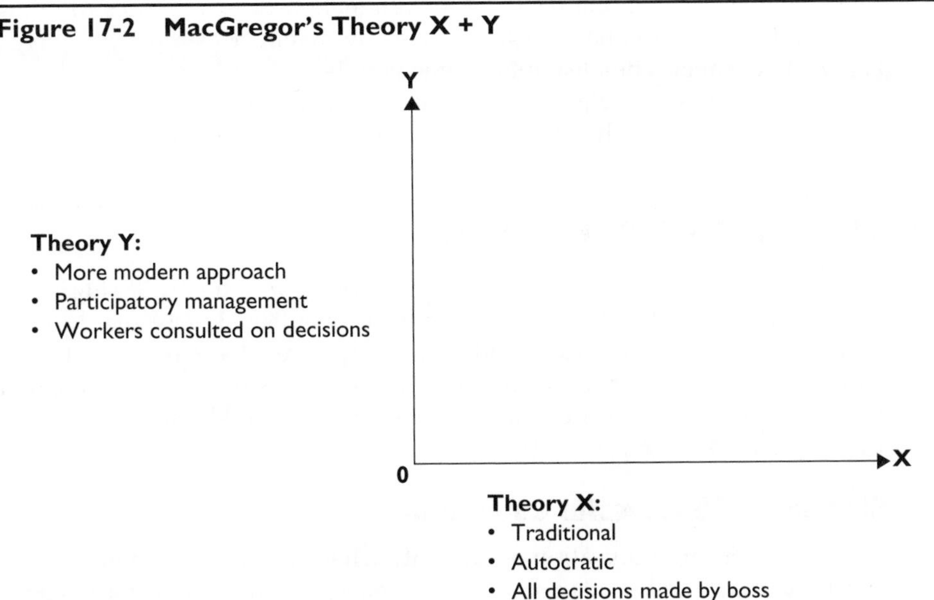

will usually set high standards of both quality and quantity that lead to greater success to the organization.

Difficulties and Payoffs of the Participatory Style

Those managers who adopt a more participatory management style will find it a stern taskmaster. Unlike Theory X, where a few top managers make all decisions, Theory Y managers at all levels must pay greater attention to setting goals, meeting worker needs, involving workers in decision making and planning as well as the action of the business, and providing useful feedback to their employees. These can be quite difficult and time-consuming tasks. Only great managers who are good leaders and communicators can accomplish this successfully. It is easier to sit on high and issue edicts as an autocratic manager. However, most managers adopt the more demanding participatory management style because the benefits of increased worker productivity, sales, and profits far outweigh the costs.

Selecting the Right Management Style

The benefits of the participatory management style (Theory Y) have made it the most widely used style in business today. Despite its wide application, it is important to remember that situations exist in which an autocratic style is best. For example, leading a platoon of soldiers on an assault of an enemy hill in wartime requires a very different management style than that used to lead a group of salespeople to meet this quarter's performance goals. However, if the building where the sales meeting is being held catches fire, a good leader would immediately switch her leadership style from participatory to autocratic in order to get everyone out of the building safely. Great managers (good leaders) adapt their style to fit the situation.

People rarely start out with a specific management style in mind. Rather, it develops over time as the result of a combination of experiences, training, and personality. Thus, it is hard to categorize any manager as a purely Theory X or Theory Y manager. The ideal management style is one that comfortably fits one's personality, yet is capable of modification and is responsive to changing situations. Great managers always seek to improve their leadership skills.

Communication and Feedback

Once a solid management structure is in place and the proper ingredients for a good motivational environment have been established, it is vital to institute a strong communication system and to develop a feedback network to keep the business moving forward. A communication system is necessary to ensure that all levels of management possess any information that could affect the organization and how they perform their job.

Elements of Successful Communication

Successful communication occurs only when an exchange of information *and* mutual understanding takes place. The first requirement is usually easily met, while the second is often more elusive. Let's look at what it takes to achieve mutual understanding when communicating.

Common Language and Perspective. A necessary condition for mutual understanding is a common language and perspective by both the sender and receiver. In today's increasingly technical world, extensive jargon minimizes the level of mutual understanding even between people in the same work unit. Everyone should be encouraged to speak and write clearly with all abbreviations preceded by full words the first time they are used. What is written may sound less technical, but if there is no mutual understanding, no communication has occurred. This problem can be reduced if all employees share a common vision of the corporate values, purpose, and objective that is repeatedly explained using the same words. This helps keep everyone focused on the same things and helps employees keep their activities in perspective.

Broad Distribution of Information. An effective communication network helps all parts of the organization move together. If a sales campaign for a product is planned, the production and logistics people need to know about it so they can be sure to have ample supplies on hand to meet the increased demand. The distribution of this type of valuable information should be widespread, so even people in the firm who would seem to have no interest in it can prepare for it. For example, if a new sales campaign is expected to cause the plant to work weekends in June, the building maintenance department should know not to schedule the repaving of the employee parking lot that month.

Use Multiple Channels and Repeat the Message. The best communication systems are those that expose their users to multiple channels and forms of communication so everyone receives and understands important information. This approach reduces the chances for bottlenecks and draws attention to information that could pass unnoticed in a single-channel system. For example, people who travel may not always have access to their e-mail, or their computers may not be working; a key person in the distribution of information may be out of town and unable to pass information along.

Direct person-to-person or telephone verbal communication is another way to supplement the formal communication system when time and accuracy are critical. In these situations, little penalty is incurred from hearing a critical message more than once, while a great loss could occur from not getting the word. When relying primarily on verbal communication, always follow up with written communication just to be sure mutual understanding has occurred.

Let Users Decide the Specifics of the Information. Designers of formal information systems need to decide what information is needed, by whom, when, and how often, which usually is best determined by asking the users of the information. Users must demonstrate a clear need for the data; otherwise, there is little reason to send it. As was seen in the section on supply chains, information must be accurate, timely, and presented in a useful form to have any value. A communication system developed by considering user needs is more likely to involve useful information.

Use Standard Procedures for Routine Matters. Routine matters often can be best handled by standard operating procedures (SOPs). These can be set up to decide who gets the minutes from the board of directors meeting, how to order office supplies, or how to change the toner cartridge in the copy machine. SOPs facilitate these items by giving exact instructions so just about anyone can do them. This way, when the person who normally changes the toner cartridge is on vacation, the copier can be kept running. The topics covered by SOPs can be extended to include policy manuals, price lists, and other official publications used by the firm.

Use of Verbal Communication. Verbal communication is a vital part of the communication system. Verbal communication is used when time is short or personal contact is needed to achieve mutual understanding. Direct contact is generally required when a major group decision is being made (such as constructing a building or entering a new line of business), leadership is called for (such as announcing a plant closing), and in all personnel matters. Usually it is wise to confirm any verbal decisions with written documentation transmitted to all parties to be sure mutual understanding has occurred.

Informal Communication (The Grapevine or Rumor Mill). In addition to the formal communication network in any organization, an informal communication network known as the grapevine or rumor mill exists. Unofficial communication channels are found among informal work groups who come together from various parts of the organization but maintain some contact with each other. Examples of these groups include carpools, golf partners, neighbors, and so on. Unofficial channels of communication are usually the quickest way to spread information in a firm. Unfortunately, they are often the greatest source of unreliable information. The successful management of official and unofficial forms of communication requires keeping official channels up to date with as much accurate information as possible to minimize the importance of unofficial channels and correct any misinformation discovered in the unofficial network as quickly as possible.

Need for Two-Way Communication. A successful communication system addresses not only the flow of information from the top down, but also the flow from the bottom up. Return flows of information (feedback) are vital to managers.

The purpose of feedback reports is to provide higher-level management with an objective assessment of progress. Whenever appropriate, they should use physical units such as quantities, volumes, and costs and include clear, concise measures of accomplishments during the reporting period. The narrative section should deal with any unusual problems or circumstances surrounding performance for that period.

While written progress reports are useful measures of performance, they should be supplemented with personal interaction whenever possible. People tend to filter out bad news when presenting reports to their bosses. To counter this, a top manager needs to do three things. First, give some form of feedback to the employees who provided the information. If people perceive that nothing ever happens to their reports, they will infer that the performance they highlight is of little value to the firm. If the feedback/communication system is established using the procedures outlined in this chapter, each report deals with a key part of the firm's performance. As such, it should be of interest to the managers and warrants some response.

Second, ask those who prepare the written report to supplement it with a brief verbal presentation and be prepared to respond to questions. Since more than half of all communication is nonverbal, seeing the expressions and body language of the report writer may tell the boss more about what is going on than the numbers in the report. It also can give the manager an opportunity to probe more deeply for the information behind the numbers, including the assumptions, calculation procedures, problems encountered, methods used to overcome them, and so on. It is rare that a written report includes everything managers need to know to be effective.

Third, practice what management expert Tom Peters calls **management by walking around**. This means that the boss does not just sit in the office and read reports. Rather, the manager walks around all over the organization and talks to everyone. In some cases, this means sitting on the loading dock and eating lunch with the shipping crew. In other cases, it can be just popping into someone's office and asking, "What are you doing that is exciting?" Once people know you do this on a regular basis and are approachable, it is amazing what can be learned that would never appear in the reports being sent to you. Many successful executives in top firms devote one or two days a week to walking around. They feel this is the only way that they will ever know what is really going on in their business. When a business fails, top management and the board of directors are often the last ones to find out they were in trouble.

Management by Objective

This chapter has emphasized the directing management function. A large part of being successful calls for strong leadership skills on the part of the manager, and a commitment to help their employees reach their full potential. This leads to happier, more productive employees who help the firm reach its purpose and objective. A technique to further these goals is **management by objective (MBO)**, a system in which employees participate in setting their own work objectives for the future.

Prerequisites to an MBO Program

MBO puts into practice many of the things already discussed in this chapter to create a work environment in which people seek to excel. Two prerequisites to a successful MBO program are strong support for the program from all levels of management and a clearly defined corporate values, purpose, and objective that are accepted as worthwhile by all. Despite its simplicity, the system is rigorous because the employees know exactly what level of performance is expected of them and their superiors know exactly what they have agreed to do to help employees achieve their objectives. It is implicit in the MBO agreement that neither side will accept a poor performance by the other.

Another prerequisite to a successful MBO system is a fair system of compensation, rewards, and penalties, in which teamwork to accomplish corporate objectives is paramount in everyone's mind. If any behavior other than cooperative behavior supportive of the corporate purpose and objective is rewarded, the system will fail. For an MBO program to work there must be consistency throughout the rewards system, worker behavior, and the firm's values, purpose, and objective.

Setting Up an MBO Program

The MBO procedure begins with supervisors and employees (individually or in teams) jointly setting their performance goals for a given period. These are set in concert with the organization's goals for the same period. An important part of this plan is determining what assistance the employees can expect from their superiors and others in the firm to reach their performance goals. The workers might be required to produce an average number of units of a certain quality per day. The manager might be required to have sufficient materials on hand to meet the workers' production rate and to have sufficient maintenance performed so the machinery can function at that rate. The two parties agree to work for the mutual benefit of the other in the accomplishment of a common corporate goal.

Advantages of Using MBO

The MBO program allows work to fulfill some of the employees' needs by giving them control and influence over their work. This system of self-control is successful only if it is carried out in a structured environment with preset physical objectives and a high level of relevant and timely feedback. Also, performance must be evaluated and dealt with appropriately. If those that fail to meet their performance objectives are dealt with harshly, others will quickly learn to set goals that can be met easily, and mediocrity will set in.

By the same token, if those that exceed their objectives and truly do exceptional work are not properly rewarded, the incentive to excel in the future will be greatly diminished for everyone. Rewards and sanctions must be given for success or failure at the stated objectives, not for some hidden agenda. Rewards should reflect the difficulty of their achievement. In the example above, if the performance requirement of an average number of units per day is a significant increase from current levels but is necessary for the business to profitably perform on a new contract, then the company, the managers, and the employees *all* should be rewarded for their efforts. For the workers and managers it may be a bonus, while for the company it can be increased profits. If the firm fails to share its good fortune or rewards workers for something else, the program will collapse quickly. Managers also have an obligation to fire consistent nonperformers who jeopardize everyone's chances of reaching their common goal.

Words of Caution

It is important to remember when using MBO that performance is an average and does not require success at every turn. A truly good manager accepts reasonable risks and occasionally fails, but over the long term her rate of success will remain high. Those managers that avoid any risk usually avoid any chances for big success.

MBO is a good complement to a program to develop a positive motivational environment. It allows employees to fulfill some of their human needs through work on a worthwhile objective in a structured environment. The success of an MBO program depends heavily on strong leadership by management at all levels. Significant benefits can accrue for everyone when the technique is implemented correctly.

LEADERSHIP AND THE SUPERIOR-EMPLOYEE RELATIONSHIP

A key element in the success of many ventures is the quality of supervisors' relationships with their employees. A highly motivated work force with faith in its mission and its superiors can make the difference between success and failure. The quality of that relationship depends heavily on the quality of the managers' leadership. The development of a good superior-employee relationship takes considerable time, interest, and effort on the part of the managers and requires careful maintenance once established since the quality of such relationships is usually judged by the most recent experience.

The cornerstones of good leadership are trust, openness, honesty, fairness, mutual respect, and common values. Good things happen when followers believe in their leaders, leaders believe in their followers, and all believe in the value of their cause.

Conveying Trust

Managers convey trust in their employees by giving them broad leeway in how they perform their work. Once workers have shown they can handle a job, a supervisor's primary responsibility is to define the requirements of the finished product and the time restrictions. They leave it up to the workers to perform the task how they see fit. This enables the employees to adapt the work to their own personal preferences within the job requirements. When the employees prove they are able to handle this freedom, all the supervisor must do is provide the necessary tools and monitor their progress.

Managers also convey trust in their employees by delegating authority. This is more than giving workers leeway in how to perform a job. It gives them full managerial control of a job. This allows an employee an opportunity to broaden her managerial skills so that she will be ready to take a management job in the future. It also gives the employee the opportunity to sample what it would be like to be a manager. Delegation frees the manager to attend to more pressing matters and should be pursued whenever possible. This is particularly valuable when the employee can perform the task as well as or better than the manager. A good example would be someone who is good at job costing. The manager can have that person perform the cost analysis for all new jobs in her area. In this case, the manager should undertake the task only if it cannot be done by the subordinate, is confidential, requires a high level of managerial prestige, or the manager could do it in less time.

Conveying Openness, Honesty, and Fairness

Supervisors convey genuine interest in the success of their employees through openness, honesty, and fairness in their dealings with them. Openness is shown by listening to both sides of disputes before making a decision and keeping employees informed about anything that could affect them. Managers show honesty and fairness in how they apply rewards and punishments and whether they defend their workers from unwarranted attacks.

How a manager handles the feedback she gives each worker influences workers' perceptions. An employee should receive at least an informal response from her supervisor to each significant activity, regardless of her performance. Feedback sessions should be short (less than five minutes), with negative feedback being given in private and the punishment fully explained. Positive feedback should be given in public and also be clearly explained. Since the goal is always to improve employee performance, the information given in informal feedback sessions should be constructive and employees should always be treated with the highest level of respect.

Fairness, openness, and honesty also should be applied to performance reviews and pay. Pay levels should be fair and published whenever possible. A worker's compensation conveys the value of that job to the firm, so it should reflect the level of responsibility, education, and performance associated with it. Adjustments in pay should be handled with care and discretion and should correspond to job performance.

Conveying Common Values

When supervisors and employees share common values, it is easier to build a good supervisor-employee relationship. Supervisors and employees can begin to measure the level of their contribution toward realizing the corporation's purpose and objective by asking three questions. The managers should ask, "What can we do to help you (the employees) do a better job?" and "What do we do that hinders you from doing a better job?" The third question should be asked by the employee and is addressed to the supervisor: "What can I do to help you do a better job?"

If these questions are answered honestly, the responses will lead both parties to focus on their common goal: the accomplishment of the firm's purpose and objective. This reflection leads to a new perspective on the other person's job that can strengthen the relationship. When supervisors and employees focus on their common values in an atmosphere of trust, openness, honesty, fairness, and mutual respect, the result should be happier, more productive employees, more satisfied customers, and greater sales and profits for the firm.

Chapter Highlights

1. Directing means leading people, not managing things. The other three management functions concern the management of things such as business plans, organizational schemes, and feedback forms.

2. Directing is the most important activity of a manager and consumes 90 percent of a manager's time. Successful directing (leadership) defines a good manager.
3. Directing is what makes business management an art supported by science.
4. How people are treated has an effect on their productivity.
5. Work can help people fulfill many of their human needs.
6. The purpose and objective of a firm as given in the business plan are the starting points for creating a work environment in which people seek to excel.
7. Jobs are developed by combining all the compatible tasks needed to accomplish a firm's purpose and objective.
8. All jobs should have a written list of tasks and quantitative measures of required performance levels.
9. Managers are responsible for providing all the things workers need to do their jobs well.
10. Managers are responsible for helping all their employees reach their full potential. Timely, relevant, and constructive feedback, both formal and informal, is a key part of this process.
11. Good leaders (good managers) use a management style that is appropriate to each situation.
12. Successful businesses have strong two-way communication systems that fully inform everyone of anything that affects the organization and their job.
13. Management by objective is one way managers can develop a productive work environment.
14. Good leadership is the basis for a good superior-employee relationship.

Chapter Quiz

1. Explain how the directing management function is different from the other three functions.
2. Explain in your own words what the phrase "directing means leading people, not managing things" means to you.
3. Define the term "leadership" in your own words. Give an example from your personal experience in which you observed good leadership. Provide an example in which you observed bad leadership and explain how it could have been improved.
4. Describe Maslow's pyramid of human needs. Can work really help people meet their needs? Explain your reasoning.
5. Describe the steps in developing a work environment in which people will seek to excel.
6. What are the managers' responsibilities in developing a good work environment? Describe the role of leadership in this process.

7. Describe the role of feedback and mentoring in a good work environment and the difference between formal and informal mentoring. Is formal or informal mentoring more important to a successful business? Explain the reasons for your choice.
8. Describe your management style and explain why you think it works best. Give your reaction to the statement that once you have found your management style, you should always stick with it.
9. Is an autocratic management style the best choice for the U.S. Marines? Explain the reasons for your answer.
10. Explain why a two-way communication system is essential to business success.
11. Explain why management by walking around is an important part of being a successful manager.
12. Explain why it is important for a formal communication system to be good enough to overcome the effect of an informal (grapevine) communication system.
13. Explain the technique of management by objective and how it can help make a firm successful.
14. Is good leadership the basis for good superior-employee relationships? Explain the reasons for your answer.
15. Why is the autocratic approach preferred by many managers?

Case 17
Yakima Valley Orchards: Part I

Don Marshall gazed out the window of his truck as he sped back to work after a meeting with his banker. He was running late, but it seemed that everything was running late this spring because of the weather. Normally, Don had been closely involved in supervising the spring work at Yakima Valley Orchards (YVO), and by this time in March most of the work was finished; but this year, between his oldest son making final college visits and his mother-in-law's declining health, he was lucky just to find time to keep things moving forward. Today had been a perfect example—instead of being in the orchards this morning and helping to get things organized, he went directly to his office to get his financials ready for the meeting with his banker.

YVO is a family-owned orchard managed by Don Marshall and jointly owned by him and his retired father, Jim. YVO has 480 acres planted in apples, with 330 acres of bearing trees and 150 acres of nonbearing trees. They also maintain some additional acreage in peaches. Don is working hard to make the orchard more efficient, but profits in the past few years have been lower than he expected.

Don had come to rely more this year than ever before on Fred Stone, his production supervisor. Don's father hired him right out of high school. Fred knows the orchard business and quickly recognizes what needs to be done. He is the kind of supervisor who keeps people jumping when he is around. If someone is not busy, Fred sees that he has a job right away! Some of the newer, younger employees do not like him, but Fred sees that they do what he tells them.

Don's father had always wanted to enlarge the peach orchards. YVO already owns an excellent 100-acre site. Unfortunately, traveling the access road to this site is difficult. Even in good weather it takes at least 30 minutes to get a crew back to it. It had always been a standing rule that idle crews were sent to this potential new orchard to remove brush and timber. About half the acreage was ready for trees, but there was no clear timetable to finish the project.

Around 3 PM Dick Kline's crew ran out of fertilizer, with about 10 acres left to treat. Checking in the office while his crew got some coffee, Dick found that both Fred and Don were gone, and nobody knew where they were.

With that information, Dick assigned the truck driver and one man to go to town for more fertilizer plus some small items on the want list. He had Jack Adams take the remaining crew of five men to the area between blocks I and II of the apple trees to remove brush. Dick got some coffee for himself, left a note for Fred Stone explaining the situation, and headed for the brush removal area.

About 4 PM, Fred and Don both pulled up at the office from different directions. Don asked Fred why he had seen the company truck headed for town, and why Dick's crew was clearing brush in the apple orchard. Fred said he did not know, but thought cleaning up that narrow strip between blocks I and II was a good idea. Don got upset and informed Fred that he thought the crew should have been working on cleaning up the new peach orchard. He wanted Fred to chew Dick out!

What happened here?

Chapter 18

Human Resource Management

Chapter Learning Objectives

- Explain the difference between human resource leadership and human resource management.
- Summarize how to determine current and future personnel needs.
- Describe why great firms generate their future leaders internally.
- Describe the best ways to recruit and retain new people.
- Explain how to conduct an effective performance review.
- Explain the best ways to determine pay levels.
- Describe why constant employee training and education is an important investment for a firm's long-term success.

Introduction

Chapter 17 dealt with the role that leadership plays in mastering the directing function, and focused on how to develop a work environment where everyone seeks to excel. This chapter is devoted to the second part of the directing function—staffing—that deals with the technical aspects of human resource management in support of leadership goals.

Staffing includes the things great managers do to find, hire, and retain the best people needed to accomplish the firm's ultimate goal of maximizing long-run profits. The objective of staffing is to have the right people with the right skills in the right places at the right time so the business can efficiently and effectively accomplish its purpose and objective today and in the future. Staffing is important because no business can ever be better than the people who run it. After all, management is accomplishing tasks through people.

Determining a Firm's Personnel Needs

Once a firm has settled on its business plan, it must transform the plan into an operating business. The first step is staffing, which focuses on developing jobs and job descriptions from the tasks needed to accomplish the firm's purpose and objective. The second step is the development of a **staffing plan** for the business by sorting these jobs into categories (such as accountants, spray truck operators, secretaries, and so on) so managers can identify their personnel needs. In the third step, a firm develops a **staff inventory** that measures how well current position descriptions meet the firm's job requirements for today and tomorrow. Successful performance of each of these staffing activities makes it easier for the firm to realize its overall purpose and objectives.

Developing Jobs and Job Descriptions

As discussed in chapter 17, job development involves combining compatible tasks from the list of things that are needed to carry out the firm's purpose and objective. Jobs are then combined in the organizing function into an interrelated network that efficiently and effectively carries out the work of the business.

Identifying Critical Tasks. Once jobs are defined and organized, a thorough evaluation determines which job positions contain critical tasks that are most important to the long-term success of the business. A **critical task** is something that must be done well if the firm is going to succeed; its poor performance will cause the firm to fail. Jobs that contain a critical task must be given special attention when organizing a business so they are never subordinated to any other task. When staffing a firm, these jobs should be given special attention to be sure that they are filled promptly by the best people. In a restaurant, for example, the executive chef's job contains many critical tasks, such as buying and preparing the food. Special efforts must be made to always employ the best chefs so the restaurant has the best chance for success.

Elements of a Job Description. A written job description should be prepared for each position in the business from the president on down. This makes everyone aware of what is expected of a given jobholder and the skills needed to perform that job. At a minimum, a job description should include:

- a job title describing the work to be performed;
- a concise listing of the tasks that must be performed;
- a listing of the education, training, experience, and other skills needed to perform the job;
- the level of authority;
- the location and any special conditions of the position;
- advancement potential;
- salary range and fringe benefits;
- a summary of how and when performance will be evaluated; and
- an explanation of how the position relates to those surrounding it and to the accomplishment of the firm's purpose and objective.

These items improve employees' understanding of their jobs and will lead to better job performance. A sample job description is given in figure 18-1.

Developing a Staffing Plan

A staffing plan is a categorized summary of jobs a firm needs to fill. For a new business, nearly all the positions must be filled. By summarizing job needs, firms can better organize recruiting efforts. This way, a firm knows it needs, for example, six chemical spray applicators that hold class III state certification licenses, two office managers, one bookkeeper, three truck drivers, and so on.

Figure 18-1 Sample Job Description

Job Title:	**Office Manager**
Location of Job:	Main Office, Hoopeston Farm Tools, Hoopeston, IL
Responsibilities:	The incumbent must be able to manage the work of a three-person office staff that includes a receptionist, bookkeeper, and secretary to the general manager of the firm. Should be knowledgeable about the farm-implement business and computer-based financial record keeping, including spreadsheets, word processing, and general business management skills. The incumbent is expected to operate in place of the general manager when she is absent. The incumbent reports directly to the general manager.
Education:	High school diploma required, associate degree in agribusiness management preferred.
Experience:	3–5 years of experience in a service-oriented business serving agriculture. Experience with all phases of farm-implement sales and services preferred.
Advancement:	Incumbent would be considered as possible successor to general manager.
Salary Range:	$25,000–$35,000 per year. Performance review given after six months, yearly thereafter.
Benefits:	401(k) retirement with employer match, medical, dental, and vision insurance available to all employees.

Developing a Staff Inventory

A staff inventory, a vital part of staffing, is an assessment of how well each position, its job description, and the current jobholder meet the firm's needs today and in the future. *The assessment is of the job, not the person holding it*. The objective is to determine if the job (as currently defined) still makes sense and will make sense in the future. For example, if a job description calls for the ability to perform typewriter repairs and the firm no longer has typewriters, the job description should be changed. Another part of the inventory looks at incumbents' age and years on the job so retirements can be anticipated. By comparing the staffing plan to the staff inventory, it is possible to determine areas where additional training of current personnel and new employees are needed.

This type of personnel planning is important for businesses of all sizes. To keep a business operating efficiently, management needs to consider differences in salary, age, management styles, employee needs, education, and so on when planning future personnel needs. This type of planning should be tied to the firm's overall planning. For example, if the firm expects to undertake a major expansion next year, it needs to know how many new workers it will need and the types of skills and experience they must have. The purpose of this type of planning is to ensure that a firm's human resources are ready to meet its needs over the long run.

RECRUITING PERSONNEL

Once a staffing plan is complete, management must turn its attention to locating and keeping good employees. This is a never-ending task that involves everyone connected with the firm. It is also an area where top management must exert its full influence to be sure the job is done right, because these decisions will profoundly affect the firm's long-term direction and profits. These are the people who will implement the firm's business plan. How well they do this depends heavily on the quality of people who are hired. This means top management must constantly strive to hire and retain the best people in all areas.

Developing Future Managers

Great organizations are constantly generating new managers internally as part of their effort to help all their employees reach their full potential. If the system is working correctly there should be several current employees who are qualified to move up to every job opening. To make sure this happens agribusinesses need to provide all their employees with additional training and education courses each year. This way the employees can grow with the firm, and keep themselves and their employers competitive.

Promoting current employees usually adds to company morale and encourages employee retention because they can see a career path within the firm. Current employees must be provided the training and experiences they need to be fully qualify for higher-level positions when they become available. When this happens, existing workers should feel that they are qualified for these better jobs. Firms should go outside the company to fill jobs for only entry-level positions or when the qualifications are beyond what is part of their current employment base.

Selection Procedure

Any hiring search should be well publicized. Good starting points are announcements to employees and employment agencies and in newspapers and trade papers. It is important to use word-of-mouth advertising to everyone—friends, neighbors, and so on—when a job is available. Some researchers have estimated that this method fills more jobs than any other, and it is certainly the least expensive. Do not rule out directly recruiting people who already have a good job and are not looking for another one. Often they are just the people needed.

The application is an important part of the hiring process and should be carefully reviewed. Verify the education and past work experience of all applicants. This can be done with a telephone call. The most important part of the review process is to check the references offered by the candidate. A letter is best, but a telephone conversation may be enough. Questions should be drawn from the job requirements given in the job description. For example, if the job requires handling large amounts of money, a question about honesty is appropriate. Attention to detail is vital if the job requires handling dangerous materials. References are normally the best source of information about a candidate's background.

When hiring, groups make better decisions than individuals. Often, it is best to set up a committee of 3–5 people. One person should be the direct supervisor, one should be a peer, and one should come from the human resource area. A member of the group with whom the candidate would be working also should have a significant say since he or she will be working closely with the new person.

The final part of the hiring process should be an on-site personal interview at the job location. This is a chance for both the applicant and the firm to see if the position is a good fit. At this point, everyone has the technical skills to perform the job. What is being examined now is the human side of the applicant. Does this person have the personality to work well with others? If this is a manager's position, does the applicant have the leadership skills needed to do the job? These intangibles are just as important to finding the right people as education and experience.

Throughout the hiring process, all applicants need to be kept informed of progress in the search and when the firm expects to fill the job. Those whose applications are not going to be considered further should be informed promptly by letter. Those still being considered but not being interviewed should be notified promptly as well after the conclusion of interviews. Finally, those interviewed but not hired need to be informed. During the whole process, the goal is to treat all applicants with the highest respect and to keep them informed about the process. Even if a person is not right for the job, she may be perfect for something else in the future. The goal is to have them think well of your organization and reapply. Remember, how you handle your job applicants tells them a great deal about how you treat your existing employees.

RETAINING PERSONNEL

Once a person becomes an employee, the reasons why she stays with the firm often involve personnel policies in areas such as promotion, performance reviews, and salary levels. Since locating a good employee is a difficult and time-consuming matter, and good workers are critical to the firm's long-term success, it is important to find ways to retain them.

Performance Appraisals

Performance appraisals must be a standard part of any job. They are one of the few ways an employee can measure his or her progress in the eyes of the boss. Bosses also should regularly provide informal feedback (both positive and negative) to all workers. Informal feedback given at the right time may do more to inspire better performance than any other form of work appraisal.

Frequency of Reviews. Performance evaluations should be given at least once a year and more frequently for new employees. New employees and holders of new jobs should be reviewed at least every three to six months during their first year. Frequent feedback allows for smaller corrections and keeps people from straying too far from desired job objectives. Appraisals can be valuable to both parties.

It is important for workers to know that they are effective and efficient employees. It gives renewed enthusiasm for the job that can lead to better future performance. For the boss, it is good to know how the job looks to the worker. It may be that what the employee has to do to complete the job is very different from the job description. The job could have been poorly defined or possibly has changed since the job description was written. Regardless, the formal appraisal gives each party a chance to explain how they see the job and the quality of work being performed. When differences exist, the appraisal gives a starting point to resolve them.

Performance Criteria. The starting point of any appraisal of employee performance is the written job description. Although it may change over time, the job description used at hiring is the best starting point for the evaluation. If the description is written properly, it includes the performance factors that the firm felt were most important in a position. The worker should be judged primarily on the level of performance of these items. Most aspects of performance can be measured in terms of how well the person handles the general areas of time, money, and people.

Performance Format. An appraisal should be written and reviewed by a direct supervisor before it is shown to the person being evaluated. The positive aspects of the person's work should be discussed first before addressing the negatives. The employee should be given a copy of the evaluation at least one day before meeting with the supervisor. This will permit a less emotional response on the part of the employee and give her a chance to collect data to respond to what is found in the report. The meeting should be conducted in a private, neutral setting so that everyone feels free to speak; for example, the employee should never be forced to sit in a chair at the side of the boss's desk. The meeting should be seen as a chance to improve the worker's performance rather than as an interrogation and should stick as much as possible to the items in the job description.

In the case of positive performance, managers need to acknowledge the good work, set new work and career goals with the worker, and ask what they can do to help the employee do a better job in the future.

Dealing with Poor Performance. When performance is poor, the manager needs to find out why. The best way to do this is to give the worker an opportunity to explain. Sometimes fault rests with the worker, but the job may be poorly defined or poorly supported by others. The goal is to find out the reasons, not assign blame.

If the problem is employee nonperformance, the manager must listen all the more. If the reason is a problem in the worker's personal life, such as a serious illness, divorce, or other family tragedy, help her obtain the necessary assistance from the appropriate social service agencies. Unless the manager has special training in this area, it is best not to try to solve the problem but to connect the person with the right people who can. If the problem is a lack of motivation, using a coworker as a mentor can be a solution when combined with setting reasonable, short-term performance improvement goals. These goals should be presented in a measurable criterion (for example, pounds sold or days reporting to work on time) together with a specific date of accomplishment. If these are not met, the worker should be terminated, since nonperformers can adversely affect the performance of others.

Performance evaluation meetings are a vital part of the directing function and a key ingredient in motivating and retaining good employees. Managers who say that performance appraisals are not worthwhile and are too time-consuming are just ducking the issue.

Terminating Workers

When job requirements are clearly laid out in a well-written job description and performance measures are reasonable and set in advance, firing decisions are more clear-cut and more easily accepted by those in the firm. If there is a system of constant feedback in place (especially for new workers), the lack of performance should not come as a surprise to the worker or the firm. The company needs to make a reasonable effort to help the person become a solid performer. However, if those efforts fail, it is best for the worker and the business to terminate that worker. The meeting where the worker is let go should always be conducted in private and carried out in a professional way.

Determining Pay Levels

Like other staffing responsibilities, determining pay levels can have a critical impact on business performance. Salary and wage levels often have a great deal to do with the value people place on certain jobs. Money is a strong but not a key motivator of performance. However, it can be a de-motivator when the worker finds his or her pay below average. Employers need to strive to keep their pay rates competitive.

The salary range for a job should be set in relation to its value to the firm. Jobs that include critical tasks should be paid more than those that do not. This is especially true if there are few good replacements available and the loss of the person would severely cripple the business. In a farm-implement dealership, the position of service manager may be a key position. Since the loss of the service manager would cause hardship for the firm, every effort should be made to keep that person working for the company. As part of this effort, the salary of the service manager may approach that of the owners. Given how vital this person is to the success of the firm, the money is well spent.

Salary ranges should be wide enough to reflect growth and increased achievement on the part of the jobholder. If the range is too narrow, people will reach the maximum quickly and feel constrained. In general, salary adjustments should be tied to performance on the tasks found in job descriptions. Bonuses are another way to reward good performance without permanently adjusting someone's pay. They can be particularly useful for rewarding performance involving a single project or activity. Using the farm-implement dealer example again, a bonus might be paid to the parts manager for efficiently implementing a new inventory system.

Fringe benefits have become an increasingly important and expensive part of workers' pay. Group medical, dental, vision, and life insurance should be considered when establishing pay levels. At higher levels of management, the benefits package often includes use of company vehicles and credit cards.

Determining pay levels and fringe benefits is an important part of staffing. Pay levels should always be set with great care and must remain at least equal to those offered by competitors. Managers need to stay up to date by subscribing to salary surveys for their area and industry. Failure to pay a proper wage can result in the loss of good workers and difficulty in hiring new ones. It is important to remember that a business can never be better than the people who work there. Always hire the best!

Training and Education

Employee training and education is an ongoing responsibility of management. As markets mature and information technology improves, firms find it increasingly important to stay on the leading edge of change. In order to remain competitive, employees must constantly upgrade their skills and be provided with the best equipment to do their jobs. A major part of this is a training budget that permits workers to regularly attend formal education and training programs. This effort also can include informal, internal development programs that prepare workers for other jobs, including managerial positions.

One form of informal, internal training is horizontal (or cross) training in which a worker learns to perform new jobs at the same level. For example, in the parts department of the implement dealer, this may mean that everyone knows how to wait on customers at the counter, take phone orders, take orders by computer, and order replacement parts from their suppliers. When cross training is used, it permits the department to operate more efficiently during busy periods even if someone is missing. It is quite aggravating to hear, "We are out of that part, and the person who knows how to order more is out until next week."

Another form of informal training is vertical training, where a worker is given a chance to do all or part of her boss's job on a temporary basis. It gives the employee a chance to see what it would be like to be the boss. It also gives the boss a means to delegate some of her work. In fact, a real test of a manager is the ability to go away for a week or two and have her unit continue to function well. Vertical training offers several advantages. First, it allows room for employees to grow and develop a taste for new tasks. Second, it gives employees a way to see what it is like to be a manager at the next level. Third, it frees the manager from many day-to-day, routine matters and gives them time to think and plan.

On the other hand, not all workers are interested in becoming a manager. Those that are should be given an opportunity to receive training so they can advance in the firm. This training can be in the functional areas of business management such as human resource management, finance, and marketing. Training can be done in the plant using experienced employees or can involve people brought in from the outside. Every employee should be encouraged to pursue ional learning as part of a philosophy of lifelong learning. Formal education, dless of the subject, helps people lead happier lives and become better think- d problem solvers. This makes them better employees. It also helps the firm achieve its goal of having the right people with the right skills at the right place at the right time so the firm can better meet its purpose and objective.

Chapter Highlights

1. Staffing consists of finding, hiring, and retaining the best people to run a business.
2. Determining a firm's personnel needs is a three-step process that includes developing jobs from tasks and job descriptions, developing a staffing plan, and conducting a staff inventory.
3. A staff inventory is an assessment of a job, not the performance of the person holding it.
4. A critical task is something that must be done well if a firm is going to succeed and will cause the firm to fail if done poorly.
5. Recruiting must be performed carefully because the people hired will execute the firm's business plan.
6. The goal of recruiting is to find the best people, wherever they are.
7. Treat all applicants for a job well because it shows them how they will be treated once they are hired.
8. Committees should select new employees.
9. Annual performance reviews must be a standard part of any job and may be conducted more often.
10. Frequent, constructive, informal feedback is the best performance motivator.
11. To keep the best employees, managers must pay at least the market rate for every job.
12. Employee training and education is an on-going responsibility of management if the firm is to keep its best employees and remain competitive.
13. Great managers are great leaders and they understand the need to help all workers reach their full potential. This is why they view the generation of the right future leaders for the firm a vital part of their job. How well they do this is often a measure of their legacy that will affect the long-run profitability of their firm.

Chapter Quiz

1. Define staffing and explain why staffing is vital to the long-term success of a business.
2. Identify and describe the three parts of determining a firm's personnel needs. Explain how they are related to the firm's business plan.
3. Explain what a critical task is and how it is handled when staffing an organization.

4. Is it better for a firm to promote from within or go outside the firm when filling a job? Explain your answer.
5. What does a firm's hiring process tell a potential employee about the business?
6. What are the most important pieces of information found on a job application form? What should a manager do with them? Explain your answer.
7. Describe the best procedure for conducting a performance review.
8. Describe how a manager should deal with an employee whose performance is very good so he or she will continue to excel.
9. Describe how a manager should deal with an employee whose performance is poor so that he or she will seek to excel in the future. When and how should a poorly performing employee be fired?
10. To keep good employees, all you have to do is pay them enough. Do you agree or disagree? Explain your answer.
11. Is it the employers' or the employees' responsibility to keep employees' job skills up to date? Explain your answer.
12. Explain why staffing is included as part of the directing business function.
13. Explain why the generation of the right future leaders for the firm is a vital part of a manager's job and how it can affect the long-run profitability of the firm.
14. Is it possible to be a great manager without being a great leader first? Explain.
15. Which is more important to the long-run success of an agribusiness, human resource leadership or human resource management? Explain.

Case 18
Yakima Valley Orchards: Part II

Tom Smiley (packinghouse and storage manager for YVO) was visibly upset as he approached Fred Stone in the orchard. He had just heard about the packinghouse, and he thought it was a cheap shot. Fred told him he did not know what he was talking about and asked him to explain.

Tom explained that Joe Long, a crew leader, had stopped by the packinghouse earlier that morning and asked him what he knew about plans to phase out the packing operation. Joe said he had heard from a reliable source that YVO was closing its packinghouse next year and hiring Hayfield Cold Storage to pack all its fruit.

Fred reassured Tom that he had not heard anything about closing the packinghouse. "Besides," Fred assured Tom, "someone with your experience would not have any problem getting another job even if our packinghouse closed." When Fred asked Tom where he heard this, Tom said it had come from Joe. To make matters worse, Tom said Joe was very upset by this news because he just bought a new house and now he does not see how he will be able to make the payments. He thought he should start looking for a new job.

Fred tracked Joe down right away and told him not to worry. He would find out what was going on. It seems that Joe got his information from Ben Williams. Ben was a tractor driver for the migrant crew and was currently working for Joe. Ben had been unhappy with his job since he came to YVO last fall. Ben has been telling everyone that he is tired of being isolated with that migrant bunch. He just does not feel at home working for YVO.

As Fred headed to the office to find Don Marshall he mumbled to himself, "I don't understand why there is so much quibbling around here all the time. Tom got one of the biggest raises last year, and he is unhappy. Joe was promoted to supervisor of migrant labor, and he is unhappy. Ben Williams, well, he is just unhappy. Why can't we all just get along?"

Which of Maslow's human needs are most important to each of these people?

How can this information help solve this problem?

Chapter 19

Personal Selling

Chapter Learning Objectives

- Explain the role of personal selling in the overall success of a business.
- Describe how all employees are a part of their firm's selling activities.
- Describe the importance of thorough product knowledge to sales success.
- Explain the importance of listening and understanding customers' needs to sales success.
- Summarize the 11 elements of successful personal selling.
- Describe the importance of trust and mutual benefit in building a long-term customer relationship.
- Explain how successful selling has its origins in the firm's purpose and objective.
- Summarize how sales can be the path to a successful business career.

Introduction

Making a sale to an agribusiness customer is the crucial final step in achieving the goal of maximizing long-term profits by profitably satisfying customers' needs. Selling is included in the directing business management function because it is the ultimate implementation of the corporate purpose and objective. All the planning, organizing, and controlling are useless until sales take place.

Every agribusiness in the Fortune 500 has products for sale. If any of these companies ceases selling, they are finished. Every employee in every department of these companies needs to understand that they are involved in selling their firm's products. All employees should understand that what they do helps their firm accomplish this. Whether working in shipping, manufacturing, billing, research and development, or marketing, all employees contribute to the firm's sales by helping to develop the right marketing mix—having the right product, at the right price, at the right place, with the right promotion—that completely fills a customer's needs. Salespeople are the final link in the value chain that completes this process.

Selling as an Internal and External Activity

Selling is usually thought of as convincing someone outside the business to buy a firm's product. However, internal selling is just as important. Internal selling keeps everyone in the business focused on profitably meeting customers' needs rather than operating without direction due to lack of motivation or entrenched practices.

The process of new product development usually starts with a bright idea. It can come from anyone, at any time, but the best sources are normally those with the closest connections to customers—namely, salespeople. Listening to customer needs is a great way to get ideas for new products and new features for existing products. Once they have a bright idea, salespeople need to sell it to others inside their company, such as top management and research and development. Internally selling a bright idea is often harder than selling the actual product. If a company is going to survive, its products and the company itself must evolve with their customers' needs.

The focus of this chapter is external business-to-business selling. This is an important activity in the agri-food system and one that many agribusiness students enter. It can involve things such as selling tomato sauce to large pizza manufacturers, cleaning solutions to dairy bottlers, resins to plastic bottle makers, and subassemblies to farm-equipment producers. Each of these products is important to the proper functioning of the agri-food system and requires strong personal selling skills. This chapter will explore and discuss the basic skills needed for personal selling.

THE ELEVEN ELEMENTS OF SUCCESSFUL PERSONAL SELLING

Regardless of the situation, there are a number of general principles that make for successful personal selling. Anyone involved in this activity needs to master each of these items.

1. Product Knowledge

A vital part of selling is matching a potential customer's needs with the virtues of your firm's products. This starts with knowing everything there is to know about your product—how it is manufactured, where the inputs come from, how shipping is handled, potential uses, technical specifications, and so on. Salespersons who have mastered this are in the best position to see how their products meet a customer's needs.

2. Listen to the Customer

Nobody likes to have products sold to him or her, but people do like to buy things that make their lives better. Salespeople need to listen carefully to what their customers' needs are, what they want, and what they cannot get. Let the customer define the reasons for the purchase. By asking questions and listening, salespeople can explain the advantages of their products in a way that directly addresses the specific needs identified by the customer.

For example, a salesperson noted numerous safety awards covering the walls of a customer's office. He mentioned this to the customer, who said safety is his highest concern because his father was disabled in an industrial accident when he was a child. When the salesperson began his presentation, he strongly emphasized the safety aspects of his firm's products and successfully made the sale. "Nobody cares how much you know until they know how much you care" is an old business saying that is appropriate here.

3. Call on the Right People

Be sure the people you speak with are those with the authority to make a buying decision. This may take some time, but be sure. In some instances, all it takes are a few simple questions: "Do you have the authority to make this purchase? If not, who does? How can I see him (or her)?"

4. Call with a Purpose

Do not waste the potential customer's time. Be sure to have all the latest information about new products, orders, inquiries, prices, delivery schedules, and so on to ensure that the customer gains some benefit from the meeting. It is recommended to call after a sale to confirm that everything that was promised was received by the customer. If there are problems, resolve them quickly to the customer's satisfaction. This will reaffirm your interest in establishing a long-term relationship rather than just making a quick sale.

5. Professional Attitude, Decorum, and Attire

All customers, including other businesses, have choices when they buy. Today it is difficult to gain a large, long-term advantage solely on product attributes. What keeps a customer coming back is good, reliable servicing of the account—helping customers use the product to their best advantage. Many people in sales suggest that they spend more time servicing accounts than selling their product.

Providing good service to an account starts with projecting a professional image. Never criticize the competition's products. It is better to point out the unique advantages of your firm's products. If a firm's employees wear formal business clothing, a salesperson must do the same. Always dress at least as well as the customer to show respect for the customer's values. If the goal is to build a long-term business relationship, shared values are a necessary starting point. In today's electronic era, professionalism also means turning off pagers, cell phones, and PDAs before meeting customers in order to give customers your full attention.

Salespeople have to be reliable and competent. They must always provide accurate, up-to-date information and deliver on all their promises regardless of costs. If the delivery of a product is promised on Wednesday, it should be there on Monday. In some firms, salespeople have become legends by the heroic efforts they have made to make a customer happy. With every firm running lean and mean, there is little room for products and salespeople who do not live up to their promises. Competitors are more than happy to fill your spot if your firm does not measure up.

As an example, a farm-equipment dealer took an urgent call late one afternoon from a producer in the middle of harvest whose machine had broken down in a field. The dealer asked the farmer exactly where the field was located and told him to stand next to the machine at 9 AM the next day, when the part would be delivered. A little before 9 AM, a small plane flew over the field and dropped a package out with a parachute. It was the needed part. The dealer had hired the plane and flown all night to the manufacturer to deliver the critical part to his customer. Under promise and over deliver!

6. Make an Appointment

When calling on a business for the first time, set things up before the visit. A letter of introduction with a follow-up telephone call is a great way to start. The letter should show the potential customer that you have done some research on them and understand their business. This also ensures that you talk to the right person. Making an appointment guarantees that the right person will be available when you call and that she will be prepared for your visit. If you are turned down for an appointment, do not throw the information away. Call again in 90 days. The customer's situation may have changed during that time and he or she might be ready to do business this time. Perseverance is a vital part of business success.

7. Get to Know Everyone

When making a sales call, talk to just about everyone you see who works for the customer. Everyone has information that could help you make a sale. The guard at the gate can tell you whose trucks are coming and going. The receptionist can tell you how busy the firm has been and which of your competitors have been visiting this firm. A quick look at the salesperson sign-in book in the lobby can tell you who has been there and who they visited. You can learn a lot by keeping your eyes and ears open and asking questions.

8. Network

Make a wide circle of friends, acquaintances, and colleagues. Do not be afraid to ask them for help when facing a problem. In some cases they can be a source of personal support. In others they can help you learn new things and provide new sales leads. It pays to be active in your community and industry trade associations to stay current on what is happening.

9. Develop a Long-Term Relationship with Your Customers

One of the biggest changes in business in recent years is the end of adversarial relationships between vendors and customers. Business leaders have come to realize the benefits of cooperating with the businesses they deal with. The concept of supply chain management, covered in chapter 12, highlights the advantages in this area. People prefer to do business with others that share their business values and like the idea that they are more than just a profitable account to their vendors.

Two fundamental parts of building this relationship are trust and mutual benefit. Each side should be confident that the other will perform as expected. An excellent way to extend trust is to minimize the risk of making a purchase by offering a full money-back guarantee, free trial periods, and free samples. Another part of building the vendor/customer relationship is learning more about each other through business entertaining such as lunches, dinners, theater trips, golf, and football games. These events help everyone learn more about what kind of person the other is. When a friendship becomes part of the business relationship, there is always a strong incentive to live up to obligations.

Keep a customer analysis on each account. Research customers and constantly update your findings. This year's great account may be next year's biggest bankruptcy and vice versa. With the Internet it is possible to quickly access all the information necessary to assess the value of your customers. Networking also can help keep your data current. If a customer is contemplating a major expansion, you need to get ready to grow with them. If they are experiencing declining sales, you need to anticipate that as well.

Keep a file on the people you deal with in each account. In addition to their names, e-mail addresses, and cell phone numbers, the file should include their likes and dislikes, best times to call, where they went to school, hobbies, children, and so on. This information helps you better understand what motivates their behavior, which is important to building a relationship.

10. Be Well-Rounded

It is always an advantage to make other people feel comfortable when they are with you. One of the best ways to do this is to be interested in whatever they do or say. You should familiarize yourself with what is going on in the world by keeping up with world events, including major sports.

11. Close the Sale

It is important to know how to close the sale and convince the customer to make a commitment to buy the product from you. With a close relationship this is easier because you know what motivates your customer. In other cases it means directly asking the customer, "What do I need to do to make this sale?" and then taking care of each obstacle raised. If the customer wants to be billed on the fifteenth rather than the first of the month, or have deliveries on Tuesdays rather than Thursdays, you can adjust. When all the obstacles are overcome, remember to ask, "Are you ready to place your order?" This seems simple, but not asking this question has resulted in lost business for many salespeople!

The Firm's Values, Purpose, and Objective

The best salespeople are those who passionately believe in the value of the products they sell. As was developed in chapter 17, a critical ingredient in developing a work environment in which everyone seeks to excel is having all workers (including salespeople) understand and accept the firm's values, purpose, and objective as having value. Thus, selling the firm's products in order to meet this quarter's sales goal should not be a firm's only concern. Improving customers' lives also should play a vital role.

For example, if a salesperson fervently believes that the pizza sauce his firm sells is the world's best, any pizza manufacturer whose goal is to make great pizza should definitely buy his firm's sauce. Purchasing his firm's sauce will help them reach their goal of making the world's greatest pizza, which will allow his firm to reach its goal of increased sales and profits. Good selling is about helping your customers solve their problems. By helping them get what they want, you get what you want.

Spencer Johnson and Larry Wilson in *The One Minute Salesperson* call this "selling on purpose"—or helping people feel good about what they bought and about themselves. With a philosophy of "our products help our customers solve their problems and make their lives better" firmly in mind, what a salesperson does takes on greater meaning. These ideals should be a prominent part of the firm's values, purpose, and objective and accepted as worthwhile by all of its employees, especially those in sales. They cannot be just empty promises; the firm must have great products and service.

SALES AS A CAREER

Sales offers an exciting and challenging job opportunity that offers independence and security. Good salespeople have the respect and admiration of others in their firm because of the importance of their efforts to the firm's overall success. A close look at any successful person reveals someone who is an effective salesperson. Many of us sold our spouses on the idea that we were the one for them. Parents sell their children on the right values. Successful scientists sell those that fund their research that it is valuable and beneficial. Top business managers sell their employees that their firm's values, purpose, and objective are worthwhile and worth their time. Even authors of textbooks such as this one sell their readers on the notion that their ideas will help them have successful business careers. Whether you enter a formal sales position or not, understanding the basic tenets of personal selling is a valuable part of anyone's business education.

CHAPTER HIGHLIGHTS

1. Personal selling is the critical final step for an agribusiness firm to achieve its goal of maximizing long-term profits by profitably satisfying customer needs.
2. Selling is considered part of the directing business management function because it is the ultimate implementation of the firm's purpose and objective.
3. Selling is both an internal and external activity because salespeople are often the best source of market information and new product ideas within a firm.
4. The first requirement for successful selling is thorough product knowledge.
5. The second requirement for successful selling is listening to customers and letting them define the reasons for buying.
6. Being an effective and efficient salesperson means calling on the right people, calling with a purpose, and having a professional attitude, decorum, and attire.

7. The objective of sales is to develop a long-term relationship built on trust and mutual benefit.
8. The best salespeople are those who are passionate about the value of their products.
9. The proper mind-set is that your firm's products make your customers' lives better.
10. By helping your customer get what they want, your firm is able to get what it wants.

CHAPTER QUIZ

1. Is personal selling a legitimate subject to be covered in a book on agribusiness management? Explain the reasons for your answer.
2. Explain why someone who works in human resources needs to know something about personal selling.
3. Explain why selling is both an internal and external activity for a firm.
4. Identify and explain types of selling other than business-to-business selling.
5. Which two elements of successful selling listed in the chapter are the most important? Explain the reasons for your answer.
6. Describe the characteristics of a successful salesperson. Explain the reasons for your answer.
7. Describe the term networking, and explain why it is important to sales success.
8. Explain why developing a long-term relationship with customers is desirable. How do football tickets and dinners affect this relationship?
9. What is the role of trust and mutual benefit in building a long-term customer relationship?
10. What does it mean to close the sale? Explain its role in personal selling.
11. How do a firm's values, purpose, and objective affect the performance of its salespeople?
12. Identify three reasons why someone seeking a career in business would select a sales position. Explain.
13. Explain the business adage that nothing happens in a business until something is sold.
14. Some firms are giving up their market research departments and replacing them with panels of salespeople. Why would they do this?
15. Will Web-based sales replace the need for personal selling? Explain the reasons for your answer.

Case 19
Mary's Migraine

Mary was excited about coming to work every day. Working for Morgan Foods had been her goal ever since she took a plant tour with her high school class. Developing new food products and processes in the laboratory really sounded exciting. It was the reason she chose food science as a major in college and completed two summer internships with them. The recruiter told her everyone starts as an entry-level, general management trainee. As a company, Morgan feels it is important for everyone to understand the full scope of what the company does. After the four-week company training program, assignments are made to a specific area within the firm.

Morgan Foods is the premier regional grower and processor of tomatoes. They produce products for most of the private-label and in-store brands of tomato products sold in the region. Management always threatened to put their products out under their own name, but never did. However, they aggressively sought business opportunities to sell their products wherever they could. The leaders of Morgan Foods thought Baba Loo Pizza offered them a great opportunity to expand their sales.

Baba Loo Pizza is a new franchise business that is growing rapidly in the region by selling a great tasting, low-fat, eastern European pizza. It has all the full flavor of regular pizza with none of the fat. The secret seems to be the garlic sauce they use. Their current tomato sauce supplier is too small to meet Baba Loo's rapidly expanding demand. Morgan just opened a new tomato processing plant with lots of unused capacity that offers good overnight highway access to all of Baba Loo's restaurants. It seems like a good fit for both firms.

At the end of the third week of the training program, Mary got a memo that seemed to end her dream. She had been assigned to the company's elite sales team that was going after a new major account—Baba Loo Pizza. This sounded exciting before she realized she had been assigned to sales. "This was not part of the deal," she thought. "I'm a scientist. I work in a laboratory. All these years of college so I can be just a sales clerk. I don't think so! Besides, I never sold anything in my life."

Mary's first reaction was to quit, but she decided to talk over her decision with her company-appointed mentor. Her mentor has long experience with Morgan in a variety of positions and seems to be happy with the firm.

Prior to the meeting, Mary put the following questions together. If you were the mentor, how would you answer them?

- How is being in sales going to help my research career?
- How is being in sales going to help me have a successful business career?
- Why do I need a college degree if I am just going to sell tomato sauce?
- If I stay and take this job, how should I prepare for my first call on Baba Loo?
- What do I need to do at my sales calls to help me make the sale?
- Once I have landed the account and made the sale, my job is over, right?

Chapter 20

Developing a Workable Approach to Agribusiness Management

Chapter Learning Objectives

- Explain why maximizing the long-term profits of a firm by profitably satisfying customer needs is central to a business's success.
- Describe the role of marketing in the success of a firm.
- Identify and explain the two golden rules of management success.
- Summarize why agribusiness management is an art supported by science.
- Summarize and explain the elements that most affect a firm's revenues, cost, and information.

Introduction

This book has presented the processes and procedures needed to accomplish managers' central goal of maximizing the firm's long-term profits by profitably satisfying their customers' needs. This central goal ties together everything a manager does. The accomplishment of this goal is a never-ending task.

To realize this central goal, agribusiness managers must operate like circus jugglers. They need to keep each part of their business moving along smoothly while devoting only a small amount of time to any one part. Like jugglers, they need effective and efficient ways to evaluate the performance of each part of the business before moving on to the next one. This is a tremendous challenge, but one that is met every day by successful agribusiness managers.

A manager must remember that a firm's customers also are seeking to maximize their own long-term profits and satisfaction from their purchases. They will buy only from firms that help them achieve that goal. Customer needs are continuously evolving, so a business must modify how it fills those needs. When a business ceases to meet its customers' needs, those customers take their business elsewhere and the business fails. Agribusinesses, like all businesses, exist only because they meet customers' needs effectively and efficiently.

Firms stay in business because they meet their customers' needs profitably. Firms must have accurate information about their operation and its costs. Since all firms seek to maximize long-term profits, they must always look for lower-cost ways to meet their customers' needs. The size of the profit margin normally reflects how well a firm meets its customers' needs.

Managers of successful agribusinesses accomplish their central goal by applying the two golden rules of management success:

1. Treat your customers the way the customer wants to be treated.
2. Be the kind of manager you would like to work for.

A commitment to the golden rules of success results in fully satisfied customers who will buy all they can from you because your products completely fill their needs, they give them great value, and your happy and productive employees always provide excellent service.

All these individual pieces need to be placed into a workable approach to agribusiness management that can be applied right away, every day. The key is to isolate those factors that have the greatest influence on revenues and costs and monitor them in ways that will permit a quick and thorough evaluation of the firm's performance.

REVENUES

Revenue is the income received from selling products. The total amount of revenue earned for a given period depends on the price charged per unit and the number of units sold. Remember that the goal is to maximize total profit rather than profit per unit. Maximizing only total revenue does not automatically lead to higher total profits since just setting low prices increases revenue, but not necessarily profits. Minimizing only total cost does not automatically work either since the best way to minimize cost is to produce nothing. The only successful way to maximize total profit is to jointly manage revenues and costs. The business world is full of firms that concentrated on only revenues (or costs) and suffered because of it.

The proper starting point for examining revenues is to review the firm's marketing plan, with special attention given to its marketing mix (the four Ps of marketing—product, price, place, and promotion). This process should include a reexamination of those unmet customer needs the firm is going to fill as stated in the firm's purpose and objective, and a comparison of that with the business's financial goals. The marketing mix involves four things a manager can control in planning his revenue expectation. Although each of these topics was covered in detail earlier in this book, let's now briefly review the key factors that typically have the greatest impact on revenues.

Changing Customer Needs

Stephen Covey, in his famous book *The 7 Habits of Highly Effective People,* reminds us that the world has three constants: change, principles, and choices. This book emphasizes teaching business principles and good decision-making procedures so managers can make informed choices. Economic principles such as the law of demand endure because they reflect universal truths. What cannot be taught is how to anticipate and respond to change—the art rather than the science of business management. Nevertheless, failure to adapt to changing customer needs is a leading cause of business failure.

Every business needs to be constantly on the lookout for changes in customers' needs as well as new and better ways to meet them. Business success demands constant attention to anticipating, understanding, and filling customer needs. Some firms require their employees to work directly with their customers so they can see firsthand what customer needs the firm is not providing and what products and services their competitors are offering. Many very successful firms spend considerable time analyzing their competitors' products and services. No firm wants to sell the perfect harness for horses while failing to note the rise of automobiles.

Expanding Market Areas

Once a firm knows what its customers want and develops a product that meets it, the next step is finding customers, whether the business is in a sparsely populated area of western Kansas or an urbanized state such as New Jersey. In the past, market areas were limited by distance. Today, the Internet makes the market area virtually unlimited. As economic units grow larger and transportation becomes less expensive, businesses can afford to reach further to buy and sell. Agribusinesses that once never sold anything to anyone more than 100 miles away now routinely service customers around the world. The size of market areas is not even limited to national borders—as demonstrated in chapter 1, if any industry has gone global it is agribusiness. E-business's ease of use and low cost make this possible. Organizations that fail to adjust to this changing reality will face higher costs for the things they buy and decreasing revenues from the things they sell.

Changing Definition of Value

Price has always been a major factor influencing customers' buying decisions, but it is not the sole reason why customers buy a product. What most buyers are looking for is value, the feeling of getting a good return for the money spent. Value is what your customers tell you it is. It cannot be imposed upon them.

The lowest price is not always the best deal. Price is just one component of the marketing mix. Pricing must be set as part of an overall marketing strategy, not in isolation. While it is important to cover all costs over the long run, setting a product's price is still essentially a marketing decision rather than an accounting decision.

Pricing depends largely on five factors: the prevailing price in the market area, the level of competition in the market area, the volume of business, the level of services provided, and how different the product is from its competitors.

If the product is a standardized commodity and involves large quantities, such as milk, grains, or crop storage, customers will be very price-conscious since a few pennies per unit can have a large effect on their profits. This is especially true if there are few competitors in the market area. However, a deviation from the market price on either end of a transaction may be good if it brings better overall value and greater profits. For example, if a grain elevator paid farmers a lower price for their crop but provided free field pick-up during harvest, its price could provide farmers with a better value than those who price using more conventional methods. It is important to find out how customers define value and provide it to them in a profitable way.

Degree of Competition

An agribusiness can have several firms in its market area and have very little competition. On the other hand, there may be only one other similar firm, but lots of competition. The level of competition in a market can be misjudged from just a quick review of the area.

Firms use both offensive and defensive strategies to compete in a market. Offensive strategies include aggressive pricing and promotion strategies such as very low prices designed to pull customers away from competitors. Bidding wars for customers often leave all the firms in a market financially drained with little change in market position unless one firm is big enough and has the will to destroy the others. Businesses use defensive strategies such as low prices and long-term contracts to keep others from entering their markets and taking their customers.

Today's competition is increasingly waged on things like level of service, credit terms, and rebates. The high level of competition in most markets makes it difficult to gain a competitive advantage in terms of products and prices. It is even hard to gain an advantage based on service since service only becomes an issue when it is less than outstanding. Agribusiness managers must be vigilant to know that their products and services are comparable to or better than those of their competitors.

Keeping Customers Aware of Your Products

Every firm must be sure its customers know about its products. This is increasingly difficult in agribusiness, where more than 1,000 new products enter the market every month. Multiple firms seek customers' business and they are constantly courting them. To attract new customers and keep old ones, businesses must promote their products effectively every day. Managers have four primary methods of attracting customers: advertising, product promotions, personal selling, and word of mouth.

Advertising is the impersonal delivery of a paid sales-creating message to a large group of people. It is a mass-media approach that usually involves newspapers, radio, television, direct mail, billboards, and handbills. It also can use product promotions such as contests, giveaways, and drawings to attract customers. The objective is to increase sales by increasing customer awareness about a firm and informing customers of the superiority of its goods and services in meeting their needs. As a part of regular evaluations of business performance, managers must assess the effectiveness of promotional efforts in increasing sales. To do this a manager should consider:

- *When to advertise.* The best time to advertise is just before customers are ready to buy. At that time, they are already in the mood to buy and are actively searching for the product. Ads should highlight the product features that are most important to customers.
- *Where to advertise.* A firm should put its message where its customers are. For small markets, it does not pay to undertake a state or national advertising campaign. Selection of the right combination of media—print, broadcast, billboard, Internet, and so on—depends on the type of business and its market.
- *How much to spend.* Advertising, like any other part of a business, must pay its own way. No set formula is universally right. The best method is to spend enough to accomplish your marketing objectives. As described in chapter 12, break-even analysis is a good way to evaluate whether sales increased enough to justify the advertising expense.

Personal selling is required in nearly every business. Personal selling includes all the activities of the people who have contact with clients or potential customers. The salesperson is a key figure in a successful promotional campaign. A salesperson can show potential customers the benefits of doing business with her firm rather than someone else. Personal friendliness, enthusiasm, persistence, a good product, and a good company are required to succeed in personal selling. In addition, a salesperson must be honest, deliver on all promises, and be well-informed and competent in all dealings with customers. Those who are not will drive business away.

Managers should provide strong support for their salespeople so they can be as effective and efficient as possible. Salespeople are a key link in the firm's promotional efforts and should be given wide latitude in modifying the firm's marketing mix in order to make a sale.

Word of mouth is the best form of advertising. A satisfied customer is the best and lowest-cost way to sell products. It is estimated that a satisfied customer tells three others about a good experience. Conversely, one that has a bad experience usually tells ten others.

Changing Credit Policies

Ninety percent of agribusiness sales are on credit. Customers generally expect it. However, credit is still a privilege. Smart managers know how to use their credit policies to increase sales. They constantly reassess the credit worthiness and level of future sales possible from each account. This year's top sales account could be next year's biggest bankruptcy and vice versa. Continuing to extend large amounts of credit to a faltering customer could prove disastrous to a firm, just as failing to give appropriate credit to an up-and-coming business could lead to a large amount of missed future sales.

Costs

Each item discussed on the revenue side of the business normally has a corresponding item on the cost side. As the old adage goes, it takes money to make money. A successful advertising program can increase sales but also may involve significant costs. Doing market research to better understand customers' needs and what drives their buying decisions should lead to bigger sales, but it is expensive.

Cost management is a major management concern. The objective of cost management is to know when changes in costs lead to greater corporate profits. Listed below are some of the procedures an agribusiness can use to evaluate changes in costs.

Evaluating Effectiveness and Efficiency

Throughout this book, the terms effectiveness and efficiency have been used to evaluate management practices. These terms have been selected carefully and linked on purpose because both must be present to be successful. These ideas also are present in the unifying management theme of this book—maximizing long-term profits by profitably satisfying customers' needs.

Maximizing long-term profits requires a firm to be economically *efficient*—to produce the maximum output per unit of input. To achieve this, firms must be sustainable. The business must use all its resources in the most efficient ways possible. Profitably satisfying customers' needs requires the firm to be *effective*—to do the right things. The achievement of the manager's central goal requires not only doing the right things, but also doing them well. This central goal makes it easier for managers to understand what is important and why it is important, and to develop a workable approach to business management.

Managers need to evaluate the effectiveness of their business by regularly updating their strategic plans and reexamining their business and marketing plans. Too many managers see these plans as one-time efforts that, once finished, are never changed or seen again. As was discussed in the revenue section, change is the one constant in our world. It is prudent to reassess everything on the cost side of the business as well as the revenue side on a regular basis to improve the firm's effectiveness and efficiency. If you do not, remember that your customers and competitors probably are.

Break-Even Analysis

A break-even point for each major product is an effective and efficient way to evaluate business performance. Break-even analysis should be performed in advance of each business year. It helps managers identify critical cost items and allows time for the development of ways to monitor and control them. If an analysis shows the break-even point to be too high a percentage of total capacity, it can give an early warning to seek ways to reduce it. Break-even analysis can help identify products that will never have profitable sales, where lower overhead is needed, or where more efficient production is required.

Plant Size

Few managers get the opportunity to build a business from the ground up. Typically, they are given the responsibility to maintain and operate an ongoing physical plant. Plant size does affect the cost of doing business. It also can limit the volume of business a firm can handle.

In the short run, a manager has to assume that the current size of the plant is fixed and learn to operate within those boundaries. Any attempt to operate the plant above its designed capacity will result in higher costs per unit due to bottlenecks, disorganization, and other inefficiencies.

When market forecasts show a sustained increase in sales, a manager needs to rationally assess the need for a larger plant so that production can keep pace with sales and costs per unit can be kept as low as possible. Well-informed managers know the efficiency limits of their plant and the operating efficiencies of their competitors. This helps them rationally plan any necessary changes in plant size.

Accounts Receivable

Sales on credit are a reality of doing business. However, lending money is a central purpose or objective of banks, not agribusinesses. Extending credit is advantageous only if it is properly managed.

Easy credit does not normally lead to greater profits. What does lead to greater profits is receiving all the money tied up in accounts receivable on time. This is easier said than done. Many managers joke that they could retire tomorrow if everyone who owes money to their business came in and paid off their account. Often, when a customer owes a large amount of money and it has not been paid for some time, it will take its business to a competitor while leaving the old debt unpaid.

A business should not apologize for a strict credit policy. A few bad accounts can severely restrict a firm's profits. The bankruptcy of a major customer with a large debt can take a firm with it. A firm's investment in accounts receivable requires the same attention and management as any other asset account.

An agribusiness manager should keep several principles in mind when evaluating and managing accounts receivable. First, customers are not afraid to ask for credit, so businesses should not be afraid to ask for payment. Second, credit is not something to which every customer is entitled; the privilege of credit must be earned. Third, establish credit and collection policies in advance and stick to them.

INFORMATION

The third area of the business that requires the manager's attention after revenues and costs is information. This side of the business has become increasingly complex as agribusinesses, their customers, and their markets have grown. Information has been further complicated by the increasing volatility of the general economy and financial markets.

Managers must begin information-system planning by taking charge of their financial affairs. They must have a plan for their financial future, including cash flow budgets, operating budgets, and capital expenditure budgets. Today's fast-moving business environment requires more than just drawing up these documents. They must serve as blueprints for action for the firm's future and be reviewed and integrated with the firm's marketing plan to meet changing situations.

Agribusiness managers need to stay abreast of changes in technology, consumer demand, weather, world politics, and the stability and solvency of their suppliers and customers. They need to be able to take this information and trace its influences on their revenues, costs, and profits in both the short and long term through an information system. The same level of precision should be applied to nonfinancial information such as sales, inventory management, and marketing. Managers who become complacent in any of these areas may place their future and their firm's future in jeopardy.

Despite their importance, many firms do not maintain good information systems. Poor records are often cited as a major factor contributing to business failure. Conversely, agribusinesses that maintain accurate and comprehensive records tend to have the highest profits and the best managers. Good records provide managers with a solid foundation for effective and efficient decision making that allows them to have an accurate picture of their firms' performance.

When evaluating the effectiveness and efficiency of an agribusiness's performance, a manager needs an information system that gives clear, firm answers to the following four questions:

1. Do the financial records produce an accurate, informative, and timely picture of the firm's financial situation and operating results?
2. Does the information system provide the data in the right form and in a timely manner needed for problem solving and decision making?
3. Are the financial statements updated at least semiannually for use by management, lenders, and others?
4. Are the accounting records audited at least annually by a qualified and unbiased outside firm to ensure the accuracy of the records and to head off any potential financial mismanagement or fraud by management or employees?

CHAPTER HIGHLIGHTS

1. The central goal of maximizing long-term profits by profitably satisfying customer needs ties together everything a manager does.
2. Top managers know how to evaluate the performance of their business effectively and efficiently.
3. Managers of successful agribusinesses accomplish their central goal by treating their customers the way the customer wants to be treated and by being the kind of manager they would like to work for.
4. A good evaluation system examines a business from three sides: revenues, costs, and information.
5. The items that most affect a firm's revenues are changes in customer demands, expanding market areas, changing definitions of value, degree of competition, product promotion, and credit policies.
6. The items that most affect a firm's costs are effectively and efficiently meeting customers' needs, evaluating the profitability of each major product, operating properly sized plants, and managing the accounts receivable.
7. In order to make good business decisions, managers must have a good information system that provides them with accurate, timely information in a usable form.
8. Accounting records must be updated frequently and audited by a qualified, unbiased outsider to ensure the records' accuracy and to head off any financial mismanagement.

CHAPTER QUIZ

1. Identify the unifying theme of this book and explain how it ties together the four management functions.
2. Explain what the golden rules of management success are and how they help an agribusiness succeed.

3. Is it better for an agribusiness to focus on maximizing total revenue or minimizing costs in order to increase profits? How does your answer fit with the central management goal given in the text? Explain the reasons for your answer.
4. Which is more important to business success—keeping customers happy or keeping employees happy? Explain the reasons for your answer.
5. What is the difference between price and value to a customer? Which is more important? Explain the reasons for your answer.
6. Explain what you think Stephen Covey meant when he said there are three constants in the world: change, principles, and choices. How does this help an agribusiness manager be more successful?
7. What is the difference between product promotion and advertising? What is the best way to advertise your products and services? Explain your answers.
8. Why is it important to the long-term success of a firm to always evaluate the effectiveness and efficiency of everything it does?
9. Accounts receivable are part of a firm's sales. Why is it discussed as a cost in this chapter?
10. Why is information given equal weight with revenues and costs when evaluating the performance of an agribusiness?
11. Explain the role of strategic management in keeping an agribusiness competitive.
12. Agribusiness has always told people that it was different than other industries. Is this true? Explain.
13. Explain what value means to customers, and how agribusinesses incorporate it into their businesses.
14. Explain why firms that achieve the maximization of long-run profits are examples of sustainable agriculture.
15. Explain why agribusinesses that maximize their long-run profits by profitably satisfying their customers' needs are considered to be efficient and effective.

CASE 20
Erin's Epiphany

Today was the first real day on her first real job. As she pulled into the parking lot of the grain elevator she was going to manage, she saw the sign on the side of the building—reserved parking for elevator manager Erin Bahn. She had never been this important before, but it felt good.

This was it. All the schools and company training programs were over. Now it was time to go to work.

She entered the office and introduced herself to the staff. Steve Jones, one of her employees, escorted her to her office. Her name was already on the door. It took about two hours for her to unload all her materials and get her computer set up the way she wanted it.

Somehow it all looked so easy in the training program. How was she ever going to mix everything she had learned about this business and business management so she would be successful?

Since you are her mentor she asks you how to go about developing a workable approach to agribusiness management. What are your suggestions?

Appendix

Tables Used in Capital Budgeting Decisions

Table 1 Compound Sum of $1: $FV = (1 + i)^n$

Period	1%	2%	3%	4%	5%	6%	7%	8%	9%	10%
1	1.0100	1.0200	1.0300	1.0400	1.0500	1.0600	1.0700	1.0800	1.0900	1.1000
2	1.0201	1.0404	1.0609	1.0816	1.1025	1.1236	1.1449	1.1664	1.1881	1.2100
3	1.0303	1.0612	1.0927	1.1249	1.1576	1.1910	1.2250	1.2597	1.2950	1.3310
4	1.0406	1.0824	1.1255	1.1699	1.2155	1.2625	1.3108	1.3605	1.4116	1.4641
5	1.0510	1.1041	1.1593	1.2167	1.2763	1.3382	1.4026	1.4693	1.5386	1.6105
6	1.0615	1.1262	1.1941	1.2653	1.3401	1.4185	1.5007	1.5869	1.6771	1.7716
7	1.0721	1.1487	1.2299	1.3159	1.4071	1.5036	1.6058	1.7138	1.8280	1.9487
8	1.0829	1.1717	1.2668	1.3686	1.4775	1.5938	1.7182	1.8509	1.9926	2.1436
9	1.0937	1.1951	1.3048	1.4233	1.5513	1.6895	1.8385	1.9990	2.1719	2.3579
10	1.1046	1.2190	1.3439	1.4802	1.6289	1.7908	1.9672	2.1589	2.3674	2.5937
11	1.1157	1.2434	1.3842	1.5395	1.7103	1.8983	2.1049	2.3316	2.5804	2.8531
12	1.1268	1.2682	1.4258	1.6010	1.7959	2.0122	2.2522	2.5182	2.8127	3.1384
13	1.1381	1.2936	1.4685	1.6651	1.8856	2.1329	2.4098	2.7196	3.0658	3.4523
14	1.1495	1.3195	1.5126	1.7317	1.9799	2.2609	2.5785	2.9372	3.3417	3.7975
15	1.1610	1.3459	1.5580	1.8009	2.0789	2.3966	2.7590	3.1722	3.6425	4.1772
16	1.1726	1.3728	1.6047	1.8730	2.1829	2.5404	2.9522	3.4259	3.9703	4.5950
17	1.1843	1.4002	1.6528	1.9479	2.2920	2.6928	3.1588	3.7000	4.3276	5.0545
18	1.1961	1.4282	1.7024	2.0258	2.4066	2.8543	3.3799	3.9960	4.7171	5.5599
19	1.2081	1.4568	1.7535	2.1068	2.5270	3.0256	3.6165	4.3157	5.1417	6.1159
20	1.2202	1.4859	1.8061	2.1911	2.6533	3.2071	3.8697	4.6610	5.6044	6.7275
21	1.2324	1.5157	1.8603	2.2788	2.7860	3.3996	4.1406	5.0338	6.1088	7.4002
22	1.2447	1.5460	1.9161	2.3699	2.9253	3.6035	4.4304	5.4365	6.6586	8.1403
23	1.2572	1.5769	1.9736	2.4647	3.0715	3.8197	4.7405	5.8715	7.2579	8.9543
24	1.2697	1.6084	2.0328	2.5633	3.2251	4.0489	5.0724	6.3412	7.9111	9.8497
25	1.2824	1.6406	2.0938	2.6658	3.3864	4.2919	5.4274	6.8485	8.6231	10.834
26	1.2953	1.6734	2.1566	2.7725	3.5557	4.5494	5.8074	7.3964	9.3992	11.918
27	1.3082	1.7069	2.2213	2.8834	3.7335	4.8223	6.2139	7.9881	10.245	13.110
28	1.3213	1.7410	2.2879	2.9987	3.9201	5.1117	6.6488	8.6271	11.167	14.421
29	1.3345	1.7758	2.3566	3.1187	4.1161	5.4184	7.1143	9.3173	12.172	15.863
30	1.3478	1.8114	2.4273	3.2434	4.3219	5.7435	7.6123	10.062	13.267	17.449
40	1.4889	2.2080	3.2620	4.8010	7.0400	10.285	14.974	21.724	31.409	45.259
50	1.6446	2.6916	4.3839	7.1067	11.467	18.420	29.457	46.901	74.357	117.39
60	1.8167	3.2810	5.8916	10.519	18.679	32.987	57.946	101.25	176.03	304.48

Source: James L. Pappas, Eugene Brigham, and Mark Hirschley, *Managerial Economics,* 4th ed., Dryden Press, Chicago, 1983.

Table I *(continued)*

Period	12%	14%	15%	16%	18%	20%	24%	28%	32%	36%
1	1.1200	1.1400	1.1500	1.1600	1.1800	1.2000	1.2400	1.2800	1.3200	1.3600
2	1.2544	1.2996	1.3225	1.3456	1.3924	1.4400	1.5376	1.6384	1.7424	1.8496
3	1.4049	1.4815	1.5209	1.5609	1.6430	1.7280	1.9066	2.0972	2.3000	2.5155
4	1.5735	1.6890	1.7490	1.8106	1.9388	2.0736	2.3642	2.6844	3.0360	3.4210
5	1.7623	1.9254	2.0114	2.1003	2.2878	2.4883	2.9316	3.4360	4.0075	4.6526
6	1.9738	2.1950	2.3131	2.4364	2.6996	2.9860	3.6352	4.3980	5.2899	6.3275
7	2.2107	2.5023	2.6600	2.8262	3.1855	3.5832	4.5077	5.6295	6.9826	8.6054
8	2.4760	2.8526	3.0590	3.2784	3.7589	4.2998	5.5895	7.2058	9.2170	11.703
9	2.7731	3.2519	3.5179	3.8030	4.4355	5.1598	6.9310	9.2234	12.166	15.916
10	3.1058	3.7072	4.0456	4.4114	5.2338	6.1917	8.5944	11.805	16.059	21.646
11	3.4785	4.2262	4.6524	5.1173	6.1759	7.4301	10.657	15.111	21.198	29.439
12	3.8960	4.8179	5.3502	5.9360	7.2876	8.9161	13.214	19.342	27.982	40.037
13	4.3635	5.4924	6.1528	6.8858	8.5994	10.699	16.386	24.758	36.937	54.451
14	4.8871	6.2613	7.0757	7.9875	10.147	12.839	20.319	31.691	48.756	70.053
15	5.4736	7.1379	8.1371	9.2655	11.973	15.407	25.195	40.564	64.358	100.71
16	6.1304	8.1372	9.3576	10.748	14.129	18.488	31.242	51.923	84.953	136.96
17	6.8660	9.2765	10.761	12.467	16.672	22.186	38.740	66.461	112.13	186.27
18	7.6900	10.575	12.375	14.462	19.673	26.623	48.038	85.070	148.02	253.33
19	8.6128	12.055	14.231	16.776	23.214	31.948	59.567	108.89	195.39	344.53
20	9.6463	13.743	16.366	19.460	27.393	38.337	73.864	139.37	257.91	468.57
21	10.803	15.667	18.821	22.574	32.323	46.005	91.591	178.40	340.44	637.26
22	12.100	17.861	21.644	26.186	38.142	55.206	113.57	228.35	449.39	866.67
23	13.552	20.361	24.891	30.376	45.007	66.247	140.83	292.30	593.19	1178.6
24	15.178	23.212	28.625	35.236	53.108	79.496	174.63	374.14	783.02	1602.9
25	17.000	26.461	32.918	40.874	62.668	95.396	216.54	478.90	1033.5	2180.0
26	19.040	30.166	37.856	47.414	73.948	114.47	268.51	612.99	1364.3	2964.9
27	21.324	34.389	43.535	55.000	87.259	137.37	332.95	784.63	1800.9	4032.2
28	23.883	39.204	50.065	63.800	102.96	164.84	412.86	1004.3	2377.2	5483.8
29	26.749	44.693	57.575	74.008	121.50	197.81	511.95	1285.5	3137.9	7458.0
30	29.959	50.950	66.211	85.849	143.37	237.37	634.81	1645.5	4142.0	10143.
40	93.050	188.88	267.86	378.72	750.37	1469.7	5455.9	19426.	66520.	*
50	289.00	700.23	1083.6	1670.7	3927.3	9100.4	46890.	*	*	*
60	897.59	2595.9	4383.9	7370.1	20555.	56347.	*	*	*	*

* *FV* > 99,999.

Table 2 Present Value of $1: $PV = 1/(1 + i)^n = 1/FV$

Period	1%	2%	3%	4%	5%	6%	7%	8%	9%	10%
1	.9901	.9804	.9709	.9615	.9524	.9434	.9346	.9259	.9174	.9091
2	.9803	.9612	.9426	.9246	.9070	.8900	.8734	.8573	.8417	.8264
3	.9706	.9423	.9151	.8890	.8638	.8396	.8163	.7938	.7722	.7513
4	.9610	.9238	.8885	.8548	.8227	.7921	.7629	.7350	.7084	.6830
5	.9515	.9057	.8626	.8219	.7835	.7473	.7130	.6806	.6499	.6209
6	.9420	.8880	.8375	.7903	.7462	.7050	.6663	.6302	.5963	.5645
7	.9327	.8706	.8131	.7599	.7107	.6651	.6227	.5835	.5470	.5132
8	.9235	.8535	.7894	.7307	.6768	.6274	.5820	.5403	.5019	.4665
9	.9143	.8368	.7664	.7026	.6446	.5919	.5439	.5002	.4604	.4241
10	.9053	.8203	.7441	.6756	.6139	.5584	.5083	.4632	.4224	.3855
11	.8963	.8043	.7224	.6496	.5847	.5268	.4751	.4289	.3875	.3505
12	.8874	.7885	.7014	.6246	.5568	.4970	.4440	.3971	.3555	.3186
13	.8787	.7730	.6810	.6006	.5303	.4688	.4150	.3677	.3262	.2897
14	.8700	.7579	.6611	.5775	.5051	.4423	.3878	.3405	.2992	.2633
15	.8613	.7430	.6419	.5553	.4810	.4173	.3624	.3152	.2745	.2394
16	.8528	.7284	.6232	.5339	.4581	.3936	.3387	.2919	.2519	.2176
17	.8444	.7142	.6050	.5134	.4363	.3714	.3166	.2703	.2311	.1978
18	.8360	.7002	.5874	.4936	.4155	.3503	.2959	.2502	.2120	.1799
19	.8277	.6864	.5703	.4746	.3957	.3305	.2765	.2317	.1945	.1635
20	.8195	.6730	.5537	.4564	.3769	.3118	.2584	.2145	.1784	.1486
21	.8114	.6598	.5375	.4388	.3589	.2942	.2415	.1987	.1637	.1351
22	.8034	.6468	.5219	.4220	.3418	.2775	.2257	.1839	.1502	.1228
23	.7954	.6342	.5067	.4057	.3256	.2618	.2109	.1703	.1378	.1117
24	.7876	.6217	.4919	.3901	.3101	.2470	.1971	.1577	.1264	.1015
25	.7798	.6095	.4776	.3751	.2953	.2330	.1842	.1460	.1160	.0923
26	.7720	.5976	.4637	.3607	.2812	.2198	.1722	.1352	.1064	.0839
27	.7644	.5859	.4502	.3468	.2678	.2074	.1609	.1252	.0976	.0763
28	.7568	.5744	.4371	.3335	.2551	.1956	.1504	.1159	.0895	.0693
29	.7493	.5631	.4243	.3207	.2429	.1846	.1406	.1073	.0822	.0630
30	.7419	.5521	.4120	.3083	.2314	.1741	.1314	.0994	.0754	.0573
35	.7059	.5000	.3554	.2534	.1813	.1301	.0937	.0676	.0490	.0356
40	.6717	.4529	.3066	.2083	.1420	.0972	.0668	.0460	.0318	.0221
45	.6391	.4102	.2644	.1712	.1113	.0727	.0476	.0313	.0207	.0137
50	.6080	.3715	.2281	.1407	.0872	.0543	.0339	.0213	.0134	.0085
55	.5785	.3365	.1968	.1157	.0683	.0406	.0242	.0145	.0087	.0053

Table 2 *(continued)*

Period	12%	14%	15%	16%	18%	20%	24%	28%	32%	36%
1	.8929	.8772	.8696	.8621	.8475	.8333	.8065	.7813	.7576	.7353
2	.7972	.7695	.7561	.7432	.7182	.6944	.6504	.6104	.5739	.5407
3	.7118	.6750	.6575	.6407	.6086	.5787	.5245	.4768	.4348	.3975
4	.6355	.5921	.5718	.5523	.5158	.4823	.4230	.3725	.3294	.2923
5	.5674	.5194	.4972	.4761	.4371	.4019	.3411	.2910	.2495	.2149
6	.5066	.4556	.4323	.4104	.3704	.3349	.2751	.2274	.1890	.1580
7	.4523	.3996	.3759	.3538	.3139	.2791	.2218	.1776	.1432	.1162
8	.4039	.3506	.3269	.3050	.2660	.2326	.1789	.1388	.1085	.0854
9	.3606	.3075	.2843	.2630	.2255	.1938	.1443	.1084	.0822	.0628
10	.3220	.2697	.2472	.2267	.1911	.1615	.1164	.0847	.0623	.0462
11	.2875	.2366	.2149	.1954	.1619	.1346	.0938	.0662	.0472	.0340
12	.2567	.2076	.1869	.1685	.1372	.1122	.0757	.0517	.0357	.0250
13	.2292	.1821	.1625	.1452	.1163	.0935	.0610	.0404	.0271	.0184
14	.2046	.1597	.1413	.1252	.0985	.0779	.0492	.0316	.0205	.0135
15	.1827	.1401	.1229	.1079	.0835	.0649	.0397	.0247	.0155	.0099
16	.1631	.1229	.1069	.0930	.0708	.0541	.0320	.0193	.0118	.0073
17	.1456	.1078	.0929	.0802	.0600	.0451	.0258	.0150	.0089	.0054
18	.1300	.0946	.0808	.0691	.0508	.0376	.0208	.0118	.0068	.0039
19	.1161	.0829	.0703	.0596	.0431	.0313	.0168	.0092	.0051	.0029
20	.1037	.0728	.0611	.0514	.0365	.0261	.0135	.0072	.0039	.0021
21	.0926	.0638	.0531	.0443	.0309	.0217	.0109	.0056	.0029	.0016
22	.0826	.0560	.0462	.0382	.0262	.0181	.0088	.0044	.0022	.0012
23	.0738	.0491	.0402	.0329	.0222	.0151	.0071	.0034	.0017	.0008
24	.0659	.0431	.0349	.0284	.0188	.0126	.0057	.0027	.0013	.0006
25	.0588	.0378	.0304	.0245	.0160	.0105	.0046	.0021	.0010	.0005
26	.0525	.0331	.0264	.0211	.0135	.0087	.0037	.0016	.0007	.0003
27	.0469	.0291	.0230	.0182	.0115	.0073	.0030	.0013	.0006	.0002
28	.0419	.0255	.0200	.0157	.0097	.0061	.0024	.0010	.0004	.0002
29	.0374	.0224	.0174	.0135	.0082	.0051	.0020	.0008	.0003	.0001
30	.0334	.0196	.0151	.0116	.0070	.0042	.0016	.0006	.0002	.0001
35	.0189	.0102	.0075	.0055	.0030	.0017	.0005	.0002	.0001	*
40	.0107	.0053	.0037	.0026	.0013	.0007	.0002	.0001	*	*
45	.0061	.0027	.0019	.0013	.0006	.0003	.0001	*	*	*
50	.0035	.0014	.0009	.0006	.0003	.0001	*	*	*	*
55	.0020	.0007	.0005	.0003	.0001	*	*	*	*	*

* The factor is zero to four decimal places.

Table 3 Present Value of an Annuity for $1 for *n* Periods: *PV* =

$$\sum_{t=1}^{n} \frac{1}{(1+i)^t} = \frac{1-\dfrac{1}{1+i^n}}{i}$$

Number of Payments	1%	2%	3%	4%	5%	6%	7%	8%	9%
1	0.9901	0.9804	0.9709	0.9615	0.9524	0.9434	0.9346	0.9259	0.9174
2	1.9704	1.9416	1.9135	1.8861	1.8594	1.8334	1.8080	1.7833	1.7591
3	2.9410	2.8839	2.8286	2.7751	2.7232	2.6730	2.6243	2.5771	2.5313
4	3.9020	3.8077	3.7171	3.6299	3.5460	3.4651	3.3872	3.3121	3.2397
5	4.8534	4.7135	4.5797	4.4518	4.3295	4.2124	4.1002	3.9927	3.8897
6	5.7955	5.6014	5.4172	5.2421	5.0757	4.9173	4.7665	4.6229	4.4859
7	6.7282	6.4720	6.2303	6.0021	5.7864	5.5824	5.3893	5.2064	5.0330
8	7.6517	7.3255	7.0197	6.7327	6.4632	6.2098	5.9713	5.7466	5.5348
9	8.5660	8.1622	7.7861	7.4353	7.1078	6.8017	6.5152	6.2469	5.9952
10	9.4713	8.9826	8.5302	8.1109	7.7217	7.3601	7.0236	6.7101	6.4177
11	10.3676	9.7868	9.2526	8.7605	8.3064	7.8869	7.4987	7.1390	6.8052
12	11.2551	10.5753	9.9540	9.3851	8.8633	8.3838	7.9427	7.5361	7.1607
13	12.1337	11.3484	10.6350	9.9856	9.3936	8.8527	8.3577	7.9038	7.4869
14	13.0037	12.1062	11.2961	10.5631	9.8986	9.2950	8.7455	8.2442	7.7862
15	13.8651	12.8493	11.9379	11.1184	10.3797	9.7122	9.1079	8.5595	8.0607
16	14.7179	13.5777	12.5611	11.6523	10.8378	10.1059	9.4466	8.8514	8.3126
17	15.5623	14.2919	13.1661	12.1657	11.2741	10.4773	9.7632	9.1216	8.5436
18	16.3983	14.9920	13.7535	12.6593	11.6896	10.8276	10.0591	9.3719	8.7556
19	17.2260	15.6785	14.3238	13.1339	12.0853	11.1581	10.3356	9.6036	8.9501
20	18.0456	16.3514	14.8775	13.5903	12.4622	11.4699	10.5940	9.8181	9.1285
21	18.8570	17.0112	15.4150	14.0292	12.8212	11.7641	10.8355	10.0168	9.2922
22	19.6604	17.6580	15.9369	14.4511	13.1630	12.0416	11.0612	10.2007	9.4424
23	20.4558	18.2922	16.4436	14.8568	13.4886	12.3034	11.2722	10.3711	9.5802
24	21.2434	18.9139	16.9355	15.2470	13.7986	12.5504	11.4693	10.5288	9.7066
25	22.0232	19.5235	17.4131	15.6221	14.0939	12.7834	11.6536	10.6748	9.8226
26	22.7952	20.1210	17.8768	15.9828	14.3752	13.0032	11.8258	10.8100	9.9290
27	23.5596	20.7069	18.3270	16.3296	14.6430	13.2105	11.9867	10.9352	10.0266
28	24.3164	21.2813	18.7641	16.6631	14.8981	13.4062	12.1371	11.0511	10.1161
29	25.0658	21.8444	19.1885	16.9837	15.1411	13.5907	12.2777	11.1584	10.1983
30	25.8077	22.3965	19.6004	17.2920	15.3725	13.7648	12.4090	11.2578	10.2737
35	29.4086	24.9986	21.4872	18.6646	16.3742	14.4982	12.9477	11.6546	10.5668
40	32.8347	27.3555	23.1148	19.7928	17.1591	15.0463	13.3317	11.9246	10.7574
45	36.0945	29.4902	24.5187	20.7200	17.7741	15.4558	13.6055	12.1084	10.8812
50	39.1961	31.4236	25.7298	21.4822	18.2559	15.7619	13.8007	12.2335	10.9617
55	42.1472	33.1748	26.7744	22.1086	18.6335	15.9905	13.9399	12.3186	11.0140

Table 3 *(continued)*

Number of Pay-ments	10%	12%	14%	15%	16%	18%	20%	24%	28%	32%
1	0.9091	0.8929	0.8772	0.8696	0.8621	0.8475	0.8333	0.8065	0.7813	0.7576
2	1.7355	1.6901	1.6467	1.6257	1.6052	1.5656	1.5278	1.4568	1.3916	1.3315
3	2.4869	2.4018	2.3216	2.2832	2.2459	2.1743	2.1065	1.9813	1.8684	1.7663
4	3.1699	3.0373	2.9137	2.8550	2.7982	2.6901	2.5887	2.4043	2.2410	2.0957
5	3.7908	3.6048	3.4331	3.3522	3.2743	3.1272	2.9906	2.7454	2.5320	2.3452
6	4.3553	4.1114	3.8887	3.7845	3.6847	3.4976	3.3255	3.0205	2.7594	2.5342
7	4.8684	4.5638	4.2883	4.1604	4.0386	3.8115	3.6046	3.2423	2.9370	2.6775
8	5.3349	4.9676	4.6389	4.4873	4.3436	4.0776	3.8372	3.4212	3.0758	2.7860
9	5.7590	5.3282	4.9464	4.7716	4.6065	4.3030	4.0310	3.5655	3.1842	2.8681
10	6.1446	5.6502	5.2161	5.0188	4.8332	4.4941	4.1925	3.6819	3.2689	2.9304
11	6.4951	5.9377	5.4527	5.2337	5.0286	4.6560	4.3271	3.7757	3.3351	2.9776
12	6.8137	6.1944	5.6603	5.4206	5.1971	4.7932	4.4392	3.8514	3.3868	3.0133
13	7.1034	6.4235	5.8424	5.5831	5.3423	4.9095	4.5327	3.9124	3.4272	3.0404
14	7.3667	6.6282	6.0021	5.7245	5.4675	5.0081	4.6106	3.9616	3.4587	3.0609
15	7.6061	6.8109	6.1422	5.8474	5.5755	5.0916	4.6755	4.0013	3.4834	3.0764
16	7.8237	6.9740	6.2651	5.9542	5.6685	5.1624	4.7296	4.0333	3.5026	3.0882
17	8.0216	7.1196	6.3729	6.0472	5.7487	5.2223	4.7746	4.0591	3.5177	3.0971
18	8.2014	7.2497	6.4674	6.1280	5.8178	5.2732	4.8122	4.0799	3.5294	3.1039
19	8.3649	7.3658	6.5504	6.1982	5.8775	5.3162	4.8435	4.0967	3.5386	3.1090
20	8.5136	7.4694	6.6231	6.2593	5.9288	5.3527	4.8696	4.1103	3.5458	3.1129
21	8.6487	7.5620	6.6870	6.3125	5.9731	5.3837	4.8913	4.1212	3.5514	3.1158
22	8.7715	7.6446	6.7429	6.3587	6.0113	5.4099	4.9094	4.1300	3.5558	3.1180
23	8.8832	7.7184	6.7921	6.3988	6.0442	5.4321	4.9245	4.1371	3.5592	3.1197
24	8.9847	7.7843	6.8351	6.4338	6.0726	5.4510	4.9371	4.1428	3.5619	3.1210
25	9.0770	7.8431	6.8729	6.4642	6.0971	5.4669	4.9476	4.1474	3.5640	3.1220
26	9.1609	7.8957	6.9061	6.4906	6.1182	5.4804	4.9563	4.1511	3.5656	3.1227
27	9.2372	7.9426	6.9352	6.5135	6.1364	5.4919	4.9636	4.1542	3.5669	3.1233
28	9.3066	7.9844	6.9607	6.5335	6.1520	5.5016	4.9697	4.1566	3.5679	3.1237
29	9.3696	8.0218	6.9830	6.5509	6.1656	5.5098	4.9747	4.1585	3.5687	3.1240
30	9.4269	8.0552	7.0027	6.5660	6.1772	5.5168	4.9789	4.1601	3.5693	3.1242
35	9.6442	8.1755	7.0700	6.6166	6.2153	5.5386	4.9915	4.1644	3.5708	3.1248
40	9.7791	8.2438	7.1050	6.6418	6.2335	5.5482	4.9966	4.1659	3.5712	3.1250
45	9.8628	8.2825	7.1232	6.6543	6.2421	5.5523	4.9986	4.1664	3.5714	3.1250
50	9.9148	8.3045	7.1327	6.6605	6.2463	5.5541	4.9995	4.1666	3.5714	3.1250
55	9.9471	8.3170	7.1376	6.6636	6.2482	5.5549	4.9998	4.1666	3.5714	3.1250

Glossary

Accounting The organized system for determining the financial position of an organization.

Accounting equation Assets = liabilities + owners' equity.

Accounting period The regular period of time between preparation of the basic financial documents.

Accounting rate of return Annual return from an investment divided by level of investment.

Accounts payable The amount of money owed by a firm to others for goods or services bought on credit and for which payment is to be made before the end of the current accounting period.

Accounts receivable The amount of money owed to a business by a customer arising from the purchase of the business's goods or services.

Accrued items Financial obligations that accumulate each day but have yet to be billed to the firm.

Activity ratio A measure of how efficiently a firm uses its resources.

Agricultural cooperative A not-for-profit organization of agricultural producers who either buy agricultural inputs and/or sell agricultural commodities.

Agri-food system The set of interacting firms involved in bringing food and fiber to consumers, including raw input suppliers, producers, processors, manufacturers, distributors, wholesalers, and retailers.

Agri-phobia Students' or parents' *unfounded* fear that someone entering the field of agriculture is throwing their life away on a dead-end career area. The reality is quite the contrary.

Amortization To pay over time, usually applied to debts.

Annuity A series of equal-sized cash flows that occur at equally spaced points in time for a known length of time.

Assembly The physical collection and movement of commodities by an individual or firm into larger lots used normally by processors, wholesalers, and so on.

Asset Items the firm either owns or controls and uses in its business.

Average cost Total cost divided by output in units.

Average product (AP) The amount of output per unit of input.

Avoidable cost A cost that does not have to be absorbed by making a decision.

Balance sheet Summarizes a firm's financial position at a given point in time and lists the firm's assets, liabilities, and net worth.

Basis The difference between the cash price of a commodity and the futures price at some point in time.

Benefit/cost (B/C) ratio The ratio of the present value of benefits to the present value of costs used in capital budgeting analysis.

Bond A contract covering a debt in which the issuer promises to make given interest payments at specified times and to repay the principal amount at the stated maturity date.

Book value The value of an asset as listed on the firm's balance sheet.

Break-even analysis The process by which a manager determines the quantity or dollar sales necessary to cover all costs at given prices.

Break-even point (BEP) The quantity of output where total cost equals total revenue (i.e., profit equals zero) at given prices.

Budget A formal, written plan detailing how the firm will use its resources, what amount of sales are expected, and so on, during some future period.

Budgeting The act of formulating a budget.

Buffer stock Inventories held as a reserve against possible shortages.

Buying function One of the nine functions of marketing; deals with how consumers acquire ownership of a product.

Capital Economic assets invested in one period that (hopefully) bring benefits for many periods in the future.

Capital budget A forecast of investment opportunities that involve cash flows that extend for two or more accounting periods.

Capital budgeting The determination of the most profitable ways to allocate capital assets between ends.

Capital rationing The situation where a firm cannot undertake all the projects with a positive net present value due to limited investment funds.

Capital structure A firm's mix of long-term liabilities and equity.

Capper-Volstead Act A 1922 act of Congress that exempts bona fide cooperative associations from federal antitrust statutes.

Carrying costs (CC) The costs of holding inventory.

Cash flow Profits after tax plus depreciation expense for the period.

Cash flow budget A forecast of the amount and timing of future cash inflows and outflows over some period of time.

Centralized decision making An organizational structure in which all of the decisions are made at the highest levels of management.

Change in quantity demanded Movement along the demand curve in response to a change in a good's own price.

Clayton Antitrust Act A federal law that prohibits combinations of firms that would lessen competition. It was the first regulation to use the word monopoly.

Collateral The assets pledged to guarantee a financial obligation.

Commodity A product with uniform characteristics so each unit looks identical to all others.

Complementary good A good or service used in conjunction with another that enhances the satisfaction of that item (e.g., sugar in coffee).

Compound interest Interest paid on interest.

Compounding The process of adding interest and determining the resulting sum of the principal and interest.

Consumer sovereignty A principle that states that consumer needs are the most important needs of the firm and must be met above all others.

Contribution Selling price per unit minus the direct cost of goods sold per unit.

Contribution margin The difference between price per unit and direct costs per unit. This difference is the contribution per unit to overhead and fixed costs.

Contribution margin percentage (CMP) The same as contribution margin except the difference is expressed as a percentage of the selling price per unit.

Controllable cost A cost that can be regulated by managers.

Controlling function One of the four functions of management; deals with measuring the progress of the firm toward the goals set in the planning function.

Cooperative Businesses owned, operated, and patronized primarily by the owners and that are operated at cost.

Corporation A state-chartered legal entity that has a legal existence apart from its owners and that issues stock.

Cost of capital The minimum rate of return a firm must earn on its investments.

Cost of goods sold The direct costs of the goods actually sold during the accounting period.

Critical tasks Those tasks that must be performed well for the agribusiness to succeed and if done poorly will cause it to fail.

Cross-price elasticity The percentage change in quantity demanded of a good or service given a known percentage change in the price of that good or service's substitute or complement.

Cross-sectional data Data from different groups or locations reflecting observations collected during the same period of time.

Current assets The items on the firm's balance sheet that are cash or will turn into cash before the end of the accounting period.

Current liabilities Debts that are payable before the end of the accounting period.

Current ratio A measure of a firm's liquidity that is determined by dividing the firm's current assets by its current liabilities.

Cyclical pattern Reoccurring patterns in price and quantity that occur over periods longer than one year.

Debenture An unsecured bond—that is, a bond not backed by specific assets but backed by the general assets of the firm.

Decentralized decision making An organizational structure where the decisions are made at the lowest levels of management possible.

Demand A series of price and quantity relationships showing how much consumers are willing and able to buy at various prices.

Depreciation The decline in market value that occurs in capital assets over time, and which reflects the "consumption" of these assets due to wear and tear, and so forth.

Derived demand The demand for one item that is largely determined by the demand for another item.

Differentiated product A product with characteristics that make it different from competing products in the eyes of consumers.

Diminishing marginal utility (returns) The situation where the consumption of additional units of a good or service adds less to total utility than previous units.

Diminishing returns, principle of States that the amount of additional output coming from the use of one more unit of input.

Directing function One of the four functions of management; deals with implementing the goals set in the planning, organizing, and controlling activities.

Discipline A branch of learning with a unified set of knowledge, such as economics, statistics, or psychology.

Discount rate The opportunity cost of money when deciding the time value of money.

Discounting In capital budgeting, the conversion of a future value to a present value by adjusting the future value by its opportunity cost.

Distribution The physical dispersal and movement of commodities by a processor or producer to the ultimate consumer.

Dividend A payment to the stockholders of a corporation from after-tax earnings.

Econometrics A mathematical model of economic behavior designed to show what factors influence an economic variable or to predict a future value of an economic variable.

Economic efficiency The point on the production function where profits are maximized. Technical efficiency is a prerequisite to economic efficiency.

Economic order quantity (EOQ) The quantity of inventory to order each time to keep total inventory costs at a minimum.

Economics The study of how scarce resources are allocated between competing ends.

Economies of scale The increase (decrease) in output when all inputs are increased (decreased) by the same proportion.

Economies of size The reduction in the average cost per unit that normally occurs as plant size is increased; arises from more efficient use of various resources.

Effectiveness Doing the right things.

Efficiency Gaining the largest return from the minimum amount of effort, expense, input, and so on; often measured by the level of output divided by the level of input required to achieve it.

Elastic demand The condition where the percentage change in quantity demanded is greater than the percentage change in price, income, and so forth.

Elasticity of demand The percentage change in quantity demanded given a known percentage change in another variable, such as own price, price of substitutes, or income.

Elasticity, own The percentage change in quantity demanded given a known percentage change in the good's own price.

Elasticity, supply The percentage change in quantity supplied in response to a known percentage change in the price of an item, price of substitutes, income, and so on.

Equimarginal allocation principle Arranging scarce resources between competing activities such that moving one unit of resources from one activity to another would not add to total output.

Equivalent annual cost (EAC) A capital budgeting technique that takes the total cost of a project and turns it into equal annual outlays using an annuity factor.

Exchange function The physical activity of buying and selling a commodity with ownership and possession passing from seller to buyer.

Explicit costs Costs that are directly traceable to a product.

Extrapolation In graphical analysis it means assuming what happened in one period will happen again in another.

Financial lease A long-term lease where the lessee pays maintenance, insurance, and taxes. Often the lessee has the option of buying the item at the end of the lease period.

Financing function One of the nine marketing functions; deals with providing the financial credit needed to carry out the marketing function until payment for the product is received.

Fixed assets The items on the firm's balance sheet that the firm owns or controls and that will last more than one accounting period.

Fixed costs Those costs that do not vary with the level of output in the short run.

Forecasting The process of developing an estimate of the future value of a variable.

Form utility The satisfaction that consumers gain from the transformation of a good from one physical form to another.

Four functions of management Planning, organizing, controlling, and directing.

Four Ps of marketing The four items that a manager can control in developing a marketing mix: product, price, place, and promotion.

Futures contract A legal contract on a commodity traded on a commodity exchange that specifies the price, quality, and quantity to be delivered at some predetermined time in the future.

General partner A person in a partnership who has decision-making responsibility and full liability for the actions of the partnership.

Grades and standards function One of the nine marketing functions; deals with standardizing the physical characteristics of the product.

Graphical analysis The presentation of data by plotting on a graph.

Gross domestic product (GDP) The total value of all the goods and services produced in a country for a specific period of time.

Gross margin Total dollar sales minus the cost of goods sold on the income statement.

Hedging Taking an equal but opposite position in the cash and futures market so as to minimize price risk.

Implicit costs Costs for which no cash outlay is required when a resource is used.

Income elasticity The percentage change in quantity demanded given a known percentage change in income.

Incremental analysis A key economic decision-making technique where the decision maker compares the change in cost with the change in income, and selects those where the change in income is greater than the change in cost.

Incremental cost A cost that changes because of a decision or the production of one more unit of output.

Inelastic demand The condition where the percentage change in quantity demanded is less than the percentage change in price, income, and so on.

Inferior goods Products whose consumption declines with rising consumer income.

Information separation One of the five barriers to consumer satisfaction; deals with not having the right information about a product for consumption.

Input Something used to produce an output.

Input sector The sector of the three-part agribusiness system that produces the inputs (such as fertilizer and chemicals) used by the production sector of agribusiness.

Insolvent When liabilities are greater than assets.

Interest The price one pays to use another's money for a specified period of time.

Internal rate of return (IRR) The discount rate that makes the present value of benefits equal to the present value of the costs in a capital budgeting case.

Inventory The amount of unsold products or inputs on hand at some point in time.

Inventory turnover ratio An activity ratio computed by dividing the cost of goods sold by inventory.

Investment tax credit A federal government tax program that permits firms to deduct some or all the cost of certain types of investments directly from their tax bill.

Law of demand States that consumers buy less of a good as the price rises, and vice versa.

Leadership The ability to motivate a group of people with diverse needs and abilities to accomplish a common objective.

Lease A contract by which the owner of an asset (the lessor) allows another party (the lessee) to use that asset for a specified period of time in return for periodic payments.

Lessee The one who leases an item from the owner.

Lessor The one who owns an item and leases it to others.

Liabilities A firm's debts.

Limited liability In the legal structure of a business, investors' financial losses are limited to what they have invested in the business.

Limited partner A person in a partnership who does not have decision-making responsibility and whose liability is limited to his/her investment.

Line position A job in the organization in which the person holding it has direct authority to make decisions.

Liquidity ratio A measure of a firm's ability to meet its debts as they come due.

Long term A time period long enough that all inputs can vary.

Long-term liabilities Debts that will not come due until after the next balance sheet is prepared.

Management Accomplishing tasks through people.

Management by objective An approach to personnel management where subordinates and their superiors jointly set the performance goals of the subordinate for the coming period.

Management by walking around A management term coined by Tom Peters, management consultant, to describe managers who do not stay in their offices, but wander around the business asking questions and talking to people to get a better idea of what is going on in their firm.

Management information system (MIS) All the activities within a firm that bring managers and others the information they need to make decisions.

Manager The one responsible for seeing that tasks are done.

Marginal analysis The process of determining the contribution of one more unit of input to the level of output, costs, and so on.

Marginal cost The change in cost associated with the production of an additional unit of output.

Marginal product (MP) The additional output possible from using one more unit of input.

Marginal revenue The change in revenue associated with the selling of one more unit of output.

Marginal utility The additional satisfaction someone receives from consuming one more unit of a product.

Market A group of buyers and sellers bargaining over the terms of exchange for goods and services.

Market information function One of the nine marketing functions; deals with keeping market participants informed about factors that could affect prices and quantities.

Marketing All of the activities that coordinate production with consumer demand.

Marketing approach The best way for producers to approach a market is by placing the profitable meeting of consumer needs at the center of everything they do.

Marketing bill The difference between what the processing-manufacturing sector pays for raw commodities and what consumers pay for food and fiber at retail.

Marketing margin The difference between the price consumers pay for a product and the price received by producers for the raw product.

Marketing mix The combination of the four Ps of marketing—product, price, place, and promotion—that a manager develops to profitably meet consumer needs.

Marketing plan A written document in which the firm examines all the items that could influence the profitable production and sale of its products.

Markup The amount or percentage added to the direct cost of goods to arrive at the selling price. Keep in mind that profit is properly figured on the selling price not the cost. Thus, 20 percent added to cost will not yield a 20 percent profit; to make a 20 percent profit, one must add 25 percent to cost.

Matrix approach An approach to organizing work where employees are responsible to two or more bosses.

Mission statement Where the firm defines its purpose and objectives.

Net cash flow The actual cash received minus actual cash paid out over a given period of time.

Net income Revenue minus expenses for a given period of time.

Net operating profit Gross margin minus operating expenses (overhead) on the income statement.

Net present value (NPV) The present value of the benefits of a project less the present value of its costs.

Net profit Net operating profit plus other income, minus other expenses on the income statement.

Net working capital Current assets minus current liabilities.

Net worth Also called owners' equity or stockholders' equity.

Notes payable Short-term unsecured loans due within the current accounting period.

Objective The part of the marketing plan that states how the firm is going to meet its purpose.

Operating expenses Expenses not directly attributed to any product or service but support the general operation of the business.

Operating lease A short-term lease where the ownership of the item remains with the lessor. Commonly used with machinery and equipment rentals.

Opportunity cost The cost of a resource as measured by its highest value in a foregone use.

Opportunity cost of money The time value of money.

Ordering cost (OC) The cost of placing an order.

Organizing function One of the four functions of management; deals with how the firm will be structured to accomplish the items set forth in the planning function.

Output Something produced from inputs.

Owners' equity (net worth) Assets minus liabilities.

Ownership separation One of the five barriers to consumer satisfaction; deals with not being able to transfer product ownership to the consumer.

Par value The stated or face value of an investment.

Partner One who shares fully in the management decisions and risk of a partnership.

Partnership A business owned by two or more people.

Payback period The time required for the benefits of a project to equal its costs.

Place utility The satisfaction that consumers receive from having a product where they want it.

Planning function One of the four functions of management dealing with all actions concerning the future of the business.

Possession utility The satisfaction that consumers receive from gaining ownership of a good or service so that they can use it.

Present value The amount of money that needs to be invested today at a known interest rate to have a given amount of money at a specified time in the future.

Price The amount paid or asked for a product.

Price determination The process used by economists to determine the factors influencing the prices of products; normally done after sales have been completed.

Price discovery The process by which a price is actually determined between a buyer and a seller during a sale.

Price (or production) index A number that represents each observation as a percentage of some standard.

Principal The original amount deposited, borrowed, or lent.

Pro forma statement A forecast of future conditions; can be prepared for cash flow budgets, balance sheets, and income statements.

Processing The conversion of products to a different form.

Processing function One of the nine marketing functions; transforms the product to a form more desired by the consumer.

Processing/manufacturing sector The sector of the three-part agribusiness system that takes raw commodities from the production sector and makes them ready for use by the final consumers.

Product mix The combination of products sold by a business.

Production The application of an input(s) to produce an output(s).

Production function A depiction of the levels of output possible from various levels and combinations of inputs.

Production process The combining of input(s) to produce an output(s).

Production sector The sector of the three-part agribusiness system where food and fiber are produced from inputs from the agricultural input sector.

Productivity Level of output divided by the level of input.

Profession A line of employment involved in applied problem solving that draws on academic disciplines to complete its work. Agribusiness management is a profession because it deals with how to efficiently and effectively meet the food needs of people. To do this it draws on such academic disciplines as economics, statistics, and psychology to do its job.

Profit Total revenue minus total cost.

Profit-and-loss (P&L) statement A summary of the revenues and expenses of a business over a given period of time. If revenues exceed expenses, there is a profit; if expenses are greater than revenues, there is a loss.

Profit maximizing production area The area under the production function between maximum efficiency and maximum output. Also called Stage II or rational production area.

Purpose The part of the marketing plan that gives a concise definition of the consumer need(s) the agribusiness firm is going to fill.

Reorder point (ROP) The quantity of inventory that should trigger an order to replenish supply.

Retailing The final step in the marketing system where products are sold to the final consumer.

Retained earnings Profits that are not paid out in dividends but are reinvested in the firm itself.

Return on investment capital (ROIC) The ratio of net profit before taxes to the level of invested capital.

Revenue Income received from the sale of products.

Risk Possibility of loss where the probabilities of various outcomes are known.

Risk-taking function One of the nine functions of marketing; deals with assuming the risk of changing prices and physical loss.

Seasonal patterns Price and quantity patterns that repeat each year due to the biological nature of agricultural production.

Selling function One of the nine functions of marketing; deals with how producers transfer ownership to consumers.

Sherman Antitrust Act A federal law that prohibits the combinations of firms; it also led to the restraint of interstate trade.

Shift in demand Change in quantity demanded at all prices in response to changes other than in the good's own price.

Short term A time period short enough that at least one input is fixed.

Shutdown point The point in the production process where a firm loses less money by ceasing operation than by continuing production.

Sole (or individual) proprietorship An unincorporated business owned by one person.

Solvency ratios The set of financial ratios that measure the relative sizes of the firm's debts to their equity.

Solvent When net worth is greater than zero, or assets are greater than liabilities on the balance sheet.

Sources and uses of net working capital statement A document that lists the firm's sources and uses of working capital over a period of time to reflect changes in the firm's liquidity.

Space separation One of the five barriers to consumer satisfaction; deals with products that are not at the right location for consumption.

Staff people An employee who has no direct authority to make decisions but does advise people who do.

Staffing inventory The section of the personnel plan that describes how well the current employees and their level of skill meet the needs of the firm today and into the future.

Staffing plan The section of the personnel plan that describes the organization's people needs by job category.

Stages of production The three stages found on a production function. In stage I, total product is increasing at an increasing rate and production is inefficient. In stage II, total product is increasing at a decreasing rate with a positive marginal product and an efficient average product. In stage III, total product is decreasing and marginal product is negative and inefficient.

Stockholders' equity Also called owners' equity or net worth.

Storage function One of the nine marketing functions; deals with holding a product between production and consumption.

Strategic management The process by which managers choose a set of strategies (broad approaches) that will allow their firm to be the first choice of their customers, employees, and investors.

Strategic plan The comprehensive step-by-step plan that explains how the firm will become the first choice of its employees, customers, and investors.

Subchapter C corporation A general type of corporation that has limited liability, many stockholders, and pays taxes on its profits.

Subchapter S corporation (S-corporation) A small, company-type of corporation that has limited liability and only a few shareholders; tax liability on profits is passed on to the shareholders.

Substitute good A product that can take the place of another.

Sunk cost A cost that cannot be recovered once made.

Supply A series of price-quantity relationships showing how much producers are willing to supply at various prices.

Supply chain The physical, financial, and information networks that involve the movement of materials, funds, and related information from acquisition of raw materials to delivery of the finished goods to the end user.

Supply chain management The management and control of all materials, funds, and information in the supply process from the acquisition of raw materials to the delivery of finished products to the end user.

Sustainable competitive advantage Something a product or firm does that consumers desire that is not quickly or easily copied by competitors.

Technical efficiency The points on the production function where the level of output per unit of input is at a maximum and cannot be obtained with fewer inputs; a prerequisite to economic efficiency.

Technology The application of science to solving everyday problems.

Time separation One of the five barriers to consumer satisfaction; deals with products not being available at the right time for consumption.

Time utility The satisfaction that consumers gain from having a product available when they want it.

Time value of money The opportunity cost of money.

Time-series data Data from one or more groups or locations reflecting observations collected over a period of time.

Total cost The sum of all fixed and variable costs of production.

Total product The amount of output produced from a production process.

Trade credit sales Short-term, unsecured, non-interest-bearing credit given to a firm by its suppliers.

Transportation function One of the nine marketing functions; deals with moving a product to a location where it can be consumed.

Trend line The positioning of a straight line on a graph so that it best captures the general direction of the data.

Uncertainty The possibility of loss where the probabilities of various outcomes are not known.

Uniform Partnership Act The general set of laws that establishes the rules under which a partnership functions.

Unitary demand The condition where the percentage change in quantity demanded is exactly equal to the percentage change in price, income, and so on.

Utility Satisfaction derived from a good or service.

Value The difference between satisfaction and dissatisfaction usually associated with the purchase and consumption of a product.

Value separation One of the five barriers to consumer satisfaction; deals with not having the product in the proper form for consumption.

Variable costs Costs that vary with the level of output in the short run.

Weighted average cost of capital The firm's overall cost of capital computed by multiplying each specific cost of capital by its percentage of the capital structure.

Working capital A firm's current assets less its current liabilities.

References

Blanchard, Kenneth H., & Johnson, Spencer. (1950). *The One Minute Manager.* New York: William Morrow.

Covey, Stephen R. (1992). *Principle-Centered Leadership.* New York: Simon & Schuster.

Covey, Stephen R. (2004). *The 7 Habits of Highly Effective People: Powerful Lessons in Personal Change.* New York: Free Press.

Drucker, Peter F. (1974). *Management: Tasks, Responsibilities, Practices.* New York: Harper & Row.

50 Years of the 500. (2004, April 5). *Fortune* 149(7).

Friedman, Milton, & Friedman, Rose. (1980). *Free to Choose.* New York: Harcourt Brace Jovanovich.

Friedman, Thomas L. (2005). *The World Is Flat: A Brief History of the Twenty-First Century.* New York: Farrar, Straus and Giroux.

Grove, Andrew S. (1996). *Only the Paranoid Survive.* New York: Doubleday.

Hallberg, Milton C. (2001). *Economic Trends in U.S. Agriculture and Food Systems Since World War II.* Ames: Iowa State University Press.

Johnson, Spencer, & Wilson, Larry. (2000). *The One Minute Salesperson.* New York: Harper-Collins.

Kinsey, Jean. The Hierarchy of Consumers' Food Preferences. University of Minnesota.

MacGregor, D. (1960). *The Human Side of Enterprise.* New York: McGraw-Hill.

Maslow, A. H. (1943). "A Theory of Human Motivation." *Psychological Review, 50,* 370–396.

Paarlberg, Don, & Paarlberg, Philip. (2000). *The Agricultural Revolution of the 20th Century.* Ames: Iowa State University Press.

Peters, Tom, & Waterman, Robert H. Jr. (1982). *In Search of Excellence: Lessons from America's Best-Run Companies.* New York: HarperCollins.

Porter, Michael E. (1980). *Competitive Strategy.* New York: Free Press.

Porter, Michael E. (1985). *Competitive Advantage.* New York: Free Press.

Index